Porsche

All the cars

Lorenzo Ardizio

All the cars
Porsche

Design
Michele Leonello

GIORGIO NADA EDITORE

Giorgio Nada Editore

Editorial executive
Leonardo Acerbi

Text and technical specifications
Lorenzo Ardizio

2013-2016 update by
Mauro Gentile

Translation
Robert Newman

Design
Michele Leonello

Graphic design project
Giorgio Nada Editore

Cover
Sansai Zappini

Photographs
Giorgio Nada Editore Archive
Porsche AG Historic Archive

© 2016 Giorgio Nada Editore, Vimodrone (Milano)

Giorgio Nada Editore s.r.l.
Via Claudio Treves, 15/17
I – 20090 VIMODRONE (Milano)
Tel. +39 02 27301126
Fax +39 02 27301454
E-mail: info@giorgionadaeditore.it
www.giorgionadaeditore.it

Allo stesso indirizzo può essere richiesto il catalogo di tutte le opere pubblicate dalla Casa Editrice

The catalogue of Giorgio Nada Editore publications is available on request at the above address

Distribution:
Giunti Editore Spa
via Bolognese 165
I – 50139 FIRENZE
www.giunti.it

Porsche. All the cars - ISBN: 978-88-7911-654-1

Index

Index

Ferdinand Porsche is one of those people who seems to have been created to become the leading character of a novel, a film. All the fundamental ingredients are there: genius, success, fame. But also the Second World War, imprisonment, exile. And the happy ending, with the first Porsche branded car to appear and a technical inheritance, both entrepreneurial and sporting, that seems to have passed unchanged to "Ferry" and on down the generations.

No less legendary and fascinating is the growth of the "family" company: Porsche has become one of the great marques in motoring, which would only partially be the merit of the reputation and prestige won by Ferdinand: it would also be due to the quality of the product, innovative ability with total loyalty to the client that would evolve over time, while always remaining loyal to themselves. And not even the links with Volkswagen – initially obligatory, then intentional, sometimes feared and rarely put into effect in a "fusion" – have been able to even scratch the surface of that exclusive and personal image of the Porsche brand.

This can be said of the 356 ancestry and even more so that of the 911. But that loyalty was taken to the extreme of possibility: the Stuttgart firm made its debut in Formula 1 with an engine derived from the 356 production unit and would dominate the World Sports Car Championship with a whole family of cars – culminating in the immortal 917 – which was also powered by an air-cooled boxer engine, related much more closely to those of their road cars than one could imagine. It challenged and beat its adversaries, as well as the prejudices. And one's thoughts can do nothing other than turn to Maranello, the den of the Porsches' most feared rivals.

But the company's life would not always be an easy one nor would it be taken for granted – not even fundamentally – which would make the Porsche that we have already outlined, even if in just these few words. At the end of the 356's career, various solutions were considered – even a four-seater of three volumes – before opting for the immediately recognisable 911.

And 20 years later, even closer to the end of an epoch, sales of the 911s began to fall in the late '70s: even though it was updated, the body is still largely the one from 1963 and seemed by this time to have expressed all of its development possibilities. And the increasingly higher power output caused major problems for the rear wheel drive car, so fascinating yet so problematical to manage in a car of such high performance.

Meanwhile, what considerably influenced the company directors' thoughts was the 924 – with its engine up front and its gearbox at the rear – which was enjoying a great success, showing itself to be technically valid and economically advantageous. So thoughts of replacing the 911 with a new model began to crystallise: one that was bigger and more comfortable, more technologically advanced and with top flight performance, the design of which had already begun before the 924 came out. In fact, the 924 was created almost by chance from a project born – yet again – in collaboration with Volkswagen and then dropped by the Wolfsburg firm.

The Porsche 928 was unveiled at the 1977 Geneva Motor Show and achieved an extraordinary level of success, winning the Car of the Year award, the only sports car to have done so until then, and it rewrote the book on which the rules for a thoroughbred grand tourer were based.

One part section of the public – and not that small, either – was obstinately devoted to the small, cantankerous and noisy 911. And that repeated once again how the car – and sports cars in particular – were much more than a means of transport, than an instrument but, quite to the contrary, it was a concentration and catalyser of excitement and passion. So that's how Porsche was forced to review the cards on the table and, together with a re-shuffle of the highest levels of the company – also decided to continue the development of the 911, a constant evolution that hasn't even been brought to a close yet and seems to have no intention of doing so. It rewrote the rules of the game version after version – some people said it also rewrote the laws of physics: from the first 356's 40 hp, the car's power output went on to the 620 hp of the 911 GT2 RS, but the engine is always there in the "wrong" place.

However, the history of Porsche is not made up of the 356 and the 911 alone: there have been many models that were much different from each other, while in parallel runs an inimitable motor sport career in every epoch and in almost all racing categories. From the number 1 to the 918 concept car, right through to a compact SUV, the name of which turned out to be the 911 R.

This book covers all – or almost all – of the models for road and racing. And to accompany this story there are all the fundamental technical details but, above all, the gorgeous, unmistakable drawings by Michele Leonello, a car designer with years of experience, especially in the Alfa Romeo Styling Centre at Arese, Milan.

Lorenzo Ardizio

 # Introduction by the designer

After careful research of the models the cars were redesigned to scale, respecting the proportions of the vehicle and its details. The drawings were made with a pencil and brush, attempting to transmit the sensation of a fast, fresh and dynamic sketch like those created in the car design centres during the research stage. Then the images were scanned and refined in a digital post-production phase. After that, the designs were checked to ensure the colours and details matched the cars described in the technical specifications. The design technique brings out the dynamism and sculptural sensation typical of the Porsches. The colour tones were blended in with reflections that accentuate the "muscles" and the sinuous surfaces of the cars from Stuttgart. With each design, one can perceive the freshness of line that emphasises the elegance, uniqueness and beauty of the cars created by the various designers that have worked at the Porsche Styling Centre.

Michele Leonello

 # Readers' note

If an expert wanted to count every Porsche model, from road cars to racers produced between 1948 to 2016, when this book was about to go to press, the result would be a number much closer to 600 than 190 that appear in this book. To them should be added the prototypes, the custom-built cars and those that were never produced; then there is a series of engines that has carved for itself a more or less important place in the great history of the automobile.

A second difficulty is caused by Porsche's traditional habit of regularly improving their products with continuous upgrades and few changes. To offer different body variants as well as even more body styles and special versions.

To keep to a reasonable number of pages of a – still substantial – book, it was, therefore, necessary to use a synthesis, a choice of the most significant or interesting models to be included. To do that, we used different criteria of selection from case to case. So sometimes cars with the same engines, other times those with the same body, others belonging to the same model year or the same motor sport category. This system of diversity is the work of the author, and is intended to offer a complete and systematic panorama, while hoping for the understanding – and asking for forgiveness up to now – of those who don't find a particular vehicle in the index; perhaps one kept with pride and passion in a private garage.

A second point concerns the criteria of the technical specifications and their compilation: given the numerous – often extravagantly numerous – versions concerning each tech spec, it was decided, case by case, to use the characteristics considered most interesting about a model. Anyway, the information should only be considered indicative, being the result of research at different sources that were often discordant.

Ferdinand and Ferry Porsche pose next to No. 1 in the courtyard of the Gmünd workshop; 8 June 1948 was the date they worked to, but soon afterwards lack of capital for the development of the car, which is the definitive, saleable version, forced them to sell the prototype to Switzerland's R. von Senger for 7,000 Swiss francs. Recovered in 1956, today the car is in the company's Stuttgart museum.

TECHNICAL SPECIFICATION

ENGINE
Central, longitudinal, 4 horizontal cylinders opposed

Bore and stroke	73.5 x 64 mm
Unitary cubic capacity	271.5 cc
Total cubic capacity	1086cc
Valve gear	overhead valves, push rods and rocker arms
Number of valves	2 per cylinder
Compression ratio	7:1
Fuel feed	2 carburettors
Ignition	coil
Coolant	forced air
Lubrication	wet sump
Maximum power	35 hp at 4000 rpm
Specific power	32.2 hp/litre

TRANSMISSION
Rear wheel drive

Clutch	dry mono-disc
Gearbox	4 speeds plus reverse, overhanging

CHASSIS
Tubular trellis

Front suspension	independent, torsion bars, double wishbones, telescopic shock absorbers
Rear suspension	independent, torsion bars, double wishbones, friction shock absorbers
Brakes	mechanical drums
Steering	screw and finger
Fuel tank	-
Tyres front/rear	-

DIMENSIONS AND WEIGHT

Wheelbase	2150 mm
Track front/rear	1290/1250 mm
Length	3860 mm
Width	1660 mm
Height	-
Weight	585 kg

PERFORMANCE

Top speed	135 kph
Power to weight ratio	16.7 hp/kg

356 No. 1   1948

The idea of creating a quick version of the Volkswagen, the people's car, rose to the top of Ferdinand Porsche's mind since 1937, but his dream was soon shattered by a cold governmental response along the lines that a quicker version of the car could not be a car of the people. The project certainly was not brought to a halt but before the Second World War the only practical example of the car would be the racing Type 64, standard bearer of the Third Reich's colours in the 1939 Berlin to Rome race. Afterwards, on 17 July 1947, a two-seaters sports car project was started in Gmünd, Austria, much of its mechanics taken from the VW – and that was the Porsche No. 1. When designing its chassis, Ferdinand opted for a light tubular steel structure on which was installed the same front and rear suspension as that of the Beetle, as was the case with the steering linkage and 4-speed transmission plus reverse. The engine was also a close cousin with the VW's 4-cylinder air cooled boxer, although many modifications took its maximum power output to 40 hp at 4000 rpm, a brilliant achievement obtained from the tiny 1131 cc unit. The principal changes were concentrated on to the head, which was redesigned to include valves in a V disposition. The engine was rotated 180° and installed centrally, with the gearbox overhanging the rear end. Despite initial difficulties, three bodies were made in a short period of time, a sleek roadster in aluminium ready for road testing in March 1948. The total weight of the car with a full fuel tank was only 596 kg and its performance was decidedly quick, so much so that, according to Mr. Porsche itself, "It went beyond our expectations. It climbed up mountains like a mountain goat and accelerated easily to 130 kph". In fact, the car's top speed was 135 kph, or 140 kph with a cockpit cover instead of a passenger.

The first 356 production coupé photographed at Gmünd. From the winter of 1948, five cars a month were produced – all hand built – and started to leave the factory; after that, the cabriolet version was added. Production came to an end on 20 March 1951 after 46 cars had left the plant, equally divided into coupés and cabrios.

TECHNICAL SPECIFICATION

ENGINE
Rear with overhang, longitudinal,
4 cylinders horizontally opposed

Bore and stroke	75 x 64 mm
Unitary cubic capacity	282.7 cc
Total cubic capacity	1131 cc
Valve gear	overhead valves, push rods and rocker arms
Number of valves	2 per cylinder
Compression ratio	7:1
Fuel feed	2 inverted Solex carburettors
Ignition	coil
Coolant	forced air
Lubrication	wet sump
Maximum power	40 hp at 4000 rpm
Specific power	35.3 hp/litre

TRANSMISSION
Rear wheel drive

Clutch	dry mono-disc
Gearbox	en bloc with differential, 4 speeds plus reverse

CHASSIS
Pressed steel

Front suspension	independent, torsion bars, double wishbones, telescopic hydraulic shock absorbers
Rear suspension	independent, torsion bars, double wishbone, telescopic hydraulic shock absorbers
Brakes	mechanical drums
Steering	screw and finger
Fuel tank	45 litres
Tyres front/rear	5.00x16/5.00x16

DIMENSIONS AND WEIGHT
Wheelbase	2100 mm
Track front/rear	1290/1250 mm
Length	3880 mm
Width	1666 mm
Height	1300 mm
Weight	745 kg (coupé)

PERFORMANCE
Top speed	140 kph
Power to weight ratio	18.6 kg/hp

356/2 Gmünd   1948

While the construction of the No. 1 went ahead with all speed, the need to modify the original ambitious project was already there, so that a more rational and economical car could be built in a small production run, but without diminishing the car's lightness or performance. "The tubular chassis was too cumbersome and expensive", said Ferry Porsche, "and we needed more space for passengers and a boot". For the new structure, they chose a boxed floorpan in steel plate, as with the Beetle. But it had to be sufficiently light so that it didn't compromise performance; "even two women could lift it", concluded Mr. Porsche. A second step back from the No. 1 was the disposition of the engine, which was made to overhang the rear axle as with the VW, a solution that would become a tradition of the marque. To compensate, the mechanically controlled brakes were replaced by a more modern and lighter hydraulic system, acquired from the British company, Lockheed. The engine was the same air cooled, 4-cylinder boxer of the No. 1, with its 40 hp at 4000 rpm and a torque of 6.5 kgm at 3300 rpm due to the fuel feed from the two Solex 26 VFJ carburettors. Benefitting from a light and compact aerodynamic body, the car's top speed increased to 140 kph. Yet again, aluminium was used for the body and that meant its weight was kept down to 680 kg, even if some of the cars' delivered weighed quite a few kilograms more. To "beat" the aluminium sheets onto the wooden shape and supervise production there was, once again, the idiosyncratic master of his profession, Friedrich Weber, who despite a number of initial problems due to the far too regular habit of enjoying a drink at a nearby tavern, had already built No. 1.

The first 356 coupé produced in the Zuffen-hausen factory. It would later be used as a company demonstrator. After having covered over 250,000 test kilometres the car, nicknamed the Wind Hound, was destroyed in an accident in August 1952: Rolf Wütherich was driving, and later he was, sadly, sitting in the passenger seat of just such a car driven by James Dean, who was killed.

TECHNICAL SPECIFICATION

ENGINE
Rear, overhanging, longitudinal
4 cylinders horizontally opposed

Bore and stroke	73.5 x 64 mm
Unitary cubic capacity	271.5 cc
Total cubic capacity	1086 cc
Valve gear	overhead valves, push rods and rocker arms
Number of valves	2 per cylinder
Compression ratio	7:1
Fuel feed	2 inverted Solex carburettors
Ignition	coil
Coolant	forced air
Lubrication	wet sump
Maximum power	40 hp at 4000 rpm
Specific power	36.8 hp/litre

TRANSMISSION
Rear wheel drive

Clutch	dry mono-disc
Gearbox	en bloc with differential, 4 speeds plus reverse

CHASSIS
Boxed steel floorpan

Front suspension	independent, torsion bars, double wishbones, hydraulic telescopic shock absorbers
Rear suspension	independent, torsion bars, double wishbones, hydraulic telescopic shock absorbers
Brakes	hydraulic drums
Steering	screw and finger
Fuel tank	52 litres
Tyres front/rear	5.00 x 16/5.00 x 16

DIMENSIONS AND WEIGHT

Wheelbase	2100 mm
Track front/rear	1290/1250 mm
Length	3850 mm
Width	1660 mm
Height	1300 mm
Weight	745 kg (coupé)

PERFORMANCE

Top speed	140 kph
Power to weight ratio	18.6 kg/hp

356 1100
1950

After the small production run of the 356 in aluminium were assembled in Gmünd in an inadequate and isolated factory – inherited from Second World War decentralisation – so real Porsche production was transferred to Zuffenhausen, the historic home of the Porsche family, near Stuttgart, from the autumn of 1949 after the area had been left free of American occupation. Among the new key developments was, certainly, the production of the body in sheet steel, mainly made necessary by the scant availability of aluminium in a Germany brought to its knees by the war. While retaining its 40 hp power output, the engine was reduced to 1086 cc so that it could become part of the 1100 cc sporting category. The first car made its appearance on the Thursday before Easter on 21 March 1951, when the 500TH 356 to see the light of day was introduced with celebration – and that was looked upon with general incredulity. As was the case with the pre-production cars from Gmünd, a cabriolet version was designed with a fold-away canvas hood, which joined the closed version from the time it was unveiled at the 1949 Geneva Motor Show. The technical characteristics of the newcomer were identical, although the body was assembled by a company called Beutler, based in Thun, Switzerland. Despite the price of the cabriolet being higher than that of the normal coupé at DM 13,400 against DM 11,400, the car was successful. Taking into account all the versions, by the end of its production in 1955, over 2,200 had been sold. Contributors to the success of the 356 were its performance, build quality and the reliability of the VW dealer network of which Porsche took advantage until 1974. And an effective marketing strategy reinforced by the company's motor sport activities, soon made the Stuttgart cars status symbols.

An evocative picture from the 1951 24 Hours of Le Mans. The 356/2 Alu Coupé driven by Auguste Veuillet and Edmond Mouche won the up to 1100 cc class and scored a brilliant 20TH place overall, the victory going to the Walker-Whitehead Jaguar XK 120. That same year a sad event shook the Porsche family: the death of Ferdinand on 30 January.

TECHNICAL SPECIFICATION

ENGINE

Rear, overhanging, longitudinal,
4 cylinders horizontally opposed

Bore and stroke	73.5 x 64 mm
Unitary cubic capacity	271.5cc
Total cubic capacity	1086 cc
Valve gear	overhead valves, push rods and rocker arms
Number of valves	2 per cylinder
Compression ratio	7:1
Ignition	coil
Coolant	forced air
Lubrication	wet sump
Maximum power	44 hp at 4200 rpm
Specific power	40.5 hp/litre

TRANSMISSION

Rear wheel drive

Clutch	dry mono-disc
Gearbox	en bloc with differential, 4 speeds plus reverse

CHASSIS

Pressed steel

Front suspension	independent, torsion bars, double wishbones, hydraulic telescopic shock absorbers
Rear suspension	independent, torsion bars, double wishbones,hydraulic telescopic shock absorbers
Brakes	mechanical drums
Steering	screw and finger
Fuel tank	45 litres
Tyres front/rear	5.00 x 16/5.00 x 16

DIMENSIONS AND WEIGHT

Wheelbase	2100 mm
Track front/rear	1290/1250 mm
Length	3870 mm
Width	-
Height	-
Weight	635 kg

PERFORMANCE

Top speed	-
Power to weight ratio	14.4 kg/hp

356 Alu Coupé 1951

The year 1951 was an historic one for Porsche, with its return to motor racing in grand style. They had already been racing for a few months, but the great turnaround was on the cards with the company's entry for the 24 Hours of Le Mans: both the great French journalist Charles Faroux and Porsche's French 356 importer Auguste Veuillet, pushed for the Stuttgart cars to compete in the race. But to aim for victory – at least in the up to 1100 cc class – the company had to develop a suitable car that turned out a higher performance and was utterly reliable. So Ferry Porsche decided to "exhume" a number of 356 Gmünds, which he was foresighted enough to have put to one side before production started at Zuffenhausen: because of their aluminium bodies weighed 635 kg, they were lighter, better styled aerodynamically and were structurally more robust. The 1086 cc engine, which was always considered highly resistant to modification, was taken to 44 hp and both wheel arches were styled in aluminium with other small modifications: but the Sarthe 356 was still close to the production car. It was driven in the race by Veuillet with Edmond Mouche and took a remarkable victory in the up to 1100 cc class, the first of a long series of wins. During the same period, a car taken to 55.5 hp established three world records – the 500 miles, the six hours and the 100 km – on the Montlhéry track just outside Paris with an average speed of slightly over 161 kph. At the same time, a 356 with a 1490 cc engine (72 hp) set eight records, among them the 72 hours at over 152 kph with its gearbox blocked – in third gear! The same two cars competed in the 51ST Liege-Rome-Liège race with the 1500 coming third overall and first in its class. And in 1953 one of the cars was entered for the Carrera Panamericana.

In 1951, an original challenge between the 356 1300 of Richard von Frankenberg, accompanied by photographer Julius Weitmann, and the Monaco-Rome express. Despite the adverse weather conditions and numerous stops to enable the photographer to take his pictures, the 356 arrived in Rome seven hours before the train, leaving the crew time to visit the Eternal City.

TECHNICAL SPECIFICATION

ENGINE

Rear, overhanging, longitudinal,
4 cylinders horizontally opposed

Bore and stroke	80 x 64 mm
Unitary cubic capacity	321.5 cc
Total cubic capacity	1286 cc
Valve gear	overhead valves, push rods and rocker arms
Number of valves	2 per cylinder
Compression ratio	6.5:1
Fuel feed	2 inverted Solex carburettors
Ignition	coil
Coolant	forced air
Lubrication	wet sump
Maximum power	44 hp at 4000 rpm
Specific power	34.2 hp/litre

TRANSMISSION

Rear wheel drive

Clutch	dry mono-disc
Gearbox	en bloc with differential, 4 speeds plus reverse

CHASSIS

Boxed steel floorpan

Front suspension	independent, torsion bars, double wishbones, hydraulic telescopic shock absorbers
Rear suspension	independent, torsion bars, double wish bones, hydraulic telescopic shock absorbers
Brakes	hydraulic drums
Steering	screw and finger
Fuel tank	52 litres
Tyres front/ rear	5.00 x 16/5.00 x 16

DIMENSIONS AND WEIGHT

Wheelbase	2100 mm
Track front/rear	1290/1250 mm
Length	3850 mm
Width	1660 mm
Height	1300 mm
Weight	745 kg (coupé)

PERFORMANCE

Top speed	160 kph
Power to weight ratio	16.9 kg/hp

356 1300 and 1300S   1951

The great success of the 356 enabled Porsche to overcome the initial production difficulties linked to the start-up of the Stuttgart factory, which had already been expanded in 1952 with the construction of Plant 2. After a good result from the 500 cars built during the first year, the objective was to double the number in 1951. That is why the car, which initially had a highly homogeneous and standardised production, was given its first update and the company began to think about creating a wider range of models. At a meeting between Ferry Porsche and Karla Rabe, the chief designer, the development phases of the 356 were established. "In 1951, we plan to produce 1,000 Type 356 cars. The distribution of the models has not yet been established between the saloons and cabriolets", said the minutes of the Rabe meeting. "The protagonist of the 1951 range will be the 1.3 litre engine with one carburettor". The main new element would be the introduction of a 44 hp 1286 cc engine with two Solex carburettors, the same ones as those on the 1.1 litre. The single carburettor engine mentioned by Rabe was judged to be of a performance capability that was too close to that of 1.1 and would not even be displayed at the 1951 Frankfurt Motor Show. In 1952, the entire range was updated: single-piece windscreens, new bumpers, a bigger rear window for the cabriolet, round rearlights and other details. The following year, the 1300S appeared: this was a car with its engine fitted with a Hirt drive shaft on roller bearings, which were to be produced by Porsche a few months later. The power unit was a 1290 cc that generated 60 hp. In 1954, the 1300 cc engine would be modified (the 1300A) with the adoption of an Alfinger drive shaft which, causing an increased stroke, forced the technicians to reduce the bore from 80 to 74.5 mm so as not to "exceed" the cubic capacity limit of the 1300 cc. At the same time, the bodies were also updated in some details.

The 540 project – or the American roadster, which has always been surrounded in mystery: the details of the car are unknown. If that car would have been of a small production run and sometimes different from the other, then the 540 was the basis for the successful generations of the Speedster. The photograph shows the extremely light and precarious hood, which had to be considered just about equal to an emergency device as bad weather protection.

TECHNICAL SPECIFICATION

ENGINE
Rear, overhanging, longitudinal,
4 cylinders horyzontally opposed

Bore and stroke	80 x 74 mm
Unitary cubic capacity	372 cc
Total cubic capacity	1488 cc
Valve gear	overhead valves, push rods and rocker arms
Number of valves	2 per cylinder
Compression ratio	8.2:1
Fuel feed	2 Solex carburettors
Ignition	coil
Coolant	forced air
Lubrication	wet sump
Maximum power	70 hp at 5000 rpm
Specific power	47 hp/litre

TRANSMISSION
Rear wheel drive

Clutch	dry mono-disc
Gearbox	en bloc with differential, 4 speeds plus reverse

CHASSIS
Boxed steel floorpan

Front suspension	independent, torsion bars, double wishbones, hydraulic telescopic shock absorbers
Rear suspension	independent, torsion bars, double wishbones, hydraulic telescopic shock absorbers
Brakes	hydraulic drums
Steering	rack and pinion
Fuel tank	52 litres
Tyres front/rear	5.00 x 16/5.00 x 16

DIMENSIONS AND WEIGHT

Wheelbase	2100 mm
Track front/rear	1290/1250 mm
Length	3950 mm
Width	1660 mm
Height	1300 mm
Weight	765 kg (coupé)

PERFORMANCE

Top speed	176 kph
Power to weight ratio	10.9 kg/hp

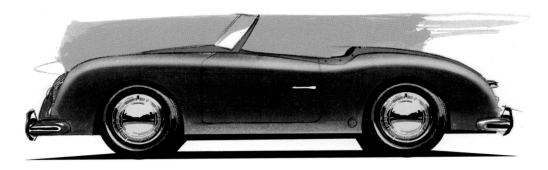

540 American Roadster 1952

Sixteen cars produced and, for many, a car of mystery are enough to ensure the 540 model and type became part of the Porsche legend, one that was also called the American Roadster, the forerunner of the of the 356 Speedster. The Roadster first appeared – even if in the USA it was often called the Speedster – in 1952, but its roots went back to the origins of Porsche itself and the Number 1, many of the features of which were repeated, like its essential lines and the windscreen that was reduced to a minimum. The mechanics were, of course, different with the engine overhanging the rear axle as on the normal 356 instead, of the central position of No. 1. This time, the initiative was that of Max Hoffman, the veteran importer to the United States of a substantial number of European marques, and his request for a car that was light with refined aerodynamics and handling, the key weapons with which to challenge the North America's home-grown giant cars as well as the sporty Jaguars and Ferraris. Those were the cars that laid down the law in the widespread challenge between gentlemen drivers, especially the Californians. The chassis was that of the normal 356, but it was reinforced to compensate for the lesser rigidity of the aluminium body styled by Heuer of Weiden, near Nuremburg. The 1300 cc power unit put out 62 hp and its consequent power to weight ratio of 11.1 kg/hp ensured top level performance. There were no fewer than three versions of the Roadster that could be distinguished, more than anything else, by the dimensions of their wheel arches, large on the first series and reduced in size on the second. They also adopted for the first time the double cooling grill on the bonnet, as would appear on the future Carrera, and the same as the 356 on the third series. The end of the American Roadster coincided with the collapse of Heuer in December 1952 which, having undervalued the times and costs, soon found out it was losing as much as DM 1,600 with every car it built.

The 1500 cc version of the 356 was also produced as a coupé, cabriolet and subsequently a Speedster, as shown in the coloured design. At the time, Porsche was in full development: in 1952 production jumped to 1,303 cars a year and the company then employed 158 people, if we exclude body builder Reutter which styled the 356. It is interesting to note that no fewer than 40 people worked in the research sector.

TECHNICAL SPECIFICATION

ENGINE

Rear, overhanging, longitudinal,
4 cylinders horizontally opposed

Bore and stroke	80 x 74 mm
Unitary cubic capacity	372 cc
Total cubic capacity	1488 cc
Valve gear	overhead valves, push rods and rocker arsms
Number of valves	2 valves per cylinder
Compression ratio	7:1
Fuel feed	2 Solex carburettors
Ignition	coil
Coolant	forced air
Lubrication	wet sump
Maximum power	55 hp at 4400 rpm
Specific power	36.9 hp/litre

TRANSMISSION

Rear wheel drive

Clutch	dry mono-disc
Gearbox	en bloc with differential, 4 speeds plus reverse

CHASSIS

Boxed steel platform

Front suspension	independent, torsion bars, double wishbones, hydraulic telescopic shock absorbers
Rear suspension	independent, torsion bars, double wishbones, hydraulic telescopic shock absorbers
Brakes	hydraulic drums
Steering	screw and finger
Fuel tank	52 litres
Tyres front/rear	5.00 x 16/5.00 x 16

DIMENSIONS AND WEIGHT

Wheelbase	2100 mm
Track front/rear	1290/1250 mm
Length	3950 mm
Width	1660 mm
Height	1300 mm
Weight	765 kg (coupé)

PERFORMANCE

Top speed	-
Power to weight ratio	13.9 kg/hp

356 1600 and 1500 S   1952

From 1952, after the debut of the sports car for the Liège-Rome-Liège and setting the records at Montlhéry, the 356 production car was also given a 1500 cc engine. In reality, some 1.5 litre 356s had already appeared nine months earlier, but they had the type 502 power unit, which was strictly derived from those used in racing, and not the type 527. It was a 1488 cc and its 60 hp output was enough to make the 356 a car that H.U. Wieselmann of the leading motoring magazine *Das Auto Motor und Sport* said, "For enthusiasts who do not drive just for the pleasure of it but also with experience, the Porsche 1.5 litre is almost the ideal creation of their dreams". After testing the car on the road, Wieselmann emphasised the breath-taking performance of the car, its lightening acceleration, but also talked of the simpler and less demanding 1.3. He wrote, "The 1.5 litre is not an amusing plaything with which one can encourage admiration and every now and then also race very fast. Instead, it is a thoroughbred, the performance of which can only be handled by a small group of drivers". Among the criticisms were the synchronisation of the gears, the difficulty of starting the car when warm and a few equipment details, observations that were quickly picked up by the factory. During the year, a new gearbox was developed and installed that was completely synchronised with Porsche's own system, while at the top of the range was the 1500 S unit that put out 70 hp. At the same time, the "old" 60 hp was replaced by a new 55 hp unit with an Alfinger drive shaft, a car that was especially mellowed in the way it operated, for which reason it was nicknamed "Dame". The brakes now had bigger 280 mm drums. While body updates continued constantly, in September 1954 Porsche started to produce all its engines (three-piece monoblock), which finally released the company from VW manufacture.

James Dean driving his 550, nicknamed "the little bastard". The actor and amateur racing driver was killed on 30 September 1955 when his 550 was involved in an accident with a Ford, whose driver was distracted. After the tragedy, the car was used for a road safety campaign, before mysteriously disappearing as it was being transported to Los Angeles.

TECHNICAL SPECIFICATION

ENGINE

Central, longitudinal,
4 cylinders horizontally opposed

Bore and stroke	85 x 66 mm
Unitary cubic capacity	374.5 cc
Total cubic capacity	1498 cc
Valve gear	4 overhead camshafts driven by counter shafts
Number of valves	2 per cylinder
Compression ratio	9.5:1
Fuel feed	2 Solex carburettors
Ignition	double, 2 coils
Coolant	forced air
Lubrication	dry sump
Maximum power	110 hp at 6200 rpm
Specific power	73.4 hp/litre

TRANSMISSION

Rear wheel drive

Clutch	dry mono-disc
Gearbox	en bloc with differential, 4 speeds plus reverse

CHASSIS

Tubular steel

Front suspension	independent, torsion bars, double wishbones, stabiliser bar, telescopic shock absorbers
Rear suspension	independent, torsion bars, double wishbones, hydraulic telescopic shock absorbers
Brakes	hydraulic drums
Steering	screw and finger
Fuel tank	-
Tyres front/rear	5.00 x 16/5.25 x 16

DIMENSIONS AND WEIGHT

Wheelbase	2100 mm
Track front/rear	1290/1250 mm
Length	-
Width	-
Height	-
Weight	550 kg

PERFORMANCE

Top speed	220 kph
Power to weight ratio	5 kg/hp

550 1500 RS   1953

Compact, light and really fast, the 550 Roadster was a sort of statement of Porsche's project philosophy, as well as the original model from which the company later drew abundantly for racing as well as its road cars. The origin? In 1950 Walter Glöckler, a Volkswagen concessionaire and racing driver, built a small roadster with a tubular chassis powered by a 1086 cc Porsche engine taken from 40 to 58 hp and fuelled by methanol, with its engine installed in a central-rear position. And it was highly successful, as Glöckler became the 1950 German champion, with evolutions of the car it remained competitive for the next two years. But in 1953 the competition had caught up and Porsche decided to compete themselves. Inspired by the Glöckler model, a tubular steel chassis was designed which, together with an aerodynamic body in aluminium of which a single example was made, formed a rigid and light structure of which a number of coupés were also built. The suspension was derived from the 356, but the engine was the work of Ernst Fuhrmann. It was a 4-cylinder air cooled boxer of 1498 cc and four overhead camshafts driven by small counter shafts, double ignition and dry sump lubrication. It had four speeds, although later a fifth would be added with a separate ratio used only to start a race; the car also had a ZF self-locking differential. Total weight was 550 kg – but that was later increased to 590 – from which the model's name came. The road car original equipment was essential and spartan, which included a small removable hood. The car was unveiled at the 1953 Paris Motor Show and the sign next to it declared its maximum power output to be 110 hp at 7000 rpm with a top speed of 225 kph. In reality, the car's top speed was "only" 220 kph with a sprint from 0-100 kph in less than 10 seconds. Later, the power output would increase to 125 hp, although various engines were used in racing to qualify for the respective categories.

The Type 597 was christened the Jagwagen or Hunter's Vehicle in an attempt to find a place in the public market. And in the '50s, with many scars of the Second World War still very much visible in Germany, it was inadvisable to refer too explicitly to the Jagwagen's use during the conflict. The engine was a detuned version of the 356 and its off-road performance was extremely good. But without the hoped for purchase by the army, only 71 were produced.

TECHNICAL SPECIFICATION

ENGINE

Rear, overhanging, longitudinal,
4 cylinders horizontally opposed

Bore and stroke	80 x 74mm
Unitary cubic capacity	372 cc
Total cubic capacity	1488 cc
Valve gear	overhead valves, push rods and rocker arms
Number of valves	2 per cylinder
Compression ratio	7:1
Fuel feed	1 carburettor
Ignition	coil
Coolant	forced air
Lubrication	wet sump
Maximum power	50 hp at 4000 rpm
Specific power	33.6 hp/litre

TRANSMISSION

4WD

Clutch	dry mono-disc
Gearbox	en bloc with differential, 4 speeds plus reverse

CHASSIS

Boxed steel floorpan

Front suspension	independent, torsion bars (adjustable), double wishbones, hydraulic telescopic shock absorbers
Rear suspension	independent, torsion bars, double wishbones, hydraulic telescopic shock absorbers
Brakes	ATE hydraulic drums
Steering	screw and finger
Fuel tank	-
Tyres front/rear	6-16/6-16

DIMENSIONS AND WEIGHT

Wheelbase	2062 mm
Track front/rear	1341/1437 mm
Length	-
Width	-
Height	-
Weight	1088 kg

PERFORMANCE

Top speed	96 kph
Power to weight ratio	21.76 kg/hp

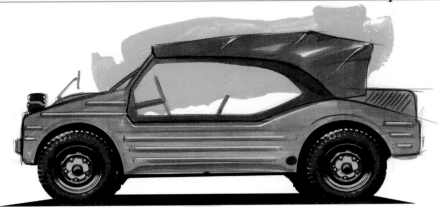

Type 597 Jagwagen   1955

At the beginning of the '50s Germany was bent on full reconstruction and Porsche attempted to meet market needs outside the 356 niche. For that reason, production began of agricultural vehicles, while in 1953 an enquiry arrived at Zuffenhausen from the new born army, now a member of NATO, that seemed like it would be a great commercial opportunity. What the military leaders wanted was a light, robust and versatile 4-wheel drive off-roader. But it had to be made inexpensively. The Porsche design studio wasn't new to this kind of task; in fact, what it called for was a vehicle similar to the wartime Type 82 Kubelwagen. Competing for this order were Goliath, of the Borgward group, and DKW. The 597 project, known as the Jagwagen, was launched on 19 December 1953 under the responsibility of Franz Xaver Reimspiess, a veteran who was the chief of Porsche's relations with the army during the war, as well as the designer of the notorious tanks from the Niebelung factory. For the mechanical element, the factory made good use of the shelves of Porsche and VW: the engine was initially the 1488 cc that put out 50 hp; then from the autumn of 1955 that was replaced by a 1582 cc. The front differential could be deactivated and the wheels had the VW Kombi's reducers to increase the vehicle's height from the ground. Off-road performance was excellent as the Jagwagen successfully took on inclines of over 60% and had good load capability. For that reason, a brochure also offered the 597 for civilian pleasure use as it was "a light cross-country vehicle able to carry four passengers up hills and slopes towards hunting lodges or fishing areas". Unfortunately, the military chiefs opted for the simpler and more economical DKW Munga and, without an army order, not even civilian production of the 597 could continue. Just 71 of them were assembled in two series as the range was updated in 1957, but almost all of them ended up being used internally, although some were sold.

Looking at the 356 from above in this picture, which was taken at the end of 1955, it is easy to see the attentive aerodynamic profiling of the body. The main aesthetic difference from the previous series was the adoption of a curved windscreen, which replaced the two-piece one. There were also improvements internally, especially in the mechanical area where a 1600 cc engine made its first appearance.

TECHNICAL SPECIFICATION

ENGINE

Rear, overhanging, longitudinal,
4 cylinders horizontally opposed

Bore and stroke	82.5 x 74 mm
Unitary cubic capacity	395.5 cc
Total cubic capacity	1582 cc
Valve gear	overhead valves, push rods and rocker arms
Number of valves	2 per cylinder
Compression ratio	7.5:1
Fuel feed	2 inverted Solex carburettors
Ignition	coil
Coolant	forced air
Lubrication	wet sump
Maximum power	60 hp at 4500 rpm
Specific power	37.9 hp/litre

TRANSMISSION

Rear wheel drive

Clutch	dry mono-disc
Gearbox	en bloc with differential, 4 speeds plus reverse

CHASSIS

Boxed steel floorpan

Front suspension	independent, torsion bars (adjustable), double wishbones, hydraulic telescopic shock absorbers
Rear suspension	independent, torsion bars, double wishbones, hydraulic telescopic shock absorbers
Brakes	hydraulic drums
Steering	screw and finger
Fuel tank	52 litres
Tyres front/rear	5.60 x 15/5.60 x 15

DIMENSIONS AND WEIGHT

Wheelbase	2100 mm
Track front/rear	1306/1272 mm
Length	3950 mm
Width	1670 mm
Height	1310 mm
Weight	820 kg (coupé and cabriolet)

PERFORMANCE

Top speed	160 kph
Power to weight ratio	13.6 kg/hp

356A 1600 and 1600S   1955

Following the principal of evolution without revolution, which is still typical of the marque, the 356 was continually updated. The new developments in the car introduced at the 1955 Frankfurt Motor Show were such that they really were those of a new series called the 356A. Next to the Coupé and Speedster at the top of the range from a price point of view, the Cabriolet was now on offer. Externally, the major new arrival was the curved windscreen to replace the V of the previous series. Inside there was a new dashboard covered in imitation leather and with three large circular instruments. The seats were also new, with reclinable backs, a rear bench seat with two makeshift places and the thick pile curly floor covering. The accessories included an elegant set of custom size suitcases for the boot, as well as a refined, leather covered headrest for the passenger. The suspension settings – now with adjustable torsion bars – had been revised, as had the driving elements and new 15 inch rims had been adopted. The 1500 cc single cam engine of the previous series was replaced by a 60 hp 1600 cc unit with a 75 hp 1600 S, its driveshaft mounted on roller bearings. The first major update of the car was in 1957. It was given a new clutch with a spring diaphragm, a single-piece gearbox and ZF worm and roller steering gear housing. The 1600 was recognisable at the rear, where the two exhaust pipes passed through the interior of the bumper bars. In 1957, the 356A Cabriolet was updated with a more generously dimensioned rear window and moveable deflectors to improve ventilation. That same year, the hardtop version went into production, equipped with a refined and efficient rigid roof group – strictly dual tone – that could be fitted as an alternative to the canvas hood.

While the previous series Speedster body was considered an experiment, with the 356A that was presented from the outset, generating favour with the American clientele for whom a lighter, more Spartan and sportier version had been considered, the Europeans were also attracted by the car's exciting performance, young lines and a well-contained price.

TECHNICAL SPECIFICATION

ENGINE

Rear, overhanging, longitudinal
4 cylinders horizontally opposed

Bore and stroke	74.5 x 74 mm
Unitary cubic capacity	322.5 cc
Total cubic capacity	1290 cc
Valve gear	overhead valves, push rods and rocker arms
Number of valves	2 per cylinder
Compression ratio	6.5:1
Fuel feed	2 inverted Solex carburettors
Ignition	coil
Coolant	forced air
Lubrication	wet sump
Maximum power	44 hp at 4200 rpm
Specific power	34.1 hp/litre

TRANSMISSION

Rear wheel drive

Clutch	dry mono-disc
Gearbox	en bloc with differential, 4 speeds plus reverse

CHASSIS

Boxed steel floorpan

Front suspension	independent, torsion bars (adjustable), double wishbones, hydraulic telescopic shock absorbers
Rear suspension	independent, torsion bars, double wishbones, hydraulic telescopic shock absorbers
Brakes	ATE hydraulic drums
Steering	screw and finger
Fuel tank	52 litres
Tyres front/rear	5.60 x 15/5.60 x 15

DIMENSIONS AND WEIGHT

Wheelbase	2100 mm
Track front/rear	1306/1272 mm
Length	3950 mm
Width	1670 mm
Height	1310 mm
Weight	820 kg (coupé and cabrio)

PERFORMANCE

Top speed	145 kph
Power to weight ratio	18.6 kg/hp (1300and 1300S)

356A 1300 and 1300S   1955

The success of the Porsche 356 was the turning point of 1955, so much so that it pushed the company's management into looking with optimism on the evolution of the model and the new 356A, which was introduced to the public in September of that year at the Frankfurt Motor Show, when the celebrated magazine *Das Auto Motor und Sport* defined it as "one of the most beautiful cars ever". And it would be one of the blue metallic 356A coupés that would become the company's 10,000TH car to leave the Porsche factory: a goal that, only a few years earlier when the undertaking began in silence in the little Gmünd workshop, seemed an impossible objective to achieve. With the launch of the 356A and the 1100 cc engine going out of production in 1954, the 1300 took over as the basic Porsche offer that was divided into two versions: the 1300 with a camshaft that rested on plain bearings and put out 44 hp, plus the 1300S and the 60 hp 1600 with roller bearings, both of which had the same power output. The engines had light alloy cylinders and heads with chromed exhausts. Three versions of the 1300 were also available, the Coupé, Cabriolet and Speedster. From the start, the latter was presented as a testimonial to Porsche's sales success, especially in international markets with the United States in the forefront. Body preparation was the same as that of its bigger 1600 sister car and in 1957 they also adopted the same updates, including a bigger, wraparound rear window and rear teardrop-shaped lights. There was a hardtop version of the Cabriolet available and a rigid roof was also designed for the Speedster: in both cases, they were well-made and finished components that were very light and practical to fit and take off; an operation that could easily be carried out by two people, using the same front clips as the canvas hood. The 1300 and 1300S production lines fell silent at the end of 1957.

The original photographic session happened in Austria and emphasised how Porsche wanted to attribute not only a sportiness to the 356A 1500GS Carrera, but also one of a true grand tourer. The car they photographed even had a sun roof. In reality, the Carrera's body was rather spartan and the engine turned out to be slightly "uncertain" at low revs as it had a decidedly sporty set-up.

TECHNICAL SPECIFICATION

ENGINE
Rear, overhanging, longitudinal,
4 cylinders horizontally opposed

Bore and stroke	85 x 66 mm
Unitary cubic capacity	374.5 cc
Total cubic capacity	1498 cc
Valve gear	4 overhead camshafts with 2 countershafts
Number of valves	2 per cylinder
Compression ratio	9.0:1
Fuel feed	2 twin choke Solex carburettors
Ignition	coil
Coolant	forced air
Lubrication	dry sump
Maximum power	100 hp at 6200 rpm
Specific power	66.7 hp/litre

TRANSMISSION
Rear wheel drive

Clutch	dry mono-disc
Gearbox	en bloc with differential, 4 speeds plus reverse

CHASSIS
Boxed steel floorpan

Front suspension	independent, torsion bars, double wishbones, stabiliser bar, telescopic shock absorbers
Rear suspension	independent, torsion bars, double wishbones, stabiliser bar, hydraulic telescopic shock absorbers
Brakes	hydraulic drums
Steering	screw and finger
Fuel tank	52 litres
Tyres front/rear	5.90 x 15/5.90 x 15

DIMENSIONS AND WEIGHT

Wheelbase	2100 mm
Track front/rear	1306/1272 mm
Length	3950 mm
Width	1670 mm
Height	1310 mm
Weight	850 kg

PERFORMANCE

Top speed	200 kph
Power to weight ratio	9 kg/hp

356A 1500 GS Carrera   1955

The Carrera name was to evoke Porsche's historic performance in the Carrera Mexicana. The 356A 1500 GS Carrera in Coupé, Cabriolet and Speedster form was presented in 1955 along with the "normal" versions of the 1300 and 1600. But under the bonnet with its two grills, was a thoroughbred engine and was a close relative of the racing unit. Although the Carrera was making its initial appearance, the first of its power units had already amazed visitors to the Paris Motor Show two years earlier, where a highly sporty racing roadster with the numbers 550 on its bonnet appeared next to the normal 356 1300S. The newcomer was presented by Porsche as more than a dream car, although the quick car with its rasping engine had a more star-studded destiny. The chrome cylinder sleeves were inserted into a light alloy crankcase, a material from which the pistons and head were also made. Lubrication is forced by a dry sump with a gear pump and the drive shaft and piston rods were mounted on roller bearings. But the most important new development was the double overhead camshaft valve gear for each cylinder bank, which enabled the car to put out 100 hp at 6200 rpm. The engine was somewhat hesitant at low revs and the body rather spartan as one expects of a sports car, especially one often used for racing. In fact, the car turned in innumerable victories in events ranging from the Mille Miglia to the Monte Carlo Rally, with dozens of these cars on the start lines, the works cars shoulder to shoulder with the often more numerous private entrants. The Carrera went out of production in 1957 and the range was split into the two versions, the De Luxe and the Grand Tourer. All in an effort to satisfy the two very different customers groups – the ones looking for a car of extremely high performance, who were a lot different from those wanting an ultra-high performance GT to prepare it for racing.

The driver from Biella, Italy, Umberto Maglioli, one of the great hillclimb and road racing specialists, gave Porsche its first win at the celebrated and fearsome Targa Florio driving a 550A 1500 RS. He crossed the finish line after 7 hours 54 minutes 52 seconds of racing at an average of 90.97 kph. Maglioli arrived in Sicily with just two mechanics and a motor sports director, yet he dominated the race, stopping for to refuel just once and no tyre changes!

TECHNICAL SPECIFICATION

ENGINE

Central, longitudinal

4 cylinders horizontally opposed

Bore and stroke	85 x 66 mm
Unitary cubic capacity	374.5 cc
Total cubic capacity	1498 cc
Valve gear	4 overhead camshafts driven by a counter shaft
Number of valves	2 per cylinder
Compression ratio	9.8:1
Fuel feed	2 Weber 40DCM1 carburettors
Ignition	double, 2 coils
Coolant	forced air
Lubrication	dry sump
Maximum power	135 hp at 7200 rpm
Specific power	90.1 hp/litre

TRANSMISSION

Rear wheel drive

Clutch	dry mono-disc
Gearbox	en block with differential, 5 speeds plus reverse

CHASSIS

Tubular steel trellis

Front suspension	independent, torsion bars, double wishbones, stabiliser bar, telescopic shock absorbers
Rear suspension	independent, torsion bars, double wishbones, hydraulic telescopic shock absorbers
Brakes	hydraulic drums
Steering	screw and finger
Fuel tank	-
Tyres front/rear	5.00 x 16/5.25 x 16

DIMENSIONS AND WEIGHT

Wheelbase	2100
Track front/rear	1290/1250 mm
Length	3601 mm
Width	1551mm
Height	1016 mm
Weight	530 kg

PERFORMANCE

Top speed	240 kph
Power to weight ratio	3.9 hp/kg

550A 1500 RS   1956

After the motor sport success of the Spyder, a profound evolution of the car was carried out for the 1956 season. The transverse longitudinals and chassis was replaced by one that was profoundly redesigned to produce a tubular trellis in steel that weighed 43 kg – 16 kg lighter than its predecessor – and that was three to five times more rigid. And because of its particular design, it allowed many more upper joints for the body, which was the same size as that of the 550. This would not force the technicians to design brackets and supports and so permitted the "skin", built by Wendler of Reutlingen, to weigh 63 kg, a massive 27 kg less than that of the 550. The 1598 cc engine also retained the double ignition twincam, with a Hirt drive shaft on roller bearings but the power output increased to 135 hp as a result of fitting a new Weber carburettor and in the increased compression rate. Revised rear suspension with anti-roll bars and bigger brakes. The car's racing debut was a win first time out, scored by Maglioli and Wolfgang von Trips in the 1000 Km of the Nürburgring. After that, the car won the year's Targa Florio driven by Maglioli again, a coupé version came fifth in the 24 Hours of Le Mans and the company scored a 1-2-3 finish in the 12 Hours of Reims. An evolution of the 550A was prepared for the end of the season and that adopted some of the future RSK's developments, as well as having its structure completely revised: its wheelbase and track were substantially reduced. The body that took those changes into account was rather ungainly, so much so that the Porsche technicians called it the Mickey Mouse. That car made its debut at the nearby Solitude circuit, but Frankenburg didn't like the braking or handling. Unfortunately, his dislike turned out to be correct a few days later in a finale at the AVUS, in which the car was destroyed in a spectacular accident when it flew over the banking. It was a miracle that the driver was uninjured. Mickey Mouse ended its career among the white flames of its magnesium body.

Huschke von Hanstein racing a 356A 1600 GS Carrera GT. After having split the Carrera's range, Porsche had the chance of offering a much lighter, very sporty version and didn't have to cure the car's gruff handling or passenger discomfort on city roads. The 110 hp of the 1500 and the 1600's 115 hp produced excellent levels of performance.

TECHNICAL SPECIFICATION

ENGINE
Rear, overhanging, longitudinal
4 cylinders horizontally opposed

Bore and stroke	85 x 66 mm
Unitary cubic capacity	374.5 cc
Total cubic capacity	1498 cc
Valve gear	4 overhead camshafts with 2 counter shafts
Numbers of valves	2 per cylinder
Compression ratio	9.0:1
Fuel feed	2 twin choke Solex carburettors
Ignition	coil
Coolant	forced air
Lubrication	dry sump
Maximum power	110 hp at 6400 rpm
Specific power	73.4 hp/litre

TRANSMISSION
Rear wheel drive

Clutch	dry mono-disc
Gearbox	en bloc with differential, 4 speeds plus reverse

CHASSIS
Boxed steel floorpan

Front suspension	independent, torsion bars, double wishbones, stabiliser bar, telescopic shock absorbers
Rear suspension	independent, torsion bars, double wishbones, hydraulic telescopic shock absorbers
Brakes	hydraulic drums
Steering	screw and finger
Fuel tank	80 litres
Tyres front/rear	5.90 x 15/5.90 x 15

DIMENSIONS AND WEIGHT

Wheelbase	2100 mm
Track front/rear	1306/1272 mm
Length	3950 mm
Width	1670 mm
Height	1310 mm
Weight	865 kg (coupé)

PERFORMANCE

Top speed	200 kph
Power to weight ratio	7.9 kg/hp

356A Carrera GT (1500 and 1600)   1957

By early 1957, the Carrera had earned a reputation for itself with its performance, but its rather twitchy handling typical of a racing car meant a sector of Porsche's clientele was dissatisfied. So after that the whole range was restyled and the model was split into two different versions destined for two different types of customer. On page three of edition 26 of *Christophorus* (spring 1957), the company's house organ, the modifications were described this way: "From now on, the Porsche Carrera will be produced in two versions to produce the Carrera GT (Grand Tourer) and the Carrera De Luxe. The GT has side windows with those of the door and rear in Plexiglas, the wraparound seats of the Speedster and lightened mounts for the bumpers. And it has no heater. Due to the adoption of inverted twin choke Solex carburettors, with separate fuel feed for each cylinder, the Carrera's production engine, which was especially tuned, has special exhausts and puts out 110 hp. A fuel tank of around 80 litres notably increases the car's autonomy. The brakes are bigger and similar to those of the 1956 Spider. These were specifically designed for racing, because the deceleration value of the original brakes is already of a good level for normal use with the car, so bigger ones are not fitted to other models". Doors, bonnet, engine cover, seats and rims even with discs (provided they were not steel discs) were in light alloy and the weight was kept down to 835 kg for the coupé and 810 kg for the Speedster, in part due to an extremely spartan body. Causing some complaints from gentlemen drivers, the GT did not arrive until the 1958 racing season, but its impressive series of victories soon meant that Porsche were forgiven. In 1958, the body shell was further lightened and the engine, now with a traditional drive shaft and plain bearings, was taken to 1582 cc by increasing the bore to generate 115 hp.

The 356A Carrera was later also offered in a more tourist configuration of a Cabriolet and Hardtop, as well as the Coupé and Speedster. But above all, the Carrera De Luxe became the faster grand tourer to which the previous version was unable to aspire, because the engine was too sporty and the car had an excessively spartan finish.

TECHNICAL SPECIFICATION

ENGINE
Rear, overhanging, longitudinal
4 cylinders horizontally opposed

Bore and stroke	87.5 x 66 mm
Unitary cubic capacity	396.8 mm
Total cubic capacity	1587.5 cc
Valve gear	4 overhead camshafts with 2 counter shafts
Number of valves	2 per cylinder
Compression ratio	9.0:1
Fuel feed	2 twin choke Solex PJJ-4 carburettors
Ignition	coil
Coolant	forced air
Lubrication	dry sump
Maximum power	105 hp at 6500 rpm
Specific power	66.1 hp/litre

TRANSMISSION
Rear wheel drive

Clutch	dry mono-disc
Gearbox	en bloc with differential, 4 speeds plus reverse

CHASSIS
Boxed steel floorpan

Front suspension	independent, torsion bars, double wishbones, stabiliser bar, telescopic shock absorbers
Rear suspension	independent, torsion bars, double wishbones, hydraulic telescopic shock absorbers
Brakes	hydraulic drums
Steering	screw and finger
Fuel tank	52 litres
Tyres front/rear	5.90 x 15/5.90 x 15

DIMENSIONS AND WEIGHT

Wheelbase	2100 mm
Track front/rear	1306/1272 mm
Length	3950
Width	1670 mm
Height	1310 mm
Weight	930 kg (coupé)

PERFORMANCE

Top speed	200 kph
Power to weight ratio	8.6 kg/hp

356A Carrera De Luxe (1500 and 1600) 1957

Taking once more the words published in number 26 of *Christophorus* in the spring of 1957, the writer said, "Shoulder to shoulder, there stands the Carrera GT and the Carrera De Luxe the engine of which, with normal city tuning, puts out 100 hp and become 105 hp with the sport set-up. In the city the Carrera De Luxe is decidedly 'softer' and rounder than the previous model. The cockpit heater has been much improved so that, with low outside temperatures and at not too high a speed, one can enjoy a warm enough interior". In fact, the heater had always been one of the weak points of the 356 and would also be so with the 911, both having air cooled engines. Among the Carrera De Luxe's characteristics there was also the opportunity of having a cabriolet body. As with the Carrera GT, in 1958 the car's cubic capacity was increased to 1582 cc for the 356A GS 1600 Carrera De Luxe with a power output of 105 hp; in this case, too, with a single piece drive shaft on plain bearings. With this version, Porsche intended to offer the more demanding client a car with a performance "almost" like the racing version, but with the greatest possible comfort. The price to be paid was the car's weight, which rose to 900 kg for the coupé and 855 kg for the Speedster. Meanwhile, Porsche intended to rationalise the Speedster's production process and decided to bring in Drauz of Heilbronn as a second outside body production unit, to work with Reutter of Stuttgart on shell construction; after a number of "transition" examples, the Speedster was definitively replaced by the more comfortable Convertible D (for Drauz), this time with a higher windscreen and wind-up windows. The new version was introduced in the autumn at the 1958 Paris Motor Show but, in reality, deliveries had already started in August.

On 24 May 1959, Edgar Barth and Wolfgang Seidel won the Targa Florio in a Porsche 718 RSK, crossing the finish line after 11 hours 02 minutes of racing at an average speed of 91.309 kph. The success of the agile and fast cars from Stuttgart that day was four-fold: second came Linge-Scagliarini in a 550A RS, followed by two Carrera 356As driven by Hanstein-Pucci and Strähle-Mahle.

TECHNICAL SPECIFICATION

ENGINE
Central, longitudinal
4 cylinders horizontally opposed

Bore and stroke	85 x 66 mm
Unitary cubic capacity	374.5 cc
Total cubic capacity	1498 cc
Valve gear	4 overhead camshafts, driven by counter shafts
Number of valves	2 per cylinder
Compression ratio	9.8:1
Fuel feed	2 Weber 46 IDM twin choke carburettors
Ignition	dual power, coil
Coolant	forced air
Lubrication	dry sump
Maximum power	148 hp at 8000 rpm
Specific power	98.8 hp/litre

TRANSMISSION
Rear wheel drive

Clutch	dry mono-disc
Gearbox	en bloc with differential, 5 speeds plus reverse

CHASSIS
Tubular steel trellis

Front suspension	independent, torsion bars, double wishbones, stabiliser bar, telescopic shock absorbers
Rear suspension	independent, double wishbones, coil spring shock absorbers
Brakes	hydraulic drums
Steering	screw and finger
Fuel tank	80 litres
Tyres front/rear	5.00 x 16/5.25 x 16

DIMENSIONS AND WEIGHT

Wheelbase	2100 mm
Track front/rear	1290/1250 mm
Length	3601 mm
Width	1511 mm
Height	890 mm
Weight	530 kg

PERFORMANCE

Top speed	240 kph
Power to weight ratio	3.5 kg/hp

718 RSK   1957

After the successful career of the 550A, a further evolution of the roadster was developed in mid-1957 which was called the 718 RSK. The K stood for the main structural modifications in relation to the 550A: the torsion bars were inclined towards the wheel and their housings were welded to the chassis near the waistline, to form a sort of K with the tubes. The body was about a dozen centimetres lower and much more tapered, so much so that its aerodynamics were 10% better. The front was more convex, with the headlights enclosed in Plexiglas and the oil radiator placed under the nose. In addition, the new regulations stipulated that a spare wheel had to be carried, the windscreen should be 100 cm wide and 20 cm high. The engine was taken to 142 hp. Among the especially significant experiments were the adoption of direct fuel injection and a Fletcher American dynamic cooling system, able to save the 8 hp needed to move the fan – but both were dropped. For the brakes, the company opted for light alloy drums with an insert in cast iron plus helical finning, which was 35% lighter than discs. After the car's debut in 1957, the following year the RSK was officially entered in major races with an engine taken to 1600 cc also available, due to a bore of 87.5 mm to generate 148 hp. The car scored many top placings and class wins, including at the Targa Florio, the Nürburgring and at AVUS. At the end of the season, the torsion bars were replaced by lighter coil springs, breaking away from Porsche road car production and "renouncing" the K in its name. Twenty examples were built in 1959, which were added to the existing 135, power was increased and the car was driven to victory in the Targa Florio as well as at the Nürburgring, where it appeared its reliability limit would compromise the car's performance at Le Mans.

The Formula 2 single seater driven by Stir-ling Moss with the Rob Walker team's typi-cal livery of blue with a white ring around the nose. After at Syracuse, Brussels, Good-wood and Pau missed by a whisker, Moss finally won at the British Aintree circuit. It was a major success, with Moss's car followed home by two more of Stuttgart's works single seaters driven by Jo Bonnier and Graham Hill.

TECHNICAL SPECIFICATION

ENGINE

Central, longitudinal,
4 cylinders horizontally opposed

Bore and stroke	85 x 66 mm
Unitary cubic capacity	374.5 cc
Total cubic capacity	1498 cc
Valve gear	4 overhead camshafts moved by counter shafts
Number of valves	2 per cylinder
Compression ratio	9.8:1
Fuel feed	2 twin choke carburettors
Ignition	double coil
Coolant	forced air
Lubrication	dry sump
Maximum power	150 hp at 7800 rpm
Specific power	100.1 hp/litre

TRANSMISSION

Rear wheel drive

Clutch	dry mono-disc
Gearbox	en bloc with differential, 6 speeds plus reverse

CHASSIS

Tubular steel trellis

Front suspension	independent, torsion bars, double wishbones, stabiliser bar, telescopic shock absorbers
Rear suspension	independent, double triangular arms, coil springs for the hydraulic telescopic shock absorbers
Brakes	hydraulic drums
Steering	screw and finger
Fuel tank	100 litres
Tyres front/rear	5.50 x 15/6.0 x 15

DIMENSIONS AND WEIGHT

Wheelbase	2200 mm
Track front/rear	1300/1260 mm
Length	3352 mm
Width	920 mm
Height	901 mm
Weight	470 kg

PERFORMANCE

Top speed	250 kph
Power to weight ratio	3.1 kg/hp

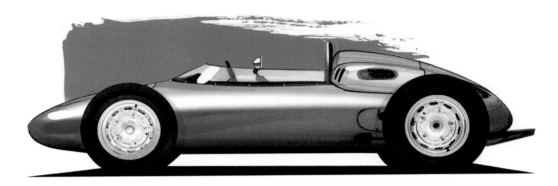

718 F2   1959

Porsche's adventure among the single seaters began in an extravagant manner: during testing for the Formula 2 Grand Prix of the Nürburgring in 1957, the quickest time was set by Edgar Barth in… an RS Spyder! Encouraged by their car's results, Porsche took another step forward the next year in its run-up to a real single-seater: a 718 RSK was heavily modified with new suspension, bigger brakes, a 150 hp engine and especially a more tapered body with a central driving position. Driven by Jean Behra, the car beat the "real" F2s at the GP of Reims and that finally pushed Porsche into developing a "real" single seater. Built during the winter of 1958 and part of 1959, the car would bring home stunning results in practice with a 9m 29s from von Trips at the Nürburgring; unfortunately, the German driver would not be so lucky at the Monaco Grand Prix debut race, where he destroyed the car by crashing into a wall after just two laps. While Stuttgart was building a new car, Jean Behra had a single seater constructed in Italy by Valerio Colotti that was similar to the one that came second at Reims driven by Hans Herrmann. Readied by Porsche, the car was test driven at Goodwood by Stirling Moss, who was excited about it, so much so that he convinced his team owner, Rob Walker, to buy one for the 1960 season, suitably painted in the Walker team's blue and white. The first win was at Aintree and other victories followed by the silver works cars driven by John Surtees, Jo Bonnier and Dan Gurney: the American gave the version with a modified body its debut at Solitude. Five of them started at the Nürburgring, competing for the Constructors' Cup, an unformal F2 championship. Bonnier's win in the 718 F2 took Porsche up to equal points with Cooper, with victory going to Zuffenhausen for the best classified car in the various races.

The task of the 356B Roadster was to follow on from the best-selling Speedster. But in 1959 there was little left of the youthful, spartan and sporty spirit of the original project. Space was made for constructional refinement, performance and comfort, yet without giving up the model's dynamic appearance, all at a reasonable price.

TECHNICAL SPECIFICATION

ENGINE

Rear, overhanging, longitudinal
4 cylinders horizontally opposed

Bore and stroke	82.5 x 74 mm
Unitary cubic capacity	395.5 cc
Total cubic capacity	1582 cc
Valve gear	overhead valves, push rods and rocker arms
Numbers of valves	2 per cylinder
Compression ratio	8.5:1
Fuel feed	2 Zenith 32 NDIX twin choke carburettors
Ignition	coil
Coolant	forced air
Lubrication	wet sump
Maximum power	75 hp at 5000 rpm
Specific power	47.4 hp/litre

TRANSMISSION

Rear wheel drive

Clutch	dry mono-disc
Gearbox	en bloc with differential, 4 speeds plus reverse

CHASSIS

Boxed steel floorpan

Front suspension	independent, torsion bars, double wishbones, stabiliser bar, telescopic shock absorbers
Rear suspension	independent, torsion bars, double wishbones, hydraulic telescopic shock absorbers
Brakes	hydraulic drums
Steering	screw and finger
Fuel tank	50 litres
Tyres front/rear	5.60 x 15/5.60 x 15

DIMENSIONS AND WEIGHT

Wheelbase	2100 mm
Track front/rear	1306/1272 mm
Length	4010 mm
Width	670 mm
Height	1330 mm (coupé)
Weight	905 kg (coupé)

PERFORMANCE

Top speed	175 kph
Power to weight ratio	12.4 kg/hp

356B   1959

As early as 1957 the Porsche management had started to think of a general renew-al of the 356A range. The tendency seemed to be to err towards ever increasing power, with the consequent evolution of the chassis and braking system. A num-ber of possibilities were considered and abandoned: pneumatic suspension, which then revealed itself to be excessively complex and expensive; and a fuel injection system, which had already been investigated at the beginning of the decade in collaboration with Bosch – and that was also judged incompatible with industrial production. So there remained the "normal" engines, the 1600 and 1600S plus the 1600 Carrera that put out 115 hp. And as far as the body was concerned, requests from the sales department for a face-lift pushed the company into exploring vari-ous routes. Among them was a variant with four headlights that was presented to top management in November 1957, but was immediately abandoned. Still, the process did not stop and the debut of the 356B was fixed for the 1959 Frankfurt Motor Show. The main variations were in the car's frontal design, the optical groups in particular. The headlights were higher and had a much more vertical inclination. The bumpers were raised in the same way and made more wrapa-round on the sides, with the lower part of the body "folded" backwards. The deflectors already in use on the Cabriolet, were also applied to the Coupé, while many more modifications made the interior more pleasant. The chalice-type, three spoke steering wheel was new. Until February 1961, the Roadster body shell was assembled by Drauz, as was the 356A Convertible D; later, production went to Anciens Etablissements d'Ieteren Frères SA of Brussels. In 1960, a cabriolet ver-sion was added with a fixed hard top welded to the body shell and that was made by Wilhelm Karmann GmbH of Osnabrück.

Graham Hill's RS60 competing in the 1960 24 Hours of Le Mans. Note the special body prepared for the event, with the windscreen and side windows forming a sort of coupé minus roof. It was an attempt to limit aerodynamic damage caused by the large regulation windscreen. To improve visibility, wipers were installed for the exterior and interior of the screen.

TECHNICAL SPECIFICATION

ENGINE

Central, longitudinal

4 cylinders horizontally opposed

Bore and stroke	87.5 x 66 mm
Unitary cubic capacity	396.7 cc
Total cubic capacity	1587 cc
Valve gear	4 overhead camshafts moved by counter shafts
Number of valves	2 per cylinder
Compression ratio	9.8:1
Fuel feed	2 twin choke carburettors
Ignition	double, 2 coils
Coolant	forced air
Lubrication	dry sump
Maximum power	160 hp at 7800 rpm
Specific power	100.8 hp/litre

TRANSMISSION

Rear wheel drive

Clutch	dry mono-disc
Gearbox	en bloc with differential, 5 speeds plus reverse

CHASSIS

Tubular steel trellis

Front suspension	independent, torsion bars, double wishbones, stabiliser bar, telescopic shock absorbers
Rear suspension	independent, double wishbones, coil springs for the hydraulic telescopic shock absorbers
Brakes	hydraulic drums
Steering	screw and finger
Fuel tank	80 litres
Tyres front/rear	5-50 x 16/5.90 x 16

DIMENSIONS AND WEIGHT

Wheelbase	2200 mm
Track front/rear	1290/1250 mm
Length	3601 mm
Width	1511 mm
Height	881 mm
Weight	550 kg

PERFORMANCE

Top speed	-
Power to weight ratio	3.4 kg/hp

718 RS60 1959

The new, 1960 season version of the Spyder was not much different from its predecessor. The eye fell immediately on the large, 25 cm windscreen imposed by FIA and the centre of various Porsche protests: it was quite a limitation for the "small" Porsche, its maximum speed 10 kph slower because of it. Another rule in the new regulations also obliged the designers to slot in a boot, which was installed at the rear of the RS60 above the engine and "hump" cover that was no longer bolted. From the mechanical point of view, the main modification to the new version was the lengthening of the wheelbase for the first time in the Spyder's history – although an exception was made for the Mickey Mouse. The engines were more or less frozen, with the 1.6 putting out 160 hp at 7800 rpm, which was a main option for clients, and the 1.5 that generated 150 hp, often used by the company to obtain good placings in motor racing's performance indices. To be able to compete in the up to 2000 category a Spyder 1.7-litre was used by the factory, powered by its 1678 cc engine (170 hp); the cubic capacity was reduced to 1608 cc for the 24 Hours of Le Mans with a bore of 88 mm. After a third place in Buenos Aires, and at Sebring, Porsche – like Ferrari – decided to retire after a disagreement with its petrol sponsor, but a "private" car driven by Jo Bonnier and Graham Hill still started – supported by German mechanics and resembling the factory car – but it retired mid-race with a broken drive shaft. Then came the two second places in the Targa Florio, where Porsche surpassed Ferrari, its main competition, and at the Nürburgring. The most prestigious race was Le Mans where, despite a massive deployment of forces, a series of breakdowns compromised the results. But a major consolation came from the Mountain Championship.

Even if the differences between the Super 90 and the 356B were reduced to a few details like the letters on the rear, the revised, more powerful engine with the Carrera's carburettors among other things, the car's layout suited the greater performance: a different set-up, bigger tyres and transverse leaf spring at the rear end.

TECHNICAL SPECIFICATION

ENGINE
Rear, overhanging, longitudinal,
4 cylinders horizontally opposed

Bore and stroke	82.5 x 74 mm
Unitary cubic capacity	395.5 xx
Total cubic capacity	1582 cc
Valve gear	overhead valves, rocker arms and push rods
Number of valves	2 per cylinder
Compression ratio	9.0:1
Fuel feed	2 twin choke carburettors
Ignition	coil
Coolant	forced air
Lubrication	wet sump
Maximum power	90 hp at 5500 rpm
Specific power	56.9 hp/litre

TRANSMISSION
Rear wheel drive

Clutch	dry mono-disc
Gearbox	en bloc with differential, 4 speeds plus reverse

CHASSIS
Boxed steel floorpan

Front suspension	independent, torsion bars, double wishbones, stabiliser bar, telescopic shock absorbers
Rear suspension	independent, torsion bars, double wishbones, hydraulic telescopic shock absorbers
Brakes	hydraulic drums
Steering	screw and finger
Fuel tank	50 litres
Tyres front/rear	5.60 x 15/5.60 x 15

DIMENSIONS AND WEIGHT

Wheelbase	2100 mm
Track front/rear	1306/1272 mm
Length	4010 mm
Width	1670 mm
Height	1330 mm (coupé and cabriolet)
Weight	935 kg (coupé and cabriolet)

PERFORMANCE

Top speed	185 kph
Power to weight ratio	10.4 kg/hp

356B 1600 Super 90   1960

Before the introduction of the 356B at the 1959 Frankfurt Motor Show, the engine range was made up of the various units with rocker arms and push rods with a power output of up to 75 hp (the 1600 S), to which were added the 105 and 115 hp Carrera De Luxe and Carrera GT models respectively with four overhead camshaft engines. Despite the performance, the latter was a little capricious in every-day use. Therefore, with the new model on the horizon, an intermediate version was considered with a performance that was not too far off that of the first Carrera but with perfect usability: it was the 1600 Super 90. The 1600 S engine with rocker arms and push rods was modified to produce bigger suction manifolds and the increased diameter of the inlet valves to 40 mm. The compression ratio went from 8.5:1 to 9:1 and the carburettors were twin choke Solex A40 PJJ4s from the 1500 GS. Maximum power went up to 90 hp at 5500 rpm with maximum torque at 12.3 kgm from 4300 rpm. The chassis was also brought up to date to handle the greater performance: Koni's sporty shock absorbers were fitted, tyres became bigger and a transverse leaf spring was installed at the rear. The latter – previously reserved for the Carrera models and later offered as an optional for the whole range – was hinged to the differential and had the task of transferring the load onto the inner wheel when the external is under pressure while cornering, reducing the oversteer, but without compromising comfort with a more rigid set-up. On the contrary, the torsion bar was reduced. The Super 90 was given enthusiastic reviews by the press starting with the long-established *Das Auto Motor und Sport*'s editor-in-chief H. U. Wieselmann, who wrote, "Porsche road cars are faster, but I don't know of any others in which one can go faster or at equal speed with the same level of safety". And he continued, "It seems that the cars are constructed in this small model factory not to earn money but to get as close as they can to technical perfection".

The 356 Carrera revised by Carlo Abarth with the help of Zagato was aimed at sporting efficiency, but its lines already revealed many trends that were to be taken up by the 911. In spite its considerable number of racing victories, the Carrera Abarth was not well received, especially not by the German press, for its constructional quality and limited aerodynamics.

TECHNICAL SPECIFICATION

ENGINE
Rear, overhanging, longitudinal
4 cylinders horizontally opposed

Bore and stroke	87.5 x 66 mm
Unitary cubic capacity	396.8 cc
Total cubic capacity	1587.5 cc
Valve gear	4 overhead camshafts, 2 counter shafts
Number of valves	2 per cylinder
Compression ratio	9.8:1
Fuel feed	2 twin choke carburettors
Ignition	coil
Coolant	forced air
Lubrication	dry sump
Maximum power	115 hp at 6500 rpm
Specific power	72.4 hp/litre

TRANSMISSION
Rear wheel drive

Clutch	dry mono-disc
Gearbox	en bloc with differential, 4 speeds plus reverse

CHASSIS
Boxed steel floorpan

Front suspension	independent, torsion bars, double wishbones, stabiliser bar, telescopic shock absorbers
Rear suspension	independent, torsion bars, double wishbones, hydraulic telescopic shock absorbers
Brakes	hydraulic drums
Steering	screw and finger
Fuel tank	80 litres
Tyres front/rear	5.90 x 15/5.90 x 15

DIMENSIONS AND WEIGHT

Wheelbase	2100 mm
Track front/rear	1306/1272 mm
Length	3980 mm
Width	1670 mm
Height	1310 mm
Weight	780 kg

PERFORMANCE

Top speed	220 kph
Power to weight ratio	6.7 kg/hp

356B 1600 GS Carrera, GTL Abarth   1960

In the early '60s it was essential to produce a competitive car for racing, and in this case every increase in power of the 4-cylinders was still not enough to compensate for too many kilograms. On 18 September 1959, the company's top management – including Ferry Porsche – met Turin car preparer Carlo Abarth, who had already worked with the Porsche family at the time of the Cisitalia Grand Prix car. Abarth was not the only person contacted, but in the end he was able to obtain an order for 20 bodies at a price of one million lire each. The starting point of the Carrera GTL (L for light) was the 356 B 1600 GS Carrera GT with its 1600 cc engine and twin overhead camshaft valve gear that put out 115 hp. But three different levels of performance were planned from the outset: the 115 hp, a second stage of 128 hp at 6500 rpm and an extreme elaboration of 135 hp at 7400 rpm. The difference was made most of all by the exhaust system, which was available in three versions: "production", "sporting" and "Sebring", obviously characterised by their noise level, each of which was much different from each other. The Abarth body, which was clearly inspired by Zagato as was later revealed by the Milanese body stylist, was aggressive and modern, setting the trend for many styling elements that would be part of the future 911, but did not produce the hoped for results, at least not on the scales or wind tunnel. Only 20 kg lighter than the Reutter coupé, the Abarth had a Cx of 0.414 against 0.296 of the first Gmünd coupé! Despite the fact that estimates at the time were much more optimistic at 0.376. The second slating of the Porsche Carrera "dressed" Italian style came from the German press, which was really severe about the car's build quality and rather caustic in its evaluation of habitability, judged "tailor made only for the Italians". But despite that, the car was still a successful racer and the 21 bodies assembled sold like hot cakes.

The RS61 was entered for the 1961 24 Hours of Le Mans with its coupé body. Porsche knew it couldn't compete against the V12 Ferraris, so it took four cars of four different cubic capacities to the Sarthe to at least score some good class placings, even if the 2-litre car still came fifth overall. The following year, the cars went back to being competitive with their 8-cylinder engines.

TECHNICAL SPECIFICATION

ENGINE
Central, longitudinal
4 cylinders horizontally opposed

Bore and stroke	87.5 x 66 mm
Unitary cubic capacity	396.7 hp
Total cubic capacity	1587 cc
Valve gear	4 overhead camshafts, driven by counter shafts
Number of valves	2 per cylinder
Compression ratio	9.8:1
Fuel feed	2 twin choke carburettors
Ignition	2 coils
Coolant	forced air
Lubrication	dry sump
Maximum power	160 hp at 7800 rpm
Specific power	100.8 hp/litre

TRANSMISSION
Rear wheel drive

Clutch	dry mono-disc
Gearbox	en bloc with differential, 5 speeds plus reverse

CHASSIS
Tubular steel trellis

Front suspension	independent, torsion bars, double wishbones, stabiliser bar, telescopic shock absorbers
Rear suspension	independent, double wishbones, coil springs for the hydraulic telescopic shock absorbers
Brakes	hydraulic drums
Steering	screw and finger
Fuel tank	80 litres
Tyres front/rear	5.50 x 15/5.90 x 15

DIMENSIONS AND WEIGHT

Wheelbase	2200 mm
Trak front/rear	1290/1250 mm
Length	3703 mm
Width	1511 mm
Height	9804 mm
Weight	550 kg

PERFORMANCE

Top speed	-
Power to weight ratio	3.4 kg/hp

718 RS61   1960

The evolution of the Spyder continued with the 1961 motor racing season on the horizon. The rear suspension was revised, the wheelbase lengthened and the track widened. The engines could be selected from 1500 cc, 1600 cc or 1700 cc, all of which had been seen during the previous season. The success of this car when driven by private entrants, especially during the latter period, was also the result of the care with which they were built: they were assembled by a team of expert mechanics, each specialised in a specific sector. If the care invested in their construction was excellent, the same couldn't be said of the built speed, so much so that many on the long waiting list went for the Carrera, which always performed well. This was also caused by increasingly restrictive regulations and ever more competitive grids, which marked the end of the Porsche Spyder. The Sebring debut would be confirmation of this tendency: the best RS61 came fifth, lapping much faster than the previous year's winning Spyder. Subsequently, the management of the works cars was partially delegated to private teams supported by Stuttgart, especially America's Camoradi. Meanwhile, Scuderia Serenissma, supported by a Porsche team manager and mechanics, entered two RS61 coupés powered by the 2-litre engine of the Carrera 2 and with a longer chassis, for the Targa Florio: the power output was similar to that of a good 1700 cc, but the torque and power generation were better. In addition, the longer chassis was ready to take on an 8-cylinder engine that was being developed and would last until the mid-60s, especially in hillclimbs where the most famous was the Spyder, nicknamed Granny, with which Edgar Barth won the 1963 and 1964 Mountain Championships. Later, there were to be the Le Mans and Nürburgring in which the RS61 was uncompetitive. That led the team manager Huscke von Hanstein, to announce Porsche's abandonment of motor racing after 1961, at least as far as the 4-cylinder sports racers were concerned.

The Carrera 2 was the maximum evolution of the 356: it was well-finished, highly reliable and, more than anything else, had performance that put it up against sports cars of double its cubic capacity. And its engines were used in many areas of motor sport, even reaching as far as Formula 1. It didn't go out of production until the arrival of the new, 6-cylinder 911.

TECHNICAL SPECIFICATION

ENGINE
Rear, overhanging, longitudinal
4 cylinders horizontally opposed

Bore and stroke	92 x 74 mm
Unitary cubic capacity	491.5 cc
Total cubic capacity	1966 cc
Valve gear	4 overhead camshafts with 2 counter shafts
Number of valves	2 per cylinder
Compression ratio	9.5:1
Fuel feed	2 twin choke carburettors
Ignition	double, with 2 coils
Coolant	forced air
Lubrication	dry sump
Maximum power	130 hp at 6200 rpm
Specific power	66.3 hp/litre

TRANSMISSION
Rear wheel drive

Clutch	dry mono-disc
Gearbox	en bloc with differential, 4 speeds plus reverse

CHASSIS
Boxed steel floorpan

Front suspension	independent, torsion bars, double wishbones, stabiliser bar, telescopic shock absorbers
Rear suspension	independent, torsion bars, double wishbones, hydraulic telescopic shock absorbers
Brakes	discs on all 4 wheels
Steering	screw and finger
Fuel tank	50 litres
Tyres front/rear	165 x 15/165 x 15

DIMENSIONS AND WEIGHT

Wheelbase	2100 mm
Track front/rear	1306/1272 mm
Length	4010 mm
Width	1670 mm
Height	1330 mm
Weight	1010 kg

PERFORMANCE

Top speed	200 kph
Power to weight ratio	5 hp/kg

356B 2000 GS Carrera 2   1961

"On really demanding roads, it is possible to reach average speeds that I prefer not to mention, because they could induce someone to overplay their hand". This quote from an article by Engelbert Männer in *Gute Fahrt* in early 1963 gives us a rather precise idea of public reaction to the launch of the fastest of the 356Bs, the 2000 GS Carrera 2. The main new development was the 1966 cc 4-cylinder boxer engine with four overhead camshafts and a bore and stroke of 92 x 74 mm. Maximum power output was 130 hp at 6200 rpm, with 16.5 kgm of torque at 4600 rpm, valves sufficient to push the 1020 kg coupé – 20 kg more for the cabriolet – to 200 kph and a 0-100 kph in 9.4 seconds. In the early '60s, that was comparable to an upmarket European sports car of double the Porsche's cubic capacity. Many clients with Carrera GTLs sent their cars to Stuttgart to have the production 1600 cc engine replace by the more modern 2-litre of the Carrera 2. Significant improvements were also made to the car's layout and even better results came from the adoption of radial ply tyres. Disc brakes were fitted to a road-going Porsche for the first time, which were produced by Porsche-Teves but were initially subject to overheating problems. The car's equipment was also rich and complete: it included a supplementary petrol-driven heater that was independent of the engine. Optional on the 356B, it turned out to be extremely useful in defrosting the windscreen after a night in the open. The 356 Carrera 2 remained in production until the launch of the 6-cylinder 911 and achieved tremendous success, given its price. Taking into account the 356 C version, 436 of these cars were built.

The chassis of the Porsche Formula 1 car for the 1961 season. The similarity between this and the RSK Spyder project is evident and from which it was directly derived, starting with the 4-cylinder type 547 engine. Despite its limits as the car waited for the readiness of the 8-cylinder boxer, it was able to do well, often taking American Dan Gurney to the podium and third in the F1 World Championship.

TECHNICAL SPECIFICATION

ENGINE

Central, longitudinal
4 cylinders horizontally opposed

Bore and stroke	85 x 66 mm
Unitary cubic capacity	374.5 cc
Total cubic capacity	1498 cc
Valve gear	4 overhead camshafts with counter shafts
Number of valves	2 per cylinder
Compression ratio	10.3:1
Fuel feed	2 twin choke carburettors
Ignition	double, 2 coils
Coolant	forced air
Lubrication	dry sump
Maximum power	190 hp at 8000 rpm
Specific power	126.8 hp/litre

TRANSMISSION

Rear wheel drive

Clutch	dry mono-disc
Gearbox	en bloc with differential, 6 speeds plus reverse

CHASSIS

Tubular steel trellis

Front suspension	independent, coil springs, double wishbones, stabiliser bar, telescopic shock absobers
Rear suspension	independent, double wishbones, coil springs for the shock absorbers, stabiliser bar
Brakes	discs on all 4 wheels
Steering	rack
Fuel tank	100 litres
Tyres front/rear	5.00 x 15/6.50 x 15

DIMENSIONS AND WEIGHT

Wheelbase	2300 mm
Track front/rear	1300/1330 mm
Length	3423 mm
Width	840 mm
Height	800 mm
Weight	450 kg

PERFORMANCE

Top speed	270 kph
Power to weight ratio	2.4 kg/hp

Type 787 1961

FIA changed the Formula 1 regulations for the 1961 season, outlawing superchargers and limiting cubic capacity to 1500 cc: in practice, the restrictions were previously those of Formula 2. Porsche, winners of the previous year's F2 Championship, realised that the development limits of the 547 engine were not far off and that, to be competitive in the maximum formula, they had to invest. It wasn't an easy decision to take and there were opposing lines of thought within the management team. In the end, the programme went ahead and with it a project for an 8-cylinder with horizontally opposed cylinders again and air cooled, just like the traditional Porsche. On 12 September 1960, the engine was started up for the first time but its power output was only 120 hp; and the 160 hp after tuning was also inadequate, being comparable to that of the much more compact 547. So for 1961 Porsche had to take remedial action, bringing back a number of the old 718 F2 units and modifying the suspension, fuel tank position and lengthening the wheelbase – but still with four cylinders and called the Type 787. The debut race in Pau ended up with two Porsche retirements. Dan Gurney had his first race for the team at Syracuse, but the Germans were beaten here by Ferrari too. After the first announcement of the 8-cylinder, Porsche took several versions of the new engine to the Monaco GP; Gurney had a 718, Hans Herrmann a transitional version between the 718 and the 787 and Jo Bonnier a 787 with a new Kugelfischer injection system, which caused a vapour lock problem, for which he retired. It seemed a no-way-out situation but to plug the gap Ferry Porsche had the racing team recover two old 718 F2 that was on its way to being sold. Despite the fact that it was obsolete, Gurney scored a series of second places that took him to third in the Championship with a great race by the American at Reims, over taken by the potent Ferrari of Giancarlo Baghetti's Ferrari on the last corner. Meanwhile, an experimental car with a slimmer body, disc brakes and a horizontal fan had made its debut at Solitude.

Dan Gurney on his way to winning Porsche's first Formula 1 GP, the Grand Prix of France at Rouen. The Porsche 804 was strongly criticised by the purists for its anonymous shape and the management for the exorbitant costs linked to the complexity of its air cooled 8-cylinder boxer. The car would never be able to really compete against its British and Ferrari adversaries.

TECHNICAL SPECIFICATION

ENGINE
Central, longitudinal
8 cylinders horizontally opposed

Bore and stroke	66 x 54.6 mm
Unitary cubic capacity	186.8 cc
Total cubic capacity	1494.4 cc
Valve gear	4 overhead camshafts powered by countershafts
Number of valves	2 per cylinder
Compression ratio	10:1
Fuel feed	4 twin choke carburettors
Ignition	dual, 4 coils
Coolant	forced air
Lubrication	dry sump
Maximum power	180 hp at 9200 rpm
Specific power	120 hp/litre

TRANSMISSION
Rear wheel drive

Clutch	dry mono-disc
Gearbox	en bloc with differential, 6 speeds plus reverse

CHASSIS
Tubular steel trellis

Front suspension	independent, torsion bars, double wishbones, stabiliser bar, telescopic shock absorbers
Rear suspension	independent, double wishbones, torsion bars, shock absorbers, stabiliser bar
Brakes	discs on all four wheels
Steering	rack
Fuel tank	100 litres
Tyres front/rear	5.00 x 15/6.50 x 15

DIMENSIONS AND WEIGHT
Wheelbase	2300 mm
Track front/rear	1300/1330 mm
Length	3600 mm
Width	-
Height	-
Weight	455 kg

PERFORMANCE
Top speed	270 kph
Power to weight ratio	2.5 kg/hp

Type 804 1962

The 804 made its debut during the 1962 Formula 1 season with its sophisticated 8-cylinder engine, which had already been discarded the year before due to its poor performance level. Meanwhile, power output increased to 178 hp, which was enough to be competitive in the F1 World Championship, but not so superior to the old 4-cylinder, which was more reliable, lighter and less expensive. The new unit had been designed with little restraint in the choice of ambitious technical developments, which did not seem to produce adequate results for all that effort (it took 220 days of specialised work to assemble one engine). And not comprising parts in common with road car production – it was a unit that couldn't be installed in a future GT – all the components had to be especially made or acquired at high prices from external suppliers. That is why a car was readied with the same chassis as the "normal" 804 but powered by the 4-cylinder 547 tuned by Michael May but was dropped just before the start of the Zandvoort GP on 20 May 1962; but an 8-cylinder engine was later installed and it became Dan Gurney's racer. The engine was not the only thing that was new to the 804; it also had a complex tubular layout, with sections reduced from 15 mm to 30 mm, two of which also acted as oil conductors. The superimposed wishbone suspension had longitudinal torsion bars and Porsche-layout disc brakes. The body was brand new, slim and modern but it was criticised due to its neutral shape, which didn't reek of a Porsche identity, except for the design of the aluminium wheels. The 804's results during the early part of the season were disastrous, so much so that continuation was in doubt, but after that Gurney turned in two great results at Rouen and Solitude that injected new life into the team. Unfortunately, lack of success during the remainder of the season meant Porsche took the decision not to pursue the project.

The 356B 2000 GS Carrera 2 GT competing in the 1963 Monte Carlo Rally, in which it won its class. Another great success was in the Rally of the Midnight Sun in Sweden. But the world of motor racing was going through considerable transformation and the results of the Carrera 2 were not as extensive as expected from a car that had few rivals among normal production cars.

TECHNICAL SPECIFICATION

ENGINE

Rear, inclined, longitudinal
4 cylinders horizontally opposed

Bore and stroke	92 x 74 mm
Unitary cubic capacity	491.5
Total cubic capacity	1966 cc
Valve gear	4 overhead camshafts, powered by countershafts
Number of valves	2 per cylinder
Compression ratio	9.8:1
Fuel feed	2 twin choke carburettors
Ignition	dual, 2 coils
Coolant	forced air
Lubrication	dry sump
Maximum power	155 hp at 6600 rpm

TRANSMISSION

Rear wheel drive

Clutch	dry mono-disc
Gearbox	en bloc with differential, 4 speeds plus reverse

CHASSIS

Boxed steel floorpan

Front suspension	independent, torsion bars, double wishbones, stabiliser bar, telescopic shock absorbers
Rear suspension	independent, torsion bars, double wishbones, hydraulic telescopic shock absorbers
Brakes	discs on all four wheels
Steering	screw and finger
Fuel tank	110 litres
Tyres front/rear	165 x 15 / 165 x 15

DIMENSIONS AND WEIGHT

Wheelbase	2100 mm
Track front/rear	1306 / 1272 mm
Length	4013 mm
Width	1554 mm
Height	1181 mm
Weight	850 kg

PERFORMANCE

Top speed	210 kph
Power to weight ratio	5.5 kg/hp

356B-C 2000 GS Carrera 2 GT   1962

If the top of the 356 range is the 130 hp Carrera 2, it was natural to cater for the interest of Porsche's many sporting clients with the car. The company's price list included a Carrera GTL Abarth, but that was a rare beast and expensive to boot. To give its customers the chance of competing with a suitable version with a road car body, the Carrera 2 GT was developed even if – given the age of the 356 – the abundance of other versions (the Abarth, but also the "old" Carrera 1500 and 1600) and the ever higher specialisation of racing, the model didn't have a long and successful motor sport career that the power of the road car could make people think. With an increased compression ratio of 9.8:1, bigger Weber 46 IDM-2 carburettors, various cross sections of valve gear diagrams and piston rods made of nitride steel it put out 140 hp at 6200 rpm or 155 hp at 6600 rpm in part due to colder Bosch spark plugs, which also needed a more extensive electrical system. The gearbox was shortened and had at least four different gear set-ups available in the list, while the differential was self-locking but optional on the GS. The final bevel gear ratio was unchanged. The body was also modified: first the 50-litre fuel tank was replaced by one of more than double that capacity at 110 litres with a filler cap, which could be opened from the outside, positioned on the bonnet. And to reduce weight, the doors, engine cover and bonnet were made of aluminium, the deflectors were fixed, the lateral and rear windows were of Plexiglas, the fronts sliding along on aluminium guides. The chrome windscreen surround was no longer and nor were the bumper bar bolts; inside, the wood-rimmed steering wheel and the absence of the passenger seat were the clearest signs of the body shell lightening process.

The only two examples of the 356 B 2000 GS-GT Dreikantschaber going into the Mulsanne corner during the 1963 24 Hours of Le Mans. During the race, the car's speed was recorded as over 239 kph, enough to explode the myth of the Abarth being fastest of the Carreras. Many hoped there would be a small production run of the car, but Porsche's attention was already focused on the future 904 in glass fibre.

TECHNICAL SPECIFICATION

ENGINE

Rear, overhanging, longitudinal
4 cylinders horizontally opposed

Bore and stroke	92 x 74 mm
Unitary cubic capacity	491.5 cc
Total cubic capacity	1966
Valve gear	4 overhead camshafts powered by countershafts
Number of valves	2 per cylinder
Compression ratio	9.8:1
Fuel feed	2 twin choke carburettors
Ignition	dual, 2 coils
Coolant	forced air
Lubrication	dry sump
Maximum power	160 hp at 6600 rpm

TRANSMISSION

Rear wheel drive

Clutch	dry mono-disc
Gearbox	en bloc with differential, 5 speeds plus reverse

CHASSIS

Boxed steel floorpan

Front suspension	independent, torsion bars, double wishbones, stabiliser bar, telescopic shock absorbers
Rear suspension	independent, double wishbones, torsion bars, hydraulic telescopic shock absorbers
Brakes	discs on all four wheels
Steering	screw and finger
Tyres front/rear	-

DIMENSIONS AND WEIGHT

Wheelbase	2100 mm
Track front/rear	1306/1272 mm
Length	-
Width	-
Height	-
Weight	820 kg

PERFORMANCE

Top speed	235 kph
Power to weight ratio	5.1 kg/hp

356B 2000 GS-GT Dreikantschaber   1963

Taking advantage of a hole in the up to 2-litre GT category regulations that required at least 100 chassis and a 1000 engines, but made no mention of the bodies, Porsche built two hybrid cars on Carrera 2 chassis suitably prepared for racing, to which they added aluminium bodies. The shells were very much like a few coupés that competed successfully on 718 RS 60-61 chassis. But while those cars had much more substantial rear uprights and a vertical rear window – or sometimes even without a rear window – two rear windows were added to the Dreikantschaber in the place of air intakes. But the number of chassis used reveal the experiment was carried out on cars that had already been in circulation for some time. They made their racing debut in the 1963 12 Hours of Sebring and finished ninth and tenth overall, a result they bettered at the Targa Florio with a third by Barth-Linge in a car with ATE disc brakes in a race won by Bonnier-Abate in a Porsche 8-cylinder. The Dreikantschaber also scored a fourth at the Nürburgring and was a major flop at Le Mans. That was despite the excellent performance by the two cars, one with disc brakes and the other with drums, when over-revving and a broken valve forced both cars to retire. The results in the Mountain Championship were not much better and in 1964 they competed at Daytona and Sebring again, in the latter of which the cars came 11TH and 12TH overall, two places behind the 904 with its glass fibre body, and still awaiting homologation. It was the end of an epoch: the complex and expensive aluminium bodies soon lost out to glass fibre and, in the same way, so did sports racers derived from the 356 road cars; they had to make way for more specialised cars that were designed especially for racing.

The 356 had enjoyed a 17-year career, with over 76,000 being sold. The evolution of its mechanics was continuous and punctual, the same with the body, an area in which the 356C foreshadowed some of the 911's styling trends. After the last of the cars left the production line in 1955 another 10 cabriolets – white with black hoods – were produced in 1966 for the Dutch police.

TECHNICAL SPECIFICATION

ENGINE

Rear, overhanging, longitudinal
4 cylinders horizontally opposed

Bore and stroke	82.5 x 74 mm
Unitary cubic capacity	395.5 cc
Total cubic capacity	1582 cc
Valve gear	overhead valves, push rods and rocker arms
Number of valves	2 per cylinder
Compression ratio	8.5:1
Fuel feed	2 twin choke carburettors
Ignition	coil
Coolant	forced air
Lubrication	wet sump
Maximum power	75 hp at 5200 rpm
Specific power	47.4 hp/litre

TRANSMISSION

Rear wheel drive

Clutch	dry mono-disc
Gearbox	en bloc with differential, 4 speeds plus reverse

CHASSIS

Boxed steel floorpan

Front suspension	independent, torsion bars, double wishbones, stabiliser bar, telescopic shock absorbers
Rear suspension	independent, torsion bars, double wishbones, hydraulic telescopic shock absorbers
Brakes	discs on all four wheels
Steering	screw and finger
Fuel tank	50 litres
Tyres front/rear	5.60 x 15/5.60 x 15

DIMENSIONS AND WEIGHT

Wheelbase	2100 mm
Track front/rear	1306/1272 mm
Length	4010 mm
Width	1670 mm
Height	1330 mm
Weight	935 kg

PERFORMANCE

Top speed	175 kph
Power to weight ratio	12.4 kg/hp

356C 1600 C 1963

The launch of the new 901 6-cylinder car, which was later permanently baptised the 911, was in the air by this time and the 356 was ready to be pensioned off. But right up until the last moment the continuous process of evolution never ceased and in 1963 the 356C was unveiled, although the untrained eye found it hard to recognise it as a new model. The only evident difference was the adoption of new rims that were still 15 inches in diameter but of different design that was necessary for them to host ATE disc brakes built under licence from Dunlop. It was not the first time such brakes had been used, as Porsche-designed discs were fitted to the Carrera 2. They amazed everyone with their efficiency and stability, but they let the water in and small production runs proved expensive. Hence the Dunlops. Various modifications were made to the chassis: first of all, the shock absorber anchorage points had to be modified – Boge or Koni adjustables, depending on the model – in readiness for the installation of the disc brakes; and the layout would be revised again. The transverse compensator bar was eliminated from the rear end as it was considered superfluous after perfecting the calibration, but it was still available as an optional for the lovers of driving completely without oversteer. At the bottom of the range, the 60 hp engine with the "Dame" push rods and rocker arms was eliminated and that was replaced by another 1600 that put out 75 hp: the power it generated was the same as the old Super, but with substantial tuning to make it work sweeter and softer, for which many Dame clients were waiting. On 28 April 1965, while the 911 was already in production, the last 356 series came out of the Stuttgart-Zuffenhausen factory; it was a white 356C 1600 C Cabriolet and to mark that fact it was "given" a bouquet of flowers. That, even if another 10 white 356 cabriolets were built in May 1966 for the Dutch police. In an honourable 17-year career, 76,302 356s were built.

The 356C lines were almost identical to those of the 356B. But under the body there was evolution without revolution, which had not stopped even when the brand new 6-cylinder 911 first appeared and the old 4-cylinder was almost ready to be pensioned off. Disc brakes, a more potent engine and a revised layout were the strong points of the C.

TECHNICAL SPECIFICATION

ENGINE

Rear, overhanging, longitudinal
4 cylinders horizontally opposed

Bore and stroke	82.5 x 74 mm
Unitary cubic capacity	395.5 cc
Total cubic capacity	1582 cc
Valve gear	overhead valves, push rods and rocker arms
Number of valves	2 per cylinder
Compression ratio	9.5:1
Fuel feed	2 twin choke carburettors
Ignition	coil
Coolant	forced air
Lubrication	wet sump
Maximum power	95 hp at 5800 rpm
Specific power	60 hp/litre

TRANSMISSION

Rear wheel drive

Clutch	dry mono-disc
Gearbox	en bloc with differential, 4 speeds plus reverse

CHASSIS

Boxed steel floorpan

Front suspension	independent, torsion bars, double wishbones, stabiliser bar, telescopic shock absorbers
Rear suspension	independent, torsion bars, double wishbones, hydraulic telescopic shock absorbers
Brakes	discs on all four wheels
Steering	screw and finger
Fuel tank	50 litres
Tyres front/rear	165 x 15/165 x 15

DIMENSIONS AND WEIGHT

Wheelbase	2100 mm
Track front/rear	1306/1272 mm
Length	4010 mm
Width	1670 mm
Height	1330 mm
Weight	935 kg

PERFORMANCE

Top speed	185 kph
Power to weight ratio	9.8 kg/hp

356C 1600 SC 1963

Introduced in 1963 with the C version, the 356C 1600 SC was externally distinguishable from the previous B model only by the wheels, which were updated to be able to install disc brakes. Inside the instrument panel – as on its little sister C – was modified in the central area, to produce a downward, which forced the company to suitably shorten the gear lever. The cabriolet's hood was updated with the adoption of a double zipper at the rear, which permitted the easy replacement of the rear window, both from inside and out. Many other detailed modifications completely deny the impression of the abandonment of the model during the final stages of its career: from the new heating lever to the handbrake dial on the dashboard and the new passenger's armrest to the repositioning of the lights and windscreen wiper switches. Further modifications were made to the seats: the fronts were slightly deeper, while the rear bench was raised a little to avoid baggage falling over during a journey; the seat backs were held in place by chains. And in the case of the 356C a dual tone hard top was added to the Cabriolet. The spartan Roadster was taken out of the 356B price list. The 1600 cc engine of the SC was replaced with another of push rods and rocker arms and went from the 75 hp of the "old" 356B to 95 hp. This power increase – the work of Hans Mezger, who would be the driving force behind the Formula 1 Tag-Porsche – was achieved by redesigning the intake and exhaust ducts, increasing the valves' diameter and upping the compression ratio due to the adoption of new pistons. The SC engine also had sodium cooled exhaust valves and a drive shaft with balanced counterweights to avoid vibration at high revs. The cylinder liners were in light alloy clad with Ferral, which was later replaced by Biral in cast iron with light alloy around them.

The Type 7 experimental prototype designed by Ferdinand Alexander Porsche, nicknamed Butzi. It was one of the various examples of styling and layout for the car that would replace the 356. But it was selected as a starting point for the 911, due to its coherence with the styling trends of the marque and its compatibility with Porsche's mechanical traditions.

TECHNICAL SPECIFICATION

ENGINE

Rear, overhanging, longitudinal
6 cylinders horizontally opposed

Bore and stroke	80 x 66 mm
Unitary cubic capacity	331.8 cc
Total cubic capacity	1991 cc
Valve gear	overhead camshaft, chain driven
Number of valves	2 per cylinder
Compression ratio	9.0:1
Fuel feed	carburettors
Ignition	coil
Coolant	forced air
Lubrication	dry sump
Maximum power	130 hp at 6100 rpm
Specific power	65.3 hp/litre

TRANSMISSION

Rear wheel drive

Clutch	dry mono-disc
Gearbox	en block with differential, 5 speeds plus reverse

CHASSIS

Unitised steel body

Front suspension	McPherson layout, longitudinal torsion bars, hydraulic telescopic shock absorbers
Rear suspension	independent, oblique arms, transverse torsion bars, hydraulic telescopic shock absorbers
Brakes	discs on all four wheels
Steering	ZF rack
Fuel tank	62 litres
Tyres front/rear	165 x 15/165 x 15

DIMENSIONS AND WEIGHT

Wheelbase	2211 mm
Track front/rear	1367/1335 mm
Length	4163 mm
Width	1610 mm
Height	1320 mm
Weight	1080 kg

PERFORMANCE

Top speed	210 kph
Power to weight ratio	8.3 kg/hp

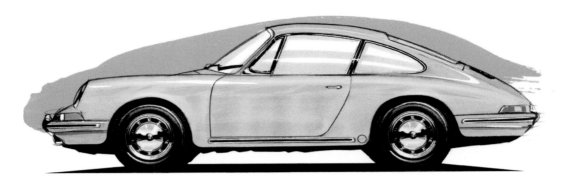

901 1963

For the replacement of the 356 many different hypotheses were considered, including a real three-volume four-seater. In the end, choice fell on the Type 7 project, the work of Ferdinand Alexander Porsche, nicknamed Butzi, the son of Ferry. The "cahier des charges" of the model to be baptised the 901 foresaw an imposition coherent with that of the 356, but with numerous variants. The 356 lines were well-known and recognisable with a vast, affectionate number of public admirers. The fundamental problem that had to be resolved was habitability: once the 2+2 formula was selected, one in which the two rear places were more than simple jump seats to maintain the performance and pleasure of driving without paying the cost in comfort and reliability with such a lively engine, it was necessary to go for a new 6-cylinder. But this brought with it a sort of category change for the car, which placed it outside what many Porsche clients could afford. Even the boot room would be among the priorities, one of the reasons for which the company opted for McPherson front suspension, as Ferry had underlined requests from many clients to be able to place at least a bag of golf clubs in the new model, which was impossible with the 356. Management was complex; no fewer than three different kind of the Type 7 were prepared before arriving at the definitive formula. There then followed 13 prototypes of the 901, which led to long test sessions with the cars camouflaged for public road use before the car's introduction at the 1963 Frankfurt Motor Show in September. But the first obstacle to what would become a sparkling career turned up even before the car went on sale. For years, Peugeot had registered all the three-number car denominations with a central 0 – including 901. Later, Porsche verified the fact that the problem only concerned production cars, so there wouldn't be any problem in naming their celebrated sports car the 904, 906 or 908, but the destiny of the heir to the 356 was already set: it would be called the 911.

Even if its styling trends did recall the 356, the new 911 offered itself as a mature car of bigger dimensions. Despite a cubic capacity of just 2-litres, it put out 130 hp, but both the chassis and engine were designed to reach even greater heights like 2.7-litres without substantial modifications and high performance with a view to its coming motor sport involvement.

TECHNICAL SPECIFICATION

ENGINE

Rear, overhanging, longitudinal
6 cylinder horizontally opposed

Bore and stroke	80 x 66 mm
Unitary cubic capacity	331.8 cc
Total cubic capacity	1991 cc
Valve gear	overhead camshaft, chain driven
Number of valves	2 per cylinder
Compression ratio	9.0:1
Fuel feed	carburettors
Ignition	coil
Coolant	forced air
Lubrication	dry sump
Maximum power	130 hp at 6100 rpm
Specific power	65.3 hp/litre

TRANSMISSION

Rear wheel drive

Clutch	dry mono-disc
Gearbox	en bloc with differential, 5 speeds plus reverse

CHASSIS

Unitised steel body

Front suspension	McPherson, longitudinal torsion bars, hydraulic telescopic shock absorbers
Rear suspension	independent, oblique arms, transverse torsion bars, hydraulic telescopic shock absorbers
Brakes	discs on all four wheels
Steering	ZF rack
Fuel tank	62 litres
Tyres front/rear	165 x 15/165 x 15

DIMENSIONS AND WEIGHT

Wheelbase	2211 mm
Track front/rear	1367/1335 mm
Length	4163 mm
Width	1610 mm
Height	1320 mm
Weight	1080 kg

PERFORMANCE

Top speed	210 kph
Power to weight ratio	8.3 kg/hp

911 1963

The 911 family's firstborn – only the designation was changed compared to the 901 – had a steel chassis and body shell, an engine that overhung beyond the rear wheels and a transaxle gearbox. The main new development over the 356, which it replaced, was the engine: once the company had opted for a 6-cylinder, given the mechanical disposition, the choice of a boxer layout was almost obligatory, while air cooling was a Porsche tradition. Due to the 2-litre cubic capacity (1991 cc, 80 x 66 mm) the unit generated 130 hp at 6100 rpm with 17.8 kgm of torque at 4200 rpm. But from the original design exercise, it was always a possibility that its capacity could reach 2.7-litres without modification should the market demand it. The combustion chambers were hemispheric with two valves in a V formation controlled by rocker arms by a camshaft for each cylinder bank, which was chain driven. The drive shaft lay on eight main bearings with dry sump lubrication. The air cooling was by a new light alloy fan with an axial blow – different to the radial system of the 356, which was less efficient but economic – and fitted coaxially to the alternator. The entire transmission, dry mono-disc clutch, five speed Porsche synchronised gearbox and the differential was contained in the sump made in a single, light alloy unit. The rear suspension kept the classic layout with oscillating half-axles, longitudinal arms and torsion bars, while the front was McPherson, which was far less bulky. The steering was by ZF constructed rack, while the four disc brakes by ATE, which had already been tried out on the 356 C, were also selected for the 911. With a completely re-designed chassis, the light alloy engine and other fine materials gave the 911 to a kerb weight of just 1080 kg, which ensured a 0-100 kph time of 9.1 seconds and a top speed – helped along by a Cx of 0.38 – of 210 kph.

A 904 Carrera GTS racing at Zolder during the 1964 Grand Prix of Limburg. The car enjoyed a most successful career driven by private entrants, while the factory team attempted experiments, like installing six and eight cylinder engines. The design, the work of Butzi Porsche, was nothing like the production cars, but it was still a milestone in sports saloons.

TECHNICAL SPECIFICATION

ENGINE

Central, longitudinal
4 cylinders horizontally opposed

Bore and stroke	92 x 74 mm
Unitary cubic capacity	491.5 cc
Total cubic capacity	1966 cc
Valve gear	4 overhead camshafts driven by counter shafts
Number of valves	2 per cylinder
Compression ratio	9.8:1
Fuel feed	2 twin choke carburettors
Ignition	dual, 2 coils
Coolant	forced air
Lubrication	dry sump
Maximum power	180 hp at 7000 rpm
Specific power	91.5 hp/litre

TRANSMISSION

Rear wheel drive

Clutch	dry mono-disc
Gearbox	en bloc with differential, 5 speeds plus reverse

CHASSIS

Boxed steel sheet

Front suspension	independent, double wishbones, coil springs, hydraulic telescopic shock absorbers
Rear suspension	independent, double wishbones, coil springs, hydraulic telescopic shock absorbers
Brakes	discs on all four wheels
Steering	screw and finger
Fuel tank	-
Tyres front/rear	5.50 x 15/6.0 x 15

DIMENSIONS AND WEIGHT

Wheelbase	2300 mm
Track front/rear	1314/1312 mm
Length	4094 mm
Width	1541 mm
Height	1066 mm
Weight	650 kg

PERFORMANCE

Top speed	263 kph
Power to weight ratio	3.6 kg/hp

904 Carrera GTS   1963

After the end of the Spyder era, Porsche made a definitive change in the sports car and GT area with its 904 – better known as the Carrera GTS – which was especially aimed at sporting clients. Right from the start it was fully aware that it had to build at least 100 of the cars for Grand Touring homologation and take its clients' needs into account to arrive at a car that wasn't too expensive, robust and easy to maintain. Although the company considered using the 911's 6-cylinder engine, it opted for the everlasting 2-litre 4-cylinder that was reliable and known to mechanics throughout the world. The chassis was made of boxed elements with a double wishbone suspension and disc brakes. Porsche dropped expensive aluminium for the body and used glass fibre, bolted and glued to a unified structure to increase overall rigidity, in principle one of the main weak points of the car. The body, heavy at just 100 kg to which 45 kg should be added for the chassis, was built by Heinkel of Speyer and designed by Ferdinand Alexander (Butzi) Porsche, father of the 911. As the 904 was a grand tourer, a road going version was also offered, with a 155 hp engine: it was driveable and versatile, but the precocious wear of the mechanics in urban use and the minor versatility of the cockpit suggested decidedly other uses. The racing version's power output soared to 185 hp, enough to push the 904 to over 250 kph with a 0-100 kph acceleration of 5.5 seconds. After producing excellent results under test at the Nürburgring, the first of the cars were sent to Sebring, where one of them scored its first class win. Meanwhile its great public success, helped along by a price of only DM 29,700 – not much for a winning car – pushed sales well beyond the 100 homologation cars. Then came the 1964 Targa Florio victory and many others, including an extraordinary second overall by Eugen Bohringer in the 1965 Monte Carlo Rally.

Apart from the slightly simplified equipment and the writing on the engine cover, there are no substantial differences between the 912 and the 911. But there was a much bigger difference in a price that was to attract those customers who liked the 356 so much and who could not afford the 6-cylinder 911, but still wanted a Porsche in their garage.

TECHNICAL SPECIFICATION

ENGINE

Rear, overhanging, longitudinal
4 cylinders horizontally opposed

Bore and stroke	82.5 x 74
Unitary cubic capacity	395.5 cc
Total cubic capacity	1582 cc
Valve gear	overhead valves, push rods and rocker arms
Number of valves	2 per cylinder
Compression ratio	9.3:1
Fuel feed	2 carburettors
Ignition	coil
Coolant	forced air
Lubrication	wet sump
Maximum power	90 hp at 5800 rpm
Specific power	56.9 hp/litre

TRANSMISSION

Rear wheel drive

Clutch	dry mono-disc
Gearbox	en bloc with differential, 5 speeds plus reverse

CHASSIS

Unified steel body

Front suspension	McPherson layout, longitudinal torsion bars, hydraulic telescopic shock absorbers
Rear suspension	independent, oblique arms, transverse torsion bars, hydraulic telescopic shock absorbers
Brakes	discs on all four wheels
Steering	ZF rack
Fuel tank	62 litres
Tyres front/rear	165 x 15/165 x 15

DIMENSIONS AND WEIGHT

Wheelbase	2211 mm
Track front/rear	1337/1317 mm
Length	4163 mm
Width	1610 mm
Height	1320 mm
Weight	970 kg

PERFORMANCE

Top speed	185 kph
Power to weight ratio	10.8 kg/hp

912   1965

The new 911 was launched from November 1963 with five cars a day being produced by Zuffenhausen. At the same time, 40 356Cs continued to roll off the same production line. The price difference between the two was considerable at DM 22,900 against DM 16,450, and when the 356 dropped out of the price list a year later, many of the company's loyal customers decided that they couldn't afford the newcomer. So in April 1965, the new 912 was unveiled and was the company's response to public demand. The chassis and body were almost exactly the same as its bigger sister, with a number of simplifications in equipment. The engine, for instance, was a 4-cylinder 1600 cc with the 356SC's push rods and rocker arms and a different level of tuning. Power output dropped from 95 hp to 90 hp at 6000 rpm, but with a notable improvement in driving elasticity. Transmission was via a 4-speed synchronised gearbox with a 5-speed available as an optional. Initially, the car was only available on the continental market as it didn't conform to a number of specific demands of the British and United States markets. The problems were resolved later and that brought the car great success in America, where already severe controls on excess speed made it a politically correct alternative to the more potent 911. There were only detail modifications to the car in 1966, but a year later the wheelbase was increased by 57 mm for better habitability. There were also new door panels, steering wheel, heating and pile floor covering, which replaced rubber, and better equipment. An EGR anti-pollution system was introduced for cars America-bound, which recycled exhaust gasses, and front stabiliser bars were no longer installed. At the same time, the Targa body became available for both the 911 and 912 and was a roadster with a fixed roll bar.

No way was the 904-8 Spyder's shape attractive, a car that earned the nickname Kanguruh for itself: the chassis was derived from that of the 904 and that shape brought back a number of aspects of the Elva-Porsche. The car wasn't successful, but it did open up a new area of attention during races in the European Mountain Championship and was the founder of a prolific new generation of "Bergspyders".

TECHNICAL SPECIFICATION

ENGINE

Central, longitudinal
8 cylinders horizontally opposed

Bore and stroke	76 x 54 mm
Unitary cubic capacity	247.6 cc
Total cubic capacity	1981 cc
Valve gear	overhead camshaft, chain driven
Number of valves	2 per cylinder
Compression ratio	10.2:1
Fuel feed	-
Ignition	-
Coolant	forced air
Lubrication	dry sump
Maximum power	260 hp at 8800 rpm
Specific power	131.2 hp/litre

TRANSMISSION

Rear wheel drive

Clutch	dry mono-disc
Gearbox	en bloc with differential, 5 speeds plus reverse

CHASSIS

Boxed in steel sheets

Front suspension	independent, overlapping wishbones, coil springs, hydraulic telescopic shock absorbers
Rear suspension	independent, overlapping wishbones, coil springs, hydraulic telescopic shock absorbers
Brakes	discs on all four wheels
Steering	screw and finger
Fuel tank	-
Tyres front/rear	-

DIMENSIONS AND WEIGHT

Track front/rear	-
Length	-
Width	-
Height	-
Weight	570 kg

PERFORMANCE

Top speed	-
Power to weight ratio	2.2 kg/hp

904-8 Spyder Kanguruh   1965

After the success of the 904 GTS, the Porsche design team's next job was to define the 906, which was to compete in racing powered by the 911's 6-cylinder engine. Meanwhile, with the 1965 European Mountain Championship coming up – one of the most important series of its kind – a Spyder was developed with an 8-cylinder power unit that placed all Porsche's bets on its lightness and compactness of the body, which was vaguely inspired by the Elva-Porsche and was certainly of unattractive appearance. So much so that it was promptly nicknamed the Kanguruh. The chassis was derived straight from the 904's, but the complete car's weight was a massive 120 kg lower at a total of 570 kg, despite the 8-cylinder engine. The 904-8's debut race was the Targa Florio, in which Mitter-Davis took third place, but the poor chassis rigidity soon meant its replacement. Two much updated Kanguruhs were later entered for the Trento-Bondone, while the first example was switched to test work: Mitter and Fischhaber capitulated to Scarfiotti's Ferrari and Hans Herrmann's Abarth, a poor result that was not bettered in subsequent races. That's why Porsche began the construction of a totally new car a few days before the Ollon-Villars hillclimb, which only retained the Kanguruh's gearbox seeing that the engine had already been updated. They opted for a tubular trellis-type chassis and new suspension, working on the new car day and night and using a number of examples bought from Colin Chapman to save time, which is why the car was called the Lotus-Porsche. The car was built just in time for the race and had no time for test work. So the result was predictable, with Mitter being beaten by Scarfiotti in the Ferrari again, the duo that eventually won the Championship. But the car's evolution continued so that, by the end of the season, weight had been reduced to 488 kg and power had risen to 250 hp: but by this time, it was too late to take revenge, although the exercise had laid down the basics for the future 910.

The 911 S's production line. Note the supplementary bumpers on the car in the foreground (the chrome bar that joins the two bumper guards, which were also bigger) and necessary for American homologation, always a key market for Porsche. Power output had increased to 160 hp and made a major leap ahead of the 356 and put the 911 firmly among the high performance GTs.

TECHNICAL SPECIFICATION

ENGINE

Rear, overhanging, longitudinal
6 cylinders horizontally opposed

Bore and stroke	80 x 66 mm
Unitary cubic capacity	331.8 cc
Total cubic capacity	1991 cc
Valve gear	overhead camshaft, chain driven
Number of valves	2 per cylinder
Compression ratio	9.8:1
Fuel feed	carburettors
Ignition	coil
Coolant	forced air
Lubrication	dry sump
Maximum power	160 hp at 6600 rpm
Specific power	80.3 hp/litre

TRANSMISSION

Rear wheel drive

Clutch	dry mono-disc
Gearbox	en bloc with differential, 5 speeds plus reverse

CHASSIS

Unitary steel construction

Front suspension	McPherson, longitudinal torsion bars, stabiliser bar, hydraulic shock absorbers
Rear suspension	independent, oblique arms, transverse torsion bars, hydraulic shock absorbers, stabiliser bar
Brakes	discs on all four wheels
Steering	ZF rack
Fuel tank	62 litres
Tyres front/rear	165 x 15/165 x 15

DIMENSIONS AND WEIGHT

Wheelbase	2211 mm
Track front/rear	1367/1335 mm
Length	4163 mm
Width	1610 mm
Height	1320 mm
Weight	1030 kg

PERFORMANCE

Top speed	225 kph
Power to weight ratio	6.4 kg/hp

911 S   1966

Introduced in 1963 and as with the 356, the 911 had already begun its continuous process of evolution without revaluation during its early years, which was typical of Porsche. In 1965 an open top version called the Targa was unveiled, a version of the body that would make history – so much so that the Targa name would be used for all the Porsches with removable and fixed pillars. But 1966 was the year of the 911 S or the Super. New nitride piston rods, new designed heads, bigger diameter valves, new camshafts and bigger carburettor jets took the 2-litre's 6-cylinder's power output to 160 hp at 6600 rpm. That moved the top speed from 210 kph to 225 kph and, partly due to a weight reduction of 50 kg to 1030 kg. To match the higher performance, the S was fitted with Koni shock absorbers and self-ventilating disc brakes, which meant the track was widened by 16 mm and 8.4 mm. New moulded light alloy rims produced by Fuchs of Meinerzhagen also made their first appearance on the 911 S: although they were designed by the Porsche Studio, headed by Ferdinand Alexander, they would be known and appreciated as Fuchs rims until the '80s. Only detailed modifications were carried out in 1967, but a DM 990 option was the first Sportomatic semi-automatic 4-speed gearbox. The following year, there were major variations: the track was further widened by 10 mm with the adoption of the new 6-inch rims and the wheelbase was increased by 57 mm by putting the rear wheels farther back. And with mechanical fuel injection plus electronic ignition, maximum power went up to 170 kph at 6800 rpm. There were also numerous continuous, well selected updates to the exterior and interior: the lateral deflectors and the supplementary heating system were no more, but a heated rear window, halogen headlights and new door panels were added.

The Porsche 906 Carrera 6 driven by Willy Mairesse and Herbert Müller winning the 1966 Targa Florio. The work of Ferdinand Piëch, a nephew of Ferry Porsche and later the CEO of VW, would be a highly successful car even if it had to move over for the more modern 910 after about a year, a car that also drew fully on the technical solutions tried out on the 906.

TECHNICAL SPECIFICATION

ENGINE

Central, longitudinal
6 cylinders horizontally opposed

Bore and stroke	80 x 66 mm
Unitary cubic capacity	331.8 cc
Total cubic capacity	1991 cc
Valve gear	overhead camshaft, chain driven
Number of valves	2 per cylinder
Compression ratio	10.3:1
Fuel feed	carburettors
Ignition	coil
Coolant	forced air
Lubrication	dry sump
Maximum power	210 hp at 8000 rpm
Specific power	105.5 hp/litre

TRANSMISSION

Rear wheel drive

Clutch	dry mono-disc
Gearbox	en bloc with differential, 5 speeds plus reverse

CHASSIS

Tubular trellis

Front suspension	overlapping wishbones, coil springs, hydraulic telescopic shock absorbers, stabiliser bar
Rear suspension	overlapping wishbones, coil springs, hydraulic telescopic shock absorbers, stabiliser bar
Brakes	discs on all four wheels
Steering	ZF rack
Fuel tank	-
Tyres front/rear	-

DIMENSIONS AND WEIGHT

Wheelbase	2300 mm
Track front/rear	1338/1402 mm
Length	4123 mm
Width	1680 mm
Height	980 mm
Weight	675 kg

PERFORMANCE

Top speed	280 kph
Power to weight ratio	3.2 kg/hp

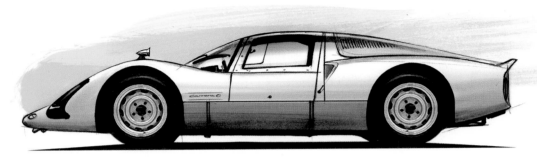

906 Carrera 6 1966

As early as 1965 it appeared evident that the long racing career of Porsche's 2-litre, 4-cylinder engine was coming to an end after so much success. There again, given the reliability problems of the 8-cylinder, it became clear that the road to take was that of the 6-cylinder boxer, derived from the 911 unit. In reality, the layout of the 906 was the same, but it wasn't only the fine tuning that was changed, so were the valves, pistons and piston rods and even the aluminium alloy casting for the lighter magnesium, shedding 54 kg. Power output also went up to 200 hp – 220 hp for the fuel injection version, which also enjoyed better torque generation at low revs. The chassis of the Carrera 6 – often called the 906 – dropped the 904's floorpan and adopted a tubular trellis chassis, but kept the earlier car's suspension: that was Ferry Porsche's decision, as he didn't want to waste the many 904 components still available in the replacement parts store. The glass fibre body was aggressive and imposing, with gullwing doors, necessary to allow the driver to climb over the large lateral fuel tanks. Fifty examples were demanded for homologation, but the tempting price of DM 45,000 soon meant orders shot up to 65 cars, although that number also includes a number of experimental 8-cylinder models. The victorious debut of the 906 Carrera 6 was at Sebring, soon after which the car won the Targa Florio, Tour de France, the 1000 Km of the Nürburgring, Le Mans, Hockenheim and Reims. For really fast tracks, Porsche experimented with a long tail for the car, with which its weight went up to 710 kg, but top speed also increased by 15 kph; new materials lightened the suspension and the beryllium disc brakes became a great success with their aluminium callipers.

The Porsche 910 being driven by Schütz-Buzzetta on the way to winning the 1967 1000 Km of the Nürburgring. The car was first built as a coupé with a removable roof group – it was removed in this case because the drivers were tall – but there were also some spiders and others with permanently fixed roofs. The "normal" 6-cylinder engine alternated with the 8-cylinders.

TECHNICAL SPECIFICATION

ENGINE
Central, longitudinal
6 cylinders horizontally opposed

Bore and stroke	80 x 66 mm
Unitary cubic capacity	331.8 cc
Total cubic capacity	1991 cc
Valve gear	overhead camshafts, chain driven
Number of valves	2 per cylinder
Compression ratio	10.3:1
Fuel feed	Bosch injection
Ignition	double, transistorised
Coolant	forced air
Lubrication	dry sump
Maximum power	220 hp at 8000 rpm
Specific power	110.5 hp/litre

TRANSMISSION
Rear wheel drive

Clutch	dry mono-disc
Gearbox	en bloc with differential, 5 speeds plus reverse

CHASSIS
Tubular trellis

Front suspension	double wishbones, coil springs, hydraulic telescopic shock absorbers, stabiliser bar
Rear suspension	double wishbones, coil springs, hydraulic telescopic shock absorbers, stabiliser bar
Brakes	discs on all four wheels
Steering	ZF rack
Fuel tank	-
Tyres front/rear	5.25 x 13/7.0 x 13

DIMENSIONS AND WEIGHT
Wheelbase	2300 mm
Track front/rear	1430/1380 mm
Length	4113 mm
Width	1680 mm
Height	980 mm
Weight	600 kg

PERFORMANCE
Top speed	265 kph
Power to weight ratio	2.72 kg/hp

910   1967

The initial intension of the 910 project was not to replace the Carrera 6 being campaigned by private entrants. On the contrary, the new car, which was an evolution of the Spyder designed for the Ollon-Villars race, had to be exclusive to the works team and was given its first time out at the 1967 Trento-Bondone. The structure was unchanged from that of the 906 (steel tubular trellis and fiberglass body), although the suspension and wheelbase were modified, the front track was widened and 13 inch rims with a central, light alloy nut were fitted. This time, the doors were hinged forward and the windscreen was bigger to conform to the new regulations. The two engines available were the 2-litre 8-cylinder that put out 270 hp, which was preferred for hillclimbs; the 901-type 6-cylinder with its 220 hp was normally used for endurance racing, like the 24 Hours of Daytona and the 12 Hours of Sebring, two events in which the 910 did well with Herrmann-Siffert fourth in both races and Mitter-Patrick taking third in Florida, preceded only by two 7-litre Fords. As Porsche had the habit of entering new cars for key races, their used cars were sold to clients, so that at the end of 1967 28 cars had been built and just before 1968 FIA decided to reduce the number of cars for homologation in the Sport Group from 50 to 25, so the 910 was automatically entered. At the Targa Florio the new 2.2-litre 8-cylinder fuel injected engine and self-ventilating disc brakes made their first appearance: the unit's power output remained at 270 hp, but the better generation of power helped the fuel injected 2.2-litre driven by Stommelen-Hawkins to win the race, followed by Cella-Biscaldi and Neerpasch-Elford in 6-cylinder 910s. At the 6 Hours of Brands Hatch, the last race of the season, Porsche experimented with new brake callipers, which meant a quicker replacement of the pads by simply removing the spring.

Gerhard Mitter, one of Porsche's star of the European Mountain Championship, driving the ultra-light 910 Bergspyder during the 1967 Freiburg-Schauinsland hillclimb. Spasmodic research into lightness led to the incredible weight – for an 8-cylinder two-seater sports racer – of 382 kg, but too much interference seriously compromised the car's road going quality.

TECHNICAL SPECIFICATION

ENGINE
Central, longitudinal
8 cylinders horizontally opposed

Bore and stroke	76 x 54 mm
Unitary cubic capacity	247.6 cc
Total cubic capacity	1981 cc
Valve gear	overhead camshaft, chain driven
Number of valves	2 per cylinder
Compression ratio	10.2:1
Fuel feed	-
Ignition	-
Coolant	forced air
Lubrication	dry sump
Maximum power	270 hp at 8000 rpm
Specific power	110.5 hp/litre

TRANSMISSION
Rear wheel drive

Clutch	dry mono-disc
Gearbox	en bloc with differential, 5 speeds plus reverse

CHASSIS
Aluminium tubed trellis

Front suspension	double wishbones, coil springs, hydraulic telescopic shock absorbers, stabiliser bar
Rear suspension	double wishbones, coil springs, hydraulic telescopic shock absorbers, stabiliser bar
Brakes	beryllium discs
Steering	ZF rack
Fuel tank	15 litres
Tyres front/rear	-

DIMENSIONS AND WEIGHT

Wheelbase	
Length	-
Width	-
Height	-
Weight	500 kg

PERFORMANCE

Top speed	-
Power to weight ratio	1.8 kg/hp

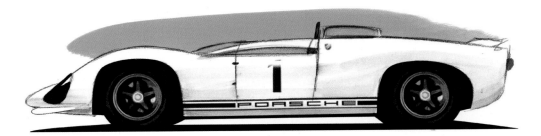

910 Bergspyder   1967

If the 910 first came out as a sports racer for endurance circuit events and hillclimbs, a brand new Bergspyder (hillclimb roadster) version was developed
with various quite substantial devices and modifications, mainly made to reduce
weight and eliminate all the superfluous elements for use in events that run for
just a few kilometres. The most substantial was the replacement of the steel tube
trellis chassis with another made in aluminium. As a result of many components
being made in titanium, a fuel tank only able to take 15 litres and a body of
sheet metal without doors, the total weight of the car was just over 500 kg. But
that was only the start of a race towards lightness that seemed to have no limit.
The extremely expensive disc brakes in beryllium, which was extremely toxic so
they had to be chromed, produced a 14 kg saving, the lightened body shell, an
engine made of magnesium and aluminium plus lighter wheels cut the car's total
weight to 419 kg. And in 1968, the car had no more alternator, lead batteries were
replaced with silver oxide units and even the front coil springs were replaced by
a Z-shaped transverse torsion bar. The result was a car that weighed a record 382
kg at the weigh-in before the start of the Montseny ascent, which enabled Gerhard
Mitter to win the European Mountain Championship due to the Bergspyder's
270 hp generated by the 8-cylinder engine. In reality, more robust fuel tanks and
heavier accumulators were fitted, leading to a weight of just under 400 kg. All the
modifications that started with a car weighing over 250 kg more seriously compromised the dynamic qualities of the two-seater, forcing the adoption of wider
tyres and larger adjustable rear spoilers before the arrival of a totally new car.

One of the most important international races to Porsche was the Targa Florio, both for the media coverage it attracted and sporting value, given the enormous technical difficulty of the severe Sicilian "route". The 907 with its 8-cylinder engine driven by Vic Elford and Umberto Maglioli – the driver from Biella, Italy, who was the first to win the Targa for Stuttgart in 1956 – is on his way to winning the 52ND Sicilian marathon in 1968.

TECHNICAL SPECIFICATION

ENGINE

Central, longitudinal
6 cylinders horizontally opposed

Bore and stroke	80 x 66 mm
Unitary cubic capacity	331.8 cc
Total cubic capacity	1991 cc
Valve gear	overhead camshaft, chain driven
Number of valves	2 per cylinder
Compression ratio	10:1
Fuel feed	Bosch injection
Ignition	double transistorised
Coolant	forced air
Lubrication	dry sump
Maximum power	220 hp at 8000 rpm
Specific power	110.5 hp/litre

TRANSMISSION

Rear wheel drive

Clutch	dry mono-disc
Gearbox	en bloc with differential, 5 speeds plus reverse

CHASSIS

Tubular trellis

Front suspension	double wishbones, coil springs, hydraulic telescopic shock absorbers, stabiliser bar
Rear suspension	double wishbones, coil springs, hydraulic telescopic shock absorbers, stabiliser bar
Brakes	discs on all four wheels
Steering	ZF rack
Fuel tank	-
Tyres front/rear	5.25 x 13/7.0 x 13

DIMENSIONS AND WEIGHT

Wheelbase	2300 mm
Track front/rear	1462/1403 mm
Length	4113 mm
Width	-
Height	-
Weight	600 kg

PERFORMANCE

Top speed	300 kph
Power to weight ratio	2.2 kg/hp

907 1967

907

1967

As the 1967 season rolled on, the 910 started to be replaced – or better, worked in the same stable as the Bergspyder adventure continued – of the new 907. Apart from some marginal modifications to the front suspension, with springs placed differently for better adjustment, and to the self-ventilating front disc brakes from its debut, the main modification compared to the 910 was in the car's aerodynamic profile, considered by the Porsche technicians one of the weak points of its predecessor. Also new was the driving position to the right of the car, considered more comfortable on clockwise circuits like most of them in the Championship. The car raced for the first time at the 1967 24 Hours of Le Mans for which Porsche went for the long tail to give it an aerodynamic penetration coefficient similar to the long tail 906 and much better than the 910. Proof of the car's efficiency was confirmed by its top speed recorded by the time keepers on the Hunaudières straight: it was 302 kph, where speeds were usually 298 kph for 6-cylinder cars like the fuel injected 901. It was a real record that enabled Siffert-Herrmann to take fifth place overall and win the performance index class. The same car took a fine fourth at Brands Hatch driven by Neerpasch-Herrmann, this time with the short body. The 2.2-litre, 270 hp 8-cylinder engine was finally installed in 1968 and was considered sufficiently reliable to also be used in endurance racing and the results soon rolled in with a triple at Daytona and a double at Sebring, the latter using cars with a gauge that indicated the wear rate of the brake pads. The 907 also made its debut in Florida, with its chassis in aluminium and wide use of titanium components: the car could have won easily if it hadn't retired with a banal alternator problem.

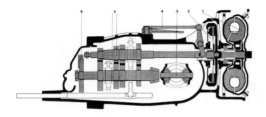

The Sportomatic gearbox, which bowed in on the 911 L. It comprised a hydraulic torque converter (1), which used the same oil of the engine circuit and had a Fichel & Sachs clutch (2): the clutch group was operated by touching the gear lever and interrupted the fuel feed to insert the desired gear. When the lever was no longer in action, the clutch and fuel feed were restored. The other points indicate the differential (3), the clutch control linkage (4), 4-speed gears (5) and the parking lock.

TECHNICAL SPECIFICATION

ENGINE

Rear, overhanging, longitudinal,
6 cylinders horizontally opposed

Bore and stroke	80 x 66 mm
Unitary cubic capacity	331.8 cc
Total cubic capacity	1991 cc
Valve gear	overhead camshaft, chain driven
Number of valves	2 per cylinder
Compression ratio	9.0:1
Fuel feed	carburettors
Ignition	coil
Coolant	forced air
Lubrication	dry sump
Maximum power	130 hp at 6100 rpm
Specific power	65.3 hp/litre

TRANSMISSION

Rear wheel drive

Clutch	dry mono-disc
Gearbox	en block with differential, 5 speeds plus reverse

CHASSIS

Unified steel structure

Front suspension	McPherson, longitudinal torsion bars, stabiliser bar, hydraulic shock absorbers
Rear suspension	independent, oblique arms, transverse torsion bars, hydraulic shock absorbers, stabiliser bar
Brakes	discs on all four wheels
Steering	ZF rack
Fuel tank	62 litres
Tyres front/rear	165 x 15/165 x 15

DIMENSIONS AND WEIGHT

Wheelbase	2211 mm
Track front/rear	1367/1335 mm
Length	4163 mm
Width	1610 mm
Height	1320 mm
Weight	1030 kg

PERFORMANCE

Top speed	215 kph
Power to weight ratio	7.9 kg/hp

911 L and 911 E   1967

With the introduction of the 160 hp 911 S in November 1967, the "old" 130 hp engine was dropped into 911 L from the following year. The body shape reflected the one used for the 911 S, but its handling made it less sporty with the smaller diameter front anti-roll bar from 13 mm to 11 mm. At the same time, the Sportomatic semi-automatic gearbox was added to the price list as a DM 990 optional. It enabled changing up or down the four gears without using the clutch which – although with some sceptical reaction – legitimised automatic transmission for sports cars. Outside handles became button operated on the whole range for safety reasons and the dashboard was in anti-reflection and bump absorbent material. Modifications were substantial the following year with the 1969 series B version and the 911 L was renamed the 911 E with the E indicating the Bosch mechanical fuel injection system, which was installed in the cars of the entire range to produce a 10 hp increase in performance. The braking system was given four self-ventilating discs with a double circuit and that brought the first widening of the track by about 10 mm, while another 10 mm were added with the adoption of 6-inch rims. In compensation, the wheelbase was lengthened by 57 mm with the rear axle being moved back, which was made possible by lengthening the suspension's wishbones and substituting the Nadella drive shaft with Löbro constant velocity joints and increasing the size of the torsion bars. The deflectors on the sidelights disappeared – with the exception of those on the Targa – at the same time as improving the ventilation system to three speeds and the addition of an electrically heated rear window. The electrical system was made more powerful and the headlights were given halogen bulbs plus emergency lights. Inside, there were new door panels, rear vision mirrors and an ashtray.

The Fuchs rims changed considerably the appearance of the 911, as can be seen in this picture; it is not difficult to understand how they entered the hearts of the enthusiasts. Porsche went back to its tradition of dividing its range into three, as was the case with the 356: entry level was the T, which was detuned and softer like the Dame variant.

TECHNICAL SPECIFICATION

ENGINE

Rear, overhanging, longitudinal
6 cylinders horizontally opposed

Bore and stroke	80 x 66 mm
Unitary cubic capacity	331.8 cc
Total cubic capacity	1991 cc
Valve gear	overhead camshaft, chain driven
Number of valves	2 per cylinder
Compression ratio	9.0:1
Fuel feed	carburettors
Ignition	coil
Coolant	forced air
Lubrication	dry sump
Maximum power	110 hp at 5800 rpm
Specific power	65.3 hp/litre

TRANSMISSION

Rear wheel drive

Clutch	dry mono-disc
Gearbox	en bloc with differential, 5 speeds plus reverse

CHASSIS

Unified steel structure

Front suspension	McPherson, longitudinal torsion bars, hydraulic telescopic shock absorbers
Rear suspension	independent, oblique arms, transverse torsion bars, hydraulic shock absorbers
Brakes	discs on all four wheels
Steering	ZF rack
Fuel tank	62 litres
Tyres front/rear	165 x 15/165 x 15

DIMENSIONS AND WEIGHT

Wheelbase	2211 mm
Track front/rear	1367/1335 mm
Length	4163 mm
Width	1610 mm
Height	1320 mm
Weight	1080 kg

PERFORMANCE

Top speed	200 kph
Power to weight ratio	9,8 kg/hp

911 T   1967

When the 911 range was expanded upwards in 1967 with the addition of the Super, it was decided to also offer a "softened" version, as was the case with the 356 with the Dame engine. This 911 was the T – the T stands for touring – with its power output reduced to 110 hp at 5800 rpm and a torque of 16 kgm at 4200 rpm, but with a much flatter power curve and lower fuel consumption than the others in the range, all to the advantage of the elasticity and economy in daily use. Power reduction was not just for commercial motivation, it was also the case that the detuned engine was less costly to build: less stress enabled the company to replace the expensive Biral wing-shaped cylinders with wings cast in light alloy with the less expensive cast iron components. In the same way, the counterweighted and equilibrated crankshaft was replaced by a more economical and lighter 6 kg one. Yet Porsche's decision to keep the head with bigger valves and the refined Weber carburettors of the 911 was characteristic of the company. At first glance, it seemed contradictory if one doesn't consider that, due to the "spartan" preparation, the T was the lightest of the 911s in production and, therefore, especially appetising with a view to setting it up for racing. The chassis included many of the 912's characteristics, which was unveiled the previous year, from which it also derived simplified equipment. But from 1968 it was possible to order the optional comfort kit, which brought the car into line with the standards of other versions and included floor carpeting, a leather covered steering wheel, hydro-pneumatic front uprights, pneumatic horns, oil pressure and indicator gauge, rubber bars on the bumpers, chrome door sills and, on request, 5.5 inch light alloy wheels. And for the USA a version was made available with an exhaust gas purification system.

Gérard Larousse in a 911 R attempting to win the 1969 Tour de France, the last racing appearance of a factory car. One of them had already broken no fewer than five long distance world and 14 international records at Monza. To face up to 20,000 kilometres non-stop, the gearbox was modified with two fifth gears to use alternately so as not to risk breakage.

TECHNICAL SPECIFICATION

ENGINE
Rear, overhanging, longitudinal
6 cylinders horizontally opposed

Bore and stroke	80 x 66 mm
Unitary cubic capacity	331.8 cc
Total cubic capacity	1991 cc
Valve gear	overhead camshaft, chain driven
Number of valves	2 per cylinder
Compression ratio	10.3:1
Fuel feed	carburettors
Ignition	dual, partially transistorised
Coolant	forced air
Lubrication	dry sump
Maximum power	210 hp at 8000 rpm
Specific power	105 hp/litre

TRANSMISSION
Rear wheel drive

Clutch	dry mono-disc
Gearbox	en block with differential, 5 speeds plus reverse

CHASSIS
Unified steel structure

Front suspension	McPherson, longitudinal torsion bars, stabiliser bar, hydraulic shock absorbers
Rear suspension	independent, oblique arms, transverse torsion bars, hydraulic shock absorbers, stabiliser bar
Brakes	discs on all four wheels
Steering	ZF rack
Fuel tank	100 litres
Tyres front/rear	185/70 x 15

DIMENSIONS AND WEIGHT

Wheelbase	2268 mm
Track front/rear	1370/1370 mm
Length	4163 mm
Width	1610 mm
Height	1320 mm
Weight	800 kg

PERFORMANCE

Top speed	230 kph
Power to weight ratio	3.8 kg/hp

911 R 2.0 1967

The suitably prepared 160 hp normal 911 and the 911 S had already competed in a number of motor sport events, especially the Monte Carlo Rally and the 1967 European Rally Championship with Vic Elford and David Stone. But at the end of 1967 Porsche introduced the 911 R 2.0 at the Hockenheim race track, a car especially designed for racing. The idea was to build a small run for private entrants at a price of DM 45,000. A total of 23 of them eventually left Zuffenhausen of which at least three were kept by the factory for use as works entries. The body shell was that of the normal production car, but the bumpers, bonnet, engine cover, doors and front wings were in glass fibre, the windscreen in thin glass, the side and rear windows in Plexiglas. The 100 litre fuel tank had an external cap for quick refuelling and the rear wings were widened to accommodate wider 7-inch tyres. All these modifications reduced the car's weight by as much as 280 kg. The chassis was only tweaked once for motor sport use, the electrical system was reinforced and there was a wide range of transmission ratios, the main modification the replacement of the production engine by that of the Carrera 6 which was detuned to 210 hp. The 911 R produced a string of victories, even if not with the works team, which soon stopped its development, except for competing with a special engine in the 1969 Targa Florio and Tour de France, the latter of which it won and was the last race of the factory 911 R. A separate matter was the car's record attempt on the banked circuit of the Monza Autodrome in November 1967, driven by Jo Siffert, Dieter Spoerry, Rico Steinemann and Charles Vogele: after numerous attempts with a privateer Carrera 6, which always broke down, Porsche offered a replacement 911 R in which the drivers broke 14 long distance records.

The 909 Bergspyder ready for its debut, which happened at the Gaisberg hillclimb with Rolf Stommelen at the wheel. Despite the technological research, the innovations and spasmodic exploration of lightness, the car would never win a race, always being beaten by the less ambitious 910. But the 909 was a true mobile laboratory when it was time to outline the 908.03.

TECHNICAL SPECIFICATION

ENGINE
Central, longitudinal
8 cylinders horizontally opposed

Bore and stroke	80 x 54.6 mm
Unitary cubic capacity	274.3 cc
Total cubic capacity	2195 cc
Valve gear	overhead camshaft, chain driven
Number of valves	2 per cylinder
Compression ratio	10.2:1
Fuel feed	Bosch injection
Ignition	dual, transistorised
Coolant	forced air
Lubrication	dry sump
Maximum power	275 hp at 8000 rpm
Specific power	125.2 hp/litre

TRANSMISSION
Rear wheel drive

Clutch	dry mono-disc
Gearbox	en bloc with differential, 5 speeds plus reverse

CHASSIS
Tubular aluminium trellis

Front suspension	double wishbones, coil springs, hydraulic telescopic shock absorbers, stabiliser bars
Rear suspension	double wishbones, coil springs, hydraulic telescopic shock absorbers, stabiliser bar
Brakes	beryllium discs
Steering	ZF rack
Fuel tank	15 litres
Tyres front/rear	-

DIMENSIONS AND WEIGHT

Wheelbase	2660 mm
Track front/rear	-
Length	3440 mm
Width	1800 mm
Height	710 mm
Weight	375 kg

PERFORMANCE

Top speed	-
Power to weight ratio	1.3 kg/hp

909 Bergspyder   1968

The 910 Bergspyder's weight was reduced to 382 kg, polishing and perfecting every detail, but many serious driveability problems emerged due to the distribution of the mass, which was not ideal, and its aerodynamic configuration. Using previous experience and wishing to design a definitive hillclimber – the European Mountain Championship was Zuffenhausen's objective – a car built specifically for that purpose was designed – the 909 Bergspyder: the engine was the same 2.2-litre 8-cylinder from the 910 taken to 275 hp and it was moved further ahead, which brought the gearbox between the power unit and the differential. That meant the driving position had to be moved forward with pedals that were in front of the forward axle. All this to move as much weight as possible to the centre of the car and improve its agility. To reduce weight, the car had an aluminium trellis chassis, the body shell was further lightened, the disc brakes were in chromed beryllium, the springs were titanium, some parts were in balsa wood and the electric wiring was in silver. The fuel tank capacity was 15 litres and it was created by welding two semi-spheres in titanium together, their thickness eight tenths of a millimetre and corroded in acid. To eliminate the fuel pump, the fuel tank itself was pressurised, inserting a rubber air chamber in the tyre tube, but that gave many fuel feed problems. So the total weight came out at 375 kg! The car first competed in the Gaisberg hillclimb driven by Rolf Stommelen but, as with the Mont Ventoux event, the 909 had to give way to the much more intensively tested 910. In addition, an accelerator blockage on 8 June 1968 cost Ludovico Scarfiotti his life during the Rossfeld event. The 909's career was short and unsuccessful, but the experienced gained with the car would become useful when designing the 908.03.

The long-tailed 908 coupé driven by Siffert-Herrmann at the 1968 24 Hours of Le Mans, from which it retired with a clutch problem. Things didn't go much better at the 1969 Sarthe race, so much so that Porsche, discouraged by fluctuating results and reliability problems, decided to retire the 908 and sell them to private entrants to concentrate all the company's energy on the development of the 917.

TECHNICAL SPECIFICATION

ENGINE
Central, longitudinal
8 cylinders horizontally opposed

Bore and stroke	85 x 66 mm
Unitary cubic capacity	374.6 cc
Total cubic capacity	2997 cc
Valve gear	twin overhead camshafts, chain driven
Number of valves	2 per cylinder
Compression ratio	10,4:1
Fuel feed	Bosch injection
Ignition	dual, transistorised
Coolant	forced air
Lubrication	dry sump
Maximum power	350 hp at 8400 rpm
Specific power	116.8 hp/litre

TRANSMISSION
Rear wheel drive

Clutch	dry mono-disc
Gearbox	en bloc with differential, 5 speeds plus reverse

CHASSIS
Tubed aluminium trellis

Front suspension	double wishbones, coil springs, hydraulic telescopic shock absorbers, stabiliser bar
Rear suspension	double wishbones, coil springs, hydraulic telescopic shock absorbers, stabiliser bar
Brakes	discs on all four wheels
Steering	ZF rack
Fuel tank	-
Tyres front/rear	-

DIMENSIONS AND WEIGHT

Wheelbase	2300 mm
Track front/rear	1484/1456 mm
Length	3540 mm
Width	1950 mm
Height	675 mm
Weight	650 kg

PERFORMANCE

Top speed	320 kph
Power to weight ratio	1.8 kg/hp

908.01 and 908.02   1968

In the summer of 1967, FIA had already made it known that it intended to limit sports racers' cubic capacity to 5-litres and 25 of them had to be built to earn homologation; prototypes were limited to 3-litres at the same time. For that reason, Porsche decided to hand its project for an 8-cylinder 3-litre to Hans Mezger, a car that first appeared as early as April 1968 in preliminary tests for the 24 Hours of Le Mans on two 907 chassis. The car's power output was 320 hp, but it would soon rise to 335 hp, while the last of them put out 370 hp. The first 908 Kurzheck (short tail) made its debut at Monza with a steel chassis, won at the Nürburgring with Siffert and Elford, but as early as Watkins Glen the first of the definitive versions appeared with an aluminium trellis chassis and 15-inch rims, which could take bigger brakes. And all of that with a weight 20 kg lower. All Porsche's energy was concentrated on the 1968 24 Hours of Le Mans, for which a new long tail body was built with extended vertical fins and a mobile wing in synthesis with the rise and fall of the rear suspension. Unfortunately, the best result was third behind a Ford GT40 and a 907 2.2. Meanwhile, the regulations changed and, given that boots and spare wheels were no longer necessary, a few 908s were transformed into roadsters, which were about 100 kg lighter but much slower. That's why the 908.02 was introduced for the 1000 Km of the Nürburgring with a new roadster body called the sole; but that generated serious stability problems despite an effective penetration coefficient. It was close to that of the long tailed coupé and 20 kph faster compared to the normal open top. A spoiler was fitted to overcome the stability problems, this time fixed as demanded by the regulations after the Hill and Rindt accidents in F1 that same year when the wings fell off. This happened after the fatal accident of Hans Laine, whose 908 just took off in a Nürburgring race.

One of the three 911 Ss prepared for the 1968 London-to-Sydney marathon. The most obvious modification was the robust external roll bar, which also acted as a roof rack for additional equipment, support for air and exhaust pipes and a frontal roo bar in case the car hit animals – a necessity after hitting a large kangaroo during a test run.

TECHNICAL SPECIFICATION

ENGINE

Rear, overhanging, longitudinal
6 cylinders horizontally opposed

Bore and stroke	80 x 66 mm
Unitary cubic capacity	331.8 cc
Total cubic capacity	1991 cc
Valve gear	overhead camshaft, chain driven
Number of valves	2 per cylinders
Compression ratio	9.8:1
Fuel feed	carburettors
Ignition	transistorised
Coolant	forced air
Lubrication	dry sump
Maximum power	160 hp at 6600 rpm
Specific power	80.3 hp/litre

TRANSMISSION

Rear wheel drive

Clutch	dry mono-disc
Gearbox	en bloc with differential, 5 speeds plus reverse

CHASSIS

Unified steel structure

Front suspension	McPherson, longitudinal torsion bars, hydraulic shock absorbers, stabiliser bar
Rear suspension	independent, oblique arms, transverse torsion bar, hydraulic shock absorbers, stabiliser bar
Brakes	disc
Steering	ZF rack
Fuel tank	200 litres
Tyres front/rear	185/70 x 15/185/70 x 15

DIMENSIONS AND WEIGHT

Wheelbase	2268 mm
Track front/rear	1353/1325 mm
Length	4163 mm
Width	1652 mm
Height	-
Weight	1300 kg

PERFORMANCE

Top speed	-
Power to weight ratio	8.1 kg/hp

911 S 2.0 London-to-Sydney   1968

The rallying career of the 911 began in 1965 with the Monte version, named after the Monte Carlo Rally. Various elaboration of the car followed for road racing. In 1968, three normal production 911 S 2.0s were substantially modified to compete in the London-to-Sydney rally-marathon: after the London start, the 98 competitors made their way towards Italy, then the Balcans, Turkey, Iran and Afghanistan to the half-way stage in Bombay. That's where the cars were loaded aboard ship bound for Australia, where they had to cross another 5,000 kilometres before crossing the Sydney finish line. When rally driver Sobieslav Zasada asked Porsche to prepare a 911 S to compete in the marathon, another two were made ready for the event for Hans Herrmann and Terry Hunter. Because hitting a kangaroo during testing in Australia caused serious damage, an imposing external roll bar was built, with a series of steel wiring to protect the windscreen. On the top was a storage room for four spare wheels and tyres, cans of fuel and a small auxiliary tank which, if the fuel system that supplied petrol to the engine broke, could provide engine fuel via gravity. The compression ratio of the production engine was dropped to 9.8:1 due to the probable need to use normal petrol along the route and the feed that the flexible exhausts were placed on the roof so that they would not be affected by ploughing through deep fords. The clutch was reinforced and the gearbox had shorter ratios; the suspension was also strengthened as were the steering components. With the survival kit, fire extinguishers, a 200-litre fuel tank and shovel, the car's weight was about 1300 kg. Hunter's 911 had to retire in Afghanistan, but Zasada finished third, Herrmann 15TH. The two cars were then sold at the finish and the one driven by Herrmann would continue a long sport career.

A gaggle of 914s parked under the large VW-Porsche sign of the factory, an emblematic image. Purists will always consider the 914 the son of a lesser god due to its close relationship with VW and for its lines, a long way from Porsche traditions as well as the central position of the engine. In reality, the 914 is a brilliant and modern car with excellent driveability.

TECHNICAL SPECIFICATION

ENGINE

Central, longitudinal
4 cylinders horizontally opposed

Bore and stroke	90 x 66 mm
Unitary cubic capacity	419.7 cc
Total cubic capacity	1679 cc
Valve gear	overhead valves, push rods and rocker arms
Number of valves	2 per cylinder
Compression ratio	8.2:1
Fuel feed	Bosch electronic injection
Ignition	electronic
Coolant	forced air
Lubrication	dry sump
Maximum power	80 hp at 4900 rpm
Specific power	47.6 hp/litre

TRANSMISSION

Rear wheel drive

Clutch	dry mono-disc
Gearbox	en bloc with differential, 5 speeds plus reverse

CHASSIS

Unified steel structure

Front suspension	McPherson, longitudinal torsion bars, hydraulic telescopic shock absorbers
Rear suspension	independent, oblique arms, transverse torsion bars, hydraulic shock absorbers
Brakes	discs on all four wheels
Steering	ZF rack
Fuel tank	62 litres
Tyres front/rear	155 x 15/155 x 15

DIMENSIONS AND WEIGHT

Wheelbase	2450 mm
Track front/rear	1337/1374 mm
Length	3985 mm
Width	1650 mm
Height	1220 mm
Weight	900 kg

PERFORMANCE

Top speed	177 kph
Power to weight ratio	11.25 kg/hp

914-4   1969

Collaboration between Porsche and Volkswagen dates back to the origin of the companies themselves and it has continued – even if in different measure – over the years for the supply of various components as well as from the commercial and service points of view. At the end of the '60s the desire of the two companies was to produce a small and modern sports car with driving pleasure as its main virtue, but one that was not excessively expensive coincided to the point that they started a project together; soon afterwards, the world was given the Volkswagen-Porsche 914. The strictly two-seater formula – even if a third passenger could be carried for short distances between the two seats – and a mid-engine appeared right from the start the best to obtain excellent handling. The car had a light chassis and, not least of all, really sporty, young and modern lines. The mechanical groups were derived from Volkswagen's mass produced models with obvious manufacturing cost benefits. The 914 was powered by a 4-cylinder 1679 cc air cooled boxer engine with electronic fuel injection built by VW with an 80 hp power output. The gearbox was a 5-speed, although a Sportomatic would become available in 1970. The car's Cx was the same as the 911's and its performance sparkled. In addition, it had modern, youthful lines with a removable glass fibre hard top and retractable headlights: habitability was also good, while the two boots could accommodate 370 litres of luggage. In 1973, the range evolved and out came the 914/2.0: the 1700 cc engine was massively revised by Porsche and that took the cubic capacity to 2-litres and the power output to 100 hp with a 190 kph top speed. The following year, the 1700 was taken definitively to 1.8 litres and power generation went up to 85 hp, 76 hp for the North American version, fed by electronic fuel injection. The 914 continued to be produced until the arrival of the 924 in 1976.

For Porsche, the 1970 24 Hours of Le Mans has become part of history. Not only did the company win with the 917 driven by Hans Herrmann and Richard Attwood, the Chasseuil-Ballot Léna 914-6 won its class and took an incredible sixth place overall. A great result for the "little" mid-engined Porsche.

TECHNICAL SPECIFICATION

ENGINE
Central, longitudinal
6 cylinders horizontally opposed

Bore and stroke	80 x 66 mm
Unitary cubic capacity	331.8 cc
Totalcubic capacity	1991 cc
Valve gear	overhead camshaft, chain driven
Number of valves	2 per cylinder
Compression ratio	8.6:1
Fuel feed	carburettors
Ignition	electronic
Coolant	forced air
Lubrication	dry sump
Maximum power	110 hp at 5800 rpm
Specific power	55.2 hp/litre

TRANSMISSION
Rear wheel drive

Clutch	dry mono-disc
Gearbox	en bloc with differential, 5 speeds plus reverse

CHASSIS
Unified steel structure

Front suspension	McPherson, longitudinal torsion bars, hydraulic telescopic shock absorbers
Rear suspension	independent, oblique arms, transverse torsion bars, hydraulic telescopic shock absorbers
Brakes	discs on all four wheels
Steering	ZF rack
Fuel tank	62 litres
Tyres front/rear	165 x 15/165 x 15

DIMENSIONS AND WEIGHT

Wheelbase	2450 mm
Track front/rear	1361/1382 mm
Length	3985 mm
Width	1650 mm
Height	1220 mm
Weight	940 kg

PERFORMANCE

Top speed	201 kph
Power to weight ratio	8.5 kg/hp

914-6   1969

If the lively, 80 hp 914-4 sold well from the start, the more potent 914-6 version introduced at the same time wasn't so lucky. Externally, the only noticeable difference was the wheel design and a number of bumper details, but under the bonnet there was a major difference. The 914-6 was powered by the lively 6-cylinder 2-litre of the 911 T. The power output of 110 hp was enough to ensure a level of performance greater than the 911 as its Cx was the same but its weight was lower; a top speed of 210 kph was 2 kph lower at night with its headlights raised. As with the 914-4 the gearbox was a 5-speed or Sportomatic from 1970. In spite of performance, the 914-6 was canibalised from the 911 T – too close to the price – and silently left the market in 1971. The car also had a brilliant if brief motor sport career: many parts of the body were made in synthetic materials, the layout was simplified and the removable roof was reinforced and screwed to the body. The car had a revised set-up, suspension and brakes with the 908's calipers. The engine was profoundly evolved and, due to light alloy cylinders, new pistons, head, shafts, piston rods and carburetors, put out 220 hp at 7800 rpm. The 914-6 won the GT Class of the 1970 24 Hours of Le Mans, in which it came sixth overall, at the 86-hour (!) Marathon de la Route and good placings at the Nürburgring and Watkins Glen. Unfortunately the racing version of the 911 S was the same price as the 914-6 at DM 49,680, but the 911's 50 hp more that came from a greater cubic capacity pushed many private entrants to the latter, encouraged that there wasn't always an up to 2-litre class in races, which would have been to the advantage of the 914. The final event in which the 914-6 competed was the 1971 Monte Carlo Rally, but Bjorn Waldegard, who had won the event twice in 911s, could only manage third.

Externally, there were few modifications to detail that distinguished the 914-8 from any other production 914: the front had bigger retractable headlamps to accommodate two small circular lights. The car's appearance was more pleasant in both open and closed configuration and an oval air intake for the radiators was slipped in half way between the bumper and the lower spoiler.

TECHNICAL SPECIFICATION

ENGINE
Central, longitudinal
8 cylinders horizontally opposed

Bore and stroke	85x 66 mm
Unitary cubic capacity	374.6 cc
Total cubic capacity	2997 cc
Valve gear	twin overhead camshafts, chain driven
Number of valves	2 per cylinder
Compression ratio	10.2:1
Fuel feed	carburettors
Ignition	electronic
Coolant	forced air
Lubrication	dry sump
Maximum power	260 hp at 7700 rpm
Specific power	86.7 hp/litre

TRANSMISSION
Rear wheel drive

Clutch	dry mono-disc
Gearbox	en bloc with differential, 5 speeds plus reverse

CHASSIS
Unified steel structure

Front suspension	McPherson, longitudinal torsion bars, hydraulic telescopic shock absorbers
Rear suspension	independent, oblique arms, transverse torsion bars, hydraulic telescopic shock absorbers
Brakes	discs on all four wheels
Steering	ZF rack
Fuel tank	62 litres
Tyres front/rear	-

DIMENSIONS AND WEIGHT

Wheelbase	2450 mm
Track front/rear	1361/1382 mm
Length	3985 mm
Width	1650 mm
Height	1220 mm
Weight	-

PERFORMANCE

Top speed	250 kph
Power to weight ratio	-

914-8   1969

In 1969, while the 914 project was still being defined, Porsche considered various ways in which to make the model more powerful and to show that the car's chassis was able to support much more power to that generated by the 4-cylinder of VW origin. So it seemed obvious as well as ambitious to use the potent 3-litre 8-cylinder boxer used in the Sport 908. In fact, the engine had been designed especially for a racing car, but a door was left open for possible road use. The unit's construction was relatively simple and economical and there was no reliability problem, despite a specific power well above 100 hp/litre. The engineers had no difficulty in finding space in the engine compartment: the supports just had to be redesigned and the fireproof wall had to be modified so that it was adapted to the bulk of the cooling fan and its air duct. In compensation, no room was taken from the boot. Together with the engine – which needed an oil radiator installed in the nose behind a new oval air intake – the 908's transaxle gearbox was installed. The suspension was set up and the rims available were those of the 911, either in metal or aluminium. Two of the cars were built, one for Ferry Porsche – who crashed his a good 10,000 kilometres before the noise law pushed them into donating it to the Porsche museum – with a carburettor engine and silencers, its power output limited to 260 hp. The second 914-8, which would never be delivered but was used by Porsche, was for Ferdinand Piëch; in that case, the exhaust silencers reduced its power by 50 hp for a total of 300 hp, but the injection and set-up were the same as the 908 racer. Performance was impressive, especially its acceleration. But the project was dropped for cost reasons and especially because of its incompatibility with the Porsche-VW agreement, on which the 914 was based.

The exterior lines of the 2.2-litre 911 were not much modified in relation to the previous series. The fog lights of the car pictured were optional. The major new development was the complete galvanising of the body shell to provide such a corrosion resistance that it was guaranteed by Porsche for no less than seven years.

TECHNICAL SPECIFICATION

ENGINE

Rear, overhanging, longitudinal
6 cylinders horizontally opposed

Bore and stroke	84 x 66 mm
Unitary cubic capacity	365.8 cc
Total cubic capacity	2195 cc
Valve gear	overhead camshaft, chain driven
Number of valves	2 per cylinder
Compression ratio	8.6:1
Fuel feed	carburettors
Ignition	battery with condenser
Coolant	forced air
Lubrication	dry sump
Maximum power	125 hp at 5800 rpm
Specific power	56.9 hp/litre

TRANSMISSION

Rear wheel drive

Clutch	dry mono-disc
Gearbox	en bloc with differential, 4 speeds plus reverse

CHASSIS

Unified steel structure

Front suspension	McPherson, longitudinal torsion bars, hydraulic telescopic shock absorbers
Rear suspension	independent, oblique arms, transverse torsion bars, hydraulic shock absorbers
Brakes	discs on all four wheels
Steering	ZF rack
Fuel tank	62 litres
Tyres front/rear	165 x 15/165 x 15

DIMENSIONS AND WEIGHT

Wheelbase	2268 mm
Track front/rear	1362/1343 mm
Length	4163 mm
Width	1610 mm
Height	1320 mm
Weight	1020 mm

PERFORMANCE

Top speed	200 kph
Power to weight ratio	8.1 kg/hp

911 T 2.2 1969

As the 912 was going out of production and the 914 went to take its place at the entry level of the range, the 911 slipped into its second stage of updating and that spawned the C series, which made its first appearance in September 1969. The most significant modification from the mechanical point of view was to increase the car's cubic capacity to 2195 cc with a larger bore that went from 80 mm to 84 mm: it wasn't so much the desire to improve overall performance, rather the need to respond to numerous requests for a "sweeter" and more elastic engine for daily use. At the entry level of the range there was the 911 T with carburettor fuel feed and a power output of 125 hp at 5800 rpm. Fuel consumption and the top speed were more or less unchanged on the 2-litre models while the liveliness and exploitability improved considerably with the 2.2. Work was done on the valve diameter, there were new piston rods and manifolds. Kerb weight was reduced by 60 kg to 1020 kg, in spite of zinc treatment for the body shell that weighed 10 kg; but the result was an enviable resistance to corrosion that was guaranteed by Porsche for seven years. The transmission was 4-speed, the self-locking differential an optional and the discs brakes were self-ventilating. Inside, the dashboard was redesigned, now with secondary switches like those of the windscreen wipers, washer, directional indicators and headlight flasher were brought together at the sides of the steering wheel so that they could be operated without the driver taking his hands from it. Many other operations further improved the standard car. With the arrival of the D series in 1971, some work was necessary on the injection and ignition to respect anti-pollution laws that had also made their way to the European market, while the versions built for the USA had been subjected to numerous such limitations for years and among them the obligation to include a ventilation system for the fuel tank.

Bjorn Waldegard's 911 ST 2.2 Rallye powered by a 180 hp production engine on its way to winning the 1970 Alpine Cup, after which he brought the World Rally Championship to Zuffenhausen. As well as the works cars, many private entrants competed with the 911 in both racing and rallying.

TECHNICAL SPECIFICATION

ENGINE

Rear, overhanging, longitudinal
6 cylinders horizontally opposed

Bore and stroke	84 x 66 mm
Unitary cubic capacity	365.8 cc
Total cubic capacity	2195 cc
Valve gear	overhead camshaft, chain driven
Number of valves	2 per cylinder
Compression ratio	9.8:1
Fuel feed	carburettors
Ignition	battery with condenser
Coolant	forced air
Lubrication	dry sump
Maximum power	180 hp at 6500 rpm
Specific power	82 hp/litre

TRANSMISSION

Rear wheel drive

Clutch	dry mono-disc
Gearbox	en bloc with differential, 5 speeds plus reverse

CHASSIS

Unified steel structure

Front suspension	McPherson, longitudinal torsion bars, hydraulic telescopic shock absorbers
Rear suspension	independent, oblique arms, transverse torsion bars, hydraulic shock absorbers, stabiliser bar
Brakes	discs on all four wheels
Steering	ZF rack
Fuel tank	62 litres
Tyres front/rear	185/70 x 15/185/70 x 15

DIMENSIONS AND WEIGHT

Wheelbase	2268 mm
Track front/rear	1374/1355 mm
Length	4163 mm
Width	1610 mm
Height	1320 mm
Weight	1020 kg

PERFORMANCE

Top speed	225 kph
Power to weight ratio	5.6 kg/hp

911 E 2.2 and 911 S 2.2   1969

The 125 hp 2.2-litre T was the base model, but for more demanding clients the E and S versions were added to the price list. The 2195 cc engine now had a mechanical fuel injection system that took the E's power output to 155 hp at 6200 rpm and the S 180 hp at 6500 rpm which, as well as the modified valve diameter, also had tailor made new piston rods and manifolds plus new forged pistons. The new technical director, Ferdinand Piëch, grandson of the founder who later became a high executive of Volkswagen, decided on a series of move that would lighten the car, including a new aluminium and magnesium alloy block and various body parts in light alloy. That was enough to drop the car's weight by over 60 kg. The transmission was a 5-speed for both the E and the S due to the installation of a new sporty gearbox with the first low down on the left. The clutch was also strengthened with a 225 mm disc and the self-locking differential with a locking factor of either 40% or 80% was an optional. The semi-automatic Sportomatic gearbox was an optional only on the S. The equipment variations reflect those of the 911 T, among others and the chance of having a rear window with an electric wiper. At the end of 1971, the range's injection system was only slightly updated so that it fell in line with new emission control limits that were spreading throughout Europe; small rubber elements were also inserted into the front and rear bumpers. The 911 S was successful in motor sports, one of its most prestigious results victory in the 1970 World Rally Championship by Bjorn Waldegard, who won that year's Monte Carlo, Swedish, Austrian and Alpine rallies plus Gérard Larrousse, who came fifth in the RAC. In 1971, a number of the cars were taken to 2.3-litres and 240 hp for circuit racing and won at Monza, Spa, the Nürburgring, Paris, Barcelona and Jarama in the Grand Touring category.

The 25 917s, which were sold for DM 140,000 with both long and short tails, lined up at Stuttgart for homologation. Because of their enormous power output, the first win was scored in 1969 but, in reality, the car was dangerous and not at all competitive. There were chassis problems, but modifications had little effect. Regardless, Porsche was not prepared to throw in the towel and the investments continued.

TECHNICAL SPECIFICATION

ENGINE

Central, longitudinal
12 cylinders horizontally opposed

Bore and stroke	85 x 66 mm
Unitary cubic capacity	374.5 cc
Total cubic capacity	4494 cc
Valve gear	twin overhead camshafts, chain driven
Number of valves	2 per cylinder
Compression ratio	10.5:1
Fuel feed	Bosch mechanical fuel injection
Ignition	double, transistorised
Coolant	forced air
Lubrication	dry sump
Maximum power	560 hp at 8300 rpm
Specific power	124 hp/litre

TRANSMISSION

Rear wheel drive

Clutch	triple dry disc
Gearbox	en bloc with differential, 5 speeds plus reverse

CHASSIS

Tubular trellis

Front suspension	double wishbones, coil springs, hydraulic telescopic shock absorbers, stabiliser bar
Rear suspension	double wishbones, coil springs, hydraulic telescopic shock absorbers, stabiliser bar
Brakes	discs on all four wheels
Steering	ZF rack
Fuel tank	120 litres
Tyres front/rear	4.25/10.20 x 15/12.5/26 x 15

DIMENSIONS AND WEIGHT

Wheelbase	2300 mm
Track front/rear	1526/1533 mm
Length	4290 mm (short tail)
Width	2033 mm
Height	920 mm
Weight	800 kg

PERFORMANCE

Top speed	320 kph
Power to weight ratio	1.4 kg/hp

917   1969

With the introduction of the new World Championship for Makes regulations in January 1968 that took the cubic capacity limit to 5-litres for sports racers – at least 25 of which had to have been produced – a team headed by Hans Mezger was nominated to design the 917. The approach to the project was conservative in many ways and was a challenge without precedent at Zuffenhausen, because until then the company's attention had been concentrated only on research into lightening cars with a medium-low cubic capacity: the chassis was an aluminium tubular trellis that was brought back after testing on the 908 and the car's lines were similar to its predecessor. The 917's engine was a traditional air cooled boxer, but with 12 cylinders and a central power take-off which, using the same number of cylinders as the 3-litre 908, turned in a cubic capacity of 4494 cc and that was likely to rise to 5-litres in the future. The car's power output was monstrous from the start: 542 hp at the first test, but it would be 580 on its race debut. Contrary to that of the 908, the chassis was more designed to be robust rather than light, given the potency and the difficulty of endurance racing. However, it still only weighed 47 kg to which the 95 kg body had to be added, 12 more with the long tail. The 25 917s were homologated with the long tail that was similar to that of the 908, with mobile wings worked by the suspension; but the long version could be removed and the short one fitted as it was more suited to tortuous circuits. Test driving and the car's early races showed off its enormous amount of power, but also its total and dangerous undrivability. There were more tests, but there didn't seem to be a solution to the problem. Gérard Mitter nicknamed the 917 the ulcer and an increasing number of drivers were not prepared to compete with the car. Meanwhile, the works team was put with those Gulf sponsored John Wyer and Louise Piëch's Porsche Salzburg (later Martini Racing).

The 917 Spyder PA during one of the last rounds of the 1969 Can-Am Championship. The car already has an adjustable rear spoiler and a front wing, which was not on the first prototype. The car, chassis number 917-028, was transformed for the 1971 season. Later, further modifications were made in line with 917-10 specifications. The sister car, 917-027, was the test car for the process.

TECHNICAL SPECIFICATION

ENGINE

Central, longitudinal
12 cylinders horizontally opposed

Bore and stroke	85 x 66 mm
Unitary cubic capacity	374.5 cc
Total cubic capacity	4494 cc
Valve gear	twin overhead camshafts, chain driven
Number of valves	2 per cylinder
Compression ratio	10.5:1
Fuel feed	Bosch mechanical injection
Ignition	double, transistorised
Coolant	forced air
Lubrication	dry sump
Maximum power	560 hp at 8300 rpm
Specific power	124 hp/litre

TRANSMISSION

Rear wheel drive

Clutch	triple dry disc
Gearbox	en bloc with differential, 5 speeds plus reverse

CHASSIS

Tubular trellis

Front suspension	double wishbones, coil springs, hydraulic telescopic shock absorbers, stabiliser bar
Rear suspension	double wishbones, coil springs, hydraulic telescopic shock absorbers, stabiliser bar
Brakes	discs on all four wheels
Steering	ZF rack
Fuel tank	180 litres
Tyres front/rear	-

DIMENSIONS AND WEIGHT

Wheelbase	2300 mm
Track front/rear	1526/1533 mm
Length	3905 mm
Width	-
Height	-
Weight	780 kg

PERFORMANCE

Top speed	320 kph
Power to weight ratio	1.4 kg/hp

917 Spyder PA   1969

The 917 found it hard to make an impression on the circuits of the World Championship for Makes due to its poor and unpredictable roadholding, so the need to publicise the Porsche brand in North America became more urgent. In addition, a new VW commercial organisation saw Porsche and Audi together on the US market, leading to a Porsche-Audi coupling in 1969. That is why competing in the highly popular Can-Am Championship seemed to offer a good opportunity, although that was dominated by the 700 hp McLaren-Chevrolets. So Porsche decided to adapt a 917 to be driven by Jo Siffert to gather experience and data with the intention of becoming more involved in Can-Am. The European 917's 4.5-litre engine and the chassis was modified just to sustain a new and simple roadster body, much inspired by that of the 908 "Sole". Total weight was 780 kg and fuel tank capacity was increased to 180 litres. But the Spyder PA was too heavy and not very powerful to be competitive immediately but, surprisingly, it was faster than the "normal" coupé. Siffert competed in a number of races with the car at the end of 1969, with a best of third place at Bridgehampton and ended the season with a fine fourth in the Championship. The 1970 season was one of pause, partly due to Porsche's substantial commitment to the World Championship of Makes, but in 1971 the Spyder PA, which had "hibernated" in California, was taken on by Vasek Polak, the PA dealer, and considerably revised: the wheelbase was shortened, the brakes were replaced with Girlings and the engine gave way to a more powerful 4.9-litre. The body was also revised and was given large tail fins. But the car's performance in the Can-Am Championship was unsatisfactory, with no fewer than seven retirements in 10 races, yet once again that experience was valuable for the further development of the car, after which Porsche returned to the Can-Am and the relative Interseries Championship in grand style in 1972 with the 917–10.

The 908.03 crewed by Brian Redman-Jo Siffert dominated the 1970 Targa Florio, followed by the sister car driven by Leo Kinnunen and Pedro Rodríguez. Despite its name, the 908.03 was a completely new car especially designed for mountain and hillclimbs and tortuous circuits. It only competed in four races in two years, but it won three of them, confirming the superiority of Porsche in this kind of competition and on the celebrated twists and turns of the Targa in particular.

TECHNICAL SPECIFICATION

ENGINE

Central, longitudinal
8 cylinders horizontally opposed

Bore and stroke	85 x 66 mm
Unitary cubic capacity	374.6 cc
Total cubic capacity	2997 cc
Valve gear	twin overhead camshafts, chain driven
Number of valves	2 per cylinder
Compression ratio	10.4:1
Fuel feed	Bosch injection
Ignition	double, transistorised
Coolant	forced air
Lubrication	dry sump
Maximum power	350 hp at 8400 rpm
Specific power	116.8 hp/litre

TRANSMISSION

Rear wheel drive

Clutch	dry mono-disc
Gearbox	en bloc with differential, 5 speeds plus reverse

CHASSIS

Aluminium tube trellis

Front suspension	double wishbones, coil springs, hydraulic telescopic shock absorbers, stabiliser bar
Rear suspension	double wishbones, coil springs, hydraulic telescopic shock absorbers, stabiliser bar
Brakes	discs on all four wheels
Steering	ZF rack
Tyres front/rear	-

DIMENSIONS AND WEIGHT

Wheelbase	2300 mm
Track front/rear	1484/1456 mm
Length	3540 mm
Width	1950 mm
Height	675 mm
Weight	545 kg

PERFORMANCE

Top speed	-
Power to weight ratio	1.5 kg/hp

908.03   1969

After having officially retired and sold the 908.02 to concentrate on the 917, Porsche realised that the big, powerful Sports that were at home on the long Le Mans straights, would be inadequate on the tortuous roads of the Targa Florio or the Nürburgring, where agility and lightness were preferred to brute force. For that reason, the 908.03 project was resuscitated which, as well as the name of its predecessors, only kept the 3-litre 8-cylinder power unit more or less unchanged. The first wind tunnel tests had already been carried out at the end of 1968, but then the project was temporarily shelved to develop the 908.02 and the 917. The disposition of the mechanical components, with its much advanced driving position, and the car's structure shared many of the concepts tested for the 909 Bergspyder. And the lightness research was no less forthcoming: the polyurethane body only weighed 12 kg and the complete car, with full lubricant, was under 545 kg. The rims were 13-inch at the front and 14.5-inch at the rear. In 1970, the 908.03 dominated the Targa Florio and the 1000 Km of the Nürburgring, the only two races in which it competed, after which it retired from racing for about a year. It was partially modified in 1971, with an 11-inch wider track at the front and 15-inch rear, 13-inch rims, rear fins and better safety equipment, which increased its weight to 565 kg. The car then competed in another two races and won the Nürburgring 100 Km again. After that, the 11 of them were built and sold to private entrants for between DM 150,000 and DM 180,000 and they used them for years in hillclimbs. An experimental 32-valve engine air cooled for the cylinders and liquid cooled for the heads was ready at the end of the 1972 Championship, but Porsche decided to retire from the World Championship for Makes and the engine was put to one side.

The 917 K sponsored by Gulf Oil of John Wyer's team was much liked by many, including the motor sport journalists, for the beauty of its lines. The picture shows the Salzburg team's 917 K driven by Louise Piëch, sister of Ferry Porsche, which would give the Zuffenhausen company its first win in the 24 Hours of Le Mans, driven by Hans Herrmann and Richard Attwood. The car was powered by a 4.5-litre 12-cylinder engine that put out 480 hp.

TECHNICAL SPECIFICATION

ENGINE

Central, longitudinal
12 cylinders horizontally opposed

Bore and stroke	85 x 66 mm
Unitary cubic capacity	408.9 cc
Total cubic capacity	4907 cc
Valve gear	twin overhead camshafts, chain driven
Number of valves	2 per cylinder
Compression ratio	10.5:1
Fuel feed	Bosch mechanical injection
Ignition	double, transistorised
Coolant	forced air
Lubrication	dry sump
Maximum power	600 hp at 8000 rpm
Specific power	122.2 hp/litre

TRANSMISSION

Rear wheel drive

Clutch	triple dry disc
Gearbox	en bloc with differential, 5 speeds plus reverse

CHASSIS

Tubular trellis

Front suspension	double wishbones, coil springs, hydraulic telescopic shock absorbers, stabiliser bar
Rear suspension	double wishbones, coil springs, hydraulic telescopic shock absorbers, stabiliser bar
Brakes	discs on all four wheels
Steering	ZF rack
Fuel tank	-
Tyres front/rear	-

DIMENSIONS AND WEIGHT

Wheelbase	2330 mm
Track front/rear	1564/1584 mm
Length	3905 mm
Width	1980 mm
Height	940 mm
Weight	800 kg

PERFORMANCE

Top speed	320 kph
Power to weight ratio	1.3 kg/hp

917 K
1970

During the 1969 season, there were many vain attempts to make the ultra-powerful 917 driveable, a car that showed it was unstable at high speed and had danger-ously unpredictable handling. To try to improve the "ulcer" as the 917 was called by Gérard Mitter, Porsche, with the support and presence of Ferdinand Piëch, organised a test session at Zeltweg after the disastrous 1000 km race: the available cars were those used during the race, a test car and a prototype of the Porsche 917 Spyder PA, which should have made their debut in the Can-Am series. The shock came when Brian Redman got out of the normal 917, tested the PA with the same engine and chassis and immediately set a lap time four seconds faster. The driver was incredulous and so was the Porsche staff: on the one hand it was clear that the stability problems, for long attributed to the chassis, were associated with the body shape. The tail was immediately modified with aluminium sheets folded to the best position, riveted and sealed with gaffer tape. After that, the 917 had an intense wedge shape with only one break in the central of the tail to cool the engine and ensure rear visibility, as demanded by FIA. Lap times were reduced even more, so Porsche was on the right road and a new version called the 917 K (kurz or short) was homologated for 1970. The car was much modified at the front, too, where there was now the characteristic three-part air intake. And a new 4.9-litre 600 hp engine made its first appearance. The 1970 season was one of triumph: the 917s dominated nine of the Championship's 10 races, among them the renowned 24 Hours of Le Mans in a car belonging to the Salzburg team driven by Herrmann-Attwood, who even overtook the more aerodynamic long tail: that was Porsche's first long-awaited victory in the French 24 Hours, which was celebrated soon afterwards by a parade of the winning 917 through the streets of Zuffenhausen.

The sketch illustrates the Porsche 917 LH that competed in the 1971 24 Hours of Le Mans in the hands of Vic Elford and Gérard Larrousse, who were forced to retire. The picture shows the Siffert-Bell sister car in the Gulf livery of John Wyer's team. In 1971, there were many improvements to the car, both mechanical and aerodynamic, which finally gave it suitable stability – even for the long tail car, which was also given ATE brakes.

TECHNICAL SPECIFICATION

ENGINE
Central, longitudinal
12 cylinders horizontally opposed

Bore and stroke	85 x 66 mm
Unitary cubic capacity	408.9 cc
Total cubic capacity	4907 cc
Valve gear	twin overhead camshafts, chain driven
Number of valves	2 per cylinder
Compression ratio	10.5:1
Fuel feed	Bosch mechanical injection
Ignition	double, transistorised
Coolant	forced air
Lubrication	dry sump
Maximum power	600 hp at 8000 rpm
Specific power	122.2 hp/litre

TRANSMISSION
Rear wheel drive

Clutch	triple dry disc
Gearbox	en bloc with differential, 5 speeds plus reverse

CHASSIS
Tubular trellis

Front suspension	double wishbones, coil springs, hydraulic telescopic shock absorbers, stabiliser bar
Rear suspension	double wishbones, coil springs, hydraulic telescopic shock absorbers, stabiliser bar
Brakes	discs on all four wheels
Steering	ZF rack
Fuel tank	-
Tyres front/rear	-

DIMENSIONS AND WEIGHT

Wheelbase	2330 mm
Track front/rear	1564/1584 mm
Length	4780 mm
Width	-
Height	-
Weight	800 kg

PERFORMANCE

Top speed	-
Power to weight ratio	1.3 kg/hp

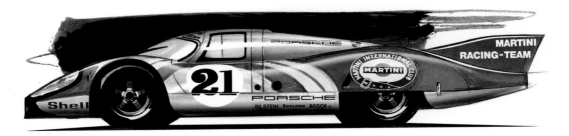

917 LH   1970

After having discovered during tests that followed the 1969 1000 Km of Zeltweg that the cause of the 917's instability problems went back to the car's aerodynamic configuration, the 917 K was designed and was shorter and lighter than its predecessor and wedge shaped, all of which greatly improved stability. Raising the tail almost up to the height of the roof itself influenced the aerodynamics negatively. The Cx increased to an uncomfortable 0.464 and the frontal section increased by 10%. But the power of the engine and the effectiveness of the chassis still ensured sufficient performance to annihilate the competition on most circuits, but there was fairly considerable concern over how the car would fare on the long straights of the Le Mans, for which top speed had to be increased. A new 4.9-litre engine was considered and the design of a new long tailed body was handed to the SERA studio – called the *langheck* or long tail. At the April tests the sides looked much rounded and shaped on the tail, but that shape plus the heavily concave front end would change substantially before Le Mans. The penetration coefficient was excellent and the top speed really high at almost 380 kph as recorded by Kurt Ahrens. Unfortunately, the stability, which had become one of the 917 K's strong points, was affected: that's why John Wyer decided not to use the long tail in the race. It was the opposite at Porsche-Salzburg, who entered two cars: one, which was sponsored by Martini, was of extravagant colouring, the work of the Anatole Lapine styling centre and that was christened the hippie car, which was one of the race's favourites. However, a series of technical problems relegated it to second place in the event, won by a 917 K. Further evolution of the 917 LH was in hand for 1971: the engine was now a 4999 cc that produced 630 hp and enabled Jackie Oliver a fastest lap average of over 250 kph and a top speed of 386 kph. But the win still went to the 917 K.

The prototype of the air cooled 16-cylinder boxer that should have powered the 917 in the Can-Am Championship. This particular inclination of the intake trumpets is caused by them being slotted between the injection pump banks. Despite the performance, Porsche would opt for the more potent – but also more difficult to run and set up – 12 cylinder with two turbochargers.

TECHNICAL SPECIFICATION

ENGINE
Central, longitudinal
16 cylinders horizontally opposed

Bore and stroke	86.8 x 70.4 mm
Unitary cubic capacity	416.5
Total cubic capacity	6665 cc
Valve gear	twin overhead camshafts, chain driven
Number of valves	2 per cylinder
Compression ratio	10.5:1
Fuel feed	Bosch mechanical injection
Ignition	double, transistorised
Coolant	forced air
Lubrication	dry sump
Maximum power	840 hp at 8300 rpm
Specific power	126 hp/litre

TRANSMISSION
Rear wheel drive

Clutch	triple dry disc
Gearbox	en bloc with differential, 5 speeds plus reverse

CHASSIS
Tubular trellis

Front suspension	double wishbones, coil springs, hydraulic telescopic shock absorbers, stabiliser bar
Rear suspension	double wishbones, coil springs, hydraulic telescopic shock absorbers, stabiliser bar
Brakes	discs on all four wheels
Steering	ZF rack
Fuel tank	180 litres
Tyres front/rear	-

DIMENSIONS AND WEIGHT

Wheelbase	2300 mm
Track front/rear	1526/1533 mm
Length	3905 mm
Width	-
Height	-
Weight	-

PERFORMANCE

Top speed	-
Power to weight ratio	-

917 16-cylinder   1970

In 1969, Porsche's involvement in the Can-Am Championship started quietly enough with the 917 Spyder PA, which stands for Porsche-Audi. It was only modified in the body and fuel tank capacity compared to the 917 that was competing in the World Championship for Makes. But the car's adversaries could have much more power, which came from over 7-litre engines. That is why Jo Siffert was able to snatch a number of good placings but without hope of victory. The definitive solution was found with turbo charging, which produced the 917-10 in 1972, but in the meantime another road had been taken: it was of a 16-cylinder engine with atmospheric fuel feed. The starting point was the 917's 12-cylinder air cooled boxer, the type 912: not even the code was changed because it was considered an evolution. In fact, the technicians limited themselves to adding another four cylinders, maintaining most of the components in common with each of the two power units. The most evident modification was the position of the two Bosch injection pumps – the same as those on the 8-cylinder 908 – in the centre above the engine, forcing the intake trumpets into an inclined position and not vertical, as on the 12-cylinder. Between 1960 and 1970, parts were made for 10 engines: depending on the cylinders used – all the variants of the 917 were available – the technicians obtained capacities of 6, 6.6, 6.7 and 7.2-litres, the latter with the cylinders of the 917 5.4 for the Interseries Championship, with a power output of over 880 hp. Tests were carried out on the bench and in a 917 Spyder PA, the 917-027 chassis, and the car was driven for a few test laps at the end of 1971 by Mark Donohue on Porsche's Weissach circuit. The American driver called the car "monstrous" and thought it was a valid alternative to the 12-cylinder turbo. Or, he opined, the 16-cylinder could be turbocharged to produce a power output close to 2000 hp! But the project was dropped and the engine went to enriching the collection at the Porsche Museum, leaving the turbo to "conquer" America.

The illustration on the right shows the livery selected for the factory 911 S 2.4, which Gérard Larrousse was to drive in the Tour de France Automobile in which he came second. In this photograph, a 911 S 2.5 of team Erwin Kremer, Porsche's Cologne concessionaire and tuner, in competition.

TECHNICAL SPECIFICATION

ENGINE

Rear, overhanging, longitudinal
6 cylinders horizontally opposed

Bore and stroke	85 x 70.4 mm
Unitary cubic capacity	399.1 cc
Total cubic capacity	2395 cc
Valve gear	overhead camshaft, chain driven
Number of valves	2 per cylinder
Compression ratio	10.3:1
Fuel feed	carburettors
Ignition	transistorised
Coolant	forced air
Lubrication	dry sump
Maximum power	245 hp at 8000 rpm
Specific power	102.3 hp/litre

TRANSMISSION

Rear wheel drive

Clutch	dry mono-disc
Gearbox	en bloc with differential, 5 speeds plus reverse

CHASSIS

Unified steel structure

Front suspension	McPherson, longitudinal torsion bars, stabiliser bar, hydraulic shock absorbers
Rear suspension	independent, oblique arms, transverse torsion bars, hydraulic shock absorbers, stabiliser bar
Brakes	discs on all four wheels
Steering	ZF rack
Fuel tank	100 litres
Tyres front/rear	7 x 15/9 x 15

DIMENSIONS AND WEIGHT

Wheelbase	2268 mm
Track front/rear	1402/1355 mm
Length	4163 mm
Width	1610 mm
Height	1320 mm
Weight	789 kg

PERFORMANCE

Top speed	240 kph
Power to weight ratio	3.9 kg/hp

911 S 2.4 Tour de France and 911 S 2.5   1971

Various racing versions of the 911 were prepared in 1970, both for track events and rallying. For the year that followed, the 911 ST 2.3 put out 240 hp and, especially on circuits, showed it was effective. However, in 1971 the company's attention was mainly concentrated on its sports racers that competed for the World Championship for Makes, the 917 at the head of the queue, and even if the company continued to support private entrants, direct involvement was reduced. The last time the works team competed was in the Tour de France Automobile: the 911 was further lightened with Plexiglas side windows, parts of the body material in plastic, shell seats and the elimination of underbody protection plus soundproofing kept the weight down to 789 kg. The cubic capacity was taken to 2395 cc using the cylinders of the ST 2.3 that were clad in hard chrome; the stroke was also increased to 70.4 mm. The car's power output went up to 240 hp at 8000 rpm, but later the car was given electronic fuel injection that took it to 260 hp. Gérard Larrousse came second in the punishing French marathon in the car. The following year, after competing in the East African Safari with a specific 911 S 2.2, a new racer was further improved and was made available to sporting customers: it was the 911 S 2.5. Starting with the production 911 S 2.4, the cubic capacity was increased to 2492 cc with the use of racing pistons that run in sleeves clad in Nikasil; that enabled the reduction of friction and the increase of power that moved on to 270 hp at 8000 rpm. Other modifications concerned the camshafts, the dual ignition head, bigger valves and polished ducts. Externally, the car could hardly be distinguished from the standard 911 S, but the suspension had a different setting, the rims were wider, the gearbox was reinforced and the body was much lightened. And given its motor sport destiny, the fuel tank was bigger and took 110 litres, while all 21 cars had a roll bar welded to the chassis.

A rear view of the 1972 911 T 2.4 emphasises the new matt black writing on the car. Even if they are not visible externally, much work on setting and better weight distribution tried to resolve the problem of lightening the nose at high speed, a problem that physiologically afflicted high performance rear engine cars.

TECHNICAL SPECIFICATION

ENGINE
Rear, overhanging, longitudinal
6 cylinder horizontally opposed

Bore and stroke	84 x 70.4 mm
Unitary cubic capacity	390.1 cc
Total cubic capacity	2341 cc
Valve gear	overhead camshaft, chain driven
Number of valves	2 per cylinder
Compression ratio	7.5:1
Fuel feed	carburettors
Ignition	transistorised
Coolant	forced air
Lubrication	dry sump
Maximum power	130 hp at 5600 rpm
Specific power	55.5 hp/litre

TRANSMISSION
Rear wheel drive

Clutch	dry mono-disc
Gearbox	en bloc with differential, 5 speeds plus reverse

CHASSIS
Unified steel structure

Front suspension	McPherson, longitudinal torsion bars, stabiliser bar, hydraulic shock absorbers
Rear suspension	independent, oblique arms, transverse torsion bars, hydraulic shock absorbers, stabiliser bar
Brakes	-
Discs on all four wheels	
Steering	ZF rack
Fuel tank	62 litres
Tyres front/rear	165 x 15/165 x 15

DIMENSIONS AND WEIGHT

Wheelbase	2271 mm
Track front/rear	1360/1342 mm
Length	4227 mm
Width	1610 mm
Height	1320 mm
Weight	1050 kg

PERFORMANCE

Top speed	205 kph
Power to weight ratio	8 kg/hp

911 T 2.4   1971

The Series E 911 was launched in 1971 with a further cubic capacity increase, testifying to Porsche's continuous update programme. By lengthening the stroke of the 2.2 6-cylinder from 66 to 70.4 mm the engine became a 2341 cc with a consequent increase in power output and performance. The 911 T for the European market and, therefore, with its fuel fed by carburettors, grew to 130 hp while the North American version with mechanical fuel injection had 10 hp more at the same 5600 rpm. The strange fact is that the new engine had to operate with normal petrol due to the increasingly rigid regulations in the USA, Porsche's main market. While performance was not sacrificed, the same couldn't be said of fuel consumption. But, given the level of the car, a more serious problem was the cars reduced stability on the straight at high speed. Changes were made to weight distribution by repositioning some secondary components to limit the lightening that had been carried out on the B and C, giving a comparison of redistribution of 42% front and 58% rear. The suspension calibration was modified and even the oil tank with its external inlet was moved forward on the E and had an external inlet concealed by a cover behind the passenger's door; later, this system was eliminated due to misunderstandings by service station staff, who mistook the oil tank cap for that of the petrol. The definitive solution came from the wind tunnel, which suggested mounting a front spoiler, initially only on the S, but it was extended to the whole range. The 5-speed gearbox was completely new, with first and second gears placed opposite each other, something new for Porsche customers who were previously forced to use the awkward first gear back-left position. The whole lubrication system was revised in 1973 and a new, exhaust layout was installed. It was no longer painted, but was entirely in stainless steel.

The characteristic front of the 911 S 2.4 with the new front spoiler fitted to reduce the front's tendency to go light at high speed. Other aspects of the model include the black plastic strips on the bumpers and the aluminium door sills. The car's wheelbase was lengthened by 3 mm in 1973 to and the oil tank was moved to behind the rear wing.

TECHNICAL SPECIFICATION

ENGINE
Rear, overhanging, longitudinal
6 cylinders horizontally opposed

Bore and stroke	84 x 70.4 mm
Unitary cubic capacity	390.1 cc
Total cubic capacity	2341 cc
Valve gear	overhead camshaft, chain driven
Number of valves	2 per cylinder
Compression ratio	8.5:1
Fuel feed	mechanical injection
Ignition	transistorised
Coolant	forced air
Lubrication	dry sump
Maximum power	190 hp at 6500 rpm
Specific power	81.1 hp/litre

TRANSMISSION
Rear wheel drive

Clutch	dry mono-disc
Gearbox	en bloc with differential, 5 speeds plus reverse

CHASSIS
Unified steel structure

Front suspension	McPherson, longitudinal torsion bars, hydraulic shock absorbers, stabiliser bar
Rear suspension	independent, oblique arms, transverse torsion bars, hydraulic shock absorbers, stabiliser bar
Brakes	discs on all four wheels
Steering	ZF rack
Fuel tank	62 litres
Tyres front/rear	185/70 x 15/185/70 x 15

DIMENSIONS AND WEIGHT

Wheelbase	2271 mm
Track front/rear	1360/1354 mm
Length	4227 mm
Width	1610 mm
Height	1320 mm
Weight	1075 kg

PERFORMANCE

Top speed	230 kph
Power to weight ratio	5.6 kg/hp

911 S 2.4   1971

With the presentation in 1971 of its 1972 model year cars, Porsche increased the cubic capacity of the 911 to 2341 cc by lengthening the stroke of the 2.2's engine. Once again, at the top of the 3-car range was the 911 S, the engine of which now put out 190 hp at 6500 rpm that took the car to a top speed of 230 kph with a 0-100 kph acceleration of seven seconds, all as a result of an increased compression ratio and a different timing. The power increase and that of its torque by over 10% was obtained despite the use of normal petrol, which caused some perplexity during refuelling. The choice was made so that the 911 would meet rigid North American regulations on emission control. The technical perfection of the engine, with its crankcase in alloy and magnesium and cylinder sleeves in Biral for better piston flow, still meant better performance, but it didn't avoid a worsening of fuel consumption; the 911 S could only cover between 5 and 7.5 kilometres with a litre of petrol. A new development was the introduction of a new 5-speed manual gearbox – with the semi-automatic Sportomatic available as an option – of the 915 type with first and second shoulder-to-shoulder; this modification was the most evident in a transmission that had been completely redesigned. In a 12-year career, it was able to support much high increases in power and was requested with insistence by rally drivers, who found the previous positioning of 1ST low left awkward. To improve high speed stability and counter the usual high speed nose lightening, the 911 S also had its oil tank placed inside its wheelbase and the filler cap close to the centre right pillar. In addition, a nose was designed with a small plastic spoiler that was most efficient as well as more attractive – so much so that it was proposed for other versions.

A 1973 911 E 2.4 Coupé with a front spoiler and light alloy rims. The Carrera RS 2.7 was unveiled that same year and the "normal" 2.4s only had detailed modifications, even if the 3 mm lengthening of the wheelbase improved performance without having to revert to questionable tricks, like moving the oil tank forward as on the 1972 car.

TECHNICAL SPECIFICATION

ENGINE

Rear, overhanging, longitudinal
6 cylinders horizontally opposed

Bore and stroke	84 x 70.4 mm
Unitary cubic capacity	390.1 cc
Total cubic capacity	2341 cc
Valve gear	overhead camshaft, chain driven
Number of valves	2 per cylinder
Compression ratio	8.0:1
Fuel feed	mechanical injection
Ignition	transistorised
Coolant	forced air
Lubrication	dry sump
Maximum power	165 hp at 6200 rpm
Specific power	70.5 hp/litre

TRANSMISSION

Rear wheel drive

Clutch	dry mono-disc
Gearbox	en bloc with differential, 5 speeds plus reverse

CHASSIS

Unified steel structure

Front suspension	McPherson, longitudinal torsion bars, stabiliser bar, hydraulic shock absorbers
Rear suspension	independent, oblique arms, transverse torsion bars, hydraulic shock absorbers, stabiliser bar
Brakes	discs on all four wheels
Steering	ZF rack
Fuel tank	62 litres
Tyres front/rear	185/70 x 15/185/70 x 157

DIMENSIONS AND WEIGHT

Wheelbase	2271 mm
Track front/rear	1372/1354 mm
Length	4227 mm
Width	1610 mm
Height	1320 mm
Weight	1075 kg

PERFORMANCE

Top speed	220 kph
Power to weight ratio	6.5 kg/hp

911 E 2.4   1971

Between the base version of the 911 T range and the potent 911 S in model year 1972 was the 911 E, with the cubic capacity of this 6-cylinder boxer engine also taken to 2.4 litres to produce 165 hp at 6200 rpm, obtained with normal, 91-octane petrol, which led to an 8.0:1 compression ratio to comply with the North American norms on emission control. Initially, the car's front was similar to that of the 2.2-litre; but later, after a critical press and public success due to a much better performance, with the spoiler fitted as standard to the 911 S, the latter was also made available as an option on the E. The gearbox was the new 915 type with 1ST and 2ND at the same level, while the semi-automatic Sportomatic box was optional. To vary the weight balance and improve the car's dynamic quality, the 911 E's oil tank was also moved to the right rear wing ahead of the axle. That meant the adoption of an oil replenishment trap flap near the central pillar, which was often confused with that for petrol by distracted service station personnel. So from the 1973 model year the oil tank was returned to behind the wing beyond the rear axle. This due to petrol pump attendant confusion and the complaints of rear passengers over the heat coming from the lubricant, which could be felt in the cab. The external cap was replaced by the usual one inside the engine compartment. This was a modification permitted by the 3 mm longer wheelbase, which ensured greater stability; at the same time, new plastic fuel tanks were used, despite some initial mass production problems. The new ATS rims also became available on the 911 E from the 1973 model year, while those for the USA had Bosch K-Jetronic fuel injection.

The Gijs van Lennep-Helmut Marko 917 K powered by a 4.9-litre engine about to win the 1971 24 Hours of Le Mans, a race in which many Porsches retired. This 917 has a new magnesium tube trellis chassis that saved 35% of the original car's weight, despite making the car more robust. The illustration on the right shows the extravagant livery of Big Bertha, the 917.20 with an experimental body developed by SERA.

TECHNICAL SPECIFICATION

ENGINE
Central, longitudinal
12 cylinders horizontally opposed

Bore and stroke	86.8 x 70.4 mm
Unitary cubic capacity	416.6 cc
Total cubic capacity	4999 cc
Valve gear	twin overhead camshafts, chain driven
Number of valves	2 per cylinder
Compression ratio	10.5:1
Fuel feed	Bosch mechanical fuel injection
Ignition	double, transistorised
Coolant	forced air
Lubrication	dry sump
Maximum power	630 hp at 8300 rpm
Specific power	126 hp/litre

TRANSMISSION
Rear wheel drive

Clutch	triple dry disc
Gearbox	en bloc with differential, 5 speeds plus reverse

CHASSIS
Tubular trellis

Front suspension	double wishbones, coil springs, hydraulic telescopic shock absorbers, stabiliser bar
Rear suspension	double wishbones, coil springs, hydraulic telescopic shock absorbers, stabiliser bar
Brakes	discs on all four wheels
Steering	ZF rack
Fuel tank	-
Tyres front/rear	-

DIMENSIONS AND WEIGHT

Wheelbase	2300 mm
Track front/rear	1526/1533 mm
Length	4140 mm
Width	-
Height	-
Weight	800 kg

PERFORMANCE

Top speed	-
Power to weight ratio	1.3 kg/hp

917 K and 917.20 1971

After the total domination of the 1970 season competition by the 917 K, which culminated with victory at the 1971 24 Hours of Le Mans, the cars were further improved. At the start of the season tests were carried out with periscope engine air intakes, which slightly reduced aerodynamic efficiency but seemed to provide performance benefits. However, the modification was dropped. A more extensive evolution of the body concerned the tail, which became lower and was given two large shark's fins, as they were called and they, finally, managed to improve the 917 K's penetration by 15% without reducing stability. Another step forward was the cubic capacity increase from 4-litres to 5. The increase was only 92 cc for a total of 4999 cc – almost the regulations' limit – but a more significant modification was the means of construction: the aluminium cylinder sleeves were no longer in Cromal but Nikasil which, reducing piston friction, ensured an increase in power output to a total of 630 hp. During the Le Mans tests, a strange looking body also appeared, which was designed by SERA and called the 917.20; it was much wider and rounded compared to the car's track and was immediately baptised Big Bertha. Later, they called it The Pig when it took to the grid with irreverent pink livery on which various pork cuts were outlined and named. The frontal section was much bigger, but the car's performance ensured an excellent race that was unfortunately nipped in the bud by an accident. A final new development appeared at the end of the season, one that was swathed in secrecy; the aluminium chassis – welded in atmospheric argon – of one of the 917 Ks was replaced with another identical one in magnesium, making the car 35% lighter. After the April tests, Derek Bell and Jo Siffert, who had not been told of this major change, still gave positive impressions of the car. One of them was fielded at Le Mans by the Martini Racing Team and won the 24-hour marathon driven by Gijs van Lennep and Helmut Marko despite the 4.9-litre engine.

Even if it wasn't officially introduced, the 916 still played an important role in Porsche's history. As a result of the revised body so that the track could be widened and the aerodynamics improved, the car looked more modern and sporty, while the interior was finished in leather and velvet. Destined for the US market, if it had been produced it would have cost more than the 911.

TECHNICAL SPECIFICATION

ENGINE

Central, longitudinal
6 cylinders horizontally opposed

Bore and stroke	84 x 70.4 mm
Unitary cubic capacity	390.1
Total cubic capacity	2341 cc
Valve gear	overhead camshaft, chain driven
Number of valves	2 per cylinder
Compression ratio	8.5:1
Fuel feed	carburettors
Ignition	electronic
Coolant	forced air
Lubrication	dry sump
Maximum power	190 hp at 6500 rpm
Specific power	81.1 hp/litre

TRANSMISSION

Rear wheel drive

Clutch	dry mono-disc
Gearbox	en bloc with differential, 5 speeds plus reverse

CHASSIS

Unified steel structure

Front suspension	McPherson, longitudinal torsion bars, hydraulic shock absorbers, stabiliser bar
Rear suspension	independent, oblique arms, transverse torsion bars, hydraulic shock absorbers, stabiliser bar
Brakes	discs on all four wheels
Steering	ZF rack
Fuel tank	-
Tyres front/rear	-

DIMENSIONS AND WEIGHT

Wheelbase	2450 mm
Track front/rear	1337/1480 mm
Length	-
Width	-
Height	-
Weight	910 kg

PERFORMANCE

Top speed	230 kph
Power to weight ratio	4.8 kg/hp

916   1972

According to Porsche's "official" story, the 916 was never in the price list, so the 11 of these cars produced should only be considered prototypes. The idea was to develop a real supercar from the 914 chassis, which had amply shown its equilibrium and dynamic quality. So the removable roof was replaced by a steel roof to increase rigidity, while long members were reinforced and covered in glass fibre. The suspension was only slightly adjusted with stabiliser bars for both axles and Bilstein shock absorbers, but the 7-inch alloy rims with their 185/70 x R15 radials forced the company to widen the wheel housings. A front spoiler was redesigned in the same way for better downforce at high speed and to house the headlights and oil radiator. The rear spoiler also had a new shape and the car's total weight panned out at 910 kg. But the major new development was the engine: it was the most powerful available at the time on the Porsche shelves, the 911 S 6-cylinder 2.4-litre that put out 190 hp at 6500 rpm. However, quite a few 916 owners replaced that power unit with the Carrera's 2.7-litre, 210 hp engine as soon as it was unveiled. The car's performance was breathtaking, with a 0-100 kph in under seven seconds and a 230 kph top speed. Of course, the brakes were the self-ventilating version of the 911 S. As well as quoting simple figures, the 916 really did have great roadholding, even better than the 911, which was at the top of the range; only some deceleration criticism was made. Perhaps for this reason and to avoid cannibalisation between the two models as well as to keep the 911 at the top, Zuffenhausen's top management dropped the project. Five of the cars went to the Porsche and Piëch families, while the remainder found their way into the most loyal clients who were really close to the marque, one of whom was in the United States.

The 911 Carrera RS 2.7 became a particular icon of both Porsche and the model range for its outstanding performance and its captivating and unmistakable aesthetics. The car enjoyed an extremely successful motor sport career and the Carrera writing along both its flanks became a must, while the duck tail rear wing was often used for the production 911 2.7.

. TECHNICAL SPECIFICATION

ENGINE
Rear, overhanging, longitudinal
6 cylinders horizontally opposed

Bore and stroke	90 x 70.4 mm
Unitary cubic capacity	447.8 cc
Total cubic capacity	2687 cc
Valve gear	overhead camshaft, chain driven
Number of valves	2 per cylinder
Compression ratio	8.5:1
Fuel feed	Bosch mechanical injection
Ignition	transistorised
Coolant	forced air
Lubrication	dry sump
Maximum power	210 hp at 6300 rpm
Specific power	78.1 hp/litre

TRANSMISSION
Rear wheel drive

Clutch	dry mono-disc
Gearbox	en bloc with differential, 5 speeds plus reverse

CHASSIS
Unified steel structure

Front suspension	McPherson, longitudinal torsion bars, hydraulic shock absorbers, stabilizer bar
Rear suspension	independent, oblique arms, transverse torsion bars, hydraulic shock absorbers, stabilizer bar
Brakes	servo discs
Steering	ZF rack
Fuel tank	85 litres
Tyres front/rear	185/0 x 15/216/60 x 15

DIMENSIONS AND WEIGHT

Wheelbase	2271 mm
Track front/rear	1372/1394 mm
Length	4147 mm
Width	1652 mm
Height	1320 mm
Weight	1075 kg

PERFORMANCE

Top speed	240 kph
Power to weight ratio	5.1 kg/hp

911 Carrera RS 2.7   1972

In 1972, Porsche's need to build a small series of cars that could be elaborated for the Grand Touring category – for which 500 had to be produced to earn homologation – which was the moment to bring back the Carrera lettering that was sort of forgotten after the introduction of the 911. The first step was to increase the cubic capacity from 2.4-litres to 2687 cc, which was achieved by taking the 6-cylinder boxer engine from a bore of 84 to 90 mm. The forged pistons were completely new and especially the cylinder sleeves in aluminium alloy with the way covered in Nikasil and, therefore, without pressed-in liners. Maximum power output went up to 210 hp at 6300 rpm with a specific power curiously lower than that of the 911 S. Handling was improved with a different suspension setting and the fitment of forged alloy rims with different sections for the front and rear ends. To improve top speed and stability a single-piece large glass fibre duck tail spoiler was mounted at the rear so that it included the entire engine cover. Pre-empting a certain reluctance of the purists to accept such an evident device of the 911's silhouette, they were given the opportunity – without dismissing the client's responsibility – to have a normal engine cover fitted. The contrary happened, because many wanted the wing on their Carrera 911s, replacing their cars' normal engine covers with the duck tail version. Lightening the car was another area in which the technicians worked: the normal seats were replaced by other Recaros, the rear suspension's articulation was in forged aluminium and the layout was simplified to the point that it saved a massive 100 kg. The 911 Carrera RS 2.7 was also available in standard Sport form, the Rennen racing version and the Touring derivative, which renounced all simplification for a richer and more comfortable car.

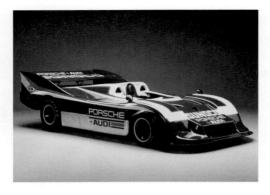

As with the 917.10, the monstrous 917.30 dominated the Can-Am Championship with its massive 1100 hp. Before it was replaced, a suitably prepared car with less aerodynamic load, faired wheels and 1500 hp was taken to the Talladega circuit in Alabama, USA, where, driven by American Mark Donohue, it established the absolute speed record for racing cars of 355.846 kph.

TECHNICAL SPECIFICATION

ENGINE
Central, longitudinal
12-cylinder turbo, horizontally opposed

Bore and stroke	86.8 x 70.4 mm
Unitary cubic capacity	416.6 cc
Total cubic capacity	4999 cc
Valve gear	twin overhead camshaft, chain driven
Number of valves	2 per cylinder
Compression ratio	6.5:1
Fuel feed	Bosch mechanical injection
Ignition	double, transisterised
Coolant	forced air
Lubrication	dry sump
Maximum power	1000 hp at 7800 rpm
Specific power	200 hp/litre

TRANSMISSION
Rear wheel drive

Clutch	triple dry disc
Gearbox	en bloc with differential, 4 speeds plus reverse

CHASSIS
Tubular trellis

Front suspension	double wishbones, coil springs, hydraulic telescopic shock absorbers, stabiliser bar
Rear suspension	double wishbones, coil springs, hydraulic telescopic shock absorbers, stabiliser bar
Brakes	discs on all four wheels
Steering	ZF rack
Fuel tank	300 litres
Tyres front/rear	-

DIMENSIONS AND WEIGHT

Wheelbase	2316 mm
Track front/rear	1620/1638 mm
Length	4562 mm
Width	2100 mm
Height	1080 mm
Weight	750 kg

PERFORMANCE

Top speed	343 kph
Power to weight ratio	0.75 kg/hp

917.10 and 917.30 1972

After Porsche's experience with the 917 Spyder PA and the retirement of the 917 from the World Championship for Makes, which limited cubic capacity to 3-litres from 1972, all of the company's motor sport energy went into a car for the Can-Am. As had happened in the World Championship with John Wyer's team, Porsche decided to associate itself with another private team and chose Roger Penske's squad for whom Indianapolis 500 winner Mark Donohue drove. The 917.10 used the 917 K chassis, which was suitably strengthened to take the over 1000 hp put out by the 12-cylinder, 5-litre unit with twin exhaust gas-powered turbochargers: previously, a 4.5-litre was tested that generated 850 hp. The transmission was reinforced and the body redesigned for greater downforce, which was evidenced by the car's enormous rear wing. Initially, the car had serious drivability problems, mainly caused by turbo lag. But at the start of the season, Donohue demonstrated the superiority of the 917 by easily winning at Mosport. Soon afterwards, Mark was involved in a frightening accident while testing at Atlanta, which put him out of action for several months: his place was taken by George Follmer who, after a great season, won the Can-Am title, while Leo Kinnunen made the Interseries title his in a similar car. The car was redesigned for 1973 so that it became the 917.30, with its cubic capacity taken to 5.4-litres for an over 1100 hp power output. The turbocharging was managed by a knob on the dashboard, baptised "the horse screw", while the wheelbase went from 2316 mm to 2500 mm and the body, in Sunoco livery, was developed together with SERA: the car's Cx dropped from the 0.65 of the 917.10 to 0.60. High values, mainly due to the massive aerodynamic devices necessary to guarantee the right amount of downforce. This time, Donohue dominated the Can-Am Championship with the car.

The 911 Carrera 2.7 was a potent car of lively performance. But the 1975 Targa version in the photograph with its roll bar painted black, was a rare beast of which few were produced. The Carrera also had window washer jets; the improvement of the 911 continued non-stop the following years with better performance and preparation.

TECHNICAL SPECIFICATION

ENGINE

Rear, overhanging, longitudinal
6 cylinders horizontally opposed

Bore and stroke	90 x 70.4 mm
Unitary cubic capacity	447.8 cc
Total cubic capacity	2687 cc
Valve gear	overhead camshaft, chain driven
Number of valves	2 per cylinder
Compression ratio	8.5:1
Fuel feed	Bosch K-Jetronic injection
Ignition	transistorized
Coolant	forced air
Lubrication	dry sump
Maximum power	145 hp at 5800 rpm
Specific power	53.9 hp/litre

TRANSMISSION

Rear wheel drive

Clutch	Dry mono-disc
Gearbox	en bloc with differential, 5 speeds plus reverse

CHASSIS

Unified steel structure

Front suspension	McPherson, longitudinal torsion bars, hydraulic shock absorbers, stabilizer bar
Rear suspension	independent, oblique arms, transverse torsion bars, hydraulic shock absorbers, stabilizer bar
Brakes	discs on all four wheels
Steering	ZF rack
Fuel tank	80 litres
Tyres front/rear	185/70 x 15/185/70 x 15

DIMENSIONS AND WEIGHT

Wheelbase	2271 mm
Track front/rear	1372/1354 mm
Length	4291 mm
Width	1610 mm
Height	1320 mm
Weight	1075 kg

PERFORMANCE

Top speed	225 kph
Power to weight ratio	7.4 kg/hp

911 2.7, S 2.7 and Carrera 2.7   1973

The 2700 cc 911 first appeared in 1973 as a continuation of the first 911 of 1963, of which it was the seventh series and available as a coupé or Targa. The T and E descriptions were dispensed with, the new 911 were of significant difference in relation to the previous models; their increased cubic capacity and the introduction of Bosch K-Jetronic electronic fuel injection meant the engines were able to better adapt themselves to market demands in terms of both elasticity and the antipollution. To the base 150 hp model were added a 175 hp of the 911 S (165 hp in 1976) and the 210 hp Carrera. The latter was added to the production line after the great success of the experimental limited edition RS in 1972, keeping its predecessor's mechanical fuel injection system that was quicker and performed better. Clients could choose between 4 and 5-speed gearboxes. Externally, the cars had new blow-absorbing bumpers in light alloy with lateral "bellows" as required by North American norms; the duck's beak spoiler was an optional on the Carrera. Inside, the seats had integral headrests and the steering wheel was padded. It was undoubtedly an aggressive car that did 0-100 kph in less than 6 seconds and the Carrera had a top speed of 240 kph. But the 911 2.7 also had a superior level of comfort for cars of its category; that was immediately emphasised by the international motoring press, which also liked the high quality external finish. The 911 coupé also had the honour of being the 250,000TH car to leave the Porsche production line since 1948; in addition, in 1975 a special series of 400 cars commemorated the 25TH anniversary of the Zuffenhausen factory.

The Porsche 911 Carrera RS 2.7 being driven by Bjorn Waldegaard in the 1974 East African Safari with the roof rack carrying anti-sand platforms. After resolving the suspension and gearbox problems that had marred the 1973 event, the Swede came close to winning a year later but, in the end, had to be happy with second place after losing time replacing a semi-axle.

TECHNICAL SPECIFICATION

ENGINE
Rear, overhanging, longitudinal
6 cylinders horizontally opposed

Bore and stroke	90 x 70.4 mm
Unitary cubic capacity	447.8 cc
Total cubic capacity	2687 cc
Valve gear	overhead camshaft, chain driven
Number of valves	2 per cylinder
Compression ratio	8,5:1
Fuel feed	Bosch mechanical injection
Ignition	double, transistorised
Coolant	forced air
Lubrication	dry sump
Maximum power	210 hp at 6300 rpm
Specific power	78.1 hp/litre

TRANSMISSION
Rear wheel drive

Clutch	dry mono-disc
Gearbox	en block with differential, 5 speeds plus reverse

CHASSIS
Unified steel structure

Front suspension	McPherson, longitudinal torsion bars, hydraulic telescopic shock absorbers
Rear suspension	independent, oblique arms, transverse torsion bar, hydraulic shock absorbers, stabiliser bar
Brakes	discs
Steering	ZF rack
Fuel tank	100 litres
Tyres front/rear	185/70 x 15/215/60 x 15

DIMENSIONS AND WEIGHT

Wheelbase	2271 mm
Track front/rear	1372/1394 mm
Length	4147 mm
Width	1652 mm
Height	1320 mm
Weight	980 kg

PERFORMANCE

Top speed	245 kph
Power to weight ratio	4. kg/hp

911 Carrera RS 2.7 Safari   1973

After a break in 1972 that followed the 1971 activity, Porsche returned to the World Rally Championship by entering the toughest and most punishing event of all, the East African Safari. Two factory cars were prepared and were driven by Waldegaard-Thorszelius and Zasada-Bien.

The Bosch fuel injected engine was similar to the production unit that put out 210 hp, while the Bosch ignition system was double with a reserve. The 5-speed transmission had a reinforced clutch and oil radiator, the differential was 40% self-locking. The steel fuel tank had a 100 litre capacity with quick-fill caps with a rubber cover. The M+ S tyres were 185/70 VR 15 front and 215/60 VR 15 rear, like those of normal production. The body shell was further lightened and ended up at 980 kg total, while the equipment included sheet metal protection below the chassis, making the car 27 cm from the ground's surface. That modification called for special Bilstein shock absorbers with a longer travel to avoid damage during major extensions of the suspension. In front of the bumpers was a protective steel bar, with other equipment including supplementary depth headlights, a pneumatic horn, a Twinmaster, reading light and special locations for helmets and road maps, as well as safety belts, a roll bar and a hoist. But the African adventure was unsuccessful for both cars as they experienced shock absorber travel trouble and serious problems with gearbox synchronisation. The synchronisation rings wore fast, so much so that they were chewed up by the gears causing breakage. The adventure was attempted again the following year with perfected cars: Waldegaard ran well, but he lost the win due to the time he took to replace a broken semi-axle.

The 911 Carrera RSR 2.8 in official Martini Racing livery photographed at Dijon in 1973. The car won first time out at the 24 Hours of Daytona and ended its career after having dominated almost all the races for which it was entered on both sides of the Atlantic, at times also powered by a 3-litre engine in anticipation of the RSR 3.0, one of which won the 1973 Targa Florio.

TECHNICAL SPECIFICATION

ENGINE
Rear, overhanging, longitudinal
6 cylinders horizontally opposed

Bore and stroke	92 x 70.4 mm
Unitary cubic capacity	476.6 cc
Total cubic capacity	2806 cc
Valve gear	overhead camshaft, chain driven
Number of valves	2 per cylinder
Compression ratio	10.3:1
Fuel feed	Bosch mechanical injection
Ignition	double transistorised
Coolant	forced air
Lubrication	dry sump
Maximum power	300 hp at 8000 rpm
Specific power	106.9 hp/litre

TRANSMISSION
Rear wheel drive

Clutch	dry mono-disc
Gearbox	en bloc with differential, 5 speeds plus reverse

CHASSIS
Unified steel structure

Front suspension	McPherson, longitudinal torsion bars, hydraulic telescopic shock absorbers
Rear suspension	independent, oblique arms, transverse torsion bars, hydraulic shock absorbers, stabiliser bar
Brakes	disc
Steering	ZF rack
Fuel tank	110 litres
Tyres front/rear	230/600 x 15/260/600 x 15

DIMENSIONS AND WEIGHT

Wheelbase	2271 mm
Track front/rear	1472/1521 mm
Length	4147 mm
Width	1652 mm
Height	1320 mm
Weight	890 kg

PERFORMANCE

Top speed	-
Power to weight ratio	2.9 kg/hp

911 Carrera RSR 2.8   1973

The designers of the 911 Carrera RS 2.7 took into account the car's likely motor sport career from the start for many of the planned 500 – the number needed to earn homologation – although public demand increased that number considerably. The Porsche racing department decided to further elaborate 57 cars in line with Group 4 specifications, and so the 911 Carrera RSR 2.8 was born.

The cubic capacity of the engine, now with a double ignition head, was taken to 2806 cc by increasing the bore by 2 mm to better exploit the opportunities provided by the regulations. Timing was revised, the compression ratio increased to 10.3:1 and the power output went up to 300 hp at 8000 rpm. The lubrication's temperature was kept under control by an oil radiator integrated into the front bumpers. The 225 mm Sachs clutch was reinforced, while the gearbox – the box in magnesium alloy – was the same as the Carrera RS' even if the gears' lubrication-ventilation system was improved; the limited slip differential was self-locking with plates, with the variable percentage of up to 80%, as was the choice for the gear ratios. The suspension was given bigger Unibal joints and an anti-roll bar, the brakes with manual brake force distribution were developed from the self-ventilating units of the 917. The body was built in thin sheet metal and freed of all that was superfluous until the weight had dropped to 890 kg and the wheel housings were widened to take 230/600 x 15 tyres front and 260/600 x 15 rear. The Carrera RSR 2.8 practically had no rivals on the race track in 1973, dominating the European Championship with Clemens Schickentanz and Claude Ballot-Léna, winners on equal points! Another was the European Mountain Championship, won by Sepp Greger, the Trans-Am series and IMSA. And on top of that, the car won the year's Targa Florio driven by Gijs van Lennep and Herbert Müller.

The market success of the 911 Turbo was enormous: it looked great and its performance was breath-taking, obtained by innovative racing technology. In only the first year on sale, the car sold 644 units in Europe (and "the rest of the world") plus 530 in the USA. The illustration shows the Turbo prototype with perforated disc brakes, which were not on the production cars.

TECHNICAL SPECIFICATION

ENGINE
Rear, overhanging, longitudinal
6-cylinder turbo, horizontally opposed

Bore and stroke	95 x 70.4 mm
Unitary cubic capacity	499 cc
Total cubic capacity	2994 cc
Valve gear	overhead camshaft, chain driven
Number of valves	2 per cylinder
Compression ratio	6.5:1
Fuel feed	Bosch K-Jetronic injection
Ignition	transistorised
Coolant	forced air
Lubrication	dry sump
Maximum power	260 hp at 5500 rpm
Specific power	88.4 hp/litre

TRANSMISSION
Rear wheel drive

Clutch	dry mono-disc
Gearbox	en bloc with differential, 4 speeds plus reverse

CHASSIS
Unified steel structure

Front suspension	McPherson, longitudinal torsion bars, hydraulic shock absorbers, stabiliser bar
Rear suspension	independent, oblique arms, transverse torsion bars, hydraulic shock absorbers, stabiliser bar
Brakes	disc
Steering	ZF rack
Fuel tank	80 litres
Tyres front/rear	205/50 x 15/225/50 x 15

DIMENSIONS AND WEIGHT

Wheelbase	2271 mm
Track front/rear	1438/1511 mm
Length	4291 mm
Width	1775 mm
Height	1320 mm
Weight	1195 kg

PERFORMANCE

Top speed	250 kph
Power to weight ratio	4.6 kg/hp

911 Turbo (930) 1974

The 911 Turbo was born of the development of the now consolidate base model and marked the moment when Porsche was able to use its turbocharged racing car experience for production cars.

The body had a profile of pronounced originality, with no chrome, homogeneity in the choice of colours for the finish of details, an imposing rear spoiler over the 6-cylinder 3000 cc boxer engine, which was turbocharged for the first time to produce 260 hp at 5500 rpm. A turbo fed by exhaust gas gave the car much greater performance if one considers the 0-200 kph took just 20 seconds with a top speed of 250 kph. Paying attention to reducing problems related to the compression also brought with it a contained turbo lag under acceleration, an immediate central drawback that was in the Zuffenhausen designers' and technicians' minds, as they had been "burnt" many times by massive turbo delay in their racing cars. Even at 2000 rpm the fluidity and meekness of the drive as well as a relative quietness, were the peculiarities that confirmed the car's classy performance, which was also evident in the pleasant interior and a substantial quantity of high quality equipment. The suspension was improved with rear arms in aluminium, Bilstein shock absorbers and bigger stabiliser bars. The brakes, which were a weak point with the 930, were the same as the 2.7's, while the gearbox only had four speeds because the larger gear wheels "stole" the fifth gear's place. Roadholding was assured even at the highest performance, by the car's aerodynamic profile, which was unmistakable and destined for a long life. Only available as a coupé, the car was available in a wide range of colours, but for the hard to please they could also have their own personal choice of colour.

One of the 106 911 Carrera RS and RSR 3.0. In fact, 100 of the cars had to be built to obtain Group 3 homologation. About half of them were road going versions, but the remainder were built and equipped for racing. The illustration shows an RSR 3.0 prepared in line with the more permissive Group 4 regulations.

TECHNICAL SPECIFICATION

ENGINE

Rear, overhanging, longitudinal
6 cylinders horizontally opposed

Bore and stroke	95 x 70.4 mm
Unitary cubic capacity	499 cc
Total cubic capacity	2994
Valve gear	overhead camshaft, chain driven
Number of valves	2 per cylinder
Compression ratio	9.8:1
Fuel feed	Bosch mechanical injection
Ignition	Transistorised
Coolant	forced air
Lubrication	dry sump
Maximum power	230 kph at 6200 rpm
Specific power	76.8 hp/litre

TRANSMISSION

Rear wheel drive

Clutch	dry mono-disc
Gearbox	en bloc with differential, free selection

CHASSIS

Unified steel structure

Front suspension	McPherson, longitudinal torsion bars, hydraulic shock absorbers, stabiliser bar
Rear suspension	independent, oblique arms, transverse torsion bars, hydraulic shock absorbers, stabiliser bar
Brakes	disc
Steering	ZF rack
Fuel tank	110 litres
Tyres front/rear	215/60 x 15/235/60 x 15

DIMENSIONS AND WEIGHT

Wheelbase	2271
Track front/rear	1437/1462 mm
Length	4235 mm
Width	1775 mm
Height	1320 mm
Weight	900 kg

PERFORMANCE

Top speed	-
Power to weight ratio	3.9 kg/hp

911 Carrera RSR 3.0   1974

The most obvious sign of the passage from the Carrera RS 2.7 and the Carrera RSR 3.0 that took place in 1974 was the disappearance of the duck tail spoiler and its replacement by another that "tray" shaped and no less prominent. To obtain Group 3 homologation at least 100 of the cars had to be built, but 106 rolled off the Zuffenhausen production line, 50 of which were road-going and the rest were prepared for motor racing. Compared to the 2.7, the engine's bore was increased to 95 mm and the cubic capacity went up to 2992.55 cc. To improve engine resistance, the crankcase, which was in magnesium alloy on the 2.7, was cast in light alloy. The cylinder liners were in light alloy with Nikasil coating, there was a butterfly for each cylinder bank and an injector for every cylinder. Power output was 230 hp. Apart from the rear spoiler and wider wheel housings for the eight-inch front tyres and the 9-11 inch rears, the chassis and body only differed by small details in relation to the Carrera 2.7. Much more significant was the modification made to 69 of the cars – 42 for European races, 15 for Team Penske and 12 built in 1975 – all of which were prepared for Group 4: the 911 Carrera RSR 3.0. Power output went up to 330 hp at 8000 rpm as a result of dual ignition, a compression ratio of 10.3:1 and Carrera 6 camshafts. The 225 mm clutch was reinforced, the set-up was more rigid in part due to the new light alloy bar that strengthened the front of the body shell, while the rims were bigger, with a 14-inch channel at the rear. In this case, too, the RSR had no rivals during the 1974 and 1975 seasons winning – among others – the European GT Championship, the Mountain title, the FIA World Cup and the IMSA series. A number of cars were also entered for the World Championship for Makes as prototypes: their power output was lower and their weight much higher to the Matra, Ferrari, Lola, Mirage and Alfa Romeo sports racers, but their tremendous reliability still weighed in their favour and they still turned in some good results.

The 911 Carrera RSR 2.1 Turbo being driven by van Lennep-Müller during the 1974 24 Hours of Le Mans. Despite the fact that it was developed from a road car, the RSR 2.1 was able to cross swords with the Alfa Romeos and Matras. The team was retired at the end of 1975 awaiting the appearance of a production car category for which the 935 was already on the stocks at Zuffenhausen.

TECHNICAL SPECIFICATION

ENGINE
Rear, overhanging, longitudinal
6-cylinder turbo, horizontally opposed

Bore and stroke	83 x 66 mm
Unitary cubic capacity	357
Total cubic capacity	2142 cc
Valve gear	overhead camshaft, chain driven
Number of valves	2 per cylinder
Compression ratio	6.5:1
Fuel feed	Bosch mechanical injection
Ignition	transistorised
Coolant	forced air
Lubrication	dry sump
Maximum power	500 hp at 7600 rpm
Specific power	233.4 hp/litre

TRANSMISSION
Rear wheel drive

Clutch	dry mono-disc
Gearbox	en bloc with differential, free selection

CHASSIS
Unified steel structure

Front suspension	McPherson, longitudinal torsion bars, hydraulic shock absorbers, stabiliser bar
Rear suspension	independent, oblique arms, transverse torsion bar, hydraulic shock absorbers, stabiliser bar
Brakes	disc
Steering	ZF rack
Fuel tank	110 litres
Tyres front/rear	245/575 x 15/340/575 x 15

DIMENSIONS AND WEIGHT

Wheelbase	2271 mm
Track front/rear	1437/1462 mm
Length	4255 mm
Width	2000 mm
Height	1320 mm
Weight	750 kg

PERFORMANCE

Top speed	310 kph
Power to weight ratio	1.5 kg/hp

911 Carrera RSR 2.1 Turbo   1974

After the 911 Carrera RSR 3.0's experience in the World Championship for Makes, challenging the open top sports racers of other constructors while waiting for the 1975 Championship, Porsche decided to increase the 911's performance by building a turbocharged car. This after the 1975 Championship when the Production Car category was expected to be introduced, but in reality it didn't appear until 1976. If the cubic capacity limit for normally aspirated cars was 3-litres, the turbos would be handicapped of 1.4-litres with their maximum allowed at 2142 cc. Using the 911 2.2's drive shaft with a 66 mm stroke and cylinders with an 83 mm bore, the company reached the permitted limit precisely. The compression ratio was reduced to 6.5:1, the con rods were in titanium, cooling was by a horizontal fan and fuel feed came from a KKK turbocharger with intercooler and a waste gate that could be regulated by the driver. Power output was 500 hp – 450 hp for six of the cars with 911/78 engines – and the top speed was 310 kph with a 0-100 kph time of 3.2 seconds. The chassis was revised with its suspension minus torsion bars, a specific set-up and rims with a 10.5-inch channel on the front and a massive 17 inches at the rear. The gearbox was the 915 type that was specially reinforced and the car had no differential. The fuel tank was in the centre behind the driving position. The body shell was also much modified: the front shield was bigger, which was where the 908's oil radiator found its home, while the rear was redesigned with a different roof group profile – in place of the rear sidelights there were two NACA air intakes – and an enormous spoiler incorporating the intercooler. The RSR could never have the agility nor the weight of its Sports Prototype adversaries, but its reliability was really impressive, having only retired twice all season. Van Lennep-Müller and Koinigg-Schurti took fine places for the Martini Racing Team, among them second in the 24 Hours of Le Mans and Watkins Glen.

The 911 Carrera 3.0 with its crankcase derived from that of the 911 Turbo replaced the Carrera 2.7. From 1977 it would have servo-assisted brakes and a new, more robust clutch. After the launch of the turbocharged version it was no longer the top-of-the-range car, but a sector of the clientele still preferred a normally aspirated engine in their car due to its quick, immediate response.

TECHNICAL SPECIFICATION

ENGINE
Rear, overhanging, longitudinal
6 cylinders horizontally opposed

Bore and stroke	95 x 70.4 mm
Unitary cubic capacity	499 cc
Total cubic capacity	2994 cc
Valve gear	overhead camshaft, chain driven
Number of valves	2 per cylinder
Compression ratio	8.5:1
Fuel feed	Bosch K-Jetronic injection
Ignition	transistorised
Coolant	forced air
Lubrication	dry sump
Maximum power	200 hp at 6000 rpm
Specific power	66.8 hp/litre

TRANSMISSION
Rear wheel drive

Clutch	dry mono-disc
Gearbox	en bloc with differential, 5 speeds plus reverse

CHASSIS
Unified steel structure

Front suspension	McPherson, longitudinal torsion bars, hydraulic telescopic shock absorbers
Rear suspension	independent, oblique arms, transverse torsion bars, hydraulic shock absorbers, stabiliser bar
Brakes	servo-assisted discs
Steering	ZF rack
Fuel tank	80 litres
Tyres front/rear	185/70 x 15/215/60 x 15

DIMENSIONS AND WEIGHT
Wheelbase	2271 mm
Track front/rear	1372/1380 mm
Length	4291 mm
Width	1652 mm
Height	1320 mm
Weight	1020 kg

PERFORMANCE
Top speed	230 kph
Power to weight ratio	5.1 kg/hp

911 Carrera 3.0   1975

Produced between 1975 and 1977, the Carrera 3.0 was a synthesis of the Porsche motor sport characteristics always associated with that name and preparation refinement never before so evident. The cubic capacity increase from 2700 to 3000 cc was clearly located in the continued research for performance excellence by the company's designers, but the 200 hp output, generated at 6000 rpm, did not ruffle the class of a car which is mainly elastic – and less noisy – in relation to its predecessors. The Bosch K-Jetronic fuel injection system, which had been perfected in relation to its consolidated application to the 911 2.7, ensured lower consumption and took its place in the pragmatic attention paid by the constructors towards the reduction in running costs. By the same token, the choice of body materials more resistant to wear, and the adoption of rust proof aluminium components. With the development of the Carrera 3.0 to testing and conception of new solutions was among the design priorities and, at the same time, reflected needs like the prospect of the car's long life, its safety and the chance of giving purchasers guarantee periods decidedly above the average. The interior was exceptional: leather-covered seats, finish and covering of the steering wheel, imitation leather or cloth interior; thermostatic control of the heating system and electric windows on the coupé. Part of the same picture was the offer to clients of three different kinds of transmission, one with a 4-speed mechanical gearbox, a 5-speed or a 3-speed Sportomatic. More or less the same as that of the 911 model, the bodies for the Carrera 3.0 Targa and Coupé proposed surrounds for the headlights and external rear vision mirrors in the same colour as the body plus matt black edges.

Unlike the first version, the 912 E was only on offer in the United States market. The European market's entry level car was the revolutionary 924 with a front engine and a transaxle layout. The difference between that and the contemporary 911 was minimum, but the purchase price and much reduced running costs contributed to the model's sales success.

TECHNICAL SPECIFICATION

ENGINE

Rear, overhanging, longitudinal
4 cylinders horizontally opposed

Bore and stroke	94 x 71 mm
Unitary cubic capacity	492.7 cc
Total cubic capacity	1971 cc
Valve gear	overhead valves, push rods and rocker arms
Number of valves	2 per cylinder
Compression ratio	7.6:1
Fuel feed	electronic injection
Ignition	electronic
Coolant	forced air
Lubrication	wet sump
Maximum power	90 hp at 4900 rpm
Specific power	45.6 hp/litre

TRANSMISSION

Rear wheel drive

Clutch	dry mono-disc
Gearbox	en bloc with differential, 5 speeds plus reverse

CHASSIS

Unified steel structure

Front suspension	McPherson, longitudinal torsion bars, hydraulic telescopic shock absorbers
Rear suspension	independent, oblique arms, transverse torsion bars, hydraulic shock absorbers
Brakes	disc
Steering	ZF rack
Fuel tank	80 litres
Tyres front/rear	165 x 15/165 x 15

DIMENSIONS AND WEIGHT

Wheelbase	2271 mm
Track front/rear	1360/1330 mm
Length	4291 mm
Width	1652 mm
Height	1320 mm
Weight	1160 kg

PERFORMANCE

Top speed	192 kph
Power to weight ratio	12.8 kg/hp

912 E   1975

The notable success of the 1964 912 would push the Porsche management to offer a car with the same spirit over ten years later. It was the 912 E, which was restricted to the USA. The car's chassis and body came from the 911 2.7, while external differences were limited to different design wheels with 165 HR 15 tyres and the writing on the engine cover. The interior had nylon carpeting on the floor and imitation leather for some parts of the seats, different handles, fixed rear window – hinged opening optional – and just a few other items. The 4-cylinder, air cooled boxer engine was the 2-litre unit of the VW-Porsche 914/2.0 fed by Bosch L-Jetronic fuel injection. The EGR system had to be revised every 30,000 miles, for which it needed a dial connected to the milometer. To respect anti-pollution norms, the exhaust also had a thermo-reactor. Maximum power output was 90 hp at 4900 rpm with 14 kgm of torque at 4000 rpm. Top speed was 180 kph. The transmission included the same 5-speed gearbox as the 911's and only differed due to 4TH and 5TH gear ratios and axle ratios; the 40% self-locking differential was optional. Customers could choose the kind of shock absorbers they wanted between Boge and Woodhead, while the braking system was of four simple discs instead of the 911's self-ventilated units. The excellent road qualities of the 912 E, together with a decidedly competitive price in the US – $3,000 less than that of the 911 S and $15,000 less than the Turbo – meant the car's immediate success, which soon went and cannibalised the 914/4: only in 1975 were no fewer than 2,092 Es produced, also helped along by the 1973-1974 oil crisis, which meant the "small" car's lightness and low fuel consumption were also trump cards.

A cutaway shows the refined technical transaxle of the 924. Despite the engine being derived from mass production – a detuned version powered also the Volkswagen LT van – its performance was lively and its behaviour safe. It was Porsche's best-seller for years, although it was not produced at Zuffenhausen but in the Audi-NSU plant at Neckarsulm.

TECHNICAL SPECIFICATION

ENGINE
Front, longitudinal
4-cylinder in line vertical

Bore and stroke	86.5 x 84.4 mm
Unitary cubic capacity	496 cc
Total cubic capacity	1984 cc
Valve gear	overhead camshaft, toothed belt
Number of valves	2 per cylinder
Ignition	electronic
Compression ratio	9.3:1
Fuel feed	electronic injection
Coolant	liquid
Lubrication	wet sump
Maximum power	125 hp at 5800 rpm
Specific power	63 hp/litre

TRANSMISSION
Rear wheel drive

Clutch	front, dry mono-disc
Gearbox	rear, en bloc with differential, 4 speeds plus reverse

CHASSIS
Unified steel structure

Front suspension	oscillating wishbones, coaxial coil springs with hydraulic telescopic shock absorbers
Rear suspension	independent, oblique arms, transverse torsion bars, hydraulic telescopic shock absorbers
Brakes front/rear	discs/ servo-assisted drums
Steering	ZF rack
Fuel tank	66 litres
Tyres front/rear	185/70 x 14/185/70 x 14

DIMENSIONS AND WEIGHT

Wheelbase	2400 mm
Track front/rear	1418/1372 mm
Length	4213 mm
Width	1656 mm
Height	1260 mm
Weight	1080 kg

PERFORMANCE

Top speed	200 kph
Power to weight ratio	8.6 kg/hp

924   1975

It should have been a Volkswagen, but the project was stopped. But Porsche, which had carried out the development, decided to go ahead on its own. From the moment it was launched, it pleased public taste, which set the car on the road to a sales record, although it never won the hearts of the Porsche purists. The new 2+2 had a front engine and the gearbox-differential group was in the rear. The two organs were connected by a rigid and solid tube in which a 20 mm diameter light transmission shaft rotated. The 4-cylinder, 2-litre in line engine was liquid cooled derived from a mass production unit. Due to the single overhead camshaft and K-Jetronic fuel injection it could generate 125 hp at 5800 rpm, sufficient to take the car to a top speed of 200 kph and a 0-100 kph time of 10.5 seconds, ensuring contained fuel consumption at the same time. The original 4-speed Audi gearbox was soon joined by a 5-speed Porsche 'box and was replaced by another 5-speed installed behind the differential in 1979. The suspension was in line with the classic Porsche layout at the rear, with McPherson on the front, a close relation to that of the VW Golf. There were front disc brakes with drums at the rear. As a result of an ideal weight distribution – 48% front and 52% rear – handling was fast and safe. The first updates came out in 1977, when equipment was influenced by the company's two 1976 world motor racing titles. The evolution continued in 1978 and, just 26 months after the 924's launch, it had sold 50,000 units, all of which rolled off the Audi-NSU Neckarsulm production line. The number had been doubled by January 1981. The following year, the car was given a rear spoiler at the base of the rear window and that improved its Cx from 0.36 to 0.33, increasing top speed by 4 kph and reducing fuel consumption.

Reinhold Jost at the wheel of the 908.03 Turbo. Many modifications would be carried out on the body, including the periscope air intake and the large rear wing: initially it was from the 917-10, but would later be designed by the Jost team. The critical year was 1975, but in 1976 along came a much hoped for win. Meanwhile, Porsche had a new weapon ready as the World Championship for Makes was nearing its end.

TECHNICAL SPECIFICATION

ENGINE

Central, longitudinal
6-cylinders turbo, horizontally opposed

Bore and stroke	83 x 66 mm
Unitary cubic capacity	374.6 cc
Total cubic capacity	2142 cc
Valve gear	twin overhead camshafts, chain driven
Number of valves	2 per cylinder
Compression ratio	6.5:1
Fuel feed	Bosch injection, KKK turbo
Ignition	double transistorised
Coolant	forced air
Lubrication	dry sump
Maximum power	450 hp at 8000 rpm
Specific power	210 hp/litre

TRANSMISSION

Rear wheel drive

Clutch	dry mono-disc
Gearbox	en bloc with differential, 5 speeds plus reverse

CHASSIS

Aluminium tube trellis

Front suspension	double wishbones, coil springs, hydraulic telescopic shock absorbers, stabiliser bar
Rear suspension	double wishbones, coil springs, hydraulic telescopic shock absorbers, stabiliser bar
Brakes	discs on all four wheels
Steering	ZF rack
Fuel tank	-
Tyres front/rear	-

DIMENSIONS AND WEIGHT

Wheelbase	2300 mm
Track front/rear	1542/1506 mm
Length	-
Width	-
Height	-
Weight	670 kg

PERFORMANCE

Top speed	320 kph
Power to weight ratio	1.5 kg/hp

908 Turbo   1975

After the 1971 season, Porsche decided to retire the works team from the World Championship for Makes. So even the almost unbeatable 908.03s were pensioned off. Most of them were sold to private entrants, who mainly raced them in hill-climbs. But four years later, a number of them returned to the World Championship with a completely new configuration. In 1975, three teams – especially the one run by Reinhold Jost, who would be the lead driver – and Martini-Porsche decided after many Interseries Championships with "traditional" cars to transform the 908 by adding a 6-cylinder turbocharger, the one that had first appeared on the 911 prototype with such success. The cubic capacity was 2142 which, multiplied by the coefficient imposed on turbos, enabled the 908 to return to the Sport Prototype category, for which normally aspirated cars of up to 3-litres were also admitted. Maximum power output was 450-500 hp and a full weight of 670 kg, which respected the regulations. Externally, there didn't seem much difference. In most cases, large periscope air intakes were fitted to feed and cool the intercooler, plus a large rear wing to ensure downforce that was originally developed for the 917–10, which had competed in the Can-Am Championship. On paper, the 908.03 Turbo looked competitive, but problems in setting up the turbo engine only brought the car a few good placings and second in the Championship table behind Alfa Romeo; they had won the title for which a 2.7 turbo was also entered. Things went better in 1976 when, despite Martini moving to the works team, the car took its first wins in both the World Championship for Makes and the Interseries.

The aggressive appearance of the 934 is mainly due to the broader wheel housings and the large air intake for the intercooler radiators. Due to the 1120 kg minimum weight imposed by the Group 4 regulations, which were not much under those for the 911, curiously the 934 would also have electric windows, complete door panels and bumpers. Despite its retirement during its Daytona debut, the 934 became unbeatable over the years.

TECHNICAL SPECIFICATION

ENGINE

Rear, overhanging, longitudinal
6-cylinder turbo, horizontally opposed

Bore and stroke	95 x 70.4 mm
Unitary cubic capacity	499 cc
Maximum cubic capacity	2994 cc
Valve gear	overhead camshaft, chain driven
Number of valves	2 per cylinder
Compression ratio	6.5:1
Fuel feed	turbo, electronic injection
Ignition	electronic
Coolant	forced air
Lubrication	dry sump
Maximum power	485 hp at 7000 rpm
Specific power	161.9 hp/litre

TRANSMISSION

Rear wheel drive

Clutch	dry mono-disc
Gearbox	en bloc with differential, 4 speeds plus reverse, free selection

CHASSIS

Unified steel structure

Front suspension	McPherson, longitudinal torsion bars, hydraulic shock absorbers, stabiliser bar
Rear suspension	independent, oblique arms, transverse torsion bars, hydraulic shock absorbers, stabiliser bar
Brakes	disc
Steering	ZF rack
Fuel tank	80 litres
Tyres front/rear	275/600 x 16/325/625 x 16

DIMENSIONS AND WEIGHT

Wheelbase	2268 mm
Track front/rear	1506/1462 mm
Length	4235 mm
Width	1775 mm
Height	1320 mm
Weight	1135 kg

PERFORMANCE

Top speed	300 kph
Power to weight ratio	2.3 kg/hp

934 Turbo   1975

The Carrera RSR period with normally aspirated engines was over, so a new version of the 911 came out in 1976; it was to compete in Group 4 and was derived from the 911 Turbo (Type 930) and assumed the name 934. The 934 name indicates that the car was prepared for Group 4, in line with the 935 and 936 denominations. Externally, the car distinguished itself from the production 930 by its three-part plastic decomposable BBS rims that meant increasing the side of the wheel housings, and by the large frontal air intakes under the bumper. But the mechanical preparation of the 934's engine was much different in that the road car's chassis and transmission showed they were able to withstand the extra power and the extra stress of track racing, so they were only slightly modified. But the brakes had the aluminium callipers of the 917, which were later adopted for the 911 Turbo in 1978. The 6-cylinder 3-litre engine with Bosch K-Jetronic fuel injection was equipped with the KKK turbocharger already used on the 917.30 – although that car had two of them – which with a charge that went up to 2.3 bar and could be regulated with the usual horse power button. That set-up took the car to generating 485 hp at 7000 rpm to produce a top speed of over 300 kph. However, during the design period, up came the need to cool the air compressed at about 150°C: there were vain attempts to install an air-to-air intercooler because they were unable to change the car's body shape due to the regulations and were unable to find the space to install one. Even though it was initially looked on with great scepticism, the solution they adopted was to put in an air-to-water exchanger with two large front radiators; all of which weighed an extra 20 kg, but the car was still within the regulation 1120 kg limit. In 1977, the car was further evolved to generate 540 hp and later to 600 hp for the more permissive IMSA regulations: it was the 934 ½ version.

Jochen Mass driving a 936, the car in its 1976 livery of Martini Racing. It was a great season that culminated in victory at Le Mans. A victory repeated the following year at the Sarthe with the 936 (see illustration) that was much revised, especially its aerodynamics as le Mans was the only race by the works team: the Cx was reduced from 0.398 to 0.37, maintaining the same downforce.

TECHNICAL SPECIFICATION

ENGINE
Central, longitudinal
6-cylinder turbo, horizontally opposed

Bore and stroke	83 x 66 mm
Unitary cubic capacity	357 cc
Total cubic capacity	2142 cc
Valve gear	overhead camshaft, chain driven
Number of valves	2 per cylinder
Compression ratio	6.5:1
Fuel feed	electronic injection, turbocharger
Ignition	electronic
Coolant	liquid
Lubrication	dry sump
Maximum power	540 hp at 8000 rpm
Specific power	252.1 hp/litre

TRANSMISSION
Rear wheel drive

Clutch	dry mono-disc
Gearbox	en bloc with differential, 5 speeds plus reverse

CHASSIS
Tubular trellis

Front suspension	independent, triangular wishbones, helical coil springs, with hydraulic shock absorbers
Rear suspension	independent, triangular wishbones, helical coil springs with hydraulic shock absorbers
Brakes	disc
Steering	ZF rack
Fuel tank	110 litres
Tyres front/rear	215/60 x 15/235/60 x 15

DIMENSIONS AND WEIGHT

Wheelbase	2410 mm
Track front/rear	1530/1480 mm
Length	-
Width	-
Height	-
Weight	700 kg

PERFORMANCE

Top speed	330 kph
Power to weight ratio	1.3 kg/hp

936 1976

In 1975 FIA continually changed the Championship regulations, while Porsche competed with cars similar to production vehicles. But, with the hypothesis of a competitive return of real sports racers, the 936 project was kicked off in great secrecy, a Group 6 car without any more links – engine apart – with the 911, the first since the time of the 917. The chassis was a tubular aluminium trellis that included some aspects of the 917's. To compensate, the company tried to lower the car: that's why the driver was in an almost lying down position. A new development was the central installation of the engine, which also had a load bearing function to perform. It was a 6-cylinder 2142 cc unit that was in the 1974 Carrera RSR Turbo, but taken to 520 hp with the gearbox derived from that of the 917. Initially the tests – as decided by Fuhrmann, who wanted to camouflage the car's existence – were carried out with a matt black prototype. And early on, together with the Martini livery, Count Rossi of Montelera, the car's sponsor, liked that colour very much and chose to keep it – until he noticed it was almost invisible to the tv cameras in fog, so it became white. The 1976 season culminated in a great win at Le Mans with Ickx and van Lennep. The following year, Porsche decided to race only at Le Mans, leaving the rest of the Championship to Alfa Romeo. The aerodynamics and engine of the 936 were revised, so that the car now had twin turbochargers and put out 540 hp. At the Sarthe a year later, after three hours, the Ickx-Pescarolo car pitted and was retired, then the Barth-Haywood Porsche likewise after pit stopping to change the injection pump. Then Furhmann asked Ickx to drive the surviving 936 and ordered the Belgian to win or break it. It looked like it would be the latter, but after a few record fragments and a touch of luck, the car won. But Porsche wouldn't be that lucky at the 1978 race in which Porsche came second or in 1979 when the Essex-liveried 936 retired.

The Stommelen-Schurti Porsche 935 at the 1976 24 Hours of Le Mans, but the next win at the Sarthe happened in 1978 – the works team raced the 936 – crewed by Ludwig-Whittington-Whittington in a 935 K-3 elaborated by Team Kremer. The K versions would be highly competitive in both Europe and the USA and many of them, like the one illustrated here, would also be sold to privateers.

TECHNICAL SPECIFICATION

ENGINE

Rear, overhanging, longitudinal
6 cylinders horizontally opposed

Bore and stroke	92 x 70.4 mm
Unitary cubic capacity	476.6 cc
Total cubic capacity	2806 cc
Valve gear	overhead camshaft, chain driven
Number of valves	2 per cylinder
Compression ratio	6.5:1
Fuel feed	mechanical injection, turbocharged
Ignition	transistorised
Coolant	forced air
Lubrication	dry sump
Maximum power	590 hp at 8000 rpm
Specific power	210.2 hp/litre

TRANSMISSION

Rear wheel drive

Clutch	dry mono-disc
Gearbox	en bloc with differential, 4 speeds plus reverse, free selection

CHASSIS

Unified steel structure

Front suspension	McPherson, longitudinal torsion bars, hydraulic shock absorbers, stabiliser bar
Rear suspension	independent, oblique arms, transverse torsion bars, hydraulic shock absorbers, stabiliser bar
Brakes	discs and servo-brake
Steering	ZF rack
Fuel tank	110 litres
Tyres front/rear	275/600 x 16/350/700 x 19

DIMENSIONS AND WEIGHT

Wheelbase	2271 mm
Track front/rear	1502/1558 mm
Length	4680 mm
Width	1970 mm
Height	1265 mm
Weight	800 kg plus 80 kg ballast

PERFORMANCE

Top speed	340 kph
Power to weight ratio	1.6 kg/hp

935 Turbo   1976

If the 934 had no rivals in Group 4, the 935 long dominated Group 5 with both the factory team and privateers, which ensured a substantial elaboration of the road-going 911 Turbo: the chassis was modified with a tubular structure, the suspension was revised without torsion bars – but with adjustable anti-roll bars –, the transmission was strengthened and Dunlop tyres in sizes 250/600 x 16 front and 350/700 rear were fitted, the latter to 19-inch rims. But the strong point was the 2808 cc turbocharged engine which, considered a handicap, put the car among the 4-litres. The double ignition and the KKK turbocharger took its power to 590 hp – although the declared output often exceeded 600 hp with a 630 hp overboost. In the beginning the much revised body used a large rear spoiler in which there was an air-to-air intercooler. Later in the 1976 season the regulations changed and limited the dimensions of the back wing, forcing Porsche to install the air-water intercooler of the 934, which caused initial reliability problems that meant Porsche only won the Championship against BMW at the last race. The 935 was further improved for the 1977 season: the big turbo was replaced by two smaller KKK units, one per cylinder bank, while the regulations now enabled the company to move the intercooler behind the flame shield – moved 20 cm farther forward – and to vary the suspension layout. By this time, power output had reached 630 hp or over 800 hp for some cars with the 3.2 and 3.3-litre engines. As well as the works team in the Martini Racing livery, many 935s were farmed out to private entrants, Loos and Kremer at the top of the list. The latter considerably modified theirs to create the 935 K: the body was lightened, the chassis strengthened with 30 metres of aluminium tubing and the intercooler was replaced by an air-to-air unit aspirated by the engine fan. Power output increased to 805 hp and one of them won the 1978 24 Hours of Le Mans.

The 928 was the result of a long, meticulous design project aimed at creating the perfect GT: it was fast, safe and comfortable, well-finished and aesthetically timeless. The result even stupefied the press, which said, "It is as if all the Porsches to date were practical exercises for the company's men to design this car".

TECHNICAL SPECIFICATION

ENGINE
Front, longitudinal
8 cylinders at V90° vertical

Bore and stroke	95 x 78.5 mm
Unitary cubic capacity	529.2 cc
Total cubic capacity	4474 cc
Valve gear	overhead camshaft, toothed belt
Number of valves	2 per cylinder
Compression ratio	8.5:1
Fuel feed	electronic injection
Ignition	electronic
Coolant	liquid
Lubrication	forced circulation
Maximum power	240 hp at 5500 rpm
Specific power	53.6 hp/litre

TRANSMISSION
Rear wheel drive

Clutch	front, dry mono-disc
Gearbox	rear, en bloc with differential, 5 speeds plus reverse

CHASSIS
Unified steel structure

Front suspension	transverse oscillating arms, coaxial coil springs with hydraulic shock absorbers, stabiliser bar
Rear suspension	transverse oscillating arms, coaxial coil springs with hydraulic shock absorbers, stabiliser bar
Brakes	discs and servo-brake
Steering	servo-assisted rack
Fuel tank	82 litres
Tyres front/rear	225/50 x 16

DIMENSIONS AND WEIGHT
Wheelbase	2500 mm
Track front/rear	1545/1514 mm
Length	4447 mm
Width	1836 mm
Height	1313 mm
Weight	1490 mm

PERFORMANCE
Top speed	230 kph
Power to weight ratio	6 kg/hp

928 1977

By the end of the '70s 911 sales were falling: even though it was updated, the body shell was still the one of 1963 and by this time the car seemed to have gone through all reasonable development possibilities. On the other hand, the 924 was so successful that consideration was given to replacing the 911 with a new model: one that was bigger and more comfortable, technologically advanced and with top performance, the design of which had already begun before the 924. After careful evaluation, conditioned by the ever more restrictive norms in anti-pollution, noise and safety terms, a transaxle layout was selected for the 928 with a large cubic capacity V8 front engine. In the beginning, the technicians considered a 5-litre unit, but the fuel crisis of the period made them err towards a cubic capacity half a litre less: a 3.9-litre unit was built that put out 184 hp (not for the American market) but that was dropped just before it was constructed. The one that fit the bill was a liquid cooled light alloy 4.5-litre V8 with single overhead camshaft valve gear that put out 240 hp at 5500 rpm and a top speed of 230 kph. Transmission was a 5-speed manual 'box or a three-speed automatic – 4-speed from 1983 – of Mercedes-Benz origin. The car was introduced at the 1977 Geneva Motor Show with extraordinary success and was even voted Car of the Year, the only sports car to have been elected so, which was the umpteenth confirmation of the technological excellence Porsche had achieved. The car was critically acclaimed but not publicly, so management decided to continue to develop the 911. Apart from the normal updates, a new version of the car was unveiled in 1979 – the 928 S. The principal innovation was a cubic capacity increase to 4664 cc that produced 300 hp at 5900 rpm – 310 in 1983 with the new Bosch LH-Jetronic injection. Two spoilers at the front and another at the base of the rear window reduced the car's Cx to 0.38 and increased its top speed to 250 kph.

In the early '80s a Zuffenhausen department was named "Special Desires" – later, it became "Porsche Exclusive" – and had the job of equipping personalised versions and variations of cars for the most demanding and well-shod of their clients. One of the specials was the Flaschschnauze with a body inspired by that of the 935, but with retractable headlights and lateral air intakes.

TECHNICAL SPECIFICATION

ENGINE

Rear, overhanging, longitudinal
6-cylinder turbo, horizontally opposed

Bore and stroke	97 x 74.4 mm
Unitary cubic capacity	549.8 cc
Total cubic capacity	3299 cc
Valve gear	overhead camshaft, chain driven
Number of valves	2 per cylinder
Compression ratio	7.0:1
Fuel feed	Bosch electronic injection
Ignition	transistorised
Coolant	forced air
Lubrication	dry sump
Maximum power	300 hp at 5500 rpm
Specific power	90.9 hp/litre

TRANSMISSION

Rear wheel drive

Clutch	dry mono-disc
Gearbox	en bloc with differential, 4 speeds plus reverse

CHASSIS

Unified steel structure

Front suspension	McPherson, longitudinal torsion bars, hydraulic shock absorbers, stabiliser bar
Rear suspension	independent, oblique arms, transverse torsion bars, hydraulic shock absorbers, stabiliser bar
Brakes	discs
Steering	ZF rack
Fuel tank	80 litres
Tyres front/rear	205/55 x 16/225/50 x 16

DIMENSIONS AND WEIGHT

Wheelbase	2272 mm
Track front/rear	1432/1501 mm
Length	4291 mm
Width	1775 mm
Height	1310 mm
Weight	1300 kg

PERFORMANCE

Top speed	260 kph
Power to weight ratio	4.3 kg/hp

911 Turbo 3.3   1977

In 1977, the success of the 911 Turbo was enough to push Porsche into evolving both the car's body and mechanics. Externally, the shape of the bumpers was changed, the engine cover was in sheet steel and the part plastic rear spoiler was revised. But more profound modifications were made under the skin: the bore was increased to 97 mm and the stroke to 74.4 mm, producing a 3299 cubic capacity. The Bosch K-Jetronic fuel injection system and the breakerless ignition helped the power output to 300 hp at 5500 rpm, also helped along by the fitment of an air-to-air heat exchanger able to cool the turbocharger's compressed air. The clutch was also revised by the adoption of a torsional shock absorber able to accept an angular variation of 34°, which was enough to absorb the gearbox's vibration at low revs. The fourth gear was made longer legged and the brakes were new: a perforated self-ventilating disc system and finned aluminium callipers – carrying the name Porsche for the first time – were added having come from the 917 after wide use on both the 934 and 935. A double exhaust outlet was fitted for the 1980 model year, and in 1982 revisions were made of the injection and fuel feed systems, leaving the car's performance unchanged but the car less thirsty. A small run of Group B cars was built that same year for private race entrants. Over the years, the Turbo 3.3 was gradually updated to meet new category norms, and a version with a sloping front became available, with retractable headlights and a modified body to be more in line with that of the 935. Air conditioning was standard from 1985 and a year later five Targa and 2670 cabriolet bodies became available. More profound and long awaited modifications were made to the 1989 versions which now had five speed gearboxes.

A cut-away of the 911 Super Carrera (SC) with its 3-litre engine shows the various improvements made over the years. Six versions were available with either a Targa or coupé body, depending on the market for which they were destined. The car for the USA was easiest to recognise, with its the large rubber strips set into the bumpers.

TECHNICAL SPECIFICATION

ENGINE
Rear, overhanging, longitudinal
6 cylinders, horizontally opposed

Bore and stroke	95 x 70.4 mm
Unitary cubic capacity	499 cc
Total cubic capacity	2994 cc
Valve gear	overhead camshaft, chain driven
Number of valves	2 per cylinder
Compression ratio	8.5:1
Fuel feed	Bosch electronic injection
Ignition	transistorised
Coolant	forced air
Lubrication	dry sump
Maximum power	180 hp at 5500 rpm
Specific power	60 hp/litre

TRANSMISSION
Rear wheel drive

Clutch	dry mono-disc
Gearbox	en bloc with differential, 5 speeds plus reverse

CHASSIS
Unified steel body

Front suspension	McPherson, longitudinal torsion bars, hydraulic shock absorbers, stabiliser bar
Rear suspension	independent, oblique arms, transverse torsion bars, hydraulic shock absorbers, stabiliser bar
Brakes	discs, servo-brakes
Steering	ZF rack
Fuel tank	80 litres
Tyres front/rear	185/70 x 15/215/60 x 15

DIMENSIONS AND WEIGHT

Wheelbase	2272 mm
Track front/rear	1369/1379 mm
Length	4291 mm
Width	1652 mm
Height	1320 mm
Weight	1160 kg

PERFORMANCE

Top speed	225 kph
Power to weight ratio	6.4 kg/hp

911 SC 3.0 1977

Despite the fact that the 924 had been launched to take its place at the bottom of the range and the 928 at the top, the 911 continued to be the fulcrum of Porsche production until the end of the '70s. With the 1978 season on the horizon, the car was updated once more – leaving the Carrera 3.0 apart – and launched the new 911 SC 3.0 which, while with a performance similar to the car it replaced, was more modern, better appointed and comfortable. The SC stood for Super Carrera, confirming the desire to bring together the strong points of the S and Carrera. The 6-cylinder, 2994 cc boxer put out a maximum of 180 hp at 5500 rpm, but more importantly it had a 27 kgm torque at 4100 rpm. The new additions were breakerless starting and the sump in Silumin instead of magnesium. The engine was available in six different versions, which made no difference to its power output, depending on the market of the model's destination. They were Europe, the United States, Japan and California, to whose anti-pollution regulations they had to meet, as well as the kind of transmission selected. Top speed was 225 kph with acceleration from 0-100 kph in seven seconds exactly. Transmission was by a 5-speed gearbox with a reinforced differential: the 3-speed Sportomatic was optional. Externally, the body was along the distinctive Carrera 3.0 lines, with wider wheel housings for 15-inch of different aspect ratios: 6-inch front, 7-inch rear; while the ultra-low tyres with 16-inch diameter wheels as optional. The engine was revised the following year, but the resultant 8 hp power increase didn't make much difference to performance. Standard equipment was much more extensive, the interior updated with both Targa and coupé bodies on offer.

After a tormented debut, the 935 Baby was sorted out; it was made more rigid, the fuel injection system was healed and the flame shield changed. After that, there wasn't much left for the opposition. But they were retired immediately afterwards; Porsche had wanted to demonstrate its technical superiority compared to that of the opposition, but by then the 911s were of over 3-litres and to race a 1.5-litre would be taking a step backwards for the marque's image.

TECHNICAL SPECIFICATION

ENGINE

Rear, overhanging, longitudinal
6-cylinder turbo, horizontally opposed

Bore and stroke	71 x 60 mm
Unitary cubic capacity	237.5 cc
Total cubic capacity	1425 cc
Valve gear	overhead camshaft, with chain and timing gear
Number of valves	2 per cylinder
Compression ratio	6.5:1
Fuel feed	mechanical injection, turbo
Ignition	transistorised
Coolant	forced air
Lubrication	dry sump
Maximum power	380 hp at 8000 rpm
Specific power	266.6 hp/litre

TRANSMISSION

Rear wheel drive

Clutch	dry mono-disc
Gearbox	en bloc with differential, 4 speeds plus reverse, free selection

CHASSIS

Aluminium tubed trellis

Front suspension	McPherson, longitudinal torsion bars, hydraulic shock absorbers, stabiliser bar
Rear suspension	independent, oblique arms, transverse torsion bars, hydraulic shock absorbers, stabiliser bar
Brakes	disc
Steering	ZF rack
Fuel tank	120 litres
Tyres front/rear	275/600 x 16/325/25 x 16

DIMENSIONS AND WEIGHT

Wheelbase	2271 mm
Track front/rear	1502/1457 mm
Length	4680 mm
Width	1970 mm
Height	1265 mm
Weight	750 kg

PERFORMANCE

Top speed	270 kph
Power to weight ratio	2.0 kg/hp

935 2.0 Turbo Baby   1977

On 5 April 1977, Fuhrmann signed an order to take a new initiative: compete in the up to 2-litre Class 1 of the DRM, the highly popular German championship. The project called for the modification of the 935: given the company's experience with the turbo, a 1425 cc 6-cylinder was designed (with a handicap of 1.4 in relation to the 1995 cc): the cylinders were redesigned to 71 x 60 mm, as were the head, valves and ducts. A KKK turbocharger with two air-to-air intercoolers – the flow of air that brushed them was favoured by a system that exploits the exhaust gas – produced 380 hp at 8200 rpm. The gearbox was the light 915/911 type without a differential. The technicians' second challenge was to close up on a minimum weight of 730 kg, over 180 kg less than the normal 935 without ballast. So they began to lighten what they could: as permitted by the regulations, only the production 911 cockpit was retained, and even that was lightened with special metals and thin glass, while as well as the axles the chassis was replaced by two aluminium tube trellises. To save oil tube weight, the radiator was moved to the back, the accelerator pedal and gear lever in titanium; the rims were in magnesium with finning to cool the brakes. The car's debut was planned for the Norisring, where Jacky Ickx' arrived after just a few laps at Porsche's Weissach test circuit. He had power generation problems, the car's gears were too long and not much rigidity: Ickx came 13TH, but he was forced to retire due to the high temperature of over 50°C in the cockpit. The body shell was 18 kg underweight, so the flame shield had been replaced by a non-insulated fibre glass panel that meant he couldn't breathe. Revenge with a perfected car was taken at Hockenheim during the Grand Prix of Germany weekend; after winning the pole position by 2 seconds, Jacky won the race with more than half a lap over Hans Heyer's Ford. And that was the 935 Baby's last race.

To make the 924 Turbo immediately recognisable, BBS alloy rims were fitted and a dual tone paint job was offered as an optional. The car's improved performance changed the 924's positioning in the marketplace, its capability now close to those of the 911 and 928. That also had beneficial effect on the car's image as it was considered a "real" Porsche, as the press confirmed.

TECHNICAL SPECIFICATION

ENGINE
Front, longitudinal
4-cylinder turbo, in line, vertical

Bore and stroke	86.5 x 84.4 mm
Unitary cubic capacity	496 cc
Total cubic capacity	1984 cc
Valve gear	overhead camshaft, toothed belt
Number of valves	2 per cylinder
Compression ratio	7.5:1
Fuel feed	electronic injection, turbo
Ignition	electronic
Coolant	liquid
Lubrication	wet sump
Maximum power	170 hp at 5500 rpm
Specific power	85.6 hp/litre

TRANSMISSION
Rear wheel drive

Clutch	front, dry mono-disc
Gearbox	rear, en bloc with differential, 5 speeds plus reverse

CHASSIS
Unified steel structure

Front suspension	control arms, coaxial coil springs with hydraulic shock absorbers, stabiliser bar
Rear suspension	independent, oblique arms, transverse torsion bars, hydraulic shock absorbers, stabiliser bar
Brakes	discs and servo-brake
Steering	ZF rack
Fuel tank	66 litres
Tyres front/rear	185/70 x 15/185/70 x 15

DIMENSIONS AND WEIGHT

Wheelbase	2400 mm
Track front/rear	1418/1392 mm
Length	4213 mm
Width	1656 mm
Height	1260 mm
Weight	1180 kg

PERFORMANCE

Top speed	225 kph
Power to weight ratio	6.9 kg/hp

924 Turbo   1978

After three years of the 924's performance with its transaxle layout, clients' requests for a more potent engine than the Volkswagen-originated 2-litre that put out 125 hp, became more and more insistent, even if its handling was considered excellent. Given the experience gathered in racing and with the 911, the best solution was turbocharging. The car's head was completely redesigned, made of an especially heat resistant alloy and had bigger valves. The KKK turbocharger had no intercooler but it did have a waste gate to control the pressure. Power output was 170 hp at 5500 rpm with a torque of 25 kgm at 3500 rpm. More than maximum power, the designer's attention was focused on research into its smooth and progressive operation suited to a production car. That, despite the fact that the car would no longer be produced at Neckarsulm but Zuffenhausen and then sent on to the Audi-NSU plant for construction. In 1980, an update of the electronic fuel injection increased top power output to 177 hp. The transmission was also modified with a more resistant clutch and a bigger diameter shaft, while the body was made suitable by the adoption of a different front spoiler to better direct air flow to the four disc brakes plus a number of air intakes to cool the radiator grill and engine cover, the left side of which was the NACA type. Compared to the normally aspirated 924, the Cx dropped from 0.36 to 0.35 with obvious benefits to performance and fuel consumption. The suspension was revised to include an anti-roll bar. In 1980, the car's insulation was also improved. Production of the 924 Turbo ended in 1982, all except for the Italian market, where it survived until 1984 after the introduction of a "super tax" for cars of over 2-litres.

The 935 Moby Dick, nicknamed due to the appearance of its front end as well as its sinuous and lengthened tail, was the most powerful and fastest 935 ever built. More importantly, it was a technical innovation mobile test laboratory, the liquid cooling of head liquid the priority, but also the pre-parers' much copied overturned gearbox. It was an ingenious interpretation of the technical regulations.

TECHNICAL SPECIFICATION

ENGINE

Rear, overhanging, longitudinal
6-cylinder turbo, horizontally opposed

Bore and stroke	95.7 x 74.4 mm
Unitary cubic capacity	535.1 cc
Total cubic capacity	3211 cc
Valve gear	twin overhead camshafts, timing gear
Number of valves	4 per cylinder
Compression ratio	7.0:1
Fuel feed	mechanical injection, turbo
Ignition	transistorised
Coolant	cylinders by forced air, heads by liquid
Lubrication	dry sump
Maximum power	845 hp at 8200 rpm

TRANSMISSION

Rear wheel drive

Clutch	dry mono-disc
Gearbox	en bloc with differential, 4 speeds plus reverse, free selection

CHASSIS

Unified aluminium structure

Front suspension	McPherson, longitudinal torsion bars, hydraulic shock absorbers, stabiliser bar
Rear suspension	independent, oblique arms, transverse torsion bars, hydraulic shock absorbers, stabiliser bar
Brakes	disc and servo-brakes
Steering	ZF rack
Fuel tank	120 litres
Tyres front/rear	275/600 x 16/350/700 x 19

DIMENSIONS AND WEIGHT

Wheelbase	2279 mm
Track front/rear	1630/1575 mm
Length	4890 mm
Width	1970 mm
Height	1265 mm
Weight	1030 kg

PERFORMANCE

Top speed	366 kph
Power to weight ratio	1.2 kg/hp

935.78 Moby Dick   1978

The extreme evolution of the 935 was by Norbert Singer in 1978: the chassis was lowered and the bottom was replaced by a fibre glass panel, interpreting a regulation brought in to help the front-engined BMW, which raised the bottom to enable the exhausts to go through: Singer raised the bottom but then... lowered the whole car. The body was reshaped for better aerodynamics, the suspension lightened and improved. The driving position was moved to the right and in the end the gearbox was overturned to lower the centre of gravity and make the perpendicular half-shafts possible. The brakes were made more powerful, but the real revolution was the engine: cubic capacity was taken to 3211 cc (95.7 x 74.4 mm) and the drive shaft was strengthened. To improve the replenishment, there were now four valves per cylinder with two camshafts for each cylinder bank, driven by cascade gearing instead of a chain. To avoid constant cylinder head gasket failure, the heads themselves were welded to the cylinders. Another problem was air cooling, which was insufficient for a 4-valve; the sort that out, they were cooled by liquid – a revolutionary step – just leaving the vertical fan the task of cooling the cylinders. The radiators were in the rear wheel housings. Fuel feed was by two KKK turbochargers with an intercooler and Kugelfischer mechanical injection. With an adjustable boost pressure of 2.8 bar, power output was 845 hp for a top speed of 366 kph. Two Moby Dicks were built, but only one raced: the victorious debut with Jochen Mass and Jackie Ickx was at the 6 Hours of Silverstone, but after holding good positions in the Le Mans for 17 hours the car was slowed as a precaution – there was a loss of oil, but at race's end this was found not to have an influence – so that it finished eighth. The 935.78's career concluded with retirements from the Norisring and Vallelunga races.

Externally, the 928 S made itself known by its front and rear spoilers, the latter at the base of the rear window, as well as by new alloy rims. The V8's performance was much evolved by increasing its compression ratio and the cubic capacity. The car's top speed of 250 kph wasn't much below the 911 Turbo 3.3's, but it was more comfortable.

TECHNICAL SPECIFICATION

ENGINE

Front, longitudinal
90° V8, vertical

Bore and stroke	97 x 78.9 mm
Unitary cubic capacity	583 cc
Total cubic capacity	4664 cc
Valve gear	overhead camshaft, toothed belt
Number of valves	2 per cylinder
Compression ratio	10:1
Fuel feed	electronic injection
Ignition	electronic
Coolant	liquid
Lubrication	forced circulation
Maximum power	300 hp at 5900 rpm
Specific power	63.8 hp/litre

TRANSMISSION

Rear wheel drive

Clutch	front, dry double-disc
Gearbox	rear, en bloc with differential, 5 speeds plus reverse

CHASSIS

Unified steel structure

Front suspension	transverse oscillating arms, coaxial coil springs with hydraulic shock absorbers, stabiliser bar
Rear suspension	transverse oscillating arms, coaxial coil springs with hydraulic shock absorbers, stabiliser bar
Brakes	discs and servo-brake
Steering	servo-assisted rack
Fuel tank	82 litres
Tyres front/rear	225/50 x 16/225/50 x 16

DIMENSIONS AND WEIGHT

Wheelbase	2500 mm
Track front/rear	1549/1521 mm
Length	4447 mm
Width	1836 mm
Height	1282 mm
Weight	1490 kg

PERFORMANCE

Top speed	250 kph
Power to weight ratio	4.9 kg/hp

928 S

1979

Right from the moment it was launched the 928 was a unanimous success with the motoring press and public. The project first came about with the veiled intention of replacing the 911, but Porsche soon realised that the 928 was for a totally different customer. Improvements continued uninterrupted in 1978, as was the company's tradition, but a widening of the range was on the horizon without forgetting the increasing attention of fuel saving, especially because the oil crisis was at its height, as was the attention now being paid to emissions: for that reason, various versions of the car were developed for the North American market. Despite the fact that the 928 was appreciated for its fluidity, the engine was one of its weak points: the 8-cylinder produced a high cruising speed and in full souplesse, but the chassis' quality could be of a much sportier performance. After having successfully tested the 944's power unit – a "half" a V8 – with a turbocharger (220 hp), with that eye very much on fuel consumption, it was decided to evolve the V8 with atmospheric fuel feed. Meanwhile, Weissach was progressing the 5-litre V8 project with a system able to deactivate four cylinders when the maximum performance was not demanded: the project was relaunched and pushed along with much energy, but inability to give necessary fluidity to the deactivation-activation process interrupted development with just three pre-production cars leased in 1982, in other words when the definitive version was due to be launched in the USA. But in 1979, the V8 was updated to take it to 4664 cc for a maximum power output of 300 hp at 5900 rpm and 310 hp in 1983 with the new Bosch LH-Jetronic fuel injection system, which led to the 928 S. Two front spoilers and one at the base of the rear window were able to chop the car's Cx to 0.38 and top speed went up to 250 kph. The car was further improved, coming close to those that were the original object of the project.

The engine called the 935.72 with its characteristic central plenum with its regulation pop-off valve. Things looked good for Formula Indy, but dubious conduct by the USAC – in conflict with the CART constructors' union – meant the Porsche unit was not so competitive and nor was the Interscope in which it had been installed, both designed to rules that were later changed.

TECHNICAL SPECIFICATION

ENGINE
Central, longitudinal
6 cylinders opposed

Bore and stroke	92.3 x 66 mm
Unitary cubic capacity	441.6 cc
Total cubic capacity	2650 cc
Valve gear	twin overhead camshafts
Number of valves	4 per cylinder
Compression ratio	9.5:1
Fuel feed	mechanical injection, turbocharger
Ignition	transistorised
Coolant	liquid
Lubrication	dry sump
Maximum power	904 hp at 8800 rpm
Specific power	341.1 hp/litre

TRANSMISSION
Rear wheel drive

Clutch	dry mono-disc
Gearbox	en bloc with differential

CHASSIS
Monocoque

Front suspension	double wishbones, hydraulic shock absorbers, stabiliser bar
Rear suspension	double wishbones, hydraulic shock absorbers, stabiliser bar
Brakes	disc
Steering	rack
Fuel tank	220 litres
Tyres front/rear	-

DIMENSIONS AND WEIGHT

Wheelbase	-
Track front/rear	-
Length	-
Width	-
Height	-
Weight	540 kg

PERFORMANCE

Top speed	350 kph
Power to weight ratio	0.6 kg/hp

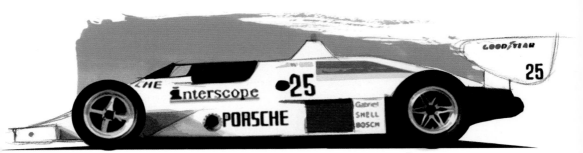

Porsche-Interscope (96B)   1979

In the spring of 1977, an "incognito" delegation left Zuffenhausen to watch the 500 Miles of Indianapolis. But this initial curiosity quickly transformed itself in into a real project, officially launched on 18 October 1978 with a budget of 250,000 dollars for the development of a Formula Indy engine, although in reality it had been started much earlier in December 1977 with a modified 935. Mark Donohue and Roger Penske provided some data on the 2.6-litre Offenhauser power unit, which put out over 830 hp, or 721 hp with turbocharging pressure limitation of 1976. The 935 unit, specially converted to methanol fuel stipulated by Formula Indy but still with the 2857 cc – 8% over the limit – that generated 890 hp and that made Porsche optimistic to the point that it reached an agreement with Jim Chapman's Interscope, which raced with a Parnelli-Cosworth driven by Danny Ongais. The 935 with its liquid cooled heads was taken to 2650 cc and given a regulation turbo, as well as methanol fuel feed: with the pressure at 22 psi 904 hp could be produced, outclassing the 4-cylinder Offy. In July 1979, it was installed in a Parnelli monocoque for testing and the project for a tailor-made chassis was begun. The real problem arose when USAC began to modify the regulations, varying the turbo pressure in line with the engine with a pop-off valve. The 4-cylinders were permitted to go up to 15 psi, the V8s just 9.25 psi, while the regulation for the 6-cylinder cars was unclear, Porsche being the only one in that area. There followed a series of misunderstandings, unofficial news, USAC inspections at Stuttgart until a 12.5 psi limit was fixed for 1980, which made the 935 engine uncompetitive. After a series of tests, it seemed clear that there was a need to radically review the unit in relation to pressure stability, but the project was dropped before that could take place.

The aggressive appearance of the 924 Carrera GTS reflected the motor racing for which it had been constructed. To be able to install a 120-litre fuel tank, the spare wheel was moved into a vertical position just behind the bumper. Often used in racing, the purpose of the car was to compete with the Carrera GTR as with the Carrera GT, which was built to homologate the Carrera GTP.

TECHNICAL SPECIFICATION

ENGINE

Front, longitudinal
4-cylinder turbo, in line, vertical

Bore and stroke	86.5 x 84.4 mm
Unitary cubic capacity	496 cc
Total cubic capacity	1984 cc
Valve gear	overhead camshaft, toothed belt
Number of valves	2 per cylinder
Compression ratio	8.5:1
Fuel feed	electronic injection, turbo
Ignition	electronic
Coolant	liquid
Lubrication	wet sump
Maximum power	210 hp at 6000 rpm
Specific power	105.8 hp/litre

TRANSMISSION

Rear wheel drive

Clutch	front, dry mono-disc
Gearbox	rear, en bloc with differential, 5 speeds plus reverse

CHASSIS

Unified steel structure

Front suspension	control arms, coaxial coil springs with hydraulic shock absorbers, stabiliser bar
Rear suspension	independent, oblique arms, transverse torsion bars, hydraulic shock absorbers, stabiliser bar
Brakes	disc and servo-brake
Steering	ZF rack
Fuel tank	120 litres
Tyres front/rear	215/60 x 15/215/60 x 15

DIMENSIONS AND WEIGHT

Wheelbase	2403 mm
Track front/rear	1420/1390 mm
Length	4323 mm
Width	1727 mm
Height	1270 mm
Weight	1180 kg

PERFORMANCE

Top speed	240 kph
Power to weight ratio	5.6 kg/hp

924 Carrera GT and GTS   1980

The prototype of the sports car based on the 924's monocoque bowed in at the 1979 Frankfurt Motor Show. And the surprise was that the name Carrera ran along its side. But the car at Frankfurt was not a simple concept, so after public success and given the intention of homologating a version of the 924 Turbo for motor racing, the next year out came a small run of 406 924 Carrera GTs, six more that necessary for the GTP category, priced at DM 60,000. Lighter by 150 kg than the Turbo due to considerably simplified equipment, the car had widened wheel housings for use with 215/60 x 16 tyres with 16-inch rims optional, a revised set-up and a series of aerodynamic modifications aimed at retaining the good 0.33 Cx of the 924. The braking system was made more effective and the engine, with its bigger KKK turbocharger now with an intercooler – cooled by the large air intake at the front end – and the 210 hp power output produced a top speed of 240 kph and a sizzling 0-100 kph time of 6.9 seconds. The next step was the Group 4 homologation of a more evolved version, which needed a production run of 50 cars – all red as it happened – later to be lined up at Zuffenhausen for FIA inspection in early March 1981. In the end, despite the DM 110,000 price, all of them were sold and total production climbed to 59. The body shell had a roll bar, boot, engine cover, doors and suspension was in aluminium, the brakes were the 911's and the set-up was revised. Power output increased to 245 hp and the top speed to almost 250 kph, but with a 32% price increase the Club Sport became available with its 275 hp at 6400 rpm. A number of 924 Carrera GTS cars were also prepared for rallying and one that was elaborated by Konrad Schmidt was driven to four wins in the German Championship by Walter Röhrl.

The 924 Carrera GTR entered for the 1981 Le Mans was, in fact, a means of drawing attention to the car and the 944's public launch with the racer's 4-cylinder 2.5-litre engine the following autumn. Once it was clear the car couldn't win, it was detuned and, driven by Jürgen Barth-Walter Röhrl, put in an almost trouble free race with few pit stops. It came 7TH overall with an average time of 184 kph.

TECHNICAL SPECIFICATION

ENGINE

Front, longitudinal
4-cylinder turbo, in line, vertical

Bore and stroke	86-5 x 84-4 mm
Unitary cubic capacity	496 cc
Total cubic capacity	1984 cc
Valve gear	overhead camshaft, toothed belt
Number of valves	2 per cylinder
Compression ratio	7.0:1
Fuel feed	electronic injection, turbocharger
Ignition	electronic
Coolant	liquid
Lubrication	wet sump
Maximum power	375 hp at 6400 rpm
Specific power	187.5 hp/litre

TRANSMISSION

Rear wheel drive

Clutch	front, dry mono-disc
Gearbox	rear, en bloc with differential, 5 speeds plus reverse

CHASSIS

Unified steel structure

Front suspension	control arms, coaxial coil springs with hydraulic shock absorbers, stabiliser bar
Rear suspension	independent, oblique arms, transverse torsion bars, hydraulic shock absorbers, stabiliser bar
Brakes	disc and servo-brake
Steering	ZF rack
Fuel tank	120 litres
Tyres front/rear	275/600 x 16/300/624 x 16

DIMENSIONS AND WEIGHT

Wheelbase	2400 mm
Track front/rear	1534/1504 mm
Length	4244 mm
Width	1745 mm
Height	1503 mm
Weight	945 kg

PERFORMANCE

Top speed	290 kph
Power to weight ratio	2.5 kg/hp

924 Carrera GTP and GTR 1980

As the Carrera GT was being homologated, its racing version was already in an advanced development stage in line with the specifics of the nascent Group B. While the monocoque was made more rigid with tubular structures, the body was integrated with glass fibre components, the track was widened, the 935's brakes had been fitted and the suspension was revised with titanium springs and Bilstein shock absorbers. The half-axles were also in titanium, while the differential was diff-lock. The engine was substantially developed, locating the KKK K27 turbocharger in the most favourable position and with the Kugelfischer injection system power output went up to 320 hp at 6200 rpm. Three of the cars were entered for the 24 Hours of Le Mans and with a top speed of nearly 290 kph, the Barth-Schurti car finished sixth. Starting from the Carrera GTS, 17 Carrera GTRs were built to compete in Group 4. Power output went up to 375 kph at 6500 rpm, while the chassis and body were further developed. But this time, the cars retired from Le Mans while holding 11TH place. Many of the cars were also prepared for IMSA and the SCCA Trans-Am. A special GTR was prepared for the 1981 24 Hours of Le Mans that would aim for victory. The engine was replaced by the 944's 2.5-litre, but in reality only the light alloy block was retained as everything else was designed specifically for the race: supercharging took power output to 510 hp at 7500 rpm. Performance was good, but reliability problems meant Porsche switched their quest for victory to the 936. So the Carrera GTR was detuned to 410 hp and entered in Hugo Boss livery for Jürgen Barth and Walter Röhrl. After having shown the car's great reliability with 21 pit stops totalling just 56 minutes their GTR came seventh.

For the first time in almost 20 years and the last 356 Cabriolet a 911 SC Cabriolet with a canvas hood was launched at the 1983 Geneva Motor Show. The opening system was highly refined and reliable even at high speed, when it didn't even worsen aerodynamic penetration. For this reason, too, the 235 kph car would become the fastest open topped car in the world.

TECHNICAL SPECIFICATION

ENGINE

Rear, overhanging, longitudinal
6 cylinders horizontally opposed

Bore and stroke	95 x 70.4 mm
Unitary cubic capacity	499 cc
Total cubic capacity	2994 cc
Valve gear	overhead camshaft, chain driven
Number of valves	2 per cylinder
Compression ratio	9.8:1
Fuel feed	Bosch electronic injection
Ignition	transistorized
Coolant	forced air
Lubrication	dry sump
Maximum power	204 hp at 5900 rpm
Specific power	68 hp/litre

TRANSMISSION

Rear wheel drive

Clutch	dry mono-disc
Gearbox	en bloc with differential, 5 speeds plus reverse

CHASSIS

Unified steel structure

Front suspension	McPherson, longitudinal torsion bars, hydraulic shock absorbers, stabiliser bar
Rear suspension	independent, oblique arms, transverse torsion bars, hydraulic shock absorbers, stabilizer bar
Brakes	disc and servo-brake
Steering	ZF rack
Fuel tank	80 litres
Tyres front/rear	185/70 x 15/215/60 x 15

DIMENSIONS AND WEIGHT

Wheelbase	2272 mm
Track front/rear	1369/1379 mm
Length	4291 mm
Width	1652 mm
Height	1320 mm
Weight	1160 kg

PERFORMANCE

Top speed	235 kph
Power to weight ratio	5.6 kg/hp

911 SC 3.0 {style=inline} 1980

In 1980, the 911 SC was given a major update aimed at better performance and fuel consumption as well as the life of the body, which was entirely treated with hot dip galvanising and guaranteed for seven years. The most significant new move was the abandonment of the obsolete normal form of fuel feed. So it was possible to increase the compression ratio from 8.6 to 9.8:1, all to the advantage of performance with power output going up to 204 hp with improved fuel consumption due to the increased thermal efficiency of the power unit. Top speed was now 235 kph and 0-100 acceleration time 6.8 seconds. And all that with an average fuel consumption in line with norm DIN 70030 of 10.4 litres per 100 km. Body equipment, the interior and mechanics were all slightly updated – a continuous process – as would be the case in the years to come. Two hundred special cars were produced in 1982, Meteor colour, wine coloured seat covering in leather and fabric – to mark Porsche's 50TH anniversary. But the major new arrival on the Porsche stand at the 1983 Geneva Motor Show with its Targas and Coupés was the 911 SC Cabriolet, over 17 years after the last rear engined open top, the 356C Cabriolet. The years had not passed uselessly; the canvas hood of the new 911 was a concentration of technology. The structure comprised three metal ribs and a self-adjusting system of steel cables. Many components were in light alloy and that helped produce a hood group that weighed less than 15 kg compared to that of the Targa. The great advantage of the new hood was its absolute ability to resist deformation, even at high speed. That ensured a perfect waterproofing hold, good soundproofing and a Cx practically identical to that of the Coupé. With a top speed of 235 kph, the 911 SC Cabriolet would become the fastest open top in the world.

The president of Porsche, Peter Schultz, at the wheel of a 936.81, which dominated the 1981 24 Hours of Le Mans driven by Derek Bell and Jacky Ickx. The idea to adapt the Formula Indy engine to the 936 chassis was initially a makeshift one, but it enabled Porsche to win another race and the technicians to see their engine development work wasn't wasted, although it never took to the track in a single seater.

TECHNICAL SPECIFICATION

ENGINE

Central, longitudinal
6-cylinder turbo, horizontally opposed

Bore and stroke	92.3 x 66 mm
Unitary cubic capacity	441.5 cc
Total cubic capacity	2649 cc
Valve gear	twin overhead camshafts, chain driven
Number of valves	4 per cylinder
Compression ratio	7.2:1
Fuel feed	electronic injection, turbo
Ignition	electronic
Coolant	head liquid, cylinders forced air
Lubrication	dry sump
Maximum power	620 hp at 8200 rpm

TRANSMISSION

Rear wheel drive

Clutch	triple dry mono-disc
Gearbox	en bloc with differential, 5 speeds plus reverse

CHASSIS

Tubular trellis

Front suspension	independent, double wishbones, coaxial coil springs with hydraulic shock absorbers
Rear suspension	independent, double wishbones, coaxial coil springs with hydraulic shock absorbers
Brakes	discs
Steering	ZF rack
Fuel tank	160 litres
Tyres front/rear	-

DIMENSIONS AND WEIGHT

Wheelbase	2400 mm
Track front/rear	1540/1515 mm
Length	4950 mm
Width	-
Height	-
Weight	780 kg

PERFORMANCE

Top speed	350 kph
Power to weight ratio	1.2 kg/hp

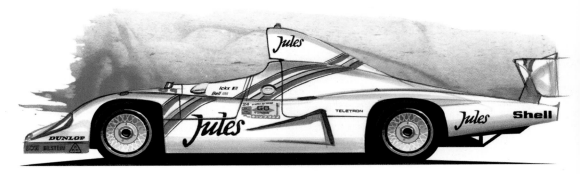

936.81 1981

In 1981, Peter Schultz became head of Porsche and during a pre-24 Hours of Le Mans meeting asked his racing team staff with which car the company would compete in the race. In an attempt to increase the prestige for their road cars at the time, a 944 turbo was prepared, but a chance of winning the first category with the car seemed out of the question. The meeting told a disappointed Schultz that the idea was to take the 936 out of the Porsche Museum and install a 96B engine recently developed for Formula Indy but soon abandoned. From the moment the 1981 French marathon admitted cars built to Group C regulations, due to come into force the following year, there were no problems in installing a 2.6 turbo which, with the handicap for turbocharged cars, was considered a 3709 cc. The most significant of the modifications concerned the fuel feed: it had to go from the methanol used in the USA to petrol. During early testing of the revised engine it churned out 740 hp, but it was immediately detuned to 630 hp, which was considered enough to be competitive. In that way, they improved the reliability in the 24 Hours and limited stress on the gearbox – which came from the 917 transaxle – and reduced fuel consumption, one of the limits imposed by Group C regulations. Only detailed modifications were made externally, except for sponsor Jules livery. Derek Bell, who was to drive with Jacky Ickx, was unable to try the car before official testing but he still set the best time in the first session. And it was never necessary to open the car's bonnet for maintenance throughout the entire race, bringing Porsche yet another victory and Ickx his fifth after he had gone back on his decision to leave Porsche. The Mass-Haywood-Schuppan car was less fortunate; it was lying second during the seventh hour but ended up 12TH after a series of problems with its clutch and fuel injection.

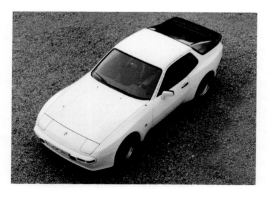

The idea to produce two different bodies for the 944 – one inspired by the 924 for the production car and a similar one for the Carrera GT – was quickly dropped, wanting to characterize the new car. For that reason, the body was derived from the sportier 924, but the wheel housings were no longer especially widened but became part of the basic body.

TECHNICAL SPECIFICATION

ENGINE

Front, longitudinal
4-cylinders in line, vertical

Bore and stroke	100 x 78.9 mm
Unitary cubic capacity	619.7 cc
Total cubic capacity	2479 cc
Valve gear	overhead camshaft, toothed belt
Number of valves	2 per cylinder
Compression ratio	10.6:1
Fuel feed	electronic injection
Ignition	electronic
Coolant	liquid
Lubrication	wet sump
Maximum power	163 hp at 5800 rpm
Specific power	65.2 hp/litre

TRANSMISSION

Rear wheel drive

Clutch	front, dry mono-disc
Gearbox	rear, en bloc with differential, 5 speeds plus reverse

CHASSIS

Unified steel body

Front suspension	control arms, coaxial coil springs with hydraulic shock absorbers, stabiliser bar
Rear suspension	independent, oblique arms, transverse torsion bars, hydraulic shock absorbers, stabilizer bar
Brakes	disc and servo-brake
Steering	ZF rack
Fuel tank	80 litres
Tyres front/rear	185/70 x 15/185/70 x 15

DIMENSIONS AND WEIGHT

Wheelbase	2400 mm
Track front/rear	1478/1476 mm
Length	4200 mm
Width	1735 mm
Height	1275 mm
Weight	1180 kg

PERFORMANCE

Top speed	220 kph
Power to weight ratio	8.0 kg/hp

944 1981

From the start of this 924 project it was clear that the agreed 100,000 VW-Audi engines to be supplied to Porsche wouldn't be enough to cover the car's entire production – not even a year, as it happened – so they began to think about a power unit that could adapt itself to the 924 body shell; one with suitable performance, little vibration from its delicate transaxle and of reduced production price. They experimented with the V6 PRV (Peugeot-Renault-Volvo) and the 5-cylinder Audi. Then, considering that there were already two engine families at Zuffenhausen – the 911's 6-cylinder boxer and the 928's V8 – management did not want to create a third. So the answer was to derive a 4-cylinder in line from one of the V8 cylinder banks. And that's how the 944 first came about in 1982: the body shell and mechanical layout were of the 924 and its styling was inspired by that introduced by the Carrera GT with either the 911's SCs rims or Fuchs as optional and just a slight revision. But the equipment was richer; initially, they considered creating two versions with only the sporty derivative in line with the Carrera GT, but the desire to distinguish the 944 from the 924 pushed them into retaining the latter. The engine was a 2.5-litre that put out 163 hp at 5800 rpm, with equilibrated Lanchester counter shafts to dampen vibration and noise. In reality, given the ambition with which the new unit was designed, the 928's V8 had little in common. Development continued over the years: in 1985 the interior and equipment were revised, the dashboard and door panels were changed and the suspension was also modified, as were the oil pump and the fuel tank, although the rims were the "telephone dial" type. In 1989 cubic capacity went up to 2.7-litres; power output increase by just 3% but the torque was better – a slight improvement in Europe but a more significant one on the North American version, which was usually penalised by the emission control regulations.

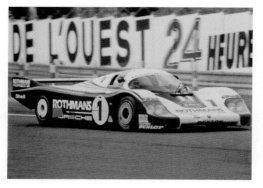

The Ickx-Bell 956 on its way to winning an unforgotten 24 Hours of Le Mans in 1982, when three of the works cars took the first three places. But that crushing win was only the tip of the iceberg. In the 1983 and 1984 seasons the 956 won 17 of the 18 races in which it competed. And they did just as well overseas run by privateers to whom many of the cars were sold.

TECHNICAL SPECIFICATION

ENGINE
Central, longitudinal
6-cylinder turbo, horizontally opposed

Bore and stroke	92.3 x 66 mm
Unitary cubic capacity	441.5 cc
Total cubic capacity	2649
Valve gear	twin overhead camshafts, chain driven
Number of valves	4 per cylinder
Compression ratio	7.2:1
Fuel feed	electronic injection, turbo
Ignition	electronic
Coolant	head liquid
Lubrication	dry sump
Maximum power	620 kph at 8200 rpm

TRANSMISSION
Rear wheel drive

Clutch	dry mono-disc
Gearbox	en bloc with differential, 5 speeds plus reverse

CHASSIS
Monocoque in aluminium

Front suspension	independent, double wishbones, coaxial coil springs with hydraulic shock absorbers
Rear suspension	independent, double wishbones, coaxial coil springs with hydraulic shock absorbers
Brakes	disc
Steering	ZF rack
Fuel tank	-
Tyres front/rear	300/625 x 15/350/680 x 15

DIMENSIONS AND WEIGHT

Wheelbase	2650 mm
Track front/rear	1648/1548 mm
Length	4770 mm
Width	2000 mm
Height	1030 mm
Weight	820 kg

PERFORMANCE

Top speed	330 kph
Power to weight ratio	1.3 kg/hp

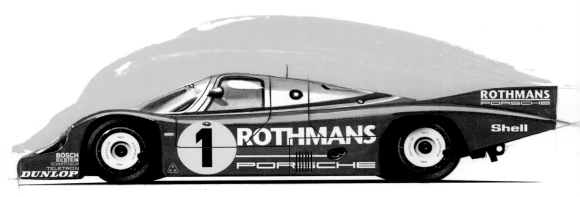

956 {style="float:left"} 1982

Group C regulations came into effect in 1982. The cars had to respect the rules concerning dimensions and proportions as well as the same safety criteria as Formula 1 cars for frontal and lateral impact, but there were no limits on development, cubic capacity or engine typology: the only obligation concerned fuel consumption. The regulation fuel tank contained 100 litres and the number of permitted refueling stops was defined. The average was about 60 litres/100 km. The first decision to be taken concerned fuel feed: the 956 was a turbocharged car, so its consumption was better, its weight less and torque was greater and it was easier to regulate the power generated during a race and, therefore, fuel consumption. The step towards the engine choice of the ex-1981 936 was a short one: it had already been tested and could put out 620 hp (580 hp when set to low consumption). The chassis was new and Venturi-type channeling on the bottom for ground effect. Despite their experience with tubular chassis, Porsche opted for a more resistant monocoque in riveted aluminium, with the body in resin strengthened with Kevlar and carbon fibre. The front suspension was derived from that of the 936, while the rear was designed taking the aerodynamics into account. After wind tunnel testing with 1:5 models, work began on a 1:1 (Cx reduced to 0.35 for the Le Mans version) in October 1981: the first tests were carried out at Paul Ricard in March 1982 and a few months later the 956 made its first public appearance in Rothmans livery. The car's first few races were tests more than anything else, but no car could stand up to the 956 at Le Mans, with an historic triple driven by Ickx-Bell, Mass-Schuppan and Holbert-Haywood. A triumph that was repeated in many other 1983 races, including the year's French marathon. The official career of the 956 lasted successfully until 1984, after which the car had a second stage of youth with the private teams.

The 1985 Carrera 911 3.2 with the optional rear spoiler, inspired by that of the Turbo. It had been part of the range from the previous year, equipped as a Turbo Look for the Coupé, which had been available since 1985 for both the Targa and Cabriolet. Goodies included the 3.3 Turbo's braking system, rims, tyres and widened wheel housings, but without the rear wing, which was optional – like the front one.

TECHNICAL SPECIFICATION

ENGINE

Rear, overhanging, longitudinal
6 cylinders horizontally opposed

Bore and stroke	95 x 74.4 mm
Unitary cubic capacity	527 cc
Total cubic capacity	3164 cc
Valve gear	overhead camshaft, chain driven
Number of valves	2 per cylinder
Compression ratio	10.3:1
Fuel feed	Bosch electronic injection
Ignition	transisitorised
Coolant	forced air
Lubrication	dry sump
Maximum power	204 hp at 5900 rpm
Specific power	68 hp/litre

TRANSMISSION

Rear wheel drive

Clutch	dry mono-disc
Gearbox	en bloc with differential, 5 speeds plus reverse

CHASSIS

Unified steel body

Front suspension	McPherson, longitudinal torsion bars, hydraulic shock absorbers, stabiliser bar
Rear suspension	independent, oblique arms, transverse torsion bar, hydraulic shock absorbers, stabiliser bar
Brakes	disc and servo-brake
Steering	ZF rack
Fuel tank	80 litres
Tyres front/rear	185/70 x 15/215/60 x 15

DIMENSIONS AND WEIGHT

Wheelbase	2272 mm
Track front/rear	1372/1380 mm
Length	4291 mm
Width	1652 mm
Height	1320 mm
Weight	1160 kg

PERFORMANCE

Top speed	245 kph
Power to weight ratio	4.7 kg/hp

911 Carrera 3.2 — 1983

The 911 Carrera 3.2 was unveiled at the 1983 Frankfurt Motor Show, a significant date for Porsche as it had introduced its first 911 2000 cc at the show 20 years earlier. The Carrera 3.2 was the task of marking an important stage in the model's evolution through the attention and effort of the designers – and the results didn't disappoint expectations. The 3200 cc gave the car the chance to use all its 231 hp, while also using less fuel due to the better connection of the fuel feed system. The ignition and fuel injection were by the Bosch Motronic system which, through an accurate taking of the head and pistons' temperature, produced an optimum regulation of the operational state of the engine. The 245 kph top speed could be reached and maintained in complete safety due to perfecting the braking system, which was adapted to the car's new level of performance, now just as reliable even in the wet. Porsche's most demanding sporty drivers liked the Carrera 3.2 right away, especially the five-speed gearbox, which had been technically perfected to make gear engagement smooth and precise. The external profile of the car was unmistakable: fog lights were incorporated into the front spoiler, the alloy rims and the Carrera logo were the most visible aspects of the new model, but attentive scrutiny revealed refined details and a prestige finish like – for the cabriolet model – the hood offered a chromatic range that was broader than the usual black and, starting from 1984, a leather rimmed steering wheel and gear knob, which were coordinated with the interior's colour. High as usual, the equipment profile included new concept seats between 1984-85 as well as a better heating system and cockpit ventilation.

The TAG-Porsche P01 engine bore ample TAG markings as stipulated in the contract, but Zuffenhausen was permitted to have a nameplate bearing the words "Made by Porsche" on it: and it was precisely a question of image that pushed through the divorce from McLaren, who were irritated by the enormous amount of publicity obtained free of cost by Porsche, although the company was to have remained in the shadows as it was amply paid for its work.

TECHNICAL SPECIFICATION

ENGINE
Central, longitudinal
80° V6 bi-turbo

Bore and stroke	82 x 47.3 mm
Unitary cubic capacity	249.8 cc
Total cubic capacity	1499 cc
Valve gear	twin overhead camshafts, timing gear
Number of valves	4 per cylinder
Compression ratio	8.7:1
Fuel feed	electronic injection, 2 turbochargers
Ignition	electronic
Coolant	liquid
Lubrication	dry sump
Maximum power	700 hp at 11,200 rpm
Specific power	466.6 hp/litre

TRANSMISSION
Rear wheel drive

Clutch	-
Gearbox	en bloc with differential

CHASSIS
Carbon fibre monocoque

Front suspension	double wishbones, hydraulic shock absorbers, stabiliser bar
Rear suspension	double wishbones, hydraulic shock absorbers, stabiliser bar
Brakes	disc
Steering	ZF rack
Fuel tank	-
Tyres front/rear	-

DIMENSIONS AND WEIGHT
Wheelbase	-
Track front/rear	-
Length	-
Width	-
Height	-
Weight	-

PERFORMANCE
Top speed	over 350 kph
Power to weight ratio	-

McLaren TAG-P01   1983

Initially, the return of Porsche to Formula 1 didn't happen because it was too expensive and without positive short term effected, but the situation changed when Ron Dennis, who had just acquired McLaren with the support of sponsor Marlboro, offered to buy engines and finance the project. The first stage saw the allocation of USD 500,000 for preliminary studies which – according to the Dennis financiers – would have brought in further funds from a technical sponsor. And that's what happened, with a USD 5 million agreement signed with TAG (Techniques d'Avant Garde) belonging to Mansour Ojjeh. After a brief investigation a 6-cylinder set-up was selected with an 80°-cylinder bank angle for minimum bulk, on which John Barnard insisted, who was designing a carbon fibre monocoque – another first – of the MP/4 with large Venturi channels on the bottom to produce ground effect. More modern materials and technologies were used for the engine to create a power unit that weighed only 150 kg, its two KKK turbochargers mounted at the sides, while it would take a year and enormous investment to have a second "mirrored" turbo. Initial tests were varied out on a modified 956, while its race debut – called a test at the time – was at Zandvoort in 1983 still with the old car. There were reliability, injection and general teething problems in 1983, but certainly not any of performance. When Niki Lauda and Alain Prost began to compete for the Formula 1 World Championship, they had 820 hp at their fingertips in races and 870 during testing, although meanwhile, the regulations were changed to abolishing wing cars, so that the TAG-Porsche's narrow angle turned out to be useless. The car only left a few crumbs for the opposition, with Lauda world champion and Prost half a point behind him! Prost dominated the 1985 season and won the title; he did it in 1986, too, but more laboriously, when the car put out 1086 hp. After that, another regulation change meant the car could no longer compete and McLaren adopted a Honda engine.

The 1983 VW Transporter that acted as a basis for the Porsche B32: at the time, many body builders offered versions of the bus that were especially refined for use an executive vehicle. The Porsche mechanics also brought the vehicle lively performance, that was superior to most of the similar vehicles on sale. The price was fixed at around DM 30,000 and there was a great deal of demand.

TECHNICAL SPECIFICATION

ENGINE

Rear, overhanging, longitudinal
6 cylinders horizontally opposed

Bore and stroke	95 x 74.4 mm
Unitary cubic capacity	527.3 cc
Total cubic capacity	3164
Valve gear	twin overhead camshafts, chain driven
Number of valves	2 per cylinder
Compression ratio	10.3:1
Fuel feed	electronic injection
Ignition	electronic
Coolant	forced air
Lubrication	dry sump
Maximum power	231 hp at 5900 rpm
Specific power	73 hp/litre

TRANSMISSION

Rear wheel drive

Clutch	dry mono-disc
Gearbox	en bloc with differential, 5 speeds plus reverse

CHASSIS

Unified steel structure

Front suspension	independent, double wishbones
Rear suspension	independent, double wishbones
Brakes	disc
Steering	-
Fuel tank	-
Tyres front/rear	-

DIMENSIONS AND WEIGHT

Wheelbase	2461 mm
Track front/rear	-
Length	4569 mm
Width	1844 mm
Height	1928 mm
Weight	-

PERFORMANCE

Top speed	190 kph
Power to weight ratio	-

VW-Porsche B32   1983

In the early '80s during prototype testing in Algiers, Porsche used a VW Transporter powered by a 914.4 cc engine to transport their instruments and spare parts. When it became necessary to replace it in 1981 a normal Transporter was bought, but it was slow, so much so that it delayed testing itself. So during a pause, Helmut Bott decided to equip the van with a 911 engine. Work started in the autumn of 1981 and a 911 SC engine which had already covered 22,000 kilometres, was transplanted into the Transporter together with a suitable gearbox, semi-axles and various control levers. And fuel tank capacity was increased, an oil tank was installed with a frontal radiator and engine compartment cooling was improved. The vehicle had to be raised 15 centimetres to take the 6-cylinder engine, the suspension was modified and the existing brakes were replaced with self-ventilating discs inside the 14-inch alloy rims. The 200 hp engine easily took the Transporter up 190 kph and a 0-100 km time of 8.3 seconds. Performance was so good that it impressed other drivers; according to Fritz Bezner it was more surprising than the Golf GTI! But it also made personnel travelling faster and more comfortable, a task for which they had previously requested the use of three different cars. The vehicle soon attracted the attention of Peter Schutz and Wolfgang Porsche, who immediately ordered another two prototypes, but this time with Carrera 3.2 engines and considered a small production run if the market showed interest. At the end of 1983 the B32 project got off the ground: it was for an initial series of 9 vehicles with the 226 hp 3.2 engine, of which five were immediately sold – one with a 928 interior, dual tone paintwork and Fuchs rims. The greatest difficulty came from the long time it took to homologate the vehicle for the US market. It was not without regret that the project was halted in 1984.

In a golden era for short production run supercars, the price of the 959 was DM 400,000 on its debut. Even if only some top data was made public, the cars sold like hot cakes. At first, deliveries were planned for 1985, but didn't happen until the end of 1987. Still, the very well-heeled didn't wait in vain: the car was the more powerful, effective and fast than was initially promised.

TECHNICAL SPECIFICATION

ENGINE

Rear, overhanging, longitudinal
6-cylinder turbo, horizontally opposed

Bore and stroke	95 x 67 mm
Unitary cubic capacity	474.8 cc
Total cubic capacity	2849 cc
Valve gear	twin overhead camshafts, chain driven
Number of valves	4 per cylinder
Compression ratio	8.3:1
Fuel feed	electronic injection, turbo
Ignition	electronic
Coolant	heads liquid, cylinders forced air
Lubrication	dry sump
Maximum power	449 hp at 6500 rpm

TRANSMISSION

4-wheel drive

Clutch	dry mono-disc
Gearbox	en bloc with differential, 6 speeds plus reverse

CHASSIS

Unified steel structure

Front suspension	McPherson, longitudinal torsion bars, hydraulic shock absorbers, stabiliser bar
Rear suspension	independent, oblique arms, transverse torsion bars, hydraulic shock absorbers, stabiliser bar
Brakes	disc, servo-brake, ABS
Steering	ZF rack
Fuel tank	84 litres
Tyres front/rear	235/45 x 17/255/40 x 17

DIMENSIONS AND WEIGHT

Wheelbase	2300 mm
Track front/rear	1504/1550 mm
Length	4260 mm
Width	1840 mm
Height	1280 mm
Weight	1450 kg

PERFORMANCE

Top speed	315
Power to weight ratio	3.2 kg/hp

959 1983

959   1983

The 959 bowed in at the 1983 Frankfurt Motor Show with the name Group B Study, but the decision to produce 200 of them for sports car racing homologation had already been announced. The turbocharged 6-cylinder boxer engine was air cooled for its cylinders and by liquid for the 4-valve heads. The car's cubic capacity was fixed at 2.85-litres so that the car would qualify for Group B albeit with a 1.4 handicap and 1.7 in 1988. The car put out 450 hp. The turbocharge system was completely new, with two blowers with reduced turbo lag, both with intercoolers located inside the rear wheel housings. Below 4200 rpm, the exhaust gas from the two cylinder banks was deviated towards the left compressor; above that rpm the gas was deviated towards the right turbocharger, making the two blowers work in parallel. The valves that regulated the flow and waste gate were electronically controlled. Transmission was permanent on all four wheels, while the manual gearbox was of six speeds and transmitted torque directly to the rear differential, which was electronically self-locking. The other extreme of the gearbox's output shaft was connected to the front differential by a multi-plate clutch, the slip factor of which was controlled by an electronic management system. When it was completely open, traction was only through the rear wheels, but when it was closed distribution was at 50% with infinite intermediate possibilities depending on the form of traction requested and the configuration selected between traction, snow and ice, rain and dry. The quadrilateral suspension had double shock absorbers which were electro-hydraulically controlled and able to vary the car's height from the ground as well as its damping effect. The self-ventilating disc brakes with ABS (perforated on the Sport version) enabled a deceleration from 300 kph in 270 metres. Top speed was 317 kph with a 0-100 kph time of just 3.7 seconds. A sports version of the car was also available and that was more spartan as it had been lightened by 100 kg.

The Carrera 4x4 during the 1984 Paris-Dakar: here, 4-wheel drive was applied to a 911 for the first time. The following year, Porsche fielded other 911s that made wide use of 959 components, including the suspension, brakes and part of the transmission, although without the refined electronic control. In part, the body was also that of the supercar, but the engine was still normally aspirated.

TECHNICAL SPECIFICATION

ENGINE
Rear, overhanging, longitudinal
6 cylinders horizontally opposed

Bore and stroke	95 x 74.4 mm
Unitary cubic capacity	527.2 mm
Total cubic capacity	3164 cc
Valve gear	overhead camshaft, chain driven
Number of valves	2 per cylinder
Compression ratio	9.6:1
Fuel feed	Bosch electronic injection
Ignition	electronic
Coolant	forced air
Lubrication	dry sump
Maximum power	225 hp at 6000 rpm
Specific power	71.1 hp/litre

TRANSMISSION
4-wheel drive

Clutch	dry mono-disc
Gearbox	en bloc with differential, 5 speeds plus reverse

CHASSIS
Unified steel structure

Front suspension	McPherson, longitudinal torsion bars, double hydraulic shock absorbers, stabiliser bar
Rear suspension	independent, oblique arms, transverse torsion bar, coil springs, double hydraulic shock absorbers, stabiliser bar
Brakes	disc and servo-brake
Steering	ZF rack
Fuel tank	120-150 litres
Tyres front/rear	201 x 15

DIMENSIONS AND WEIGHT
Wheelbase	2280 mm
Track front/rear	1420/1366 mm
Length	4290 mm
Width	1630 mm
Height	1470 mm
Weight	1215 kg

PERFORMANCE
Top speed	210 kph

911 Carrera 4x4 Paris Dakar   1984

In anticipation of the attention Porsche would pay to 4-wheel drive in the future, three 911 3.2s were prepared during the winter of 1984 Paris-Dakar with a 4-wheel drive transmission system and officially called the 953. The engine was only slightly modified so that it functioned with low quality petrol available en route: the compression ratio went down, as did the power output from 231 to 225 hp, but to compensate a DME electronic management system was adopted for the first time. The clutch was strengthened and the gearbox was given a radiator, but the real news was the transmission shaft which was in a rigid tube to reach the front differential. Four-wheel drive could be inserted by the driver and was divided 31% front and 69% rear. The front suspension was also strengthened with double wishbones arms and shock absorbers, while the rear coil springs helped the torsion bars. Set-up was heightened to 120 mm, while the Dunlop tyres were 205 mm on 15-inch rims on both axles with the two spares inside the cockpit. The body was much strengthened with steel plates to resist the marathon's stress as well as being modified for the 4-wheel drive, while the bumpers, bonnet, engine cover and doors were in plastic and carbon fibre with the windows in Plexiglas. Fuel tank capacity was 120 litres, with another 120 litres in the cockpit, bringing dry weight to 1200 kg. Serviced by two MAN trucks and sponsored by Rothmans, the three cars were driven by Ickx-Metge with the third as a donator of components driven by Porsche employees Kussmaul-Lehner. Metge won, with Ickx sixth and the reserve car 26TH. In 1988, the three cars were taken over by Jacques Lafitte's team and painted green for the Paris-Dakar of that year.

The highly talented 1985 Porsche factory team of Jacky Ickx, Hans Joachim Stuck, Derek Bell and Jochen Mass won many races in the 962C, but not the 24 Hours of Le Mans. However, the privateers turned in some significant wins, including victory in the IMSA Championship. The illustration shows the Holbert Racing 962, which won the first race at Mid-Ohio on 10 June 1984 plus four other events, driven by Derek Bell and Al Holbert.

TECHNICAL SPECIFICATION

ENGINE

Central, longitudinal
6-cylinder turbo horizontally opposed

Bore and stroke	93 x 70.4 mm
Unitary cubic capacity	478.1 cc
Total cubic capacity	2869 cc
Valve gear	twin overhead camshafts, chain driven
Number of valves	2 per cylinder
Compression ratio	7.5:1
Fuel feed	electronic injection, turbocharger
Ignition	electronic
Coolant	liquid
Lubrication	dry sump
Maximum power	680 hp at 8200 rpm
Specific power	237 hp/litre

TRANSMISSION

Rear wheel drive

Clutch	dry mono-disc
Gearbox	en bloc with differential, 5 speeds plus reverse

CHASSIS

Aluminium monocoque

Front suspension	independent, double wishbones, coil springs, hydraulic shock absorbers
Rear suspension	independent, double wishbones, coil springs, hydraulic shock absorbers
Brakes	disc
Steering	rack
Fuel tank	120 litres
Tyres front/rear	325/625 x 17/350/680 x 19

DIMENSIONS AND WEIGHT

Wheelbase	2770 mm
Track front/rear	1634/1548 mm
Length	4770 mm
Width	2000 mm
Height	1030 mm
Weight	850 kg

PERFORMANCE

Top speed	-
Power to weight ratio	1.2 kg/hp

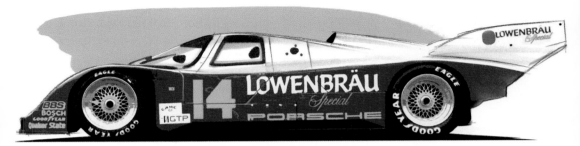

962 and 962C   1984

If the 956 was designed for Group C, substantial modifications were necessary for the IMSA series: the chassis had to be replaced – for safety sake, the pedals had to be placed inside the wheelbase – and an engine derived from that of the 935 (2869 cc) was installed, but with a single turbo. To compensate, as there was no fuel consumption limit, power output was easily taken to 650 hp. The new car was named the 962 of which tests started at Paul Ricard in mid-1984, soon after which came a long series of victories. Later, the car used a 3.2-litre engine (720 hp), but from 1987 a limit of 3-litres was fixed by IMSA, so the 2994 cc engine was used. At the same time, development began on the 962C, the version for Group C European races which had adopted the same safety regulations as IMSA and had further reduced fuel consumption to 51 litres per 100 km. So the 956 power unit was perfected and the Bosch Motronic injection differently calibrated, while the body was adapted, fully drawing on the 956, especially at the rear, where the wheels had grown to 19-inch. The 962C won two races right away, but the anxiously awaited 24 Hours of Le Mans was a disaster for the 962, although the race was won by the Joest team's 956. Meanwhile, testing went ahead on the PDK double clutch engine, which was slow and unreliable at first. Then both factors were improved to the point that the car scored a much hoped for win, even if in shorter races. A PDK 962C was also fielded at Le Mans, but it had to retire on the 41ST lap, leaving victory to the car with the traditional gearbox driven by Bell-Stuck-Holbert. The same team in the same car also dominated the 1987 French marathon. And, as Ferry Porsche said, "When we win Le Mans, we then sell double the usual number of cars in America". In fact, 105 962s were sold to privateers up to 1991.

At the end of its highly successful career, the 944 Turbo, with better 250 hp mechanics, suspension and brakes, was also turned into a cabriolet with its body built by the American Sunroof Company, its hood operated electrically for the US an optional feature for the rest of the world. The company initially considered a Targa version.

TECHNICAL SPECIFICATION

ENGINE

Front, longitudinal
4-cylinder turbo in line

Bore and stroke	100 x 78.9 mm
Unitary cubic capacity	619.7 cc
Total cubic capacity	2479 cc
Valve gear	overhead camshaft, toothed belt
Number of valves	2 per cylinder
Compression ratio	8.0:1
Fuel feed	electronic injection, turbocharger
Ignition	electronic
Coolant	liquid
Lubrication	wet sump
Maximum power	220 hp at 5800 rpm
Specific power	88 hp/litre

TRANSMISSION

Rear wheel drive

Clutch	front, dry mono-disc
Gearbox	rear, en bloc with differential, 5 speeds plus reverse

CHASSIS

Unified steel structure

Front suspension	double wishbones, coaxial coil springs with hydraulic shock absorbers, stabiliser bar
Rear suspension	independent, oblique arms, transverse torsion bars, hydraulic shock absorbers, stabiliser bar
Brakes	disc and servo-brake
Steering	ZF rack
Fuel tank	80 litres
Tyres front/rear	205/55 x 16/225/50 x 16

DIMENSIONS AND WEIGHT

Wheelbase	2400 mm
Track front/rear	1477/1451 mm
Length	4230 mm
Width	1735 mm
Height	1275 mm
Weight	1280 kg

PERFORMANCE

Top speed	245 kph
Power to weight ratio	5.8 kg/hp

944 Turbo and Turbo S   1985

The 944 Turbo was launched at the end of January 1985. Externally, it had a bumper shield that was completely revised for aerodynamic reasons and had bigger air intakes plus one for the intercooler, and that gave the car's front end a more modern look. The rear spoiler was bigger, while the aerodynamic profile was also applied under the bumpers to improve underbody air flow and reduce resistance. Initially, the engine was given a KKK turbocharger with intercooler without major modifications to its structure, with the exception of the installation of an oil radiator in the area of the "usual" oil-water exchanger integrated into the crankcase. Later, during endurance tests, the turbocharger's roller bearing was liquid-cooled, the cylinder block was enlarged by 1 mm and the head revised for greater heat dissipation – including ceramic port liners – and the oil pan. Power output went up to 220 hp and 0-100 kph acceleration to 5.9 seconds and that took the 944 Turbo's performance close to the 911's. From 1986, the 944 was offered in Turbo Cup form with 250 hp and an especially prepared chassis for motor racing, which was used for a mono-marque series. A year later, Porsche management explored the possibility of offering a road-going version with the 250 hp mechanics: the engine only needed slight changes, while the chassis was further perfected with Koni adjustable set-up, the 928 S4's brakes and specific 16-inch rims. The new car was named the 944 Turbo S but the S didn't appear on the body because from 1989 the specifications of the Turbo S were those of the normal Turbo. The last evolution of the turbocharged 944 appeared in February 1991 with the introduction of the 944 Turbo Cabriolet with the 250 hp mechanics of the ex-Turbo S and an open body by ASC of Weinsberg.

The 924 S could only be told from the 924 by its alloy "telephone dial" rims designed by Porsche's head of its styling centre, Anatole Lapine. The mechanics were much improved though with the adoption of an engine that was highly elastic and silent as well as potent. But this was the swansong of the best-selling Porsche, which was born all those years ago from an aborted VW project: it went out of production at the end of 1988.

TECHNICAL SPECIFICATION

ENGINE
Front, longitudinal
4 cylinders in line

Bore and stroke	100 x 78.9 mm
Unitary cubic capacity	619.7 cc
Total cubic capacity	2479 cc
Valve gear	overhead camshaft, toothed belt
Number of valves	2 per cylinder
Compression ratio	9.7:1
Fuel feed	electronic injection
Ignition	electronic
Coolant	liquid
Lubrication	wet sump
Maximum power	150 hp at 5800 rpm
Specific power	60 hp/litre

TRANSMISSION
Rear wheel drive

Clutch	front, dry mono-disc
Gearbox	rear, en bloc with differential, 5 speeds plus reverse

CHASSIS
Unified steel structure

Front suspension	double wishbones, coaxial coil springs with hydraulic shock absorbers, stabiliser bar
Rear suspension	independent, oblique arms, transverse torsion bars, hydraulic shock absorbers, stabiliser bar
Brakes	disc with servo-brake
Steering	ZF rack
Fuel tank	66 litres
Tyres front/rear	195/65 x 15/195/65 x 15

DIMENSIONS AND WEIGHT

Wheelbase	2400 mm
Track front/rear	1420/1393 mm
Length	4211 mm
Width	1684 mm
Height	1275 mm
Weight	1210 kg

PERFORMANCE

Top speed	215 kph
Power to weight ratio	8.0 kg/hp

924 S   1985

The last 924 was launched in July 1985; a month later the production line began to assemble its heir – the 924 S, which was unveiled at the Frankfurt Motor Show soon afterwards. Externally, the body only had new "telephone dial" light alloy rims similar to those designed five years earlier by Tony Lapine for his own 924. But while the body shell was considered valid and was not changed, modifications were more extensive under the skin: the engine was replaced by a 4-cylinder in line 2479 cc unit from the 944, detuned by 10 hp to 150 hp. In reality, the car's development with the 2.5-litre power unit started in 1979 with a launch date of 1981. But Peter Schutz, who had just been appointed Porsche's president, decided to delay marketing the car to avoid cannibalization of the 944. However, with the launch of the 924 S it was difficult to interpret precisely what was the company's range of front end engines: if the 928 was undoubtedly at the top, then the 944 and 924 S took on similar positions as they were only slightly distinguished by the fact that the latter, although with better performance and more comfort due to the fluidity of the power unit, kept the body and interior of the old 924; and that was with all the well-known defects because of the economical origins of the car. To balance the situation out, the car's price was much lower while its performance, with only 10 hp less, were not so different. But in 1978, the gap was closed when the 924 S was given the basic 2.5-litre, 160 hp 944 normally aspirated engine. And the equipment and set-up were improved. However, that was it: after 16,282 cars sold, the last one rolled off the production line in September and made way for the 924 S2 with its renewed body.

A rally version of the 959 in, as usual, Rothmans livery and photographed during its debut event, the 1985 Rally of the Pharaons. The event was only a dress rehearsal for the 1986 Paris-Dakar, in which Ickx and Metge took the first two places, with their support vehicle in sixth. The third vehicle is usually entered so that it could donate its components to the front runners when necessary.

TECHNICAL SPECIFICATION

ENGINE

Rear, overhanging, longitudinal
6-cylinder turbo horizontally opposed

Bore and stroke	95 x 67 mm
Unitary cubic capacity	474.8 cc
Total cubic capacity	2849 cc
Valve gear	twin overhead camshafts, chain driven
Number of valves	4 per cylinder
Compression ratio	8.0:1
Fuel feed	electronic injection, turbo
Ignition	electronic
Coolant	head liquid, cylinders forced air
Lubrication	dry sump
Maximum power	400 hp at 6500 rpm

TRANSMISSION

4-wheel drive

Clutch	dry mono-disc
Gearbox	en bloc with differential, 6 speeds plus reverse

CHASSIS

Unified steel structure

Front suspension	McPherson, longitudinal torsion bars, double hydraulic shock absorbers, stabiliser bar
Rear suspension	independent, oblique arms, transverse torsion bars plus springs, double hydraulic shock absorbers, stabiliser bar
Brakes	disc, servo-brake, ABS
Steering	ZF rack
Fuel tank	120-150 litres
Tyres front/rear	205 x 18

DIMENSIONS AND WEIGHT

Wheelbase	2300 mm
Track front/rear	1500/1550 mm
Length	4260 mm
Width	1840 mm
Height	1490 mm
Weight	1260 kg

PERFORMANCE

Top speed	210 kph

959 Paris-Dakar   1985

After the disappointing results of the 911 hybrid with 959 components in the 1985 Paris-Dakar, development of the racing 959 was completed. This time, the engine was a refined 6-cylinder with a liquid-cooled 4-valve head and two turbochargers that worked with reduced turbo lag, depending on the rotation revolutions. Only the compression ratio is lowered to "digest" the low octane fuel available during the rally, which could otherwise have damaged the pistons in an unmodified engine. Power output dropped to 400 hp. The transmission was modified with a strength-ened clutch and much shorter gear ratios – top speed went down from over 315 kph to 210 kph – and the sophisticated multiple disc clutch was replaced by a rigid connection between the rear wheels. The driver was still able to modify the torque distribution between the two axles by interacting with the electronically-controlled longitudinal differential. The suspension was given reinforced arms and double shock absorbers that worked in parallel, the brakes were from the production car, light alloy rally rims were 18 inches in diameter and the front and rear tyres were of 205 section width. This was a normal precaution for the African marathons, during which it was often difficult to obtain replacements. A detuned, 390 hp 959 debuted in the 1985 4,000 km Rally of the Pharaons, which started and finished in Cairo. The best placement was by the support team of Roland Kussmaul and Eckehard Kiefer, preceded only by an off-roader powered by a 928 engine! Next came the murderous, 14,000 km 1986 Paris-Dakar, which was won again by Metge-Lemoyne; they were followed home by the Ickx-Brasseur sister car and the 959 component donor crewed by Kussmaul-Unger, who took sixth place.

The 928 S4 in the Weissach wind tunnel. Because of this work, the car's Cx dropped to 0.34, 0.352 when the radiator's air intake was completely open, a 13% reduction. The 928 S4 was the fastest normally aspirated production car in the world as well as being an elegant and refined, comfortable grand tourer, with an irreproachable road behaviour.

TECHNICAL SPECIFICATION

ENGINE

Front, longitudinal
90° V8

Bore and stroke	100 x 78.9 mm
Unitary cubic capacity	619.6 cc
Total cubic capacity	4957 cc
Valve gear	twin overhead camshafts, toothed belt
Number of valves	4 per cylinder
Compression ratio	10:1
Fuel feed	electronic injection
Ignition	electronic
Coolant	liquid
Lubrication	forced circulation
Maximum power	320 hp at 6000 rpm
Specific power	65.3 hp/litre

TRANSMISSION

Rear wheel drive

Clutch	front, dry dual disc
Gearbox	en bloc with differential, 5 speeds plus reverse

CHASSIS

Unified steel structure

Front suspension	double wishbone, coaxial coil springs with hydraulic shock absorbers, stabiliser bar
Rear suspension	double wishbone, coaxial coil springs with hydraulic shock absorbers, stabiliser bar
Brakes	disc and servo-brake
Steering	servo-assisted rack
Fuel tank	82 litres
Tyres front/rear	225/50 x 16/245/45 x 16

DIMENSIONS AND WEIGHT

Wheelbase	2500 mm
Track front/rear	1551/1546 mm
Length	4447 mm
Width	1836 mm
Height	1292 mm
Weight	1580 kg

PERFORMANCE

Top speed	270 kph
Power to weight ratio	4.9 kg/hp

928 S4 and Club Sport 1986

After the 1979 launch of the 928 S the car was under continual development, so that a sports version competed in the 24 Hours of Le Mans. In addition, a laboratory car was built with which to study new technical solutions. But the real new development arrived in 1986 with the launch of a new engine with 4 valves per cylinder and twin overhead camshafts. A 5-litre 32-valve 292 hp engine had already made its debut in the USA with a new interior and the unofficial name of S3, because the 1984 4.7-litre 16-valve was called the S2. The objective of American 4-valves per cylinder was to reduce emissions rather than to increase performance. On the contrary, with the new head, the 4.7-litre 928 S4 put out 320 hp, although in Australia that dropped to 300 hp up to 1989. The clutch on the manual gearbox was strengthened and the torque converter was made bigger on the automatic; the interiors and exteriors were also slightly revised. A pre-series 928 S4 was taken to the Bonneville salt flats by Al Holbert on 7 August 1986, when it set a flying start kilometre and mile of 276.69 kph and 275.37 kph respectively, records that made the car the fastest normally aspirated vehicle in the world for 1987. Later, the same car exceeded 180 mph at the Nardò circuit in Italy during an unofficial test. A Club Sport version appeared in 1988 and that was 100 kg lighter, while a less spartan Special Equipment S4 was built for the British market with the specific technique of the Club Sport and the normal interior. The car had a revised set-up and wider wheel housings with Bridgestone tyres, self-locking differential and simplified equipment in which the last remaining comfort were the electric windows. The engine's timing was also revised and the power – even if declared at 320 hp – rose to 330 hp at 6200 rpm.

The completely white 959/961 that won the GT class of the 1986 24 Hours of Le Mans and took seventh overall in a race dominated by the Bell-Holbert-Stuck 962C. Although homologation in Group B was a long way off as the required 200 units had not yet been built, Porsche did not wish to give up the prestigious shop window that racing offered.

TECHNICAL SPECIFICATION

ENGINE
Rear, overhanging, longitudinal
6-cylinder turbo, horizontally opposed

Bore and stroke	95 x 67 mm
Unitary cubic capacity	474.8 cc
Total cubic capacity	2849 cc
Valve gear	twin overhead camshafts, chain driven
Number of valves	4 per cylinder
Compression ratio	9.5:1
Fuel feed	electronic injection
Ignition	electronic
Coolant	head liquid, cylinders forced air
Lubrication	dry sump
Maximum power	680 hp at 7800 rpm

TRANSMISSION
4-wheel drive

Clutch	dry mono-disc
Gearbox	en bloc with differential, 6 speeds plus reverse

CHASSIS
Unified steel structure

Front suspension	McPherson, longitudinal torsion bars, hydraulic shock absorbers, stabiliser bar
Rear suspension	independent, oblique arms, transverse torsion bars, hydraulic shock absorbers, stabiliser bar
Brakes	disc
Steering	ZF rack
Fuel tank	120-150 litres
Tyres front/rear	280/640 x 17

DIMENSIONS AND WEIGHT

Wheelbase	2310 mm
Track front/rear	1522/1580 mm
Length	4380 mm
Width	1890 mm
Height	1260 mm
Weight	1150 kg

PERFORMANCE

Top speed	340 kph

961   1986

Even if the 959 had been presented to the public as a hypothetical Group B car, by the start of 1986 Porsche was a long way from producing the 200 homologation cars. However, they decided to enter a car for the IMSA/GTX category of the 24 Hours of Le Mans, which accepted bi-turbo engine cars with a cubic capacity up to 3164 cc. Due to its considerable preparation, the new car was called the 961. Although derived from the production power unit, compression ratio was increased to 9.5:1 and turbocharger pressure went up to 2.25 bar that led to its 640 hp output for a top speed of 340 kph. The clutch was replaced by a racing Sachs, although the gearbox was unchanged with longer ratios by simply varying the axle ratio at both the front and rear where the viscous coupling unit gave way to a rigid connection between the wheels. The set-up was revised and lowered 10 mm for track use. At the same time, the body was rebuilt in glass fibre and widened by 50 mm, paying special attention – given the speed in play – to avoid all lift problems. The brakes were the 962C's discs and the Dunlop tyres 280/640s were fitted to 17-inch magnesium rims, and in 1987 to 19-inch. There was no time to hammer out a sponsorship agreement before the car's first race, so the 959/961 competed in a completely white livery bearing just the Porsche name and those of technical sponsors Dunlop and Shell. In 1986, Metge-Ballot Léna won their class and took a brilliant seventh place overall in a race without problems. The following year, the car's power output was upped to 680 hp and Rothmans came on board as the sponsor: unfortunately, an incorrect downshift meant the car over-revved that stopped the engine and disintegrated the transmission. The blockage of the four wheels that followed put the car into the barrier, where it was destroyed by fire – but without injuring the driver.

The 911 Carrera 3.2 Club Sport was launched to offer sporting customers a car that was already lightened and in racing set-up, especially in the many mono-marque championships organised by the various Porsche clubs across the world. The rest of the range was still continually updated and improved, which led to celebrations in 1988 to mark the 250,000TH 911 built.

TECHNICAL SPECIFICATION

ENGINE
Rear, overhanging, longitudinal
6-cylinders horizontally opposed

Bore and stroke	95 x 74.4 mm
Unitary cubic capacity	527.3 mm
Total cubic capacity	3164 cc
Valve gear	overhead camshaft, chain driven
Number of valves	2 per cylinder
Compression ratio	10.3:1
Fuel feed	Bosch electronic injection
Ignition	electronic
Coolant	forced air
Lubrication	dry sump
Maximum power	231 hp at 5900 rpm
Specific power	73.1 hp/litre

TRANSMISSION
4-wheel drive

Clutch	dry mono-disc
Gearbox	en bloc with differential, 5 speeds plus reverse

CHASSIS
Unified steel structure

Front suspension	McPherson, lower oblique arms, coil springs, hydraulic shock absorbers, stabiliser bar
Rear suspension	independent, oblique arms, coil springs, hydraulic shock absorbers, stabiliser bar
Brakes	disc, servo-brake, ABS
Steering	ZF rack
Fuel tank	85 litres
Tyres front/rear	205/55 ZR 16/225/50 ZR 16

DIMENSIONS AND WEIGHT

Wheelbase	2272 mm
Track front/rear	1398/1405 mm
Length	4291 mm
Width	1652 mm
Height	1320 mm
Weight	1160 kg

PERFORMANCE

Top speed	245 kph
Power to weight ratio	5.0 kg/hp

911 Carrera 3.2 and Club Sport   1986

In 1986, the 911 was given its usual slight update and improvements. Especially a guarantee against corrosion was extended to 10 years, a duration not offered by any other constructor. The Carrera's set-up was slightly revised with a bigger anti-roll bar and stabiliser; the Turbo Look rear wheels now had a 9-inch channel. Inside, the seats were lowered by 20 mm, but more relevant new developments were introduced the following year: while the cabriolet had an electrically controlled hood, the Carrera was given a new generation gearbox, which replaced the type 915 after more than ten years. The G50 was a completely new unit, with a first-time box and perfected mechanics, drawing from technology developed for the 959. The availability of the gears was also changed, with reverse top left and fifth top right. The new transmission meant the transverse bar had to be redesigned. The 1987 model year brought the range offer of the 911 Carrera 3.2 Club Sport: while being a 231 hp production car, the engine had a rather high rev limiter producing 6840 against 6570 rpm and more rigid supports. The set-up included sports shock absorbers and a more simplified equipment to reduce the car's weight to 1160 kg: the air conditioning and electric windows were also eliminated. In 1988, the 911 achieved a double anniversary: 250,000 cars had rolled off the Zuffenhausen production line in the car's 25TH anniversary of manufacture, which began in 1963. That is why a small series of 875 911 Carrera 3.2 specials went into production, with their bodies in a special metallic diamond colour, rims colour-keyed, blue-silver leather interior and autographed by Ferry Porsche on the back of the front headrests. The "normal" Carrera went back to Fuchs rims with a 7-inch channel at the front and an 8-inch rear.

The illustration shows the 911 Carrera 3.2 Speedster Club sport prototype that was built in 1987 with a faired cockpit, a car that never went into production. The picture shows the aggressive appearance of the Speedster with its faired hood and inclined windscreen and emphasised in its turbo look configuration with wider wheel housings and equipment derived from the Turbo.

TECHNICAL SPECIFICATION

ENGINE
Rear, overhanging, longitudinal
6-cylinders horizontally opposed

Bore and stroke	95 x 74.4 mm
Unitary cubic capacity	527.3 cc
Total cubic capacity	3164 cc
Valve gear	overhead camshaft, chain driven
Number of valves	2 per cylinder
Compression ratio	10.3:1
Fuel feed	electronic injection
Ignition	electronic
Coolant	forced air
Lubrication	dry sump
Maximum, power	231 hp at 5900 rpm
Specific power	69.4 hp/litre

TRANSMISSION
Rear wheel drive

Clutch	dry mono-disc
Gearbox	en bloc with differential, 5 speeds plus reverse

CHASSIS
Unified steel structure

Front suspension	McPherson, lower arms, coil springs, hydraulic shock absorbers, stabiliser bar
Rear suspension	independent, lower arms, coil springs, hydraulic shock absorbers, stabiliser bar
Brakes	disc, servo-brake
Steering	ZF rack
Fuel tank	85 litres
Tyres front/rear	205/55 x 16/255/50 x 16

DIMENSIONS AND WEIGHT

Wheelbase	2272 mm
Track front/rear	1398/1405 mm
Length	4291 mm
Width	1652 mm
Height	1220 mm
Weight	1210 kg

PERFORMANCE

Top speed	245 kph
Power to weight ratio	5.2 kg/hp

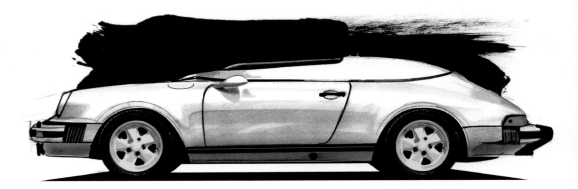

911 Carrera 3.2 Speedster   1986

A 911 with a body that harked back to the styling trends of the 356 Speedster was started in 1982, when Helmuth Bott had a prototype built with an extremely small wraparound windscreen, which also continued on the doors, as was often seen on some sports cars of the '50s. The concept was fascinating, but there were many problems to sort out, starting with visibility and weather protection. A limited series of 200 "Palm Beach" or "Bel Air" cars was planned, but more urgent needs meant the project was abandoned, left in a drawer and the prototype was consigned to a Weissach garage – until 17 March 1987. That's when president Peter Schutz visited the styling centre and took the car in hand again. A Club Sport version of a Speedster concept car was presented at that same year's Frankfurt Motor Show, with fairing on the cockpit that left only the driver's position uncovered, a car that never saw the light of day. But it was a public success that meant a Speedster version was proposed for the 1989 model year, which also celebrated the 25TH anniversary of the marque. The closed hood was protected by glass fibre fairing that outlined two "humps" behind the headrests; when it was opened it was only an emergency system, given the difficulty of assembling it and its minimum efficiency e.g. complaints about the inflation of the hood and noise at high speed. Porsche itself defined the car as "light foldable cover for emergencies"; but despite its appearance when closed it was really not bad looking and it was emphasised how the Speedster was "a car essentially designed for good weather". The windscreen was reduced, inclined and was easily removed with the help of simple tools. Starting with the cabriolet's body shell, a total of 2102 to 2104 of the Speedsters were built, of which between 161 and 171 had the "tight" body and not the Turbo Look.

Launched in 1989, the 944 S2 had the same body as the 944 Turbo, with its characteristic front end with integrated bumpers. Later, an S3 version was also developed, but the number of mechanical modifications – productive and aesthetic – for the new version were such that they pushed Porsche into calling it by a new name: the 968.

TECHNICAL SPECIFICATION

ENGINE
Front, longitudinal
4-cylinders in line, vertical

Bore and stroke	100 x 78.9 mm
Unitary cubic capacity	619.7 cc
Total cubic capacity	2479 cc
Valve gear	twin overhead camshafts, toothed belt
Number of valves	4 per cylinder
Compression ratio	10.9:1
Fuel feed	electronic injection
Ignition	electronic
Coolant	liquid
Lubrication	wet sump
Maximum power	190 hp at 6000 rpm
Specific power	76 hp/litre

TRANSMISSION
Rear wheel drive

Clutch	front, dry mono-disc
Gearbox	rear, en bloc with differential, 5 speeds plus reverse

CHASSIS
Unified steel structure

Front suspension	double wishbone, coaxial coil springs with hydraulic shock absorbers, stabiliser bar
Rear suspension	independent, oblique arms, transverse torsion bars, hydraulic shock absorbers, stabiliser bar
Brakes	disc and servo-brake
Steering	ZF rack
Fuel tank	80 litres
Tyres front/rear	195/65 x 15/195/65 x 15

DIMENSIONS AND WEIGHT

Wheelbase	2400 mm
Track front/rear	1478/1476 mm
Length	4230 mm
Width	1735 mm
Height	1275 mm
Weight	1280 kg

PERFORMANCE

Top speed	228 kph
Power to weight ratio	6.7 kg/hp

944 S and S2 1986

As was often the case with Porsche, not long after the launch of the 944, an engine evolution was already under way, even if the common parts were few at about 50 components in total. The 4-cylinder 2.5-litre was ideally derived from a V8 cylinder bank of the 928. For that reason, a 16-valve 4-cylinders in line version was under development in parallel with that of a 32-valve for the 928 S4. The technology was the same as that used for the V8 with a bigger belt, as it had to drive two shafts, that ran the exhaust camshaft, which was in turn connected to the intake one via a small chain at the cylinder bank centre between the second and third cylinders. Initially, 163 hp were generated, practically the same as the 8-valve version, which made a new head useless. For that reason, the unit was profoundly developed up to a 192 hp output, precisely half between the 944 and the 220 hp of the 944 Turbo. At the same time, various versions of an automatic gearbox were under the microscope as it was still not available on the Turbo or S. As a VW transmission was unavailable and with the ZF agreement no more, many tests with optimum results were conducted with the brand new PDK with a double clutch: it was fast, pleasant to use and able to substantially reduce fuel consumption. Unfortunately, reliability problems advised against a production run. Meanwhile, the 944 was taken to 2.7 litres in 1989 and the company wanted to do the same thing with the 944 S2's 16-valve. But, faced with this opportunity and with the competition ever fiercer, it was decided to move on directly to the 3-litre, which enabled Porsche to better exploit the 4-valves per cylinder's "breathing". The S2 also had a better chassis and a more efficient body for the Turbo, while the 944 S2 was also given a Cabriolet version.

After abandoning the Porsche 2708 chassis, Stuttgart's adventure in Formula Indy continued with a March chassis. Given the poor 1989 results March prepared a car specifically for Porsche, permitting Teo Fabi to achieve his first placings and his first win, concluding the Championship in fourth place. Unfortunately, everything changed in 1990.

TECHNICAL SPECIFICATION

ENGINE
Central, longitudinal
V8

Bore and stroke	88.2 x 54.2 mm
Unitary cubic capacity	331.1 cc
Total cubic capacity	2649.2 cc
Valve gear	twin overhead camshafts, timing gear
Number of valves	4 per cylinder
Compression ratio	-
Fuel feed	electronic injection, turbocharger
Ignition	electronic
Coolant	liquid
Lubrication	dry sump
Maximum power	750 hp at 11,200 rpm
Specific power	283.1 hp/litre

TRANSMISSION
Rear wheel drive

Clutch	dry mono-disc
Gearbox	6 speeds plus reverse

CHASSIS
Composite monocoque

Front suspension	independent, hydraulic shock absorbers, stabiliser bar
Rear suspension	independent, hydraulic shock absorbers, stabiliser bar
Brakes	disc
Steering	rack
Fuel tank	-
Tyres front/rear	9.5/25 x 15/14.5/27 x 15

DIMENSIONS AND WEIGHT

Wheelbase	2800 mm
Track front/rear	1710/1620 mm
Length	4660 mm
Width	2010 mm
Height	980 mm
Weight	703 kg

PERFORMANCE

Top speed	over 360 kph
Power to weight ratio	0.93 kg/hp

Porsche 2708   1987

Management of Porsche's motor sport activity in the United States was in the hands of Al Holbert in 1985, when he pushed the company once more towards the Indy Championship, this time as the constructor of the whole car. That meant the choice had to be a V8 engine: all the competing teams had that layout as the idea of a V8 for road cars began to gather momentum. On 23 October 1985, the project was called the 2708 and was approved by Peter Schutz. The regulations included a fuel consumption limit as well as a restriction on turbocharging pressure of 7.9 psi for 1988 through a pop-off valve, although this was difficult to interpret. The 2708 drew fully on the technology used for the V6 TAG and on 11 December 1986 the unit was finally run on the test bench, while a sponsorship agreement was reached with Quaker State. Engine development work proceeded, but work on the rest of the car with its monocoque in composite was much delayed: it wasn't until 16 September 1987 that the first all-white car took to the Weissach test track, while a dummy car in official livery went on show at Nazareth, where it was planned it would compete in its first race. After a discouraging time setting up the car, it eventually made its debut at Laguna Seca in October 1988, but what had been described as a season of development produced no results, to the point that, with the engine's performance taken as read, March and Lola monocoques were acquired for a comparison, which ended up in favour of the March, so the Porsche monocoque was dropped. The results were no better, turning the spotlight on the power unit's deficiencies, but with planned development and a new March monocoque produced to order and called the 89P for 1989. That combination enabled Teo Fabi, who had taken over from Al Unser, to score the car's first win and a good 4TH place in the Championship. Things looked good for 1990, but March got the monocoque completely wrong so Porsche could do nothing other than retire. A loser for the first time.

The PEP doesn't look good from the outside, but the idea of a real mobile laboratory that could be adapted to various forms of mechanics seemed like it would be a success. Unfortunately, the Weissach technicians found that the sensations the PEP transmitted were "little representative of a real car": so they continued to use production cars for testing.

TECHNICAL SPECIFICATION

ENGINE

Basic: rear, overhanging, longitudinal
6 cylinders horizontally opposed

Bore and stroke	variable
Unitary cubic capacity	variable
Total cubic capacity	variable
Valve gear	1-2 overhead camshafts
Number of valves	2-4 per cylinder
Compression ratio	-
Fuel feed	-
Ignition	-
Coolant	-
Lubrication	-
Maximum power	variable
Specific power	variable

TRANSMISSION

Rear, 4WD

Clutch	-
Gearbox	variable

CHASSIS

Central monocoque in aluminium

Front suspension	interchangeable
Rear suspension	interchangeable
Brakes	disc, servo-brake
Steering	ZF rack
Fuel tank	20 litres
Tyres	variable

DIMENSIONS AND WEIGHT

Wheelbase	variable
Track front/rear	variable
Length	-
Width	-
Height	-
Weight	variable

PERFORMANCE

Top speed	variable
Power to weight ratio	variable

Porsche Experimental Prototype 1987

Among the various projects developed at Weissach in the '80s, one in particular merits attention, the 1987 PEP or Porsche Experimental Prototype. The idea was to design a laboratory car able to be adapted to various mechanical layouts and to permit the dynamic testing of ideas very different from each other to produce immediate feedback on the concept under the magnifying glass. It was an "adaptable" car, according to Helmut Flegl's definition of it. The heart of the PEP or 2696 was a central aluminium monocoque with fuel and oil tanks at the rear. Two tubular steel structures were installed front and rear to which suspension that had to be tested from time to time could be fitted, while the mounts were designed so that torsional rigidity could be varied, as could weight distribution by bolting on ballast at different points, as well as the track and wheelbase. The basic imposition of the drive train was an all-wheel drive 911 rear engine (connected by a telescopic tube that enabled the testers to vary the wheelbase and engine disposition) that would simulate rear or all-wheel drive. The matt black painted body was of a compact coupé with doors, door pillars, the roof group and windscreen of the 944, but with a glass fibre body. Instrumentation came from the 928 and there was a large wing at the rear that could simulate various aerodynamic configurations. Porsche publicised the PEP strongly as a definitive solution to the cost problem and complex prototypes. But when it came down to it, it was not so effective because its behaviour and feedback were not too realistic so they couldn't be regarded as reliable. And PEP was not suitable for presentations because it transmitted a "precarious" impression, starting with its noise levels, which were hardly representative of a real car.

Despite having studied various kinds of style including those by Giorgetto Giugiaro at Italdesign, the one selected was that of Porsche's own styling centre headed by Harm Lagaay. It faithfully took up once more many of the 911's styling trends and proportions, also looking ahead to a number of lines that were later adopted for the 993 and 996. The project's failure caused enormous financial damage.

TECHNICAL SPECIFICATION

ENGINE
Front, longitudinal
80° V8

Bore and stroke	92 x 68 mm
Unitary cubic capacity	452 cc
Total cubic capacity	3616 cc
Valve gear	twin overhead camshafts, chain driven
Number of valves	4 per cylinder
Compression ratio	-
Fuel feed	electronic injection
Ignition	electronic
Coolant	liquid
Lubrication	dry sump
Maximum power	300 hp at 7000 rpm
Specific power	83.3 hp/litre

TRANSMISSION
Rear wheel drive

Clutch	-
Gearbox	6 speed automatic plus reverse

CHASSIS
Unified steel structure

Front suspension	independent, coil springs, hydraulic shock absorbers, stabiliser bar
Rear suspension	independent, coil springs, hydraulic shock absorbers, stabiliser bar
Brakes	disc, servo-brake, ABS
Steering	rack
Fuel tank	-
Tyres front/rear	-

DIMENSIONS AND WEIGHT

Wheelbase	2826 mm
Track front/rear	-
Length	-
Width	-
Height	-
Weight	1740 kg

PERFORMANCE

Top speed	270 kph
Power to weight ratio	5.8 kg/hp

989 — 1988

With the low end of the Porsche range always under pressure from Japanese competitors, at the end of the '80s the company decided to invest USD 550 million in the development and industrialisation of a model that was to take its place above the 911. It was to be a high performance, medium-large saloon. The mechanics and cab were defined in record time, while the company's styling centre and Italdesign offered various styles: if the Italian proposal called the 932 was a sporting saloon that was pleasant and unmistakably Porsche, the German one was a most faithful revisit to 911 style, lengthened and with four doors. The in-house proposal was accepted by management as design of the 80° V8 began, a liquid cooled 3616 cc unit that put out 300 hp, although a 3.6 320 hp was considered as was a 4.2-litre 344 hp plus the drop to a V6 and supercharging. The transmission, manual, Tiptronic or PDK if available, was on the front axle with the engine, while traction could have been all-wheel drive with rear wheel steering. Testing the mechanics began using a Mercedes 300 CE body shell. Performance was excellent, but at the end of 1991 doubts about its feasibility started to grow, reinforced by the fact that the "father" of the project, Ulrich Bez, had left the company. The 989 turned out to be expensive to produce 20% more than forecast and extremely expensive in the marketplace where there was not much space for cars that cost over DM 150,000. Then a contraction of the market pushed Porsche into launching the small Boxster project so that it was a short step to completely abandoning the project. In the autumn of 1992 an attempt was made to recover part of the investment by selling the excellent V8 to other constructors, but that was in vain. Porsche had been hit hard: over USD 150 million had gone without a single car being produced and with serious consequences to the health of the entire company.

The 968, the last evolution of the 924 body shell, was also offered from launch day in Cabriolet form. By then, it was a mature car that was fast and able to compete with the best the opposition had to offer. The aesthetics were improved, so increasing the family feeling with others in the model range. It would leave its place to the Boxster, founder of a new generation of "small" Porsches.

TECHNICAL SPECIFICATION

ENGINE
Front, longitudinal
4 cylinders in line, vertical

Bore and stroke	104 x 88 mm
Unitary cubic capacity	747.5 cc
Total cubic capacity	2990 cc
Valve gear	twin overhead camshafts with toothed belt
Number of valves	4 per cylinder
Compression ratio	11:1
Fuel feed	electronic injection
Ignition	electronic
Coolant	liquid
Lubrication	wet sump
Maximum power	240 hp at 6200 rpm
Specific power	80 hp/litre

TRANSMISSION
Rear wheel drive

Clutch	front, dry mono-disc
Gearbox	rear, en bloc with differential, 6 speeds plus reverse

CHASSIS
Unified steel structure

Front suspension	double wishbone, coaxial coil springs with hydraulic shock absorbers, stabiliser bar
Rear suspension	independent, oblique arms, transverse torsion bars, hydraulic shock absorbers, stabiliser bar
Brakes	disc, servo-brake, ABS
Steering	ZF rack
Fuel tank	80 litres
Tyres front/rear	205/55 x 16/225/50 x 16

DIMENSIONS AND WEIGHT

Wheelbase	2400 mm
Track front/rear	1478/1450 mm
Length	4320 mm
Width	1735 mm
Height	275 mm
Weight	1335 kg

PERFORMANCE

Top speed	245 kph
Power to weight ratio	5.5 kg/hp

968 1989

Various new engine options were being studied as the 944 neared the end of its career. There was a 16-valve turbo, a new V6 derived from the Formula Indy V8 and even a 6-cylinder in line BMW derivation. In the end, the conservative decision was a simple development of the existing power unit. But special attention was reserved for the 944 S2's 16-valve 4-cylinder 3-litre. To begin with, it was given the VarioCam variable valve timing system, so bigger valves and an 11:1 compression ratio, all of which took power output to 240 hp at 6200 rpm. The complex aspiration system was redesigned, as were cooling, lubrication, new forged connecting rods and to reduce vibration, a dual mass flywheel was installed. There were also new developments on the transmission front, with the manual gearbox being replaced by a new 6-speed unit that had been developed with Audi. Of the automatics, the PDK was shelved for good after it gave problems on the 944, so the 911's Tiptronic was adapted for the 911. The differential was 40% self-locking and the brakes came from the 944 Turbo, with a cooling conveyor applied to the suspension arms; the 16-inch rims – 17-inch were optional – in the Cup design. The body was also much revised, especially the front, which now had round headlights to increase – according to Harm Lagaay, who had just returned from BMW – the family feeling with the 911 and 928. The Cx improved as were the aesthetics on both the coupé and cabriolet. Initially, the new model was to be called the 944 S3, but extensive modifications – with 82% of components new – and with production moved to Zuffenhausen, led management to launching a totally new model that was now the 968.

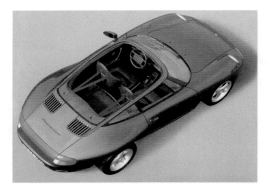

An unusual image of the Panamericana concept car with its unusual roof group, which could either be open or closed creating various configurations. The colour combination was also different and caused considerable discussion at the time of the car's launch, especially the extravagant shapes of the prototype's styling, which would become a milestone in the development of the new 911.

TECHNICAL SPECIFICATION

ENGINE
Central, longitudinal
6-cylinder turbo, horizontally opposed

Bore and stroke	93 x 70.4 mm
Unitary cubic capacity	478.1 cc
Total cubic capacity	2869 cc
Valve gear	twin overhead camshafts, chain driven
Number of valves	2 per cylinder
Compression ratio	7.5:1
Fuel feed	electronic injection, turbo
Ignition	electronic
Coolant	liquid
Lubrication	dry sump
Maximum power	680 hp at 8200 rpm
Specific power	237 hp/litre

TRANSMISSION
Rear wheel drive

Clutch	dry mono-disc
Gearbox	en bloc with differential, 5 speeds plus reverse

CHASSIS
Aluminium monocoque

Front suspension	independent, double wishbone, coaxial coil springs with hydraulic shock absorbers
Rear suspension	independent, double wishbone, coaxial coil springs with hydraulic shock absorbers
Brakes	disc
Steering	ZF rack
Fuel tank	120 litres
Tyres front/rear	-

DIMENSIONS AND WEIGHT

Wheelbase	2770 mm
Track front/rear	1634/1548 mm
Length	4770 mm
Width	-
Height	-
Weight	850

PERFORMANCE

Top speed	-
Power to weight ratio	1.2 kg/hp

Panamericana   1989

Ulrich Bez had just returned to Porsche in 1989 and he found there was a dire need to renew the 911, the image of which had slipped and was not doing well in the market. So, working side-by-side with the head of the company's styling centre Harm Lagaay, a futuristic concept car called the Panamericana was created and was unveiled at that year's Frankfurt Motor Show, where it caused a sensation. The name, of course, was inspired by the '50s Carrera Panamericana from which the various Carrera took their name and its purpose, according to Lagaay, was to "show that Porsche is always able to create new trends in terms of shape, colour and trim". The starting point was a production Carrera 4, but the style – derived from a sketch by stylist Steve Murkett – was of a sort of dune buggy based on a 911. A tubular exoskeleton made up the windscreen profile and doors, to which was fixed a fold-able sunroof which, combined with plastic panels, can turn into five different con-figurations between open and closed. Other characteristics of the glass fibre body were the concave wheel housings leaving the tyres and all-new rims in view much more than usual, inspired by a number of Italian open top sports cars of the '50s. Along the sides ran two crossed ribs that gave the car an unmistakable elegance, emphasised on the concept car so as not to give away the styling of the future 911 993, which was under development at the same time. The colour selected was frog green with the roof group profiles in pink. The interior was in leather combinations of four colours. Officially, the concept car should have been – the usual – birthday present for Ferry Porsche, who would have been 80 in September. But it was judged "grotesque" by him, somewhat embarrassing between him and Ulrich Bez as the designer later said. According to Lagaay, it was a problem of understanding: many were frightened of the idea of it being the heir to the 911.

A cut-away from a catalogue in which Porsche indicated modifications to the 911 for its adoption of 4-wheel drive. The picture shows the new 3.6-litre engine and its new 5-speed gearbox and the transmission return shaft housed in a rigid tube. Also note the electric seat adjusters which, together with a new air conditioning system, enhance the Carrera 4's equipment.

TECHNICAL SPECIFICATION

ENGINE
Rear, overhanging, longitudinal
6 cylinders horizontally opposed

Bore and stroke	100 x 76.4 mm
Unitary cubic capacity	600 cc
Total cubic capacity	3600 cc
Valve gear	overhead camshaft, chain driven
Number of valves	2 per cylinder
Compression ratio	10.3:1
Fuel feed	Bosch electronic injection
Ignition	dual, electronic
Coolant	forced air
Lubrication	dry sump
Maximum power	250 hp at 6100 rpm
Specific power	69.4 hp/litre

TRANSMISSION
4-wheel drive

Clutch	dry mono-disc
Gearbox	en bloc with differential, 5 speeds plus reverse

CHASSIS
Unified steel structure

Front suspension	McPherson, lower oblique arms, coil springs, hydraulic shock absorbers, stabiliser bar
Rear suspension	independent, oblique arms, coil springs, hydraulic shock absorbers, stabiliser bar
Brakes	disc, servo-brake, ABS
Steering	ZF rack
Fuel tank	77 litres
Tyres front/rear	205/55 x 16/225/50 x 16

DIMENSIONS AND WEIGHT

Wheelbase	2272 mm
Track front/rear	1380/1374 mm
Length	4250 mm
Width	1652 mm
Height	1310 mm
Weight	1450 kg

PERFORMANCE

Top speed	260 kph
Power to weight ratio	5.4 kg/hp

911 Carrera 4 (964) 1989

The new 911 series called the 964 made its debut as a coupé, symbol of the marque and the 4WD tradition, already hinted at with the 959 supercar and destined to substantially influence the car's future. The new Carrera 4 was based on the same structure – suitably adapted to make room for transmission towards the front axle of the "normal" 911, but many modifications were carried out to both the mechanics and body. Externally, the had had more flowing surfaces, bumpers integrated into the body and an electrically controlled rear spoiler that emerged at over 80 kph. That also brought substantial improvements on the aerodynamic front, with the car's Cx dropping from 0.42 to a remarkable 0.32. The body was available both as a coupé and Targa. From the mechanical point of view, the suspension was revised which, while maintaining the overall layout, had large, light alloy coil springs at both the front and rear plus Bilstein shock absorbers. The 4WD system called for a central differential at the exit from the 5-speed gearbox with an electronically-controlled multi-disc clutch that automatically shared torque on both axles: when the ABS sensors noted a skid, more torque was sent to the axle with the best traction. In the case of the rear axle, a similar device in the differential also gave an ideal distribution between the right and left wheels. The Carrera 4's new concept 3.6-litre engine with a dual ignition head put out 250 hp at 6000 rpm had a top speed of 260 kph. The car was built in a new area of the factory on the other side of Bundesstrasse, with the raw body shells passing through the paint section via an elevated bridge. Just before the 911 964 went out of production, the new Carrera 4 Turbo Look came out and combined 4WD specifics with the aesthetics of the 911 Turbo.

The 1992 911 Carrera 2 already had a 3.6-litre engine, five spoke rims and teardrop rear vision mirrors. The 964 gave the unified body its debut, with both the 4WD version and the rear wheel drive of common ilk. The style was also renewed with smoother integrated bumpers that made the 911's lines more modern and captivating.

TECHNICAL SPECIFICATION

ENGINE
Rear, overhanging, longitudinal
6 cylinders, horizontally opposed

Bore and stroke	100 x 76.4 mm
Unitary cubic capacity	600 cc
Total cubic capacity	3600 cc
Valve gear	overhead camshaft, chain driven
Number of valves	2 per cylinder
Compression ratio	10.3:1
Fuel feed	Bosch electronic injection
Ignition	dual, electronic
Coolant	forced air
Lubrication	dry sump
Maximum power	250 hp at 6100 rpm
Specific power	69.4 hp/litre

TRANSMISSION
Rear wheel drive

Clutch	dry mono-disc
Gearbox	en bloc with differential, 5 speeds plus reverse

CHASSIS
Unified steel structure

Front suspension	McPherson, lower oblique arms, coil springs, hydraulic shock absorbers, stabiliser bar
Rear suspension	independent, oblique arms, coil springs, hydraulic shock absorbers, stabiliser bar
Brakes	disc, servo-brake, ABS
Steering	ZF rack
Fuel tank	77 litres
Tyres front/rear	205/55 x 16/225/50 x 16

DIMENSIONS AND WEIGHT

Wheelbase	2272 mm
Track front/rear	1380/1374 mm
Length	4250 mm
Width	1652 mm
Height	1310 mm
Weight	1350 kg

PERFORMANCE

Top speed	260 kph
Power to weight ratio	5.4 kg/hp

911 Carrera 2 (964) 1989

When it was time to replace the Carrera 3.2 and with a wealth of 959 four-wheel drive experience behind them, Porsche decided that the 911 should become available as a 4WD. Initially, they considered creating a body especially for the task, which could have been adapted to accommodate front traction, leaving the Carrera 2 – that's how the two-wheel drive version would have been called – the old Carrera body shell. A second possibility would have been to build one single chassis, the same for both versions: apart from the development costs, which would have more quickly amortised given the larger numbers of cars built, one obstacle seemed to be the front differential's bulk, which took space from the boot. The problem was resolved with a new and more rational plastic fuel tank that made better use of the available space. And that brought about the "Einheitskarosserie" or unified body, which could house both the power steering and the ABS. To mark the change of generation towards the new 964 and while generally maintaining the 1963 shape of the car, it was revised to include new, rounded and integrated bumpers: although there had been no major modifications, the launch of the Audi 100 at the start of the '80s with its Cx of 0.29 brought in new standards that made the old 911's Cx 0.40 obsolete. The objective that faced Porsche management was to achieve a Cx of 0.32, which was obtained by redesigning the plastic and fairing the car's bottom helped along by a brand new rear spoiler that could be electrically retracted: closed, it would simply be the rear grill but above 80 kph it would raise automatically, reducing aerodynamic resistance and uncover a second grill that ensured a greater airflow to the engine compartment without needing to resort to unsightly vents. Below 15 kph, the wing automatically lowered itself to blend in with the body.

The aggressive image of the 928 GTS makes the car look more modern and attractive, but for many purists the modifications compromised the original purity of the design created – in perfect "Origami" style in vogue at the time of its launch – by Anatole Lapine. The GTS was the last in the 928 line after 61,056 cars had been built between 1978 and 1985.

TECHNICAL SPECIFICATION

ENGINE
Front, longitudinal
90° V8, vertical

Bore and stroke	100 x 78.9 mm
Unitary cubic capacity	619.6 cc
Total cubic capacity	4957 cc
Valve gear	twin overhead camshafts, toothed belt
Number of valves	4 per cylinder
Compression ratio	10.0:1
Fuel feed	electronic injection
Ignition	electronic
Coolant	liquid
Lubrication	forced circulation
Maximum power	330 hp at 6200 rpm
Specific power	66 hp/litre

TRANSMISSION
Rear wheel drive

Clutch	front, dry twin disc
Gearbox	rear, en bloc with differential, 5 speeds plus reverse

CHASSIS
Unified steel structure

Front suspension	double wishbone, coaxial coil springs with hydraulic shock absorbers, stabilisers bar
Rear suspension	double wishbones, coaxial coil springs with hydraulic shock absorbers, stabiliser bar
Brakes	disc, servo-brake, ABS
Steering	servo-assisted rack
Fuel tank	82 litres
Tyres front/rear	225/50 x 16/245/45 x 16

DIMENSIONS AND WEIGHT

Wheelbase	2500 mm
Track front/rear	1551/1546 mm
Length	4520 mm
Width	1836 mm
Height	1282 mm
Weight	1580 kg

PERFORMANCE

Top speed	275 kph
Power to weight ratio	4.7 kg/hp

928 GT and GTS   1989

At the end of 1988, Porsche knew 928 Club Sports were not selling as well as expected. So a new GT version was immediately launched: the engine was a slightly higher tuned version of the Club Sport, but the compression ratio had increased to 10:1 and that enabled the company to obtain official homologation for a power output of 330 hp at 6200 rpm. The minimum was at too high revs for an automatic gearbox, which was no longer available. Standard equipment included a self-monitoring system with tyre pressure sensors. In 1990, the PSD electronically controlled differential, originally developed for the 959, was also adopted. The market success of the new car was reasonable but not brilliant, much due to the dated conception of the GT. So Porsche considered a restyling as well as increasing engine power to 5.4, 5.6 and 6-litres. Meanwhile, the idea to launching a new generation of engines derived from the unit developed for Formula Indy was beginning to gather impetus. But modest sales and other investments made at Zuffenhausen steered the management towards a more conservative choice. So the 928 was unveiled in 1992 in its final coming, the GTS. The 5.4 engine generated 350 hp – 10 hp more than indicated by the company – and generated it better to enable the company to bring back automatic transmission to the range. Suspension and brakes were improved and enlarged at the front due to space left by new 17-inch Cup alloy rims to which were fitted 225/45 ZR 17 front and 255/40 ZR 17 rear similar to those on the 911 Carrera. The bigger size tyres forced the company to redesign the wheel housings, especially the rear, giving the car a more "muscular" look. The tail panel came in for similar treatment and bore the name Porsche on an insert between the optical groups, with the denomination 928 GTS just above, and the spoiler was painted in the same colour as the car.

The dashboard of the 911 Carrera 2 with 4-speed Tiptronic automatic transmission: using the various options of the selectors on the left, the 'box works automatically. But with the lever in the right side selector it can be used as a sequential gearbox, choosing gear changes by moving the lever forward or backwards. The Tiptronic automatic gearbox was also installed in the GT.

TECHNICAL SPECIFICATION

ENGINE
Rear, overhanging, longitudinal
6 cylinders horizontally opposed

Bore and stroke	100 x 76.4 mm
Unitary cubic capacity	600 cc
Total cubic capacity	3600 cc
Valve gear	overhead camshaft, chain driven
Number of valves	2 per cylinder
Compression ratio	10.3:1
Fuel feed	Bosch electronic injection
Ignition	dual, electronic
Coolant	forced air
Lubrication	dry sump
Maximum power	250 hp at 6100 rpm
Specific power	69.4 hp/litre

TRANSMISSION
Rear wheel drive

Clutch	torque converter
Gearbox	Tiptronic, en bloc with differential, 4 speeds plus reverse

CHASSIS
Unified steel structure

Front suspension	McPherson, lower oblique arms, coil springs, hydraulic shock absorbers, stabilisers bar
Rear suspension	independent, oblique arms, coil springs, hydraulic shock absorbers, stabiliser bar
Brakes	disc, servo-brake, ABS
Steering	ZF rack
Fuel tank	77 litres
Tyres front/rear	205/55 x 16/225/50 x 16

DIMENSIONS AND WEIGHT

Wheelbase	2272 mm
Track front/rear	1380/1374 mm
Length	4250 mm
Width	1652 mm
Height	1310 mm
Weight	1350 kg

PERFORMANCE

Top speed	260 kph
Power to weight ratio	5.4 kg/hp

911 Carrera 2 Tiptronic   1990

During the new 911's development stage, a new VW automatic gearbox was considered, although the design was delayed. Much more attention was given to the possible production of the double clutch PDK, which had been tested on the 962 C for some time: the project was taken up several times, thinking of selling it to other constructors, but it was eventually dropped due to development difficulties. ZF had designed an automatic 4-speed box with a hydraulic torque converter at the same time, and that was much more modern and faster that previously. Obviously, it wasn't easy to install into the unusual 911 body shell, for which the Porsche technicians were forced to design a new box with a counter shaft run by a cascade of three helical gears which, running in parallel with the gearbox, turned towards the differential. Initially, a variation was considered for the Carrera 4, but that was dropped due to its excessive development costs. As well as the normal hydraulic-mechanical means of operation, the ZF gearbox was operated by an electronic control unit connected to the ABS system, the Motronic – therefore also receiving information on the throttle movements – and to a lateral acceleration sensor; receiving information from those three systems, the transmission takes driving style into account, at the same time avoiding undesired changes when the car was cornering under lateral acceleration of more than 0.4 g. There were five different operational logics, from the most economical to the sportiest, with the gearbox able to adapt itself automatically. The major new development, which would set a trend, was the opportunity of using the gearbox manually in sequence by moving the lever to the right and moving it either forward or backwards: it was due to this characteristic that the name Tiptronic was chosen, which also had the advantage of not recalling the presence of the converter – one of the least appreciated aspects of the old Sportomatic.

The picture shows a 911 Carrara 2 Cup racing in 1990; at the same time as the highly popular DTM, the Porsche Carrera Cup racing enjoyed great success. The illustration shows the Carrera 4 Leichtbau; all 20 of them were sold in the United States, the cars specially prepared by Jürgen Barth's team.

TECHNICAL SPECIFICATION

ENGINE

Rear, overhanging, longitudinal
6 cylinders horizontally opposed

Bore and stroke	100 x 76.4 mm
Unitary cubic capacity	600 cc
Total cubic capacity	3600 cc
Valve gear	overhead camshaft, chain driven
Number of valves	2 per cylinder
Compression ratio	10.3:1
Fuel feed	Bosch electronic injection
Ignition	dual, electronic
Coolant	forced air
Lubrication	dry sump
Maximum power	265 hp at 6100 rpm
Specific power	75 hp/litre

TRANSMISSION

Rear wheel drive

Clutch	dry mono-disc
Gearbox	en bloc with differential, 5 speeds plus reverse

CHASSIS

Unified steel structure

Front suspension	McPherson, lower oblique arms, coil springs, hydraulic shock absorbers, stabiliser bar
Rear suspension	independent, oblique arms, coil springs, hydraulic shock absorbers, stabilisers bar
Brakes	disc, servo-brake, ABS
Steering	ZF rack
Fuel tank	77 litres
Tyres front/rear	245/60 x 17/265/630 x 17

DIMENSIONS AND WEIGHT

Wheelbase	2272 mm
Track front/rear	1380/1374 mm
Length	4250 mm
Width	1652 mm
Height	1250 mm
Weight	1210 kg

PERFORMANCE

Top speed	270 kph
Power to weight ratio	4.5 kg/hp

911 Carrera CUP and 4 Leichtbau   1990

After the success of the 944 Turbo Cup, the Porsche Carrera Cup was instituted in 1990 with regulations formulated by the company and races often taking place in conjunction with those of the popular DTM. The company produced 911 Carrera 2 Cup cars for the series, the engines for which came from the assembly line to ensure they were of the same power and were prepared to obtain a higher output above 15 kW. In addition, they had no air filters or flywheels. The control units were sealed and after the races some of them were randomly sent to Weissach to avert manipulation. The suspension was the same as the road cars, but the Bilstein shock absorbers were adjustable, as were the springs and anti-roll bars, while the braking system was replaced by that of the 911 Turbo even if the ABS could be deactivated to avoid "misunderstandings" of the system in particular race situations. The body was unchanged, except for the use of thin glass for the side and rear windows, operations that, as a result of the elimination of underbody protection and anti-rumble material, reduced the cars' weight by 140 kg. The input for the construction of the Carrera 4 Leichtbau came from an American client in search of a 911 prepared for club racing that was a good performer but fairly economical to run. The request was made in 1988, but it was only two years later that Jürgen Barth's team came up with the car that would become the Lightweight as a result of a 24% reduction in mass compared to the production Carrera 4. With its lighter body and doors in aluminium plastic components, a 911 Turbo-style rear wing and an engine suitably tuned, the car could produce 265 hp. The gearbox was toughened and made shorter, using the experience of the 953 Paris-Dakar, while the central and rear differentials were operated manually, instead of being in automatic mode. Together with the 917's brakes and roll bar, the car was race ready. Although it was never added to the price list, 20 of them were built for the US market.

The development of the 969, a derivative of the 911 able to add itself to the top of the range and replace the 911 Turbo, began as early as 1984. The set-up and body fully owe their allegiance to the 959, which came out at the same time. It was decided to leave it in production for the 1991 model year but subsequently, the company opted for a more conservative alternative: the "normal" 911 Turbo.

TECHNICAL SPECIFICATION

ENGINE

Rear, overhanging, longitudinal
6 cylinders, horizontally opposed

Bore and stroke	-
Unitary cubic capacity	600 cc
Total cubic capacity	3500 cc
Valve gear	twin overhead camshafts, chain driven
Number of valves	4 per cylinder
Compression ratio	-
Fuel feed	electronic injection, bi-turbo
Ignition	dual, electronic
Coolant	head liquid, cylinders air
Lubrication	dry sump
Maximum power	370 hp
Specific power	105.7 hp/litre

TRANSMISSION

4-wheel drive

Clutch	dry mono-disc
Gearbox	-

CHASSIS

Unified steel structure

Front suspension	independent, coil springs, hydraulic shock absorbers stabiliser bar
Rear suspension	independent, coil springs, hydraulic shock absorbers, stabiliser bar
Brakes	disc, servo-brake, ABS
Steering	rack
Fuel tank	-
Tyres front/rear	-

DIMENSIONS AND WEIGHT

Wheelbase	-
Track front/rear	-
Length	4200 mm
Width	1850 mm
Height	1300 mm
Weight	-

PERFORMANCE

Top speed	300 kph
Power to weight ratio	-

969   1990

It should have gone to the top of the range to replace the 911 Turbo and 16 prototypes were built, developed and tested across the world, as was Porsche's tradition. The production system was already tooled up and it seemed the 969 was ready to make its debut. But, suddenly, the project was abandoned in a period of substantial economic uncertainty that stopped numerous studies, among them the 928 Cabriolet. The 969 was based on the 911 Carrera 4 chassis, has a 6-cylinder 3.5-litre engine that put out around 370 hp with air-cooled cylinders and a 4-valve head by liquid, in line with the system developed in racing and installed in the 959 production car. The supercar also handed down to the 969 its traditional but simplified 4WD system, while for the transmission system the company opted for the ambitious dual clutch PDK gearbox with a sequential function. The car's low and tapered body line also derived from the 959, with its lateral air intakes and typical curved rear wing. On the Nardò track in southern Italy, the 969 exceeded 300 kph and, at a price of close on DM 200,000, it should have been produced at a rate of 2500 a year. The management of the car, which started in 1984, was not linear: after having hypothesised the use of a 3.3-litre engine – almost a direct descendent of the 911 – 4-valves per cylinder head air cooling problems immediately arose, and that pushed the technicians towards a liquid cooled boxer. There was also the idea of installing a V8 unit in the 969 derived from the Formula Indy engine, for which an experiment was carried out. In fact, the management were thinking of replacing all the 911's 6-cylinder boxer power units with a V8. After that, a V8 road car engine project for the 969 began, one which, reduced to a V6 should have powered the 911 family, but in this case, too, a stalemate was reached.

After an interruption in the 969 project, which eventually came to nothing, a turbo-charged finally returned to the 911 range in 1991, this time based on the 964 body. Power increased, even if not all Porsche's clients were satisfied, but the Turbo was always recognisable by its wider wheel housings and large rear spoiler, which gave it an aggressive look.

TECHNICAL SPECIFICATION

ENGINE

Rear, overhanging, longitudinal
6-cylinder turbo, horizontally opposed

Bore and stroke	97 x 74.4 mm
Unitary cubic capacity	549.8 cc
Total cubic capacity	3299 cc
Valve gear	overhead camshaft, chain driven
Number of valves	2 per cylinder
Compression ratio	7.0:1
Fuel feed	electronic injection, turbo
Ignition	electronic
Coolant	forced air
Lubrication	dry sump
Maximum power	320 hp at 5750 rpm
Specific power	96.9 hp/litre

TRANSMISSION

Rear wheel drive

Clutch	dry mono-disc
Gearbox	en bloc with differential, 5 speeds plus reverse

CHASSIS

Unified steel structure

Front suspension	McPherson, lower oblique arms, coil springs, hydraulic shock absorbers, stabiliser bar
Rear suspension	independent, oblique arms, coil springs, hydraulic shock absorbers, stabiliser bar
Brakes	disc, servo-brake, ABS
Steering	ZF rack
Fuel tank	77 litres
Tyres front/rear	205/50 x 17/255/40 x 17

DIMENSIONS AND WEIGHT

Wheelbase	2272 mm
Track front/rear	1442/1499 mm
Length	4250 mm
Width	1775 mm
Height	1310 mm
Weight	1470 kg

PERFORMANCE

Top speed	270 kph
Power to weight ratio	5.4 kg/hp

911 Turbo (964) and 911 Turbo 3.6   1991

Having abandoned the ambitious 969 project, Porsche decided to produce a turbo-charged version of the 911 starting from a new body shell developed for the 964. The body was adapted to the styling trends now typical of the Turbo: wider wheel housings for tyres of 205/50 ZR 17 front and 255/40 ZR 17 rear, fitted to new-style alloy rims. The rear vision mirrors were tear-shaped and the rear spoilers were of more generous dimensions due to the new integrated intercooler. Inside, the heater was improved and airbags were standard equipment. From the mechanical point of view, the 6-cylinder, 3.3-litre turbocharged boxer was brought back with 20 hp more for a total of 320 hp, despite the fact that the new unit had to respect the even more rigid exhaust emissions and noise regulations. The head gasket was changed and was now in hardened steel, the fan belt and alternator were separate and the Bosch K-Jetronic injection system was installed with the lambda sensor already used in the USA. The gearbox was a 5-speed and the differential was self-locking. Due to car's greater weight and more gentle power generation, some cus-tomers coming from the "old" and violent Turbo 3.3 declared themselves dissatis-fied: that's why a 355 hp optional unit was offered. The Turbo was updated many times as the years passed, but the real news was made in 1993 with the appearance of the 3.6-litre Turbo. The old 3.3 unit had been dropped, a refugee from a genera-tion past, while the new 3.6 was derived straight from the Carrera 4's 6-cylinder. Power output went up to 360 hp and the performance increase meant a further lowering of the set-up, the adoption of a front strut bar and bigger tyres, now fit-ted to new 18-inch decomposable rims. Fuel consumption was higher, so Porsche met their clients' request for a bigger, 92-litre fuel tank as an optional.

The Arrows-Footwork F1 car with a V12 Porsche engine competed in six Grands Prix in 1991, but was often unable to qualify. Much of the responsibility for this was attributed to the engine's poor power output and its weight. The initiative was a defeat for Porsche: for the first time, the company threw in the towel, making a terrible dent in its image so soon after the failure of its Formula Indy adventure.

TECHNICAL SPECIFICATION

ENGINE
Central, longitudinal
12-cylinder 80° V8

Bore and stroke	86x 50.2 mm
Unitary cubic capacity	291.5 cc
Total cubic capacity	3498 cc
Valve gear	twin overhead camshafts, timing gear
Number of valves	4 per cylinder
Compression ratio	-
Fuel feed	electronic injection
Ignition	electronic
Coolant	liquid
Lubrication	dry sump
Maximum power	670 hp at 13,500 rpm
Specific power	191.4 hp/litre

TRANSMISSION
Rear wheel drive

Clutch	dry
Gearbox	en bloc with differential, 6 speeds plus reverse

CHASSIS
Carbon fibre monocoque

Front suspension	double wishbones, hydraulic shock absorbers, stabiliser bar
Rear suspension	double wishbones, hydraulic shock absorbers, stabiliser bar
Brakes	disc
Steering	rack
Fuel tank	-
Tyres front/rear	-

DIMENSIONS AND WEIGHT

Wheelbase	-
Track front/rear	1806/1676 mm
Length	-
Width	-
Height	-
Weight	500 kg

PERFORMANCE

Top speed	350 kph
Power to weight ratio	0.7 hp/litre

Footwork-Porsche FA12 1991

The newspaper headlines gave no escape: after a 40-year motor sport career with numerous successes and with the ability to tenaciously take on critical situations to finally win, Porsche left Formula 1 as a loser, damaging its credibility as a company. After the huge success with McLaren, the new management headed up to Arno Bohn and Ulrich Bez decided to return to Formula 1 with a 3.5-litre V12 engine. But this time, the company was not commissioned to produce a new power unit, it was a Porsche initiative which, as soon as a rough outline was ready, the company went hunting for a team in whose cars to install it. As all the top teams were already committed to suppliers, Stuttgart was forced to go for a mid-grid team thinking – and this would be a demonstration of a lack of competency of Bez and Bohn in the racing world – they would easily become successful and would then attract the attention of one of the top teams. Hans Mezger sketched out the characteristics of the new V12 engine with an 80° angle between the cylinder banks so as to take up once more many of the TAG V6 elements. In practice, it would just comprise two paired V6s due to the central PTO, which left the teams' technicians to which the project was proposed rather perplexed given the weight and bulk of such an imposition, Adrian Newey more than anyone else. After a series of contact with van Rossem's Onyx, an agreement for the 1991 season was finally reached with Arrows – now called Footwork and in the hands of Japanese businessman Wataru Ohashi. Development continued but once ready at last, the V12 turned out to be heavy, cumbersome and well below the agreed 700 hp. There followed rather disheartening tests with the old Arrows A11C after which the FA12 was prepared, a car that was driven in 1991 by Michele Alboreto and Alex Caffi. But with a series of non-qualifications, breakdowns and tail end placings it was a failure which ended in Porsche's retirement from Formula 1.

The 1992 911 Carrera RS took up the idea – launched with the Carrera RS 2.7 in 1973 – of an extremely fast road car, which could become a perfect starting point for motor sport elaboration. As well as the European versions aimed at various types of clientele, an RS America in the illustration was aimed at the US market with its fixed rear spoiler.

TECHNICAL SPECIFICATION

ENGINE

Rear, overhanging, longitudinal
6 cylinders horizontally opposed

Bore and stroke	100 x 76.4 mm
Unitary cubic capacity	600 cc
Total cubic capacity	3600 cc
Valve gear	overhead camshaft, chain driven
Number of valves	2 per cylinder
Compression ratio	11.3:1
Fuel feed	electronic injection
Ignition	double, electronic
Coolant	forced air
Lubrication	dry sump
Maximum power	260 hp at 6100 rpm
Specific power	72.2 hp/litre

TRANSMISSION

Rear wheel drive

Clutch	dry mono-disc
Gearbox	en bloc with differential, 5 speeds plus reverse

CHASSIS

Unified steel structure

Front suspension	McPherson, lower oblique arms, coil springs, hydraulic shock absorbers, stabiliser bar
Rear suspension	independent, oblique arms, coil springs, hydraulic shock absorbers, stabiliser bar
Brakes	disc, servo-brake, ABS
Steering	ZF rack
Fuel tank	77 litres
Tyres front/rear	205/50 x 17/255/40 x 17

DIMENSIONS AND WEIGHT

Wheelbase	2272 mm
Track front/rear	1379/1380 mm
Length	4275 mm
Width	1652 mm
Height	1270 mm
Weight	1220 kg

PERFORMANCE

Top speed	260 kph
Power to weight ratio	4.7 kg/hp

911 Carrera RS   1992

Starting from the 911 Carrera 2, out came the 911 Carrera RS 3.6 in 1992, a lightened and more powerful version of the production car that was aimed at an especially demanding clientele or those searching for a car ready to be elaborated for racing. Power output was taken to 260 hp by a careful selection of its pistons, coupling and a different mapping, while the 5 hp lost compared to the Carrera Cup were attributed to the air filter and the exhaust silencer. The flywheel was lightened by 7 kg – except on the Touring. The Carrera RS was available in three versions: the Basic, with simplified equipment and lightened; the Touring, with a wealth of equipment, rear seats, power steering and sound deadening; the Sport or NGT from the category in which it was homologated, and which was destined to race, with its welded roll bar, racing clutch with a sintered Ceram disc and shell seats as on the Basic. The RS's gearbox was strengthened and the self-locking differential was up to 20% under acceleration and 100% in deceleration. The suspension was revised, lowering the set-up by 40%, making the springs and shock absorbers more rigid and using spherical metal bearings for greater precision, even if running comfort felt it notably. The braking system was that of the 911 Turbo with ABS, but the functioning logic was revised on the basis of sporting needs, causing a number of tantrums when used on rough roads. The 17-inch rims in Cup style were in magnesium, which saved 11 kg per car and were fitted with 205/50 tyres on the front and 225/40 rear. The body's wheel housings were widened, but the rear spoiler was the production extractable version. Due to the lightening exercise – the engine cover was in aluminium – the car weighed 1220 kg. A total of 2282 cars were assembled, while the RS America version was prepared for the USA, with a 250 hp production engine, specific rims and a fixed rear spoiler.

Unveiled at the 1992 Geneva Motor Show, the 911 Turbo S had air intakes in the rear wings and those up front in place of fog lights. Only 86 of the cars were built, but they were a useful starting point for motor sport elaboration. With breath-taking performance, the car's comfort was terrible.

TECHNICAL SPECIFICATION

ENGINE

Rear, overhanging, longitudinal
6-cylinder turbo, horizontally opposed

Bore and stroke	97 x 74.4 mm
Unitary cubic capacity	549.8 cc
Total cubic capacity	3299 cc
Valve gear	overhead camshaft, chain driven
Number of valves	2 per cylinder
Compression ratio	7.0:1
Fuel feed	electronic injection, turbo
Ignition	electronic
Coolant	forced air
Lubrication	dry sump
Maximum power	381 hp at 6000 rpm
Specific power	115.1 hp/litre

TRANSMISSION

Rear wheel drive

Clutch	dry mono-disc
Gearbox	en bloc with differential, 5 speeds plus reverse

CHASSIS

Unified steel structure

Front suspension	McPherson, lower arms, coil springs, hydraulic shock absorbers, stabiliser bar
Rear suspension	independent, lower arms, coil springs, hydraulic shock absorbers, stabiliser bar
Brakes	disc, servo-brake, ABS
Steering	ZF rack
Fuel tank	92 litres
Tyres front/rear	225/40 x 18/265/35 x 18

DIMENSIONS AND WEIGHT

Wheelbase	2272 mm
Track front/rear	1440/1481 mm
Length	4275 mm
Width	1775 mm
Height	1250 mm
Weight	1290 mm

PERFORMANCE

Top speed	290 kph
Power to weight ratio	3.4 kg/hp

911 Turbo S and Turbo S2   1992

A year after the launch of the 911 Turbo at the 1992 Geneva Motor Show, an even quicker version was introduced, called the Turbo S and with a power output of 381 hp at 6000 rpm. The increase was achieved with a modified camshaft, polished ducts and with a turbocharger pressure of 0.9 bar. To ensure reliability, a second oil radiator was installed in the front left wheel housing, replacing the usual air conditioning exchanger. The suspension was revised and the set-up lowered by 40 mm, the rims were 18-inch Cup specials fitted with ultra-low profile 235/40 tyres front and 265/35 rear. The rim dimensions also helped host bigger brake callipers and they were cooled by ducts leading from the air intakes that replaced the front sidelights, which were now part of the overall optical groups. Another two air intakes were also built into the rear wheel housings *à la* 959 and they improved engine cooling. The body was lightened by the same criteria adopted for the Carrera RS, including the elimination of the power steering. Performance was incredible, with a top speed of 290 kph and a dash from 0-100 kph in 4.7 seconds; and roadholding was excellent, but turbo lag was rather evident and made controlling oversteer demanding. As with the Carrera RS, comfort was not good. Twenty 911 Turbo S2s were put together for the United States as options for the normal Turbo costing USD 11,072, especially designed to meet IMSA Supercar regulations: the Turbo S engine was lowered into the normal Turbo chassis, with 17-inch Cup monolithic rims. Strangely, the power output declared by the company was 322 hp, but the motoring press estimated it was over 370 hp, closing in on an effective 381 hp! Stuck and Haywood won four IMSA races and the title in the car.

Lightened with thoroughbred handling and with a really strong appearance – on the sides was enormous Club Sport lettering – the sports version of the 968 was offered at a low price in relation to the rest of the range, while the equipment, which was initially cut to the quick, could be improved through the optional list. The car was a success.

TECHNICAL SPECIFICATION

ENGINE

Front, longitudinal
4-cylinders in line, vertical

Bore and stroke	104 x 88 mm
Unitary cubic capacity	747.5 cc
Total cubic capacity	2990 cc
Valve gear	twin overhead camshafts, toothed belt
Number of valves	4 per cylinder
Compression ratio	11:1
Fuel feed	electronic injection
Ignition	electronic
Coolant	liquid
Lubrication	wet sump
Maximum power	240 hp at 6200 rpm
Specific power	80 hp/litre

TRANSMISSION

Rear wheel drive

Clutch	front, dry mono-disc
Gearbox	rear, en bloc with differential, 6 speeds plus reverse

CHASSIS

Unified steel structure

Front suspension	double wishbones, coaxial coil springs with hydraulic shock absorbers, stabiliser bar
Rear suspension	independent, oblique arms, transverse torsion bars, hydraulic shock absorbers, stabiliser bar
Brakes	disc, servo-brake, ABS
Steering	ZF rack
Fuel tank	80 litres
Tyres front/rear	225/40 x 17/255/35 x 17

DIMENSIONS AND WEIGHT

Wheelbase	2400 mm
Track front/rear	1473/1450 mm
Length	4320 mm
Width	1735 mm
Height	1255
Weight	1335 kg

PERFORMANCE

Top speed	254 kph
Power to weight ratio	5.3 hp/kg

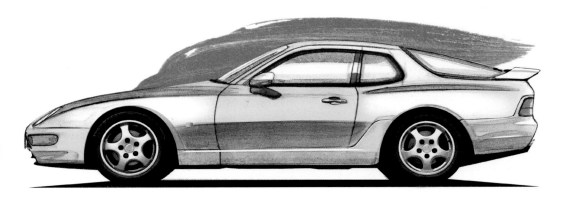

968 Club Sport   1993

After the unenthusiastic experience with the 928 Club Sport, Porsche came up with the new 968 Club Sport for the 1993 model year in which the modifications compared to the "normal" version were much more extensive than those carried out on the top of the range 928. The mechanics were the same, with the 3-litre 4-cylinder 16-valve engine that put out 240 hp and 305 Nm of torque, but the body lost all things superfluous: electric seats and mirrors, headlight washers, driver's airbag, automatic air conditioning and most of the sound proofed panels. With no air conditioning, the battery was also smaller. The rear seats and relative loudspeakers disappeared, while the fronts were fixed and shell shaped in plastic, even if it was possible to order the normal ones as zero cost optionals, as most of the equipment that had been removed. The operation saved 50 kg and, while certainly not being a light car, its 1335 kg were distributed 48.5% front and 51.5% rear. The set-up was lowered 20 mm and Cup Design 17-inch rims – with a 7.5-inch channel at the front and 9-inch rear – were in the same colour as the body, with the exception of the silver car, which had black wheels. An even more rigid set-up was available on request, as were the self-locking differential and a braking system with perforated discs. Even though it was well designed, the cabrio version of the Club Sport was never produced. Performance was lively, with a top speed of 254 kph and a 0-100 kph time of 6.1 seconds and according to *Auto Motor und Sport*, it was able to challenge the 911 – and its price was decidedly lower than that of the normal 968 at 13 million lire less on the Italian market; all of which meant the car was a great international success. Even in Britain, where a slightly less spartan version was available, the Metropolitan Police acquired several in 1994.

The 911 IMSA in Brumo livery competing in the 1993 12 Hours of Sebring. Attention paid to the IMSA Championship was extremely high, as was the case with all the American series. After the negative image created by its retirement from Formula Indy and F1, Porsche needed to re-establish its prestige in US motor sport, without making mistakes.

TECHNICAL SPECIFICATION

ENGINE

Rear, overhanging, longitudinal
6-cylinder turbo, horizontally opposed

Bore and stroke	100 x 76.4 mm
Unitary cubic capacity	600 cc
Total cubic capacity	3600 cc
Valve gear	overhead camshaft, chain driven
Number of valves	2 per cylinder
Compression ratio	7.5:1
Fuel feed	electronic injection, turbo
Ignition	electronic
Coolant	forced air
Lubrication	dry sump
Maximum power	370 hp at 6000 rpm
Specific power	102.7 hp/litre

TRANSMISSION

Rear wheel drive

Clutch	dry mono-disc
Gearbox	en bloc with diff, 5 speeds plus reverse, free choice

CHASSIS

Unified steel structure

Front suspension	McPherson, lower arms, coil springs, hydraulic shock absorbers, stabiliser bar
Rear suspension	independent, lower arms, coil springs, hydraulic shock absorbers, stabiliser bar
Brakes	disc, servo-brake, ABS
Steering	ZF rack
Fuel tank	61 litres
Tyres front/rear	225/40 x 18/265/35 x 18

DIMENSIONS AND WEIGHT

Wheelbase	2272 mm
Track front/rear	1440/1481 mm
Length	4275 mm
Width	1775 mm
Height	1250 mm
Weight	1430 mm

PERFORMANCE

Top speed	280 kph
Power to weight ratio	3.8 kg/hp

911 Turbo 3.6 IMSA   1993

After the victories of 1991 and 1992 with the 911 Turbo 3.3, Porsche decided to prepare a new version of the 911 for the 1993 season of the IMSA GTX Super-car series, one with a 3.6-litre engine. In this case, too, though, the company's involvement in United States motor sport was not directed by Stuttgart but a private team, as it had done successfully so many times in the past. In this case it was Brumo, whose cars could easily be recognised from their white, blue and red livery on the bonnet. But Porsche's "semi-official" support was evident also in the choice of drivers, who alternated at the wheel: Hans Joachim Stuck, Hurley Haywood and Walter Röhrl. The type M64 3600 cc engine was normal production, but the pistons, camshafts and the K-Jetronic fuel injection were all redesigned for racing, as was the turbocharging system. The racing clutch had sintered gaskets and, while maintaining the structure of the production unit, the gearbox was able to adopt specific ratios race by race. As with the previous seasons, the differential self-locked 20% with blades under acceleration while, to help the driver with changes, it locked completely under deceleration, some-times rather violently. The production suspension was optimised and adjustable in line with each track, the brakes were more powerful with Porsche designed aluminium callipers. The category's regulations did not permit the evolution of the car's body: not only did they define the external shape, including the rear wing, but they also imposed a very high minimum weight of 1440 kg. The fuel tank was limited to 61 litres and the cockpit had to have a welded roll bar cage, fire extinguishers and lightened Recaro seats. One of the most severe limitations was the use of Bridgestone road tyres in size 225/40 ZR 18 front and 235/35 ZR 18 rear. But, once again, the 911 dominated the Championship.

The 911 Turbo S GT Le Mans photographed during a pit stop with Walter Röhrl at the wheel. The large rear wing had two supplementary air intakes in its pillars. And it also had a pneumatic jack system with raised the whole car including all four wheels at the same time, cutting pit stop time.

TECHNICAL SPECIFICATION

ENGINE

Rear, overhanging, longitudinal
6-cylinder turbo, horizontally opposed

Bore and stroke	95 x 74.4 mm
Unitary cubic capacity	527.3 cc
Total cubic capacity	3164 cc
Valve gear	twin overhead camshafts, chain driven
Number of valves	4 per cylinder
Compression ratio	-
Fuel feed	electronic injection, turbo
Ignition	transistorised
Coolant	head liquid, cylinders forced air
Lubrication	dry sump
Maximum power	475 hp at 7500 rpm

TRANSMISSION

Rear wheel drive

Clutch	dry mono-disc
Gearbox	en bloc with differential, 5 speeds plus reverse, free selection

CHASSIS

Unified steel structure

Front suspension	McPherson, lower arms, coil springs, hydraulic shock absorbers, stabiliser bar
Rear suspension	independent, lower arms, coil springs, hydraulic shock absorbers, stabiliser bar
Brakes	disc, servo-brake, ABS
Steering	ZF rack
Fuel tank	120 litres
Tyres front/rear	225/40 x 18/265/35 x 18

DIMENSIONS AND WEIGHT

Wheelbase	2272 mm
Track front/rear	1450/1480 mm
Length	4250 mm
Width	-
Height	-
Weight	1000 kg

PERFORMANCE

Top speed	280 kph
Power to weight ratio	2.1 kg/hp

911 Turbo S GT Le Mans   1993

Regulations were created by the Automobile Club de l'Ouest organisers of the 1993 24 Hours of Le Mans, that christened a new GT class that enabled any homologated car from any "credible" country – especially with regard to emission rules – to compete, provided the vehicles maintained their production car structure and – in part – the external shape of the body. In recompense, the engine could be seriously elaborated, even with a turbocharger or replaced by one made by the same constructor. This norm adapted itself well to the 911 Turbo S, with its 6-cylinder 3.3-litre engine of 381 hp and its set-up, which was already 40 mm lower, had more powerful brakes as well as an already modified body, even with air intakes for the rear brakes. However, to ensure better performance, the engine was given two turbochargers with intercoolers, the air intakes for which were in the rear wing pillars. The wing could be modified, unlike the rest of the body. The car's cubic capacity had to be reduced to 3164 cc and in practice, was an engine that was similar to that of the 962 IMSA, which had post combustion systems used to maintain the high speed of the turbine under deceleration and therefore eliminating typical turbo lag even if it did consume more fuel. But having had to use two 24 mm restrictor inlets, the car's power output was reduced to 475 hp at 7500 rpm. Even if the chassis were adjustable, it still took on the technology of that from the production Turbo S, but the body was lightened by a huge 350 kg to weigh in at 1000 kg, the minimum weight permitted by the rules. The transmission used the type G50 production gearbox that was modified with an additional cooling pump with radiator, while the differential was 40% self-locking. A regulation also limited the maximum width of the tyres to 12 inches: so the car ran on 18-inch BBS decomposable rims fitted with Goodyear tyres of 9.5 and 11 inches.

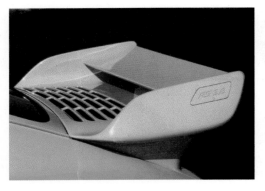

The rear spoiler of the 3.8-litre 911 Carrera RS, of which only a few were produced in 1993, 51 of them transformed into Carrera RSRs to compete in various categories of motor racing that limited power output using aspiration restrictors, but if not limited it would generate 375 hp. It won the GT Class of the 1993 and 1994 24 Hours of Le Mans and the 1993 24 Hours of Spa.

TECHNICAL SPECIFICATION

ENGINE
Rear, overhanging, longitudinal
6 cylinders horizontally opposed

Bore and stroke	102 x 76.4 mm
Unitary cubic capacity	624 cc
Total cubic capacity	3746 cc
Valve gear	overhead camshaft, chain driven
Number of valves	2 per cylinder
Compression ratio	11.8:1
Fuel feed	Bosch electronic injection
Ignition	double, electronic
Coolant	forced air
Lubrication	dry sump
Maximum power	350 hp at 7000 rpm
Specific power	92.1 hp/litre

TRANSMISSION
Rear wheel drive

Clutch	dry mono-disc
Gearbox	en bloc with differential, 5 speeds plus reverse

CHASSIS
Unified steel structure

Front suspension	McPherson, lower arms, coil springs, hydraulic shock absorbers, stabiliser bar
Rear suspension	independent, multi-link layout, coil springs, hydraulic shock absorbers, stabiliser bar
Brakes	disc, servo-brake, ABS
Steering	ZF rack
Fuel tank	77 litres
Tyres front/rear	205/40 x 18/265/35 x 18

DIMENSIONS AND WEIGHT

Wheelbase	2272 mm
Track front/rear	1444/1535 mm
Length	4275 mm
Width	1652 mm
Height	1270 mm
Weight	1200 kg

PERFORMANCE

Top speed	280 kph
Power to weight ratio	3.4 kg/hp

911 Carrera RS 3.8 and RSR 3.8   1993

To take the place of the Carrera RS 3.6, in 1993 the bore of the 6-cylinder boxer engine was taken to 102 mm to deliver a cubic capacity of 3746. So the new power unit was installed in a body derived from that of the Turbo, with wheel housings widened, the suspension of the RS 3.6, but with doors in aluminium, more powerful brakes as on the Turbo S and bigger 18-inch rims. The car weighed 1210 kg together with a full tank of 92 litres of fuel. And a new rear fixed bi-plane, single piece glass fibre spoiler was installed. As a result of a series of improvements, like the six throttle valves located near the bigger valves, the ducts polished, the compression ratio increased to 11.6:1 and a second oil radiator, the power of the RS 3.8 road car was 300 hp at 6500 rpm. The gearbox had steel synchronisation and the differential self-locked to 40%. As well as the basic model costing DM 220,000 with only air bags and a radio as optionals, there was also the Club Sport that cost DM 10,000 more but it had a roll bar, racing belts, a fire extinguisher, racing pads and a sintered clutch. Obviously, the RS, which was rigid and noisy, was mainly the starting point for the RSR racer: for DM 270,000 Porsche supplied the car ready to race and to confirm that, the winner of its category in the 1993 24 Hours of Le Mans was one of those RSRs hat had just been delivered and was completely unaltered. In line with the categories of other races, though, the car had to be modified to comply with the regulations: as well as the norm on the adoption or not of a catalyser, many classes imposed the use of an aspiration flange to limit power. At Le Mans in 1993, with a 48 mm restrictor, the RSR still put out 360 hp and with the 39 mm imposed by the FIA only 315 hp compared to 375 hp of the unlimited car. Other regulations limited power, as in the German GT Championship, for which output was fixed at 325 hp; failure to do so meant fuel would be limited.

This air cooled car in the photograph was the last real 911 to many; to others, the multi-link rear suspension and sloping headlights, betrayed the original idea. However, while not revolutionary, the 993 series marked a change in the 911's evolution as it became so fast, safe and comfortable, befitting '90s grand tourers, raising sales and the image of the marque.

TECHNICAL SPECIFICATION

ENGINE

Rear, overhanging, longitudinal
6 cylinders horizontally opposed

Bore and stroke	100 x 76.4 mm
Unitary cubic capacity	600 cc
Total cubic capacity	3600 cc
Valve gear	overhead camshaft, chain driven
Number of valves	2 per cylinder
Compression ratio	11.3:1
Fuel feed	Bosch electronic injection
Ignition	double, electronic
Coolant	forced air
Lubrication	dry sump
Maximum power	272 hp at 6100 rpm
Specific power	75.5 hp/litre

TRANSMISSION

Rear wheel drive

Clutch	dry mono-disc
Gearbox	en bloc with differential, 6 speeds plus reverse

CHASSIS

Unified steel structure

Front suspension	McPherson, lower arms, coil springs, hydraulic shock absorbers, stabiliser bar
Rear suspension	independent, multi-link layout, coil springs, hydraulic shock absorbers, stabiliser bar
Brakes	disc, servo-brake, ABS
Steering	servo-assisted ZF rack
Fuel tank	71.5 litres
Tyres front/rear	205/55 x 16/245/45 x 16

DIMENSIONS AND WEIGHT

Wheelbase	2272 mm
Track front/rear	1405/1444 mm
Length	4245 mm
Width	1735 mm
Height	1300 mm
Weight	1370 kg

PERFORMANCE

Top speed	270 kph
Power to weight ratio	5 kg/hp

911 Carrera 2 (993)   1993

The 911 was given quite an injection of youth with the 964 but at the start of the '90s the market became even more demanding and Porsche's excellence wasn't so excellent any more according to some of the motoring press: performance was still good, but roadholding was sometimes not up to scratch. In addition, the car was very noisy, especially due to vibration transmitted to the body shell by the suspension which, more than anything else, testified to the fact that its design harked back to 1963. That's why a new 993 series Coupé was introduced at the 1993 Frankfurt Motor Show; the Cabriolet would be presented just before the 1994 show at Geneva. Externally, the body was modernised and made sportier, in part due to the company's experience with the controversial Panamericana: it was lower, wider, its optical groups were more inclined and the bumpers were completely integrated with the body. From the mechanical point of view, the main feature was the replacement of the traditional rear suspension with a modern multi-link layout, fixed to a light auxiliary chassis in aluminium. That way, the system was able to deliver optimum dynamic performance without transmitting noise or vibration to the body. The engine was massively updated and power output rose to 272 hp, while the gearbox had six speeds, but still weight like the "old" unit as it was built of light alloy, and the Tiptronic was improved. A new Targa body bowed in during the autumn of 1995 at Frankfurt, this time with a sophisticated glass roof that could be slid back but lined up perfectly with the body when it was closed. The Carreras were given more power at 285 hp due to a variable aspiration system called Varioram. As was the case with the Turbo Look, the Carrera S combined its aspirated mechanics with the Turbo body from 1997. On 15 July 1996, the 993 became the millionth Porsche to have been produced; it was for the Police and was handed over to them by Ferry Porsche himself.

With more "wicked" aesthetics drawn in full from the styling trends set by the Club Sport, the 968 Turbo S had a rear spoiler the centre of which could be adjusted to an excursion of over 10°. But only 17 of 968 Turbo RSs were built with their 350 hp power units, of which four were in racing configuration. That was far fewer than Porsche's planned 50-100 cars costing DM 228,000 each.

TECHNICAL SPECIFICATION

ENGINE

Front, longitudinal
4-cylinder turbo, in line, vertical

Bore and stroke	104 x 88 mm
Unitary cubic capacity	747.5 cc
Total cubic capacity	2990 cc
Valve gear	twin overhead camshafts, toothed belt
Number of valves	4 per cylinder
Compression ratio	11:1
Fuel feed	electronic injection, turbo
Ignition	electronic
Coolant	liquid
Lubrication	wet sump
Maximum power	305 hp at 5400 rpm
Specific power	101.6 hp/litre

TRANSMISSION

Rear wheel drive

Clutch	front, dry mono-disc
Gearbox	rear, en bloc with differential, 6 speeds plus reverse

CHASSIS

Unified steel structure

Front suspension	double wishbones, coaxial coil springs with hydraulic shock absorbers, stabiliser bar
Rear suspension	independent, oblique arms, transverse torsion bars, hydraulic shock absorbers, stabiliser bar
Brakes	disc, servo-brakes, ABS
Steering	ZF rack
Fuel tank	80 litres
Tyres front/rear	235/40 x 18/265/35 x 18

DIMENSIONS AND WEIGHT

Wheelbase	2400 mm
Track front/rear	1478/1450 mm
Length	4320 mm
Width	1735 mm
Height	1255 mm
Weight	1350 kg

PERFORMANCE

Top speed	290 kph
Power to weight ratio	4.4 kg/hp

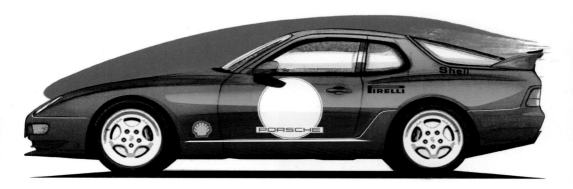

968 Turbo S and Turbo RS 1993

In September 1992, a project was launched at Porsche for a turbocharged version of the 968 with a view to its further motor racing involvement, perhaps a mono-marque championship. When the car was unveiled for the 1993 model year, its name was the 968 Turbo S, even if it didn't have a "normal" turbo. The head of the 944 Turbo was adapted on the basis of 3-litres and due to the KKK liquid cooled turbo, power output rose to 305 hp at 5400 rpm with an even more impressive torque of 500 Nm at just 3000 rpm. So top speed also went up to 290 kph and a 0-100 kph time of 4.7 seconds. The transmission was adapted to this higher performance with a non-bi-mass flywheel, a stronger clutch, new gear ratios and a 75% self-locking differential. The lower set-up was inspired by that of the 968 Club Sport, the brakes were made more powerful and given ABS and the rims were bigger at 18-inch in Cup design fitted with tyres of sections 235/40 front and 265/35 rear. Externally, the Turbo S stood out for its bigger air intake to serve the intercooler and two small NACA intakes on the bonnet, while the rear spoiler was bigger with an adjustable centre. The car was priced at DM 175,000 and production began in April 1993. For sporting clients, the Weissach racing department also offered the Turbo RS with a bigger intercooler and a 337 hp output, exactly that permitted by ADAC regulations that imposed a 4 hp per kilogram of weight rule, the Turbo RS weighing 1350 kg. Without a limiter, power went up to 350 hp. The car had a racing clutch, the suspension was on Unibal, the anti-roll bars could be adjusted and the wheels were bigger. Also included for racing was a cage-type anti-roll bar and an extinguisher. Porsche expected to produce between 50 and 100 Turbo RSs but in the end they totalled only 17, just four of them, comprising a prototype and three cars, equipped for racing.

After an initial attempt based on the Carrera 3.2, in 1994 the 911 was offered with a sporty and attractive two-seater open body with a lower windscreen and an occasional hood, all to relive once more the Speedster legend. Many components were in common with the first of the Speedster generation, but others were improved. Unfortunately, the car was unsuccessful, partially due to its price.

TECHNICAL SPECIFICATION

ENGINE

Rear, overhanging, longitudinal
6 cylinders, horizontally opposed

Bore and stroke	100 x 76.4 mm
Unitary cubic capacity	600 cc
Total cubic capacity	3600 cc
Valve gear	overhead camshaft, chain driven
Number of valves	2 per cylinder
Compression ratio	11.3:1
Fuel feed	Bosch electronic injection
Ignition	dual, electronic
Coolant	forced air
Lubrication	dry sump
Maximum power	250 hp at 6100 rpm
Specific power	69.4 hp/litre

TRANSMISSION

Rear wheel drive

Clutch	dry mono-disc
Gearbox	en bloc with differential, 6 speeds plus reverse

CHASSIS

Unified steel structure

Front suspension	McPherson, lower arms, coil springs, hydraulic shock absorbers, stabilisers bar
Rear suspension	independent, multi-link layout, coil springs, hydraulic shock absorbers, stabiliser bar
Brakes	disc, servo-brake, ABS
Steering	ZF rack, servo-assisted
Fuel tank	77 litres
Tyres front/rear	205/50 x 17/255/40 x 17

DIMENSIONS AND WEIGHT

Wheelbase	2272 mm
Track front/rear	1380/1374 mm
Length	4250 mm
Width	1652 mm
Height	1280 mm
Weight	1350 kg

PERFORMANCE

Top speed	260 kph
Power to weight ratio	5.4 kg/hp

911 Speedster (964)   1993

A few years after its launch, the 964 series of the 911 experienced a severe drop in sales and that pushed the management into coming up with new versions. The idea of a Club Sport was shot down and the Speedster project was resurrected. One was displayed at the Paris Motor Show in October 1992 – even if it was started more than three years earlier. The starting point was the body shell of the 911 964, but the company attempted to "recycle" many of the superstructures already used for the "old" Speedster, with the Carrera 3.2 floorpan. Fritz Bezner's team was given the task of improving the quality level and appeal of the coming car. Starting from the Carrera 2 Cabriolet using both the manual transmission and the Tiptronic automatic gearbox, the doors were replaced by the lighter ones from the Carrera RS, as well as the Cabriolet's black leather covered seats, although they were optional. It was also possible to order an internal finish – gear lever, handbrake, rear seat coverings and dashboard – in the same colour as the exterior. Wheels were also available in the same colour in the Cup design. The hood was hand operated and folded back under an original glass fibre cover, with two domed headrests. It was the quality of the hood that surprised the motoring press when compared with the previous generation of the Speedster: it was well made and was of excellent wind and rain protection, even if it was considered just an emergency component on this kind of car. Initially, the project included the production of a Turbo Look version, but the idea was rejected in mid-August 1992; however, about 20 of them were built by Rolf Sprenger. Partially because of its price, which was mid-way between those of the Coupé and Cabriolet, the Speedster was a modest success, with just 925 sold between 1993 and 1994.

The Dauer-Porsche 962 LM of Hurley Haywood, Yannick Dalmas and Mauro Baldi on its way to winning the 1994 24 Hours of Le Mans after a long battle with the Toyota. Although almost identical to the 962 C, the car entered was a much discussed extreme interpretation of the regulations for the GT category together with the McLaren F1, which was not entered.

TECHNICAL SPECIFICATION

ENGINE
Central, longitudinal
6 cylinders, horizontally opposed

Bore and stroke	95 x 70.4 mm
Unitary cubic capacity	500 cc
Total cubic capacity	2994 cc
Valve gear	twin overhead camshafts, chain driven
Number of valves	4 per cylinder
Compression ratio	-
Fuel feed	electronic injection, bi-turbo
Ignition	electronic
Coolant	liquid
Lubrication	dry sump
Maximum power	600 hp at 7700 rpm
Specific power	200 hp/litre

TRANSMISSION
Rear wheel drive

Clutch	dry mono-disc
Gearbox	en bloc with differential, 5 speeds plus reverse

CHASSIS
Unified steel structure

Front suspension	double wishbones, coil springs, hydraulic shock absorbers, stabiliser bar
Rear suspension	double wishbones, coil springs, hydraulic shock absorbers, stabiliser bar
Brakes	disc, servo-brake, ABS
Steering	ZF rack
Fuel tank	120 litres
Tyres front/rear	-

DIMENSIONS AND WEIGHT

Wheelbase	-
Track front/rear	-
Length	4995 mm
Width	2000 mm
Height	-
Weight	1000 kg

PERFORMANCE

Top speed	365 kph
Power to weight ratio	1.6 kg/hp

Dauer-Porsche 962 LM   1994

The enormous number (148) of 962s built – of which 105 had the original Porsche chassis – led various tuners to equip some of them as road cars, by which time the car's motor sport career was nearing its end. Among them was Ekkehard Zimmerman, who was able to obtain a German homologation, as well as driver Vern Schuppan with his Anglo-Japanese 962 CR with its 3.3-litre air cooled twin turbo engine and prepared by Andial. A third tuner was able to attract Porsche's attention to his project, racing driver Jochen Dauer. At the same time, the 24 Hours of Le Mans regulations admitted some cars with a corresponding road car production, although with a minimum weight and fuel feed restrictions to reduce maximum power. Norbert Singer's idea proposed to new design director Horst Marchart was simple: Porsche would have supported Dauer to obtain road car homologation for a version of the 962, which would then be entered for Le Mans as a GT. He was given the OK of Porsche's board of directors in March 1994 and the car was prepared and homologated in Germany, to then be checked out by Alain Bertaut of the Automobile Club de l'Ouest, whose job it was to verify its admissibility. There were a number of objections to transforming a racing car into one for road use to then transfer it back to being a racing car again. While a second "excuse" to exclude the car from Le Mans was the absence of bumper bars – the obligation of which was contradicted by Singer after successfully having the car homologated by the Germans and with a number of road cars already on the roads around Paris! The 600 hp 962 LM was admitted even though it "went against the spirit of the regulations" and at the end of the 24-hour race it came first and third, despite the absence of official support from Porsche and Joest.

The 993 series 911 Carrera RS was available in two versions: one exclusively for motor racing and the "softer" one for road use. The illustration shows a 911 Carrera Cup with its fixed rear spoiler that had an adjustable wing with which to compete in the Supercup Championship, a supporting series for the European Grands Prix. The Carrera Cup cars for DTM supporting events had an electrically retractable spoiler.

TECHNICAL SPECIFICATION

ENGINE

Rear, overhanging, longitudinal
6 cylinders horizontally opposed
Bore and stroke 102 x 76.4 mm

Unitary cubic capacity	624 cc
Total cubic capacity	3746 cc
Valve gear	overhead camshaft, chain driven
Number of valves	2 per cylinder
Compression ratio	11.3:1
Fuel feed	Bosch electronic injection
Ignition	double, electronic
Coolant	forced air
Lubrication	dry sump
Maximum power	300 hp at 6500 rpm
Specific power	78.9 hp/litre

TRANSMISSION

Rear wheel drive

Clutch	dry mono-disc
Gearbox	en bloc with differential, 6 speeds plus reverse

CHASSIS

Unified steel structure

Front suspension	McPherson, lower arms, coil springs, hydraulic shock absorbers, stabiliser bar
Rear suspension	independent, multi-link layout, coil springs, shock absorbers, stabiliser bar
Brakes	disc, servo-brake, ABS
Steering	ZF rack, servo-assisted
Fuel tank	92 litres
Tyres front/rear	225/40 x 18/265/35 x 18

DIMENSIONS AND WEIGHT

Wheelbase	2272 mm
Track front/rear	1413/1452 mm
Length	4380 mm
Width	1890 mm
Height	1300 mm
Weight	1270 kg

PERFORMANCE

Top speed	277 kph
Power to weight ratio	4.2 kg/hp

911 Carrera Cup, Cup RSR and RS   1994

Already on the cards in 1994, an identical series of 911 Cup cars were built for various mono-marque events and, with a number of modifications, for the GT3 categories of other championships. While the body shells were produced at Zuffenhausen with roll bars that stiffened the body by 20%, the mechanics were installed at the Weissach racing department. Cubic capacity increased to 3745.7 cc with an increase in stroke for a power output of 315 hp. The production clutch was made more robust for motor sport use, as was the gearbox's synchroniser. The body was lightened with bonnet and engine cover in aluminium and the weight was limited to 1120 kg. Tyres for the Supercup Championship were Pirelli in sizes 234/645 x 18 front and 285/645 x 18 rear; the set-up was revised and made adjustable. For the GT3 class of the Japanese Championship – it was later used in others series – the Cup 3.8 RSR was created with the specifics of the Carrera Cup, but with its engine increased in power output to 340 hp at 7000 rpm with new timing and the absence of silencers. The 911 RS Carrera was presented as a 1995 model year car, a version set up for 993 series races: the 6-cylinder had a cubic capacity of 3744 cc that put out 300 hp, plus an impressive torque due to the Varioram aspiration system. The set-up was lowered by 30 mm front and 40 mm rear, stiffened and with the ability to be set up to suit each circuit, while the body was lightened both externally with engine cover and boot in aluminium, and internally where specific equipment was reduced to the bone. The Carrera RS was available in two different versions: the basic for road use with a more refined interior, bi-mass fly-wheel and "softer" mechanics; in this case, the rear wing was fixed with a grill similar to that of the normal Carrera. The Club Sport was ready to race as was the marque's tradition, had a fixed wing with double lateral air intakes to cool the engine bay and fuel feed. Inside, there was a roll bar cage and airbags were optional.

With the 993 series Carrera 4, Porsche corrected the teething trouble of youth that afflicted the previous model. There was a new transmission, multi-link suspension at the rear, all of which finally gave the right feel at the wheel of the 911 4WD. Its modern appearance and the quality of finish did the rest. For the more demanding customers, there was the Carrera 4S, heir of the Turbo Look and the new Targa.

TECHNICAL SPECIFICATION

ENGINE
Rear, overhanging, longitudinal
6 cylinders, horizontally opposed

Bore and stroke	100 x 76.4 mm
Unitary cubic capacity	600 cc
Total cubic capacity	3600 cc
Valve gear	overhead camshaft, chain driven
Number of valves	2 per cylinder
Compression ratio	11.3:1
Fuel feed	Bosch electronic injection
Ignition	double electronic
Coolant	forced air
Lubrication	dry sump
Maximum power	272 hp at 6100 rpm
Specific power	75.5 hp/litre

TRANSMISSION
4-WD

Clutch	dry mono-disc
Gearbox	en bloc with differential, 6 speeds plus reverse

CHASSIS
Unified steel structure

Front suspension	McPherson, lower arms, coil springs, hydraulic shock absorbers, stabiliser bar
Rear suspension	independent, multi-link layout, coil springs, shock absorbers, stabiliser bar
Brakes	disc, servo-brake, ABS
Steering	ZF rack, servo-assisted
Fuel tank	73 litres
Tyres front/rear	205/55 x 16/ 245/45 x 16

DIMENSIONS AND WEIGHT

Wheelbase	2272 mm
Track front/rear	1405/1444 mm
Length	4245mm
Width	1735 mm
Height	1300 mm
Weight	1420 kg

PERFORMANCE

Top speed	270 kph
Power to weight ratio	5.2 kg/hp

911 Carrera 4 (993) 1995

With the 968 and 928 out of play and with the Boxster still to be launched, the determinate role to be played by a new generation of the 911 seemed clear: it was called the 993. If the task of the technicians and designers was difficult for the Carrera 2, it was even more so for the 4WD version, which had been the subject of much criticism both internally and by the motoring press. Speaking of the 964, Ulrich Bez said, "With its suspension mounted directly to the body shell, noise was terrible. And the 4x4 doesn't drive like a Porsche: it doesn't even go as well as a Mercedes 4-Matic: the faster one, especially on roads in bad condition".

So because of all that, the system was massively revised before the launch in 1995: this time, the car was based on a simple viscose disc coupling on the front differential and that, in turn, was redesigned to produce an overall weight saving of about 50 kg. The main objective was, indeed, to limit weight as well as to give the car a safer road behaviour, better mobility when exiting a corner, where the previous Carrera 4 was extremely lazy, and, in general, a better return from all the mechanics, with a minor loss in power. The gearbox was the new synchronised 6-speed with the 'box in light alloy, while the rear differential was self-locking and had ABD, an automatic braking system that intervened independently on the two wheels, simulating a further differential self-locking effect. The engine was the same as the Carrera 2's, but for 1996 it had 13 hp more due to the Varioram system of variable length aspiration ducts. That same year, out came the Targa bodied version with its roof in sliding glass and equipped as the Carrera 4S with the Turbo's body but with a normal extractable wing. And it would be a Carrera 4S Mexico Blue that was the last 993 to be built on 31 March 1998.

The modern lines of the 911 Turbo, the latest of the species, and air cooled. In 1997, a kit went on offer to take its power output to 430 hp and the top speed broke the 300 kph barrier, all priced at DM 235,000. In 1998, a 199 Turbo S went on offer in the American market with air intakes on the rear wing and the wheel housings.

TECHNICAL SPECIFICATION

ENGINE
Rear, overhanging, longitudinal
6 cylinders horizontally opposed

Bore and stroke	100 x 76.4 mm
Unitary cubic capacity	600 cc
Total cubic capacity	3600 cc
Valve gear	overhead camshaft, chain driven
Number of valves	2 per cylinder
Compression ratio	8.0:1
Fuel feed	electronic injection, bi-turbo
Ignition	dual, electronic
Coolant	forced air
Lubrication	dry sump
Maximum power	408 hp at 5750 rpm
Specific power	113.3 hp/litre

TRANSMISSION
4-WD

Clutch	dry mono-disc
Gearbox	en bloc with differential, 6 speeds plus reverse

CHASSIS
Unified steel structure

Front suspension	McPherson, lower arms, coil springs, hydraulic shock absorbers, stabiliser bar
Rear suspension	independent, multi-link layout, coil springs, shock absorbers, stabiliser bar
Brakes	disc, servo-brake, ABS
Steering	ZF rack, servo-assisted
Fuel tank	73 litres
Tyres front/rear	205/40 x 18/245/40 x 18

DIMENSIONS AND WEIGHT

Wheelbase	2272 mm
Track front/rear	1411/1504 mm
Length	4275 mm
Width	1795 MM
Height	1285 mm
Weight	1500 kg

PERFORMANCE

Top speed	290 kph
Power to weight ratio	3.6 kg/hp

911 Turbo (993) 1995

Unveiled in 1995 for the 1996 model year, the 911 Turbo series 993 embodied numerous new developments over the previous generation, starting with permanent 4WD. The 3.6-litre engine was derived from that of the aspirated Carrera unit, but the piston rods were more robust, the aspiration ducts bigger, the exhaust ones covered with Portliner ceramic to better dissipate head heat and the camshafts were also new. Fuel feed was by two turbochargers, one for each cylinder bank and each with its own intercooler: the two air masses were united before the throttle and the exhaust gas before the silencer. The Bosch Motronic M5.2 injection-ignition system had been improved. Power output jumped to 408 hp with a new and even more impressive torque of 540 Nm at 4500 rpm, value that meant the car needed a bigger clutch and a hydraulic servo-assistance system to lighten pedal load. In addition, it was decided to give the Turbo the Carrera 4 four-wheel drive system to better manage road performance. The 4TH, 5TH and 6TH ratios were lengthened and the gearbox had a more effective lubrication-cooling system. The differential was bladed self-locking, 25% in traction and 40% in deceleration, assisted by the electronic ABD system. The Turbo's chassis was reinforced in a number of areas – the modifications would be extended to other versions – the set-up was lowered and the rims with hollow spokes made using a new technology that meant a 30% weight saving. The brakes were self-ventilated discs and perforated with a servo-brake for each circuit. The Turbo body's Cx was reduced to ø.34 despite bigger front air intakes and the spoiler due to a better profiling of the bumpers and sills. And the lift was virtually nil on both axles.

The 911 GT2 EVO was the most extreme 993 and was prepared under GT1 class regulations, which permitted a 600 hp power output. It was lightened and made more powerful and derived from the rear-wheel drive 911 GT2; many more of them were built than the 25 cars needed for homologation, while only a small percentage of them stayed in road-going configuration (see illustration).

TECHNICAL SPECIFICATION

ENGINE
Rear, overhanging, longitudinal
6 cylinders horizontally opposed

Bore and stroke	100 x 76.4 mm
Unitary cubic capacity	600 cc
Total cubic capacity	3600 cc
Valve gear	overhead camshaft, chain driven
Number of valves	2 per cylinder
Compression ratio	8.0:1
Fuel feed	electronic injection, bi-turbo
Ignition	electronic
Coolant	forced air
Lubrication	dry sump
Maximum power	544 hp at 5750 rpm
Specific power	151.1 hp/litre

TRANSMISSION
Rear wheel drive

Clutch	dry mono-disc
Gearbox	en bloc with differential, 6 speeds plus reverse

CHASSIS
Unified steel structure

Front suspension	McPherson, lower arms, coil springs, hydraulic shock absorbers, stabiliser bar
Rear suspension	independent, multi-link layout, coil springs, shock absorbers, stabiliser bar
Brakes	disc, servo-brake, ABS
Steering	ZF rack
Fuel tank	100 litres
Tyres front/rear	265/640 x 18/340/670 x 18

DIMENSIONS AND WEIGHT

Wheelbase	2272 mm
Track front/rear	1411/1504 mm
Length	4275 mm
Width	1795 mm
Height	1285 mm
Weight	1150 kg

PERFORMANCE

Top speed	310 kph
Power to weight ratio	2.1 kg/hp

911 GT2 and 911 GT2 EVO 1995

Before the introduction of the 911 Turbo between 1994 and 1995, the 911 GT2 was developed to compete in the GT2 class of the BPR, so at Le Mans where this regulation was accepted. Compared to the Turbo, the most obvious modification was the elimination of front wheel drive, with traction coming out of the rear wheels. But the engine was similar, except for a different turbo pressure that took the car's power output to 430 hp. The racing version was given a TAG injection-ignition system and that increased output to over 450 hp on the racers, depending on the suction restrictions of the individual regulations. The production car had a dual-mass flywheel and a Bosch system for an overall weight of 1290 kg, while the racer stopped at 1150 kg with its roll bar, jacks to raise the car and a 100-litre safety fuel tank. The suspension was mounted on Unibal and could be adjusted in line with the Carrera Cup layout; rims were 18-inch and they hosted 380 mm disc brakes. The body stood out for its characteristic rear front deflector with upward curved ends and the rear wing in which there were two triangular air intakes in the pillars. Performance came close to that of the 959, with a top speed of 296 kph and a 0-100 kph speed of 4 seconds dead, with 0-200 kph in 13.3 seconds. In 1995, the Porsche entry succumbed to the McLarens and Ferraris in the top category, but it did well in GT2, so for the 1996 season out came the GT2 EVO, that respected GT1 regs: the restrictors were 40.4 mm, minimum weight 1150 kg and the bigger tyres – 265/645 x 18 front and 325/680 x 18 rear. Power output went up to more than 600 hp at 7000 rpm, partially achieved by increasing turbo pressure and, in a determinate way, substantially revising the whole engine. The body was lightened, substituting the metal panels with others in Kevlar and with more extreme aerodynamic devices.

After the 962-derivative Dauer-Porsche had won the 1994 24 Hours of Le Mans, the company also enjoyed success in 1996 and 1997 with a hybrid car, the chassis of which was TWR and the engine Porsche, all run by Joest Racing. The photograph shows Michele Alboreto, who shared the car with Tom Kristensen and Stefan Johansson, on his way to victory in the 1997 event.

TECHNICAL SPECIFICATION

ENGINE
Central, longitudinal
6 cylinders horizontally opposed

Bore and stroke	95 x 70.4 mm
Unitary cubic capacity	500 cc
Total cubic capacity	2994 cc
Valve gear	twin overhead camshafts, chain driven
Number of valves	4 per cylinder
Compression ratio	-
Fuel feed	electronic injection, bi-turbo
Ignition	electronic
Coolant	liquid
Lubrication	dry sump
Maximum power	540 hp at 7700 rpm
Specific power	180 hp/litre

TRANSMISSION
Rear wheel drive

Clutch	dry mono-disc
Gearbox	en bloc with differential, 5 speeds plus reverse

CHASSIS
Carbon fibre monocoque

Front suspension	independent, coil springs, hydraulic shock absorbers, stabiliser bar
Rear suspension	independent, coil springs, hydraulic shock absorbers, stabiliser bar
Brakes	disc
Steering	rack
Fuel tank	80 litres
Tyres front/rear	-

DIMENSIONS AND WEIGHT

Wheelbase	-
Length	-
Width	-
Height	-
Weight	890 kg

PERFORMANCE

Top speed	-
Power to weight ratio	1.6 kg/hp

TWR-Porsche WSC95   1995

To aim for victory in the IMSA series and the Le Mans, at the end of 1994, a "real" GT1 was needed. Chassis research soon led Porsche to Valparaiso, the American HQ of Tom Walkinshaw's TWR, linked to Jaguar. Two March chassis were bought from March for Jaguar in 1991 as they had already competed in the World Sports Car Championship powered by Cosworth engines and won with Jaguar, after which came Judd and Mazda engines. All considered, adapting the chassis to the Porsche 962 power unit was considered possible. So a project called WSC95 got under way in September 1994, with the monocoque in carbon fibre designed by Ross Brawn. The coupés were transformed into open tops, with a front wing – which was later removed due to the regulations, as was the shaped bottom with Venturi channels – a large rear wing and a prominent periscope air intake to chill the intercooler, as well as two further small periscope air vents to feed the turbocharger, "fringed" with 34.5 mm restrictors that limited power output to 540 hp. The first tests at Charlotte were worrying as were the preliminaries at Daytona, where the Ferrari 333SPs were 2-3 seconds faster. They believed Porsche was hiding the cars' real performance capability, with the IMSA judges penalising the WSC95 further with 32 mm restrictors for an output of 460 hp and 100 kg of ballast. There was nothing the TWR-Porsches could do: Horst Marchart deserted Daytona and Sebring and took the cars back to Weissach, where they were prepared for Le Mans. The adventure was interrupted when Porsche decided to build its own GT1; then Joest came forward and obtained two cars – in the case of victory, he would have "won" one. Three days in Weissach's wind tunnel showed up many problems, but in France, Reuter, Wurz and Jones dominated the 24 Hours. And the following year, Porsche's face was saved by the great victory of the Joest WSC95. Evolved for 1998 and name changed to LMP1 98, the car retired.

Only one road-going 911 GT1/96 was produced and subsequently completed, for 1996 and was sold for DM 1,500,000 as that was all that was needed for homologation, to which had to be added the two chassis for racing use. The appearance of the car tended to recall as much as possible the styling trends of the 911, of which the doors and optical groups front and back were retained.

TECHNICAL SPECIFICATION

ENGINE
Central, longitudinal
6 cylinders horizontally opposed

Bore and stroke	95 x 74.4 mm
Unitary cubic capacity	527.3 cc
Total cubic capacity	3164 cc
Valve gear	twin overhead camshafts, chain driven
Number of valves	4 per cylinder
Compression ratio	9.0:1
Fuel feed	electronic injection, bi-turbo
Ignition	electronic
Coolant	liquid
Lubrication	dry sump
Maximum power	600 hp at 7200 rpm
Specific power	187.5 hp/litre

TRANSMISSION
Rear wheel drive

Clutch	dry mono-disc
Gearbox	en bloc with differential, 6 speeds plus reverse

CHASSIS
Unified steel structure

Front suspension	double wishbones, Bilstein spring shock absorbers, stabiliser bar
Rear suspension	double wishbones, Bilstein spring shock absorbers, stabiliser bar
Brakes	disc, servo-brake
Steering	ZF rack
Fuel tank	100 litres
Tyres front/rear	27/68 x 18/30/70 x 18

DIMENSIONS AND WEIGHT

Wheelbase	2500 mm
Track front/rear	1380/1550 mm
Length	4683 mm
Width	1964 mm
Height	1173 mm
Weight	1050 kg

PERFORMANCE

Top speed	320 kph
Power to weight ratio	1.7 kg/hp

911 GT1 (993)   1996

At the start of the '90s, Porsche attention paid to the various GT categories assumed a greater relevance. They went after the various mono-marque championships as well as BPR and IMSA-GT. And it was the GT1 category that most attracted the attention of the Stuttgart directors, a category in which it was possible to compete for outright victory in the most famous races, with the 24 Hours of Le Mans at the top of the tree. The 911 GT1 project began with the 1996 season on the horizon and it was necessary to build a few road cars to obtain homologation, even if only a limited number. The starting point was the floorpan of the 911 993, but the ample concessions of the regulations permitted the company to create a real racing car. Everything superfluous was dispensed with and the car was given a roll bar cage that also acted as part of the chassis, while the body itself was made in composite materials, carbon fibre and Kevlar. Unusually, the engine was installed in a central-rear position and as a starting point its basis was that of the 3163 cc 911 Turbo S GT, which was adequate enough to adopt liquid cooling. The technological reasoning in this case was stronger than Porsche's consolidated tradition as far as air cooling went. The engine had two turbochargers with intercoolers, but as the car would also be competing against normally aspirated racers, two 37.5 mm-diameter suction limiters had to be used and they reduced the unit's maximum power output by 50 hp for a total of 600 hp at 7200 rpm, as against 544 hp for the road-going version. There was a manual 6-speed gearbox and pushrod layout for the suspension, carbon fibre disc brakes and an 1120 kg weight for the road goer, which was equipped with lights, heated rear view mirrors, a catalyser and equipment in line with the road code. The two 911 GT1s came second and fourth in the 1996 24 Hours of Le Mans, victory going to the TWR-Porsche WSC95.

This cut-away of the new Boxster shows the imposition of the mid-engine as well as many points in common with the 911 996, starting with the front end. Even if technically valid, transaxle cars were dropped in favour of a younger and more rational model able to increase sales and improve Porsche's image. It would become an icon.

TECHNICAL SPECIFICATION

ENGINE
Central, longitudinal
6 cylinders horizontally opposed

Bore and stroke	85.5 x 72 mm
Unitary cubic capacity	413.3 cc
Total cubic capacity	2480 cc
Valve gear	twin overhead camshafts, chain driven
Number of valves	4 per cylinder
Compression ratio	11:1
Fuel feed	electronic injection
Ignition	electronic
Coolant	liquid
Lubrication	dry sump
Maximum power	204 hp at 6000 rpm
Specific power	81 hp/litre

TRANSMISSION
Rear wheel drive

Clutch	dry mono-disc
Gearbox	en bloc with differential, 5 speeds plus reverse

CHASSIS
Unified steel structure

Front suspension	McPherson, lower arms, coil springs, hydraulic shock absorbers, stabilisers bar
Rear suspension	McPherson, lower arms, coil springs, hydraulic shock absorbers, stabilisers bar
Brakes	disc and servo-brake
Steering	ZF rack
Fuel tank	64 litres
Tyres front/rear	205/55 x 16/225/50 x 16

DIMENSIONS AND WEIGHT

Wheelbase	2415 mm
Track front/rear	1466/1527 mm
Length	4315 mm
Width	1778 mm
Height	1290 mm
Weight	1252 kg

PERFORMANCE

Top speed	245 kph
Power to weight ratio	6.13 kg/hp

Boxster   1996

With the 968 and 928 going out of production, in the early '90s the Porsche range was based solely on the 911, which was in need of deep revision, starting with the air cooled engine. After the flop of the 989, the idea of a new, smaller, more economical car than the 911 gathered ground, but one able to share many of the veteran's components to lower production costs. So at the 1993 Detroit Motor Show, an attractive concept car called the Boxster made its appearance (boxer plus roadster). The design was inspired by a number of styling trends typical of the marque, but with attention – as was stated at the time – to remain in touch with the concept of a light and lively roadster, which had led to the creation of the No. 1 in 1948. With lines only slightly simplified compared to the prototype, the definitive car was launched in 1996, a vehicle that posed as an entry level Porsche. The Boxster had the hard task of resolving the company's situation after a period of deep crisis, due in particular to the narrow profit margins determined by excessive production costs. So the car was designed in a more efficient manner, able to share many components with the 911 – including the entire front end, right through to the doors – and to be less expensively assembled at Zuffenhausen and the Finnish factory at Valmet Automotive. The consultancy provided by Toyota, which was initially received with diffidence, turned out to be fundamental in Porsche achieving its objectives. The Boxster was a mid-engined roadster, with a 6-cylinder, for the first time liquid cooled boxer unit with twin overhead camshafts and four valves per cylinder. Its weight was equally distributed on the two axles and its road behaviour was excellent. All that without sacrificing habitability or comfort. The power unit, which shared its structure with that of the 911 996, was a 2.5-litre with a 201 hp output and a top speed of 240 kph and a 0-100 kph time of 6.9 seconds.

The picture shows the 911 GT1/98 crewed by Laurent Aiello, Allan McNish and Stéphane Ortelli. At long last, the car was able to score Porsche's 16TH overall win in the 1998 24 Hours of Le Mans. The illustration is of the road-going 911 GT1/97 and, compared to its predecessor, had the new optical groups of the 996 to retain that family feeling of the rest of the range.

TECHNICAL SPECIFICATION

ENGINE
Central, longitudinal
6 cylinders horizontally opposed

Bore and stroke	95 x 74.4 mm
Unitary cubic capacity	527.3 cc
Total cubic capacity	3164 cc
Valve gear	twin overhead camshafts, chain driven
Number of valves	4 per cylinder
Compression ratio	9.0:1
Fuel feed	electronic injection, bi-turbo
Ignition	electronic
Coolant	liquid
Lubrication	dry sump
Maximum power	600 hp at 7200 rpm
Specific power	187.5 hp/litre

TRANSMISSION
Rear wheel drive

Clutch	3 carbon discs
Gearbox	en bloc with differential, 6 speeds plus reverse

CHASSIS
Carbon fibre monocoque

Front suspension	double overlapping wishbones, springs, Bilstein spring shock absorbers, stabiliser bar
Rear suspension	double overlapping wishbones, Bilstein spring shock absorbers, stabiliser bar
Brakes	disc, servo-brake
Steering	ZF rack
Fuel tank	100 litres
Tyres front/rear	265/645 x 18/305/645 x 18

DIMENSIONS AND WEIGHT

Wheelbase	2700 mm
Track front/rear	1460/1548 mm
Length	4980 mm
Width	1990 mm
Height	1140 mm
Weight	950 kg

PERFORMANCE

Top speed	330 kph
Power to weight ratio	1.5 kg/hp

911 GT1 (996)   1997

Losing the 1997 24 Hours of Le Mans was a searing disappointment for Porsche: the GT1 easily led the race until one was involved in an accident during the 16TH hour and the other went out in hour 21 with a broken oil radiator. As well as some detailed modifications, the 1997 car's body was updated with the 911 996's new, lengthened headlights as standard to maintain that family feeling. The 6-speed gearbox became sequential and the front track was widened, while the aerodynamics were perfected. But a completely new car was developed for 1998 and that car did score a 1-2 finish in the 1998 Le Mans. Weight was reduced by a new carbon fibre monocoque to weigh just 950 kg and, despite the reduction of the suction limiters' diameter by 1.8 mm, power output increased by 50 hp. A reduction in cubic capacity was considered at first and that would have allowed – given the curious FIA regulations – a power increase, but later that was taken to 3198 cc. The fuel tank was behind the cockpit, lengthening the wheelbase and producing a better profile of the rear end. The push rod front suspension had elongated triangles for an optimum geometry and were fixed directly to the monocoque, while the brakes had 6-piston callipers. After a series of wind tunnel test, the 911 GT1 took to the Weissach test track on 23 February 1998 with Bob Wollek at the wheel and he immediately judged it to be more of a racer than its predecessor. The initial races of the season weren't all that encouraging, but the declared objective was Le Mans: the two works cars finished first and second at the Sarthe, with the Aiello-McNish-Ortelli GT1 the winner and its sister car on its tail, driven by Müller-Wollek-Alzen. Twenty-one road cars were built in 1997 and six racers, but only one road goer and five racing cars came out in 1998, the regulations dictating that they had to be sold to privateers, in this case to Zakspeed.

For many purists the 996, with its newly-designed liquid cooled engine wasn't a real 911. It was most certainly a grand tourer that was fast and comfortable, in line with – if not ahead of – its time. Among its most discussed characteristics was the shape of the car's front optical groups that weren't circular but lengthened, including the side-lights and indicators.

TECHNICAL SPECIFICATION

ENGINE
Rear, overhanging, longitudinal
6 cylinders horizontally opposed

Bore and stroke	96 x 78 mm
Unitary cubic capacity	563 cc
Total cubic capacity	3387 cc
Valve gear	twin overhead camshafts, chain driven
Number of valves	4 per cylinder
Compression ratio	11.3:1
Fuel feed	Bosch electronic injection
Ignition	electronic
Coolant	liquid
Lubrication	dry sump
Maximum power	300 hp at 6800 rpm
Specific power	88.2 hp/litre

TRANSMISSION
Rear wheel drive

Clutch	dry mono-disc
Gearbox	en bloc with differential, 6 speeds plus reverse

CHASSIS
Unified steel structure

Front suspension	McPherson, lower arms, coil springs, hydraulic shock absorbers, stabiliser bar
Rear suspension	independent, multi-link layout, coil springs, hydraulic shock absorbers, stabiliser bar
Brakes	disc, servo-brake, ABS
Steering	ZF rack, servo-assisted
Fuel tank	65 litres
Tyres front/rear	205/55 x 17/255/40 x 17

DIMENSIONS AND WEIGHT

Wheelbase	2350 mm
Track front/rear	1455/1500 mm
Length	4430 mm
Width	1795 mm
Height	1305 mm
Weight	1320 kg

PERFORMANCE

Top speed	280 kph
Power to weight ratio	4.4 kg/hp

911 Carrera (996)   1998

For the first time, the body of the 911 was redesigned with the launch of the 996 series in 1998, but even with numerous and substantial evolutions the car had always remained the same since 1963. Outside, the body was more streamlined and tapered, the new interior more refined and richly equipped. The front optical groups were new and lengthened as on the Boxster, with which the 911 was developed. The car was 18.5 centimetres longer, 3 cm wider and its wheelbase was lengthened by 7.8 cm, all to the advantage of habitability and safety in case of an impact. At the same time, its weight had dropped by an impressive 50 kg compared to the 993 series, its torsional rigidity increased by 50% and its Cx was down to 0.30. The McPherson front suspension layout and rear multi-link were a repeat of the 993's, but with a perfected calibration and set-up, as well as wide use of light alloy. Another fundamental new development – enough to make the purists turn up their noses – was the installation of a liquid cooled 6-cylinder boxer engine with two radiators in the front. That had already been the case with the front engine Porsche, the Boxster and the company's racing cars, but never with a road-going 911. The modifications were made necessary by the ever increasing performance requested, but also to respect noise level norms that had come into force in the meantime. The engine was a 3387 cc 4-valves per cylinder with twin overhead camshafts with Variocam. Completely in aluminium, it had cylinder blocks in Lokasil with the sliding surfaces hardened by silicon. The 996 put out a maximum of 300 hp at 6800 rpm for a top speed of the Carrera 2 coupé of 280 kph. When it was launched, Coupé and Cabriolet versions were also on offer, the latter with an electric hood and an ejectable roll bar, a 6-speed manual gearbox or the new 5-speed Tiptronic. From 2000, it became available with optional Porsche Stability Management system.

The body of the 911 Carrera 4 could be told, in particular, by the front optical groups, in which the directional indicators had no orange glass but were completely grey with only the bulb coloured. The rears were in white-grey glass, where there was lettering on the engine cover and brake supports in a titanium colour. The engine was also the same as that of the 3.4 cc 300 hp Carrera.

TECHNICAL SPECIFICATION

ENGINE
Rear, overhanging, longitudinal
6 cylinders horizontally opposed

Bore and stroke	96 x 78 mm
Unitary cubic capacity	563 cc
Total cubic capacity	3387 cc
Valve gear	twin overhead camshafts, chain driven
Number of valves	4 per cylinder
Compression ratio	11.3:1
Fuel feed	Bosch electronic injection
Ignition	electronic
Coolant	liquid
Lubrication	dry sump
Maximum power	300 hp at 6800 rpm
Specific power	88.2 hp/litre

TRANSMISSION
Rear wheel drive

Clutch	dry mono-disc
Gearbox	en bloc with differential, 6 speeds plus reverse

CHASSIS
Unified steel structure

Front suspension	McPherson, lower arms, coil springs, hydraulic shock absorbers, stabiliser bar
Rear suspension	independent, multi-link layout, coil springs, hydraulic shock absorbers, stabiliser bar
Brakes	disc, servo-brake, ABS
Steering	ZF rack, servo-assisted
Fuel tank	65 litres
Tyres front/rear	205/55 x 17/225/40 x 17

DIMENSIONS AND WEIGHT

Wheelbase	2350 mm
Track front/rear	1455/1500 mm
Length	4430 mm
Width	1795 mm
Height	1305 mm
Weight	1375 kg

PERFORMANCE

Top speed	280 kph
Power to weight ratio	4.5 kg/hp

911 Carrera 4 (996)   1999

After the sensation of the 996 launch, its body redesigned and its engine liquid cooled, the great new development of the 1999 model year was the commercialisation of the new 911 Carrera 4, which took the place of the previous 993-based model. The engine was still the Carrera's, with rear wheel drive. Its 3.4-litres put out 300 hp and the only change was the adoption of an electronically controlled accelerator, which was needed to interact with the PSM electronic stability control and offered better fuel consumption and torque generation as it was able to optimise the throttle's opening. The car could be had with a 6-speed manual or a 5-speed Tiptronic S of ZF origin gearbox and also usable sequentially. If the 4WD system was conceptually inspired by that of the 993, with its viscose coupling integrated into a separate sump of the front differential, a new aspect was the uncovered cardan transmission shaft and not contained in a rigid tube. That made useful space in the central tunnel in which to fit the tubes that carries the cooling liquid to the front radiators. Another advantage was weight saving: in spite of the generous dimensions of the organs – management of superior power of the Turbo was planned – the weight increase compared to the Carrera was only 55 kg. Torque distribution to the two axles was variable: in normal conditions, only 5% of traction came from the front axle, but that could increase progressively to as much as 40% as the rear end begins to slide, both in cases of slippery surfaces and brusque acceleration. The chassis had the same suspension as the Carrera; it was just set up differently. An optional was a more rigid and sporty chassis. In 2000 a special Millennium series was produced with a sporty set-up and top equipment in a special violet-chrome colour for the body.

A 2003 version of the 911 GT3: the most obvious modification compared to the previous series was the replacement of the original bi-plane rear spoiler with a much simpler and sportier unit. At a slight disadvantage in daily use, in which the system was too rigid and the engine uncertain at low speeds, the GT3 was a valid starting point for motor sport elaboration.

TECHNICAL SPECIFICATION

ENGINE
Rear, overhanging, longitudinal
6 cylinders horizontally opposed

Bore and stroke	100 x 76.4 mm
Unitary cubic capacity	599.6 cc
Total cubic capacity	3598 cc
Valve gear	twin overhead camshafts, chain driven
Number of valves	4 per cylinder
Compression ratio	11.7:1
Fuel feed	Bosch electronic injection
Ignition	electronic
Coolant	liquid
Lubrication	dry sump
Maximum power	350 hp at 7200 rpm
Specific power	100 hp/litre

TRANSMISSION
Rear wheel drive

Clutch	dry mono-disc
Gearbox	en bloc with differential, 6 speeds plus reverse

CHASSIS
Unified steel structure

Front suspension	McPherson, lower arms, coil springs, hydraulic shock absorbers, stabiliser bar
Rear suspension	independent, multi-link layout, coil springs, hydraulic shock absorbers, stabiliser bar
Brakes	disc, servo-brake, ABS
Steering	ZF rack, servo-assisted
Fuel tank	89 litres
Tyres front/rear	225/40 x 18/285/30 x 18

DIMENSIONS AND WEIGHT
Wheelbase	2350 mm
Track front/rear	1475/1495
Length	4430 mm
Width	1765 mm
Height	1270mm
Weight	1350 mm

PERFORMANCE
Top speed	302 kph
Power to weight ratio	3.7 kg/hp

911 GT3   1999

Destined for racing but also homologated for road use, the 911 GT3 went into production at Zuffenhausen from May 1999. Its equipment was bleak and some technical decisions were decidedly of the racing type. The 6-cylinder engine was taken to 3.6-litre and with the GT1's crankshaft, Nikasil lined damp sleeves, piston rods in titanium, racing pistons, dry sump lubrication with a separate tank, a compression ratio of 11.7:1, timing, Variocam calibration and an optimised exhaust, the car put out 360 hp for a top speed of 302 kph and a 0-100 kph time of 4.8 seconds. The road-going version had a dual mass flywheel, while the Clubsport a rigid but lightened element; the gearbox was derived from that of the GT2. The differential was a bladed self-locking unit (40%-60%). The chassis was lowered 30 mm compared to the Carrera and the suspension was adjustable; the brakes were bigger and the decomposable wheels were 18-inch. The GT3's body was lightened, the 86-litre fuel tank occupied almost all of the boot, and that forced Porsche to adopt a repair kit as there was no space for the spare wheel. The seats were shell-shaped, could not be reclined and were 28 kg lighter. While a radio and air conditioning were optional, a Clubsport version was also available with a roll bar cage and racing equipment, including a fire extinguisher, seats with 6-point seat belts and a battery master switch. After a year's pause, in 2003 out came the 911 GT3 with an updated body to meet the new regulations introduced in 2002, and frontal optimisation with a 0.30 Cx and that had 21 hp more. Then out came the extreme GT3 RS, specifically developed for racing and equipped with carbon-ceramic brakes as standard. More effective than normal steel discs, these had the advantage of weighing a quarter of the normal and would become optional for the whole range. Only slighter improvements were made on the 2004 versions. In total, 4689 road-going 911 GT3s were produced between 1999 and 2004, to which those for motor racing should be added.

The Carrera GT was a true supercar, which was an heir to the 959 and, like its predecessor, it was to show the potential of the marque. Both were derived from motor racing and adopted the best technology had to offer. The breath-taking shape was by Harm Lagaay, who chose an open body to astonish the motoring world.

TECHNICAL SPECIFICATION

ENGINE
Central, longitudinal
68° V10

Bore and stroke	96 x 76 mm
Unitary cubic capacity	550 cc
Total cubic capacity	5500 cc
Valve gear	twin overhead camshafts, chain driven
Number of valves	4 per cylinder
Compression ratio	12:1
Fuel feed	electronic injection
Ignition	electronic
Coolant	liquid
Lubrication	dry sump
Maximum power	549 hp at 8000 rpm
Specific power	99.8 hp/litre

TRANSMISSION
Rear wheel drive

Clutch	dry mono-disc
Gearbox	en bloc with differential, 6 speeds plus reverse

CHASSIS
Monocoque in carbon fibre

Front suspension	double wishbones, coil springs, hydraulic shock absorbers, stabiliser bar
Rear suspension	double wishbones, coil springs, hydraulic shock absorbers, stabiliser bar
Brakes	disc, servo-brake
Steering	ZF rack
Fuel tank	90 litres
Tyres front/rear	265/30 x 19/335/30 x 20

DIMENSIONS AND WEIGHT

Wheelbase	2700 mm
Track front/rear	1620/1570 mm
Length	4556 mm
Width	1915 mm
Height	1192 mm
Weight	1380 kg

PERFORMANCE

Top speed	330 kph
Power to weight ratio	2.2 kg/hp

Carrera GT   2000

Presented at the 2000 Geneva Motor Show as a dream car, the prototype of the Carrera GT was so successful there that it pushed the Porsche management into designing a "real" car to offer the public as a "showdown". In reality, the roots of the decision go much farther back to motor racing: at the end of the '90s, after the 911 GT1 was put out of play by new regulations, Porsche brought out a new sports racer for the 24 Hours of Le Mans which, in turn, exhumed a V10 engine that had been secretly designed in 1992 for the Footwork F1 car and then dropped. This project was also deferred to concentrate on the emergent Cayenne, so it seemed everything was put on hold. Until the 2000 turnaround, that is. The cubic capacity of the V10 was taken to 5733 cc, which generated 612 hp at 8000 rpm. The transmission was rear wheel drive and entrusted to a 6-speed manual gearbox with a ceramic clutch. The chassis was a carbon fibre and composites monocoque, the suspension's double wishbone push rod and the brakes were carbon-ceramic. The body was a two-seater roadster with a mid-engine, could be closed off with a carbon fibre hard top that weighed just 2.5 kg born of the most advanced aerodynamic research. Just 1380 kg was the car's weight and its top speed was up there at 330 kph, with a 0-100 kph time of 3.9 seconds and could have broken the 200 kph barrier in seven seconds more. The Carrera GT's handling was impeccable having been sorted by ex-World Rally Champion Walter Röhrl and did not sacrifice reliability or comfort. Despite its prohibitive price of USD 440,000, the last car left the Leipzig factory on 6 May 2006 after Porsche had announced the previous August that production would be stopped before achieving the target of 1500 cars, due to new homologation norms in the USA. That 6 May car was the last of a total 1270 Carrera GTs to be produced.

The Boxster S distinguished itself from the basic model from the rear, with its double terminal central exhaust. At the front, the most obvious modification was the introduction of a central air intake in the bumper bar. The car had 17-inch rims with 18-inchers available on request. The front end was revised with larger air intakes in 2003. Inside, there was a three spoke sporty steering wheel, which was standard.

TECHNICAL SPECIFICATION

ENGINE

Central, longitudinal
6 cylinders horizontally opposed

Bore and stroke	93 x 78 mm
Unitary cubic capacity	529.8 cc
Total cubic capacity	3179 cc
Valve gear	twin overhead camshafts, chain driven
Number of valves	4 per cylinder
Compression ratio	11.0:1
Fuel feed	Bosch electronic injection
Ignition	electronic
Coolant	liquid
Lubrication	dry sump
Maximum power	249 hp at 6250 rpm
Specific power	77.8 hp/litre

TRANSMISSION

Rear wheel drive

Clutch	dry mono-disc
Gearbox	en bloc with differential, 6 speeds plus reverse

CHASSIS

Unified steel structure

Front suspension	McPherson, lower arms, coil springs, hydraulic shock absorbers, stabiliser bar
Rear suspension	McPherson, lower arms, coil springs, hydraulic shock absorbers, stabiliser bar
Brakes	disc, servo-brake, ABS
Steering	ZF rack, servo-assisted
Fuel tank	64 litres
Tyres front/rear	205/50 x 17/255/40 x 17

DIMENSIONS AND WEIGHT

Wheelbase	2415 mm
Track front/rear	1455/1508 mm
Length	4315
Width	1780 mm
Height	1290 mm
Weight	1295 kg

PERFORMANCE

Top speed	260 kph
Power to weight ratio	5.2 kg/hp

Boxster S   2000

While the cubic capacity of the Boxster was increased to 2.7-litres or 228 hp, the substantial and immediate sales success of the car in 2000 pushed Porsche into going ahead with a development of the car leading up to the Boxster S's launch. Initially, the newcomer was to be a 2.9-litre, but later the company opted for 3179 cc, which was obtained with a 93 mm bore, only 3 mm less than the 3.4 Carrera; that enabled the technicians to use the bigger sister car's head with larger valves. Compression ratio stood at 11:1 for a power output of 249 hp at 6250 rpm. The 6-speed manual gearbox- the automatic Tiptronic S was also available – now had sixth. To handle the increased power of about 25% over the Boxster, only the set-up was revised as it was lowered 15 mm and a bigger anti-roll bar was added. The brakes came from the Carrera and the car had 17-inch rims with 18-inchers optional. The more evident external modifications included the central twin exhaust terminal and internally a central air intake that fed the third radiator for the 3.2-litre engine: however, the new aperture had an effect on the Cx, which became worse at 0.32. Inside – the modifications were also extended to the Boxster – the quality of plastic was improved, replacing the shinier with the more pleasant soft touch material; the three-spoke steering wheel was standard. For two years, the Boxster S remained unchanged, but in 2003 it was given a real facelift, which was unveiled at Grottaferrata, near Rome: there was a new bumper shield from which protruded an air intake that was bigger and finned, an improved hood and a more efficient retractable rear spoiler; the lateral air intakes also protruded more and two rear exits were added. The engine was revised and was given the Variocam variable timing system and that took power output to 260 hp, with notable torque benefits. The set-up was also slightly revised, made more rigid and lowered 10 mm.

The new generation 911 Turbo dispensed with the extreme aesthetic aspects of the previous series. Designed by Pinky Lai, the 996 series Turbo was of slender and discreet lines despite the large air intake and the wheel housings' "muscles". A restyling of the front optical groups began with this model – they had always been one of the controversial elements of the 911 – which was later extended to the entire range.

TECHNICAL SPECIFICATION

ENGINE
Rear, overhanging, longitudinal
6 cylinders horizontally opposed

Bore and stroke	100 x 76.4
Unitary cubic capacity	599.6 cc
Total cubic capacity	3598 cc
Valve gear	twin overhead camshafts, chain driven
Number of valves	4 per cylinder
Compression ratio	9.4:1
Fuel feed	electronic injection, twin turbo
Ignition	electronic
Coolant	liquid
Lubrication	dry sump
Maximum power	420 hp at 6000 rpm
Specific power	116.6 hp/litre

TRANSMISSION
Rear wheel drive

Clutch	dry mono-disc
Gearbox	en bloc with differential, 6 speeds plus reverse

CHASSIS
Unified steel structure

Front suspension	McPherson, lower arms, coil springs, hydraulic shock absorbers, stabiliser bar
Rear suspension	independent, multi-link layout, coil springs, hydraulic shock absorbers, stabiliser bar
Brakes	disc, servo-brake, ABS
Steering	ZF rack, servo-assisted
Fuel tank	64 litres
Tyres front/rear	225/40 x 18/295/30 x 18

DIMENSIONS AND WEIGHT

Wheelbase	2350 mm
Track front/rear	1475/1495 mm
Length	4435w mm
Width	1830 mm
Height	1295 mm
Weight	1540 kg

PERFORMANCE

Top speed	305 kph
Power to weight ratio	3.6 kg/hp

911 Turbo (996) 2000

When the 996 series of the 911 Turbo was launched in 2000, it went to the top of the range for both its performance and equipment. It also had modified and recognisable lines: the flanks were leaner and flowing, with the large rear wheel housings widened but well integrated to the overall body design. Sporty touches were the two lateral air intakes just behind the doors, which carried air to the heat exchangers to be expelled down low, behind the rear wings. Then the rear was enhanced by an elegant spoiler that looked vaguely like a duck's tail and that became a servo-assisted bi-plane at over 120 kph, raising the upper part by 65 mm. The most distinctive area of the car was the whole front, where the bumper shield had two enormous lateral air intakes and a smaller one in the centre able to cool a radiating area that had gone up by 50% compared to the Carrera. The strongpoint of the 911 Turbo was its 3.6-litre engine with two turbochargers. It put out 420 hp at 6000 rpm, which testifies to the unit's refined construction: lubrication was by dry sump, the unit had eight main bearings, double valve springs and the Variocam Plus variable timing system, which also integrated a means of varying the raising of the valves (3 or 10 mm) via special hydraulic tappets, able to integrate with two special profile camshafts. The transmission was borrowed – with the appropriate modifications – from the Carrera 4's, as was the suspension, even if with a different set-up and layout lowered by 30 mm. The brakes were bigger – front discs 330 mm – with a DM 15,000 option of a PCCB system with carbon-ceramic discs that were 20 kg lighter. A more powerful 450 hp, 620 Nm torque version came out in 2004, called the Turbo S. And a 911 Turbo Cabriolet became available in both the power outputs, the chassis of which was only 70 kg heavier, despite it being more rigid than the Coupé's.

The 911 GT2 was also available in Club-sport form, which distinguished itself by having a more efficient, lighter rear wing for which carbon fibre was used; it had air intakes in its supports, as well as a roll bar bolted to the body and transformable into a cage with just a few modifications. The car's 462 hp could be brought to a standstill by the PCCB braking system with carbon ceramic discs.

TECHNICAL SPECIFICATION

ENGINE

Rear, overhanging, longitudinal
6 cylinders horizontally opposed

Bore and stroke	100 x 76.4 mm
Unitary cubic capacity	599.6 cc
Total cubic capacity	3598 cc
Valve gear	twin overhead camshafts, chain driven
Number of valves	4 per cylinder
Compression ratio	9.4:1
Fuel feed	electronic injection, twin-turbo
Ignition	electronic
Coolant	liquid
Lubrication	dry sump
Maximum power	462 hp at 5700 rpm
Specific power	128.3 hp/litre

TRANSMISSION

Rear wheel drive

Clutch	dry mono-disc
Gearbox	en bloc with differential, 6 speeds plus reverse

CHASSIS

Unified steel structure

Front suspension	McPherson, lower arms, coil springs, hydraulic shock absorbers, stabiliser bar
Rear suspension	independent, multi-link layout, coil springs, hydraulic shock absorbers, stabiliser bar
Brakes	disc, servo-brake, ABS
Steering	ZF rack, servo-assisted
Fuel tank	89 litres
Tyres front/rear	235/40 x 18/ 315/30 x 18

DIMENSIONS AND WEIGHT

Wheelbase	2355 mm
Track front/rear	1455/1495 mm
Length	4450 mm
Width	1830 mm
Height	1275 mm
Weight	1440 kg

PERFORMANCE

Top speed	315 kph
Power to weight ratio	3.1 kg/hp

911 GT2   2000

The 911 Turbo was a really fast and refined grand tourer, so for Porsche's racing customers the GT2 was developed, its performance superior to its road-going sister and with strictly rear wheel drive, although it could still be homologated for road use. The Turbo's engine was spiced up with a more effective fuel feed and turbocharging plus a modified exhaust system. So power output rose to 462 hp – it became 483 hp in 2004 – but without penalising fuel consumption to be in line with emission rules. The transmission was exclusively manual at 6 speeds, which was derived from that of the 993 series 911 GT2, modified with the GT3 lubrication method and an externally mounted water-oil exchange system. The ratios came from the 911 Turbo and the differential was 40% self-locking under acceleration and 60% in deceleration. Suspension was derived from the GT3, with a modified calibration in relation to the greater power output: the set-up was 70 mm lower than the normal Carrera. Brakes were the Porsche PCCB ceramic composites, which were standard equipment for the first time: discs were enlarged to 350 mm and the mono-block 6-pot callipers with six pumps meant the car could use modified pads, which gave 40% more friction surface. The ABS was the sporty version of the GT3, but PSM was not available. Externally, the GT2 had a new front bumper shield with optimised air intakes and a profile that was able to reduce lift. For that reason, the air that passed through the central radiator was made to blow upwards through a vent before the engine compartment, in a low pressure area. There was a new wing at the rear with air intakes in the pillars. The cockpit was simplified and the absence of the back bench meant a 28 kg weight saving for a 1440 kg total. And the Clubsport was also available with a lightened racing set-up and roll bar.

For Porsche, it was an audacious project essential to the company's survival: but in just a few years, the Cayenne became one of the most liked of vehicles for its design and performance. The project was known as the E1 in development, after which various names were suggested, like Colorado, Verera, Roxster and even Bugatti. Initially meant for Bratislava production, that was later switched to Leipzig.

TECHNICAL SPECIFICATION

ENGINE
Front, longitudinal, V8

Bore and stroke	93 x 83 mm
Unitary cubic capacity	563.8 cc
Total cubic capacity	4511 cc
Valve gear	twin overhead camshafts, chain driven
Number of valves	4 per cylinder
Compression ratio	11.5:1
Fuel feed	electronic injection
Ignition	electronic
Coolant	liquid
Lubrication	dry sump
Maximum power	340 hp at 6000 rpm
Specific power	75.5 hp/litre

TRANSMISSION
4WD

Clutch	-
Gearbox	en bloc with engine, automatic at 6 speeds plus reverse

CHASSIS
Unified steel structure

Front suspension	quadrilaterals, air springs, electronically controlled shock absorbers, stabiliser bar
Rear suspension	multi-link, air springs, electronically controlled shock absorbers, stabiliser bar
Brakes	disc, servo-brake, ABS
Steering	ZF rack, servo-assisted
Fuel tank	100 litres
Tyres front/rear	255/55 x 18

DIMENSIONS AND WEIGHT
Wheelbase	2855
Track front/rear	1647/1662 mm
Length	4786 mm
Width	1928 mm
Height	1699 mm
Weight	2355 kg

PERFORMANCE
Top speed	242 kph
Power to weight ratio	6.9 kg/hp

Cayenne S and Cayenne   2001

Porsche's third front was opened up in 2001 with a literal revolution: the company's new Cayenne was a five door SUV. The decision to go ahead with the project was an audacious but necessary one to broaden its horizons as an independent manufacturer and not become the marketing sector of some colossal of the industry, as MD Wendelin Wiedeking put it. In fact, a project for a Porsche "Range Rover" had already begun for the first time in the early '70s and taken up again at other times. Finally, the decision to go ahead was taken in the '90s before arriving at the definitive solution, although there were a number of attempts to reach agreement with other manufacturers to lower development and industrialisation costs, top of the list Mercedes-Benz which was having great success with its ML. The development of the Cayenne was not entirely Porsche's idea, as an agreement with Porsche's "cousin" VW was signed in 1998: The Cayenne and the VW Touareg – later the Audi Q7 – were born of a common floorpan. But the similarity between the two stopped at a number of transmission groups and part of the chassis. The engine, design, performance and personality were completely different: the Cayenne was a completely new car with a strong personality. It would become a status symbol and a sales success, linked with a record profit margin that exceeds 10% and became the company's cure-all. Almost five metres long, two wide and 1.7 high, heavy at 2.5 metric tons, the Cayenne is a luxurious SUV of outstanding design and high performance, but it is also an unexpectedly good off-roader. Soon after its launch, the press accused Porsche of over-engineering the car, having designed – almost – a real off-road vehicle aimed at a clientele unlikely to leave asphalt roads in search of adventure. Unveiled in 2001, the Cayenne S is powered by a 4.5-litre V8 engine that produces 340 hp. To this was added a "basic" model in 2005 called simply the Cayenne, which has a 3.2-litre V6 unit capable of 250 hp and originated by VW.

The key distinguishing mark of the Cayenne Turbo is its front end, with the two larger lateral air intakes to chill the engine's two air-to-air intercoolers and the engine cover's two power bumps. The 450 hp put out by the V8 make the car the world's fastest SUV, a record that was underlined in 2002 with a power increase to generate 500 hp, enough to carry the car to 270 kph.

TECHNICAL SPECIFICATION

ENGINE
Front, longitudinal, V8

Bore and stroke	93 x 83 mm
Unitary cubic capacity	563.8 cc
Total cubic capacity	4511 cc
Valve gear	twin overhead camshafts, chain driven
Number of valves	4 per cylinder
Compression ratio	9.5:1
Fuel feed	electronic injection, bi-turbo
Ignition	electronic
Coolant	liquid
Lubrication	dry sump
Maximum power	450 hp at 6000 rpm
Specific power	99.7 hp/litre

TRANSMISSION
4WD

Clutch	-
Gearbox	en bloc with engine, automatic, 6 speeds and reverse

CHASSIS
Unified steel structure

Front suspension	quadrilaterals, air springs, electronically controlled shock absorbers, stabiliser bar
Rear suspension	multi-link, air springs, electronically controlled shock absorbers, stabiliser bar
Brakes	disc, servo-brake, ABS
Steering	ZF rack, servo-assisted
Fuel tank	100 litres
Tyres front/rear	255/55 x 18

DIMENSIONS AND WEIGHT

Wheelbase	2855 mm
Track front/rear	1647/1662 mm
Length	4786 mm
Width	1928 mm
Height	1699 mm
Weight	2355 kg

PERFORMANCE

Top speed	270 kph
Power to weight ratio	5.2 kg/hp

Cayenne Turbo　　　　　　　　2001

The top of the range 4.5-litre V8 Cayenne was given two IHI turbochargers with intercooler, after which it put out 450 hp at 6000 rpm. The engine was further evolved with forged pistons that were cooled by jets of oil, double valve exhaust springs and a refined exhaust manifold system. The turbochargers had integrated wastegate valves and operated by Bosch Motronic. A small reserve tank was created to lubricate the turbos and that was able to work in optimum manner, even at inclinations and stress typical of offroaders. The sump was designed with the same thought in mind -for extreme use. Given the performance and weight of the vehicle – the force demanded at top speed and maximum load was precisely double that required by the Boxster in the same conditions – the self-ventilated front discs were of 350 mm diameter and 34 mm thick, with mono-block 6-piston callipers of six pistons. The usual self-ventilated discs to improve cooling had to be dropped because in off-road use the perforations could retain stones or mud, damaging the system. The Cayenne's 4WD was electronically operated by Porsche Traction Management, which could distribute 100% of torque to both axles. The Turbo also had Porsche Active Suspension Management, which was optional on the S, and was a pneumatic suspension system integrated with the shock absorbers' electronic control and able to adapt itself to the differing terrain conditions and driving style. At the same time as an equipment update, the engine was revised in 2002 and its output went up to 500 hp for a top speed of 270 kph and a 0-100 kph time of 5.3 seconds; the brakes were made more powerful with 380 mm and 358 mm discs respectively. That improvement kit could also be bought in the aftermarket as part of the equipment programme for 14,760 euros, to which the cost of installation had to be added.

Thea bodies of the 911 range were updated for the 2002 model year, especially the front end where the criticised optical groups, nicknamed fried eggs, were replaced by halogens on the Turbo. And bi-xenon headlights were optional on all models. The front shield was revised, given bigger air intakes and the Cabriolet – as shown in this picture with the optional hardtop – had a heated rear window in glass that could be removed.

TECHNICAL SPECIFICATION

ENGINE
Rear, overhanging, longitudinal
6 cylinders horizontally opposed

Bore and stroke	96 x 82.8 mm
Unitary cubic capacity	599.3 cc
Total cubic capacity	3596 cc
Valve gear	twin overhead camshafts, chain driven
Number of valves	4 per cylinder
Compression ratio	11.3:1
Fuel feed	electronic injection
Ignition	electronic
Coolant	liquid
Lubrication	dry sump
Maximum power	320 hp at 6800 rpm
Specific power	88.8 hp/litre

TRANSMISSION
Rear wheel drive

Clutch	dry mono-disc
Gearbox	en bloc with differential, 6 speeds plus reverse

CHASSIS
Unified steel structure

Front suspension	McPherson, lower arms, coil springs, hydraulic shock absorbers, stabiliser bar
Rear suspension	independent, multi-link layout, coil springs, hydraulic shock absorbers, stabiliser bar
Brakes	disc, servo-brake, ABS
Steering	ZF rack, servo-assisted
Fuel tank	64 litres
Tyres front/rear	205/50 x 17/255/40 x 17

DIMENSIONS AND WEIGHT

Wheelbase	2350
Track front/rear	1465/1465 mm
Length	4430 mm
Width	1765 mm
Height	1305 mm
Weight	1345 kg

PERFORMANCE

Top speed	280 kph
Power to weight ratio	4.2 kg/hp

911 3.6 (996)   2002

The main mechanical new development of the 2002 911 range was the increase in cubic capacity to 3596 cc, achieved by augmenting the stroke to 82.8 mm. As a consequence, power output went up to 320 hp, in part due to the new connecting rods, pistons and the adoption of the VarioCam Plus system that varies timing and adjusts the rise of the valves through tappets that are able to "select" two possible cam profiles on the shaft. The system of "returnless" fuel feed was also new, permitting the avoidance of fuel vapours in the fuel tank. The 911s now respected the Euro3/D4 norm, which enjoyed fiscal benefits in some countries. The clutch and gearbox were unchanged, except for some strengthening work, given the greater engine torque. A Carrera 4S came out in 2002, the mechanics of which were those of the Carrera 4, but the body and chassis came from the Turbo; the set-up was lowered by 10 mm, brakes became more powerful and 18-inch rims were adopted, while the PSM stability control system was now standard as on the Carrera 4 and optional on the two-wheel drive. Outside, modifications were mainly made to the car's front end where, to a bumper shield slightly revised with bigger air intakes, the much criticised front optical groups – as per those of the Boxster, like all the front of the car – with more oval units of halogen technology. Bi-xenon lights were optional and derived from the 911 Turbo. The rear parking sensors ran along the bumpers. There were only minor changes to the interior. The 40 Year version's power output was increased to 345 hp in 2003 and was a limited series of only 1,963 of the Carrera 2, fitted out to commemorate the 1963 launch of the first 911. The improvement was mainly due to the engine's perfected fuel feed system and electronic management, with the additional responsibility of respecting the ever more restrictive emission norms. The power kit was later extended to the whole range.

The new Targa body made its debut in 2002, but only on the two-wheel drive Carrera; as with the 1996 993 series, the system was based on an all-glass roof group, of which the upper part could be opened and slid to the rear. Another new aspect was the introduction of a kind of pavilion roof, with the opportunity of taking off the whole rear window to obtain access to the boot.

TECHNICAL SPECIFICATION

ENGINE
Rear, overhanging, longitudinal
6 cylinders horizontally opposed

Bore and stroke	96 x 82.8 mm
Unitary cubic capacity	599.3 cc
Total cubic capacity	3596 cc
Valve gear	twin overhead camshafts, chain driven
Number of valves	4 per cylinder
Compression ratio	11.3:1
Fuel feed	electronic injection
Ignition	electronic
Coolant	liquid
Lubrication	dry sump
Maximum power	320 hp at 6800 rpm
Specific power	88.8 hp/litre

TRANSMISSION
Clutch	dry mono-disc
Gearbox	en bloc with differential, 6 speeds plus reverse

CHASSIS
Unified steel structure

Front suspension	McPherson, lower arms, coil springs, hydraulic shock absorbers, stabiliser bar
Rear suspension	independent, multi-link layout, coil springs, hydraulic shock absorbers, stabiliser bar
Brakes	disc, servo-brake, ABS
Steering	ZF rack, servo-assisted
Fuel tank	64 litres
Tyres front/rear	225/40 x 18/295/30 x 18

DIMENSIONS AND WEIGHT
Wheelbase	2350 mm
Track front/rear	1455/1475 mm
Length	4435 mm
Width	1830 mm
Height	1295 mm
Weight	1485 kg

PERFORMANCE
Top speed	280 kph
Power to weight ratio	4.6 kg/hp

911 Carrera Targa (996)　　　2002

Four years after the 911 Targa went out of production as the first to introduce a sliding glass roof, in 2002 out came the same body on the shell of the 911 996 as a two-wheel drive only. More than anything else, the designers plan was to correct the main defects of the previous series: excessive aerodynamic noise with the roof closed and the poor rigidity of the bodyshell, sufficient to make the body and the interior squeak. As far as the belt line, the car was the same as the coupé, but its windscreen was much more inclined. The whole roof group was fixed to an auxiliary frame that extended from the screen to the engine cover, ensuring all was perfectly rigid. The roof and the rear window were both in laminated glass that absorbed ultra-violet rays – the thickness was, respectively, 7.45 mm and 3.85 mm – and formed an uninterrupted 1.54 square metre transparent surface, with the exception of a crosspiece at the level of the central pillars. Pressing a button on the dashboard, the roof lowered itself and ran for 50 cm under the rear window, opening up a vast portion of "sky". At the front of the car there emerged a deflector to avoid excessive turbulence. There was also an electrically controlled small curtain for the sunroof, which was to protect those in the car from direct sunlight and the cold of winter. Another new aspect was access to the rear bench seat – where there were the emergency seats, in this case even smaller due to the presence of the sunroof – via the rear window, which opened electrically as if it were a small door, operated by a switch in the door compartment and with a remote control. The car was about 80 kg heavier than the coupé, although the declared performance was the same as the Cabriolet, but the centre of gravity was much higher, so the technicians fitted a bigger roll bar.

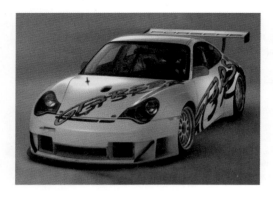

The illustration shows the 2003 911 GT3 RS road going car: it had a welded roll bar and a special body and a kit was provided by Porsche for sports preparation. In the photograph is the 2004 911 GT3 RSR in standard presentation livery. It was powered by a 445 hp engine, had a 6-speed sequential gearbox and a lightened body that weight 1,100 kg in running order with full tanks.

TECHNICAL SPECIFICATION

ENGINE
Rear, overhanging, longitudinal
6 cylinders horizontally opposed

Bore and stroke	100 x 76.4 mm
Unitary cubic capacity	599.6 mm
Total cubic capacity	3598 cc
Valve gear	twin overhead camshafts, chain driven
Number of valves	4 per cylinder
Compression ratio	11.7:1
Fuel feed	Bosch electronic injection
Ignition	electronic
Coolant	liquid
Lubrication	dry sump
Maximum power	381 hp at 7400 rpm
Specific power	105.8 hp/litre

TRANSMISSION
Rear wheel drive

Clutch	dry mono-disc
Gearbox	en bloc with differential, 6 speeds plus reverse

CHASSIS
Unified steel structure

Front suspension	McPherson, lower arms, coil springs, hydraulic shock absorbers, stabiliser bar
Rear suspension	independent, multi-link layout, coil springs, hydraulic shock absorbers, stabiliser bar
Brakes	disc, servo-brake, ABS
Steering	ZF rack, servo-assisted
Fuel tank	89 litres
Tyres front/rear	235/40 x 18/295/30 x 18

DIMENSIONS AND WEIGHT

Wheelbase	2355 mm
Track front/rear	1455/1488 mm
Length	4435 mm
Width	1770 mm
Height	1275 mm
Weight	1360 kg

PERFORMANCE

Top speed	306 kph
Power to weight ratio	3.5 kg/hp

911 GT3 RS and RSR
2003

Derived from the normal 911 GT3, the RS was for Grand Touring motor racing, in which the preparations in relation to production cars were reduced to a minimum, of which at least 25 had to be built for homologation purposes. With the GT3 RS, Porsche wanted to offer an almost ready version for racing, one that was able to fully exploit the opportunities offered by the regulations. As a result of a sportier preparation with the VarioCam system and the Motronic 7.8, revolutions per minute went up and so did the car's power output, which was now 381 hp at 7400 rpm. The clutch, with a dual-mass flywheel, and the gearbox were unchanged, even with specific ratios. Top speed was 306 kph and its 0-100 kph time 4.4 seconds. The brakes were more powerful with six pot mono-block callipers at the front, four at the rear and 350 mm discs front, 330 mm rear. The PCCB system with carbon-ceramic discs was optional. Set-up was lowered by 30 mm and the body lightened. The cooling flow was revised and at the front the hot air was directed upwards, where it exited from vents among the optical groups and the base of the windscreen, which also improved downforce by the new rear spoiler. The racing GT3 RSR was equipped in line with ACO30 regulations in 2004, permitting the car to compete at Le Mans, but kits were available to transform the car to FIA norms. The power output, often limited in races by fuel feed restrictors, were different depending on the category, increased to 445 hp with a racing clutch and a 6-speed sequential gearbox with straight tooth gearing and self-locking differential. The suspension retained the basic layout, but with redesigned racing components, as were the brakes with 380 mm discs front and 355 mm rear: carbon-ceramics were banned. The body's aerodynamics were heavily revised, as was safety and was lightened to 1,100 kg with a full fuel tank.

In the photograph is the Boxster S, marking 50 years of the 550 Spyder and displaying the 18-inch Carrera dual tone rims, which were also on the 911 40 Years Edition. The air intake grills along the flanks are metallic grey, as are the front optical group frames. The original twin exhaust terminal stands out at the rear with the two exits one on top of the other. The interior was also revised.

TECHNICAL SPECIFICATION

ENGINE

Central, longitudinal
6 cylinders horizontally opposed

Bore and stroke	93 x 78 mm
Unitary cubic capacity	529.8 cc
Total cubic capacity	3179 cc
Valve gear	twin overhead camshafts, chain driven
Number of valves	4 per cylinder
Compression ratio	11.0:1
Fuel feed	Bosch electronic injection
Ignition	electronic
Coolant	liquid
Lubrication	dry sump
Maximum power	265 hp at 6200 rpm
Specific power	82.8 hp/litre

TRANSMISSION

Rear wheel drive

Clutch	dry mono-disc
Gearbox	en bloc with differential, 6 speeds plus reverse

CHASSIS

Unified steel structure

Front suspension	McPherson, lower arms, coil springs, hydraulic shock absorbers, stabiliser bar
Rear suspension	McPherson, lower arms, coil springs, hydraulic shock absorbers, stabiliser bar
Brakes	disc, servo-brake, ABS
Steering	ZF rack, servo-assisted
Fuel tank	64 litres
Tyres front/rear	225/40 x 18/265/35 x 18

DIMENSIONS AND WEIGHT

Wheelbase	2415 mm
Track front/rear	1455/1514 mm
Length	4320 mm
Width	1780 mm
Height	1280 mm
Weight	1320 kg

PERFORMANCE

Top speed	266 kph
Power to weight ratio	4.9 kg/hp

Boxster S 50 Years of the 550 Spyder   2004

A special series of the Boxster S was dedicated to the 50TH anniversary of the 550 Spyder. A total of 1,953 units of the new car were produced to coincide with the 1953 launch of the 550 Spyder. The body was in the Carrera GT's silver grey rims were 18-inch dual colour light alloy rims as on the Carrera with the Porsche logo set into the centre. They were the same as those on the 911 40 Years, another 2004 newcomer to commemorate 40 years of Stuttgart's symbolic model, which also shared like coloured aspects with the Boxster details including the lateral grills of the air intakes, the front optical group frames and the brake callipers. The hood was also new in the exclusive cacao colour, the same as the leather interior and the and the carpeting material; but they were also available in the more conventional black with dark grey leather. The much detailed interior shared the same colour as the body, the central tunnel and the rear seat material. On the dashboard was a commemorative badge on which featured the car's celebratory serial number. The new twin terminal exhaust terminals at the rear were clear to see as they were on top of e ach other which, as well as their characteristic shape, were developed to provide a special sound. Mechanically, the 3.2-litre engine was taken from 260 hp to 266 hp and torque increased to 310 Nm at 4600 rpm: top speed was 266 kph at 6200 rpm with a 0-100 kph time of 5.7 seconds. The 6-speed manual gearbox had ratios that were shortened by 15% for greater liveliness, although the car was also available with a Tiptronic S 'box with steering wheel controls, but that reduced top speed to 264 kph and the 0-100 kph time went up to 6.4 seconds. The set-up was revised and lowered 10 mm, while the track was widened by 5 mm. There were 4-pot mono-block callipers with four pumping units for the brakes, the front discs were 318 mm and the rears 299 mm. Standard equipment included Litronic headlights, an on-board computer and PSM stability control.

The oval shaped optical groups made their comeback in 2004 on the 911 997 series, even if they seemed to be round when seen from the front. This follows bitter criticism of the lengthened lights of the 996. Now, sidelights and indicators were in two small groups sunken into the front bumpers. The rear design and interior were also new.

TECHNICAL SPECIFICATION

ENGINE
Rear, overhanging, longitudinal
6 cylinders horizontally opposed

Bore and stroke	96 x 82.8 mm
Unitary cubic capacity	599.6 cc
Total cubic capacity	3596 cc
Valve gear	twin overhead camshafts, chain driven
Number of valves	4 per cylinder
Compression ratio	11.3:1
Fuel feed	Bosch electronic injection
Ignition	electronic
Coolant	liquid
Lubrication	dry sump
Maximum power	325 hp at 6800 rpm
Specific power	90.2 hp/litre

TRANSMISSION
Rear wheel drive

Clutch	dry mono-disc
Gearbox	en bloc with differential, 6 speeds plus reverse

CHASSIS
Unified steel structure

Front suspension	McPherson, lower arms, coil springs, hydraulic shock absorbers, stabiliser bar
Rear suspension	independent, multi-link layout, coil springs, hydraulic shock absorbers, stabiliser bar
Brakes	disc, servo-brake, ABS
Steering	ZF rack, servo-assisted
Fuel tank	64 litres
Tyres front/rear	235/40 x 18/265/40 x 18

DIMENSIONS AND WEIGHT

Wheelbase	2360 mm
Track front/rear	1486/1534 mm
Length	4427 mm
Width	1808 mm
Height	1310 mm
Weight	1395 kg

PERFORMANCE

Top speed	285 kph
Power to weight ratio	4.2 kg/hp

911 Carrera and Carrera S (997)   2004

Introduced in 1963, the continual evolution of the 911 continued in 2004 with the launch of the 997. Better aerodynamics took the Cx down to 0.28, a record for Porsche, which compensated for the slightly larger front end, in part due to a slightly wider track. To reduce weight, the doors were made of light alloy as was the boot lid and that enabled the company to limit the car's weight to a little over that of the previous model while substantially improving the body shell's passive resistance. Inside, habitability had been improved with sportier and better profiled seats that were lowered 10 mm. Instrumentation was updated as was safety, which now included lateral airbags and the curtain-type in the doors. Only the Carrera of the 997 range was presented at first, with its two-wheel drive and a power output of 325 hp, together with the Carrera S, powered by a new version of the 6-cylinder boxer taken to 3.8 litres for 355 hp. Both were offered in Coupé and Cabriolet versions. If the 3.6 was practically unchanged in respect of the previous series. The increase in cubic capacity of the 3.8 was achieved with a bore increased to 99 mm to generate a cubic capacity of 3824.2 hp; due to the use of 98 octane fuel and anti-detonation sensors, the compression ratio was 11.8:1 and power increased by 30 hp, as did torque, which went up to 400 Nm at 4600 rpm. Both the manual 6-speed gearbox and the Tiptronic S became more robust even though with unchanged rations. The suspension was revised and the track widened, while the brakes were given discs that were 330 mm thicker. Carrera rims were 18-inch, the Carrera S 19 inch. The entire 997 series was unveiled at the 2006 Geneva Motor Show, where the Carrera S became available with a new 3.8-litre engine the power of which was increased to 381 hp for a top speed of 300 kph.

The second generation Boxster had a much revised body which, especially at the front, recalled many of the Carrera GT's styling aspects, breaking away from those of the 911, of which it retained only the doors and rear vision mirrors. Around 80% of the new car's components were new, and the code-type gearbox also became the 587.

TECHNICAL SPECIFICATION

ENGINE
Central, longitudinal
6 cylinders horizontally opposed

Bore and stroke	85.5 x 78 mm
Unitary cubic capacity	447.8 cc
Total cubic capacity	2687 cc
Valve gear	twin overhead camshafts, chain driven
Numbers of valves	4 per cylinder
Compression ratio	11.1:1
Fuel feed	Bosch electronic injection
Ignition	electronic
Coolant	liquid
Lubrication	dry sump
Maximum power	240 hp at 6400 rpm
Specific power	88.5 hp/litre

TRANSMISSION
Rear wheel drive

Clutch	dry mono-disc
Gearbox	en bloc with differential, 5 speeds plus reverse

CHASSIS
Unified steel structure

Front suspension	McPherson, lower arms, coil springs, hydraulic shock absorbers, stabiliser bar
Rear suspension	McPherson, lower arms, coil springs, hydraulic shock absorbers, stabiliser bar
Brakes	disc, servo-brake, ABS
Steering	ZF rack, servo-assisted
Fuel tank	64 litres
Tyres front/rear	205/55 x 17/235/50 x 17

DIMENSIONS AND WEIGHT

Wheelbase	2415 mm
Track front/rear	1490/1534 mm
Length	4329 mm
Width	1801 mm
Height	1295 mm
Weight	1370 kg

PERFORMANCE

Top speed	256 kph
Power to weight ratio	5.7 kg/hp

Boxster and Boxster S (MY 2005)   2004

At the Paris Motor Show in September 2004, the second generation of the Boxster and Boxster S made their debut for the 2005 model year. Both engines had the same cubic capacity, but with power output increased to 240 hp for the Boxster's 2.7-litre and 280 hp for the 3.2-litre S. As a result, top speed went up to 268 and 256 kph. As well as modifications to the exhaust and the electronics, the main new development was the use of the VarioCam system. The chassis was updated while maintaining the same basic layout: carbon-ceramic brakes were available as an option, but the PSM stability control was standard. The body, which boasted of an excellent 0.29 Cx, was revised at the front with oval headlights, bigger air intakes at the sides and at the rear of different design. The interiors were also redesigned and were now more similar to the 911's and the same for both versions, although the Boxster S could always be recognised by its double exhaust terminal and 18-inch rims. In 2007, the power output of the 2.7-litre went up by 5 hp with the VarioCam Plus, while the Boxster S was given a 295 hp,3.4-litre engine that would accelerate from 0-100 kph in 5.4 seconds and top 272 kph. A final facelift came out for 2009 with slight modifications to the bumpers, exhausts and rear vision mirrors, which were bigger and in line with recent new norms. From the mechanical point of view, the 3.4-litre Boxster S was given direct fuel injection, taking its power output to 310 hp. The "old" 2.7-litre Boxster, which now had a third front air intake like the S, went on to a new 2.9-litre that generated 255 hp and spec to 263 kph. Both cars manual gearboxes were now 6-speed, but the brand new PDK automatic with double clutch also became available to take the place of the Tiptronic S. Initially, the selection of ratios could be made through special rocker switches on the steering wheel, but in 2010 they were replaced by a gearbox that had the more traditional paddles.

The RS Spyder defended Porsche's colours in both Europe and the United States from 2006 to 2010 in the LMP2 class of the Le Mans Championship and the American Le Mans Series. In 2012, the company announced it would build a new car able to compete for victory at the Sarthe: it would eventually be Porsche's 17TH victory in the French marathon. The last in 1998 was with the 911 GT1.

TECHNICAL SPECIFICATION

ENGINE
Central, longitudinal
90° V8

Bore and stroke	100 x 76.4 mm
Unitary cubic capacity	420.8 cc
Total cubic capacity	3397 cc
Valve gear	twin overhead camshafts, chain driven
Number of valves	4 per cylinder
Compression ratio	-
Fuel feed	electronic injection
Ignition	electronic
Coolant	liquid
Lubrication	dry sump
Maximum power	503 hp at 10,300 rpm
Specific power	148 hp/litre

TRANSMISSION
Rear wheel drive

Clutch	dry mono-disc
Gearbox	en bloc with differential, 6 speeds plus reverse

CHASSIS
Carbon fibre monocoque

Front suspension	double wishbone, torsion bars, gas shock absorbers, stabiliser bar
Rear suspension	double wishbone, torsion bars, gas shock absorbers. stabiliser bar
Brakes	carbon-ceramic discs
Steering	servo-assisted rack
Fuel tank	89 litres
Tyres front/rear	20/65 x 18/31/71 x 18

DIMENSIONS AND WEIGHT

Wheelbase	-
Track front/rear	-
Length	4650 mm
Width	2000 mm
Height	1068 mm
Weight	775 kg

PERFORMANCE

Top speed	329 kph
Power to weight ratio	0.65 kg/hp

RS Spyder   2005

After leaving the Le Mans Prototype category in 1999, Porsche marked its return to motor racing with a "real" sports racer in the last race in the 2005 American Le Mans Series at Laguna Seca, where the RS Spyder won the cadet LMP2 class – but apart from the car's power output and weight the Porsche was similar to LMP1 in which it competed for outright victory. The chassis of the RS Spyder was a monocoque in Carbon Fibre Reinforced Plastic, as was the body with honeycomb and aluminium inserts with an overall weight of 775 kg produced with Carbotech. The engine, with a sequential gearbox that played a weight bearing role, was a new V8 with 90° cylinder banks of 3.4-litres that put out 480 hp, an output limited by a 44 mm suction flange. A carbon fibre structure fixed to the gearbox sustained the push rod rear suspension, with a minimum weight fixed at 775 kg and a fuel tank of 90 litres. The engine was updated in 2007 and power output went up to 503 hp, while in 2008 the reduction of the flange meant a power output of 476 hp, although mid-season the car's power went up to 503 hp again with direct injection, which actually reduced fuel consumption; but it increased the car's weight to 800 kg for the ALMS Championship and 825 kg in the LMS, in which the fuel tank capacity was reduced to 80 litres. In 2009, the ALMS demanded a reduction in wing width from 200 cm to 160 cm to limit performance. The RS Spyder won its class in the ALMS Championship in 2006, 2007 and 2008, when it also competed in Europe's Le Mans Series and it won the LMP2 category of the 24 Hours of Le Mans for two consecutive years. But the car's golden year was 2008, when Bernhard-Dumas-Collard won the 12 Hours of Sebring outright, seeing off fearful competition from the LMP1 cars – the Audi R10 TDI and the Peugeot 908 HDI FAP. The RS Spyder's last season was in 2010 ALMS only, in which it had come second in its class by the end of the championship.

After the launch of the two-wheel drive series 997 of the 911, the 996-based Carrera 4s were still on sale with 996 specifics, but finally the new versions were unveiled in 2005. A perfected Targa body also made a comeback and was the first with 4WD.

TECHNICAL SPECIFICATION

ENGINE

Rear, overhanging, longitudinal
6 cylinders horizontally opposed

Bore and stroke	99 x 82.8 mm
Unitary cubic capacity	637.3 cc
Total cubic capacity	3824 cc
Valve gear	twin overhead camshafts, chain driven
Number of valves	4 per cylinder
Compression ratio	11.8:1
Fuel feed	Bosch electronic injection
Ignition	electronic
Coolant	liquid
Lubrication	dry sump
Maximum power	355 hp at 6600 rpm
Specific power	93.4 hp/litre

TRANSMISSION

4WD

Clutch	dry mono-disc
Gearbox	en bloc with differential, 6 speeds plus reverse

CHASSIS

Unified steel structure

Front suspension	McPherson, lower arms, coil springs, hydraulic shock absorbers, stabiliser bar
Rear suspension	independent, multi-link layout, coil springs, hydraulic shock absorbers, stabiliser bar
Brakes	disc, servo-brake, ABS
Steering	ZF rack, servo-assisted
Fuel tank	64 litres
Tyres front/rear	235/35 x 19/305/30 x 19

DIMENSIONS AND WEIGHT

Wheelbase	2360 mm
Track front/rear	1486/1534 mm
Length	4427 mm
Width	1808 mm
Height	1300 mm
Weight	1475 kg

PERFORMANCE

Top speed	288 kph
Power to weight ratio	4.1 kg/hp

911 Carrera 4 and Carrera 4S (997)   2005

A year after the launch of the two rear wheel drive 997 911s, the range was expanded with the arrival of 4WD models, the Carrera 4 and the Carrera 4S. The rear track of the Carrera 4s was 14 mm wider, the front just 2 mm more so, as they had to accommodate 295/35ZR18 tyres compared to the Carrera's smaller 265/40ZR18s. That meant the rear wheel housings had to be widened by 44 mm, giving the car a much more aggressive appearance, but also worsening the Cx quite a lot, as it went from 0.28 to 0.30. The engine was the same liquid-cooled 6-cylinder inherited from the 996 and that could put out 325 hp. Due to the negative aerodynamic effect, the car's top speed dropped from 285 to 280 kph. With the exception of the 4WD system, the Carrera 4S shared the Carrera S's mechanics and had a new 6-cylinder, 3.8-litre boxer that generated 355 hp. Both were offered in Coupé and Cabriolet versions, but in 2007 out came the Targa, which was exclusively 4WD. As with the previous Targa, the roof was made up of two laminated glass panels, of which the centre one could slide back and the one at the rear by compass as if it were a small hatchback. The design had been much improved, with the window frames extending back as far as the engine cover. The car weighed 115 kg more than the coupé and that lowered performance. Both the 6-speed manual gearbox and the Tiptronic S automatic were made more robust, while the brakes now had discs that were 330 mm thicker. On the suspension front, there were two, one that was "passive" and the other that could be adjusted with PASM. The rims were 18 inches in diameter with 19-inch for the Carrera 4 S, which was also available with a new 3.8-litre, 381 hp engine that took the car's top speed to 288 kph.

The Cayman was the first "small" coupé to be produced by Porsche after the front engine 968 left the scene. The chassis was derived from the second generation Boxster's, while the body was different at the rear and the upper area, where the canvas hood was replaced by a rigid, tapered roof group able to take the body shell's torsional rigidity to a level of excellence.

TECHNICAL SPECIFICATION

ENGINE
Central, longitudinal
6 cylinders horizontally opposed

Bore and stroke	96 x 78 mm
Unitary cubic capacity	564.5 cc
Total cubic capacity	3387 cc
Valve gear	twin overhead camshafts, chain driven
Compression ratio	11.1:1
Number of valves	4 per cylinder
Fuel feed	Bosch electronic injection
Ignition	electronic
Coolant	liquid
Lubrication	dry sump
Maximum power	295 hp at 6250 rpm
Specific power	86.7 hp/litre

TRANSMISSION
Rear wheel drive

Clutch	dry mono-disc
Gearbox	en bloc with differential, 6 speeds plus reverse

CHASSIS
Unified steel structure

Front suspension	McPherson, lower arms, coil springs, hydraulic shock absorbers, stabiliser bar
Rear suspension	McPherson, lower arms, coil springs, hydraulic shock absorbers, stabiliser bar
Brakes	disc, servo-brake, ABS
Steering	ZF rack, servo-assisted
Fuel tank	65 litres
Tyres front/rear	235/40 x 18/265/40 x 18

DIMENSIONS AND WEIGHT

Wheelbase	2415 mm
Track front/rear	1486/1528 mm
Length	4341 mm
Width	1801 mm
Height	1305 mm
Weight	1415 kg

PERFORMANCE

Top speed	275 kph
Power to weight ratio	4.7 kg/hp

Cayman S   2005

Pictures and advance information about the new Porsche Cayman had been cir-
culating since May 2005, but to actually see the car enthusiasts had to wait until
the Frankfurt Motor Show in September of that year. The car went on sale in
2006 and was produced at Zuffenhausen and the company's Valmet Automotive
plant in Uusikaupunki, Finland. The Cayman was a two-seater coupé built on
the second generation Boxster 987's monocoque, with which it also shared the
interior, much of the body design – even if, as is often the case the modifications
were noticeable – and the mechanics. The greater torsional rigidity of the Cayman, achieve with its more rigid roof group, permitted a more precise suspension set-up and even better road behaviour. Like its open top cousin, as well as
the luggage compartment up front the new car had a rear "boot" just above the
engine. The first version was the Cayman S with its new, 3.4-litre, water cooled
6-cylinder boxer mid-engine that produced 295 hp at 6250 rpm. It was derived
from that of the 3.2 Boxster S unit, but with the VarioCam Plus variable valve
timing and adjustment system. Top speed was 272 kph and its standing start
0-100 kph time was 5.4 seconds, a performance that was not too far off the 911's,
which was often in difficulty on the handling front by its rear end weight, and
the perfect balance of the Cayman S. Specials were the Cayman S Porsche Design
Edition 1, of which 777 were produced with black bodies, interior in Alcàntara
and a case with objects including a Porsche Design chronograph; then there was
the Cayman S Sport in 2008 having been presented as a 2009 model year car of
which 700 were produced and had a sporting aspect plus a new exhaust that
took power output to 303 hp.

The GT3 version of the 997 had a 3.6-litre engine that put out 415 hp, which even exceeded the performance of the previous generation's GT3 Cup. Even quicker was the GT3 RS which could be homologated for road use, but offered a useful base for motor racing elaboration. The GT3 range was in continual evolution.

TECHNICAL SPECIFICATION

ENGINE
Rear, overhanging, longitudinal
6 cylinders horizontally opposed

Bore and stroke	100 x 76.4 mm
Unitary cubic capacity	600 cc
Total cubic capacity	3600 cc
Valve gear	twin overhead camshafts, chain driven
Number of valves	4 per cylinder
Compression ratio	12.0:1
Fuel feed	Bosch electronic injection
Ignition	electronic
Coolant	liquid
Lubrication	dry sump
Maximum power	415 hp at 7600 rpm
Specific power	115.2 hp/litre

TRANSMISSION
Rear wheel drive

Clutch	dry mono-disc
Gearbox	en bloc with differential, 6 speeds plus reverse

CHASSIS
Unified steel structure

Front suspension	McPherson, lower arms, coil springs, hydraulic shock absorbers, stabiliser bar
Rear suspension	independent, multi-link layout, coil springs, hydraulic shock absorbers, stabiliser bar
Brakes	disc, servo-brake, ABS
Steering	ZF rack, servo-assisted
Fuel tank	64 litres
Tyres front/rear	235/35 x 19/305/30 x 19

DIMENSIONS AND WEIGHT

Wheelbase	2360 mm
Track front/rear	1497/1558 mm
Length	4460 mm
Width	1852 mm
Height	1280 mm
Weight	1375 kg

PERFORMANCE

Top speed	310 kph
Power to weight ratio	3.3 kg/hp

911 GT3 and 911 GT3 RS   2006

The new generation 911 GT3 was launched at the Geneva Motor Show for the 2006 model year, even if a small number had been assembled for the 2005 Supercup Championship. The passing of time and the various categories in which the car would compete brought about a vast family of models, with characteristics that were often only slightly different from each other. The 3.6-litre engine no longer had the VarioCam Plus system that regulated the height of the valves, but did keep the variable valve timing method with a new variable aspiration system and exhaust. So maximum power output became 415 hp (115 hp per litre) with a maximum torque, which could be adjusted with the "Sport" button, of 405 Nm at 5500 rpm. The flywheel was dual-mass and the gearbox a manual 6-speed with reduced stroke and reinforced synchronisation. The set-up was revised with adjustable suspension and active PASM system shock absorbers, while the brakes were available with both steel discs with PCCB or carbon-ceramics. Rims were 19 inch. The body was lightened with aluminium doors, special bumpers, bigger miniskirts and a fixed rear wing. The Clubsport package also included shell-shaped seats, a roll bar, 6-point safety belts, a fire extinguisher and a battery disconnect switch. As well as the GT3, there was the GT3 RS, with sportier characteristics, but it could still be homologated for road use: the body was the Carrera 4's with its bigger wheel housings, although the engine was the same as the GT3's. The bi-mass flywheel was replaced by a lighter unit – with the exception of cars for the USA – that ensured a more violent accelerator response. The set-up was further perfected and lowered 30 mm compared to the Carrera, the track was wider and the wheelbase longer due to the split rear arms. The bumper shield had bigger air intakes and the rear wing was in carbon fibre. The body was further lightened with plastic components, the rear window in polycarbonate and the boot and engine covers were made of light alloy.

Only a few details distinguish the Cayman from its big sister, the Cayman S, and they included a single central exhaust plus lettering in titanium. Despite its 50 hp less, the car's performance was still lively, in part due to the extraordinary torsional and flexural rigidity of the body shell and the careful profiling of the body, all of which took its Cx down to an excellent 0.29.

TECHNICAL SPECIFICATION

ENGINE
Central, longitudinal
6 cylinders horizontally opposed

Bore and stroke	85.5 x 78 mm
Unitary cubic capacity	447.8 cc
Total cubic capacity	2687 cc
Valve gear	twin overhead camshafts, chain driven
Number of valves	4 per cylinder
Compression ratio	11.3:1
Fuel feed	Bosch electronic injection
Ignition	electronic
Coolant	liquid
Lubrication	dry sump
Maximum power	245 hp at 6500 rpm
Specific power	94.2 hp/litre

TRANSMISSION
Rear wheel drive

Clutch	dry mono-disc
Gearbox	en bloc with differential, 6 speeds plus reverse

CHASSIS
Unified steel structure

Front suspension	McPherson, lower arms, coil springs, hydraulic shock absorbers, stabiliser bar
Rear suspension	McPherson, lower arms, coil springs, hydraulic shock absorbers, stabiliser bar
Brakes	disc, servo-brake, ABS
Steering	ZF rack, servo-assisted
Fuel tank	65 litres
Tyres front/rear	205/55 x 17/235/50 x 17

DIMENSIONS AND WEIGHT

Wheelbase	2415 mm
Track front/rear	1490/1534 mm
Length	4341 mm
Width	1801 mm
Height	1305 mm
Weight	1330 kg

PERFORMANCE

Top speed	260 kph
Power to weight ratio	5.4 kg/hp

Cayman   2006

With a strategy that was not so widespread, Porsche launched the Cayman S in 2005 with the intention of bringing out an entry level version later. The car was simply called the Cayman and was unveiled in 2006, powered by a water cooled 6-cylinder, 2.7-litre boxer engine that put out 245 hp at 6500 rpm with a torque of 273 Nm at between 4600 and 6000 rpm. It had variable timing and adjustment of the valve lift by VarioCam Plus, which had already been used on the Boxster. The engine could only be accessed in the workshop, but it was possible to top up the oil and water through two pipe mouths at the base of the boot. There were three options available for the transmission, as the Cayman could accommodate a 5-speed manual gearbox as standard that took it from 0-100 kph in 6.1 seconds and a top speed of 258 kph. The optionals were a 6-aspeed derived from the Cayman S returning a maximum of 260 kph with the same 0-100 kph acceleration with better ratios for a livelier drive, and a Tiptronic S with a torque converter, which would take the car to 253 max and 0-100 kph in 7 seconds dead. The braking system was the same as that of the Cayman S, while the suspension could have the PASM system as optional. Externally, there was not a lot of difference between the Cayman and the S; the light alloy rims with split spokes were 17-inch, the brake callipers were painted black, the lettering was in titanium colour, the black "lips" around the front spoiler and the oval shaped central exhaust terminal – those were the main differences. The body turned in a Cx of 0.29 and practical needs were not forgotten: ahead of the front axle there was a 150-litre boot and there was another behind the rear axle of 260 litres.

The 4-litre GT3 RSR for the 2012 season. The starting point was the GT3 road car, but considerable elaboration turned it into a real racer. The range also included the GT3 R, which was fielded as a GT3, while the RSR competed in the GT2 category: the difference in modification was reflected in the price of the two cars – 304,000 euros for the R and 498,000 euros for the RSR.

TECHNICAL SPECIFICATION

ENGINE
Rear, overhanging, longitudinal
6 cylinders horizontally opposed

Bore and stroke	102 x 76.4 mm
Unitary cubic capacity	632.5 cc
Total cubic capacity	3795 cc
Valve gear	twin overhead camshafts, chain driven
Number of valves	4 per cylinder
Compression ratio	14.5:1
Fuel feed	electronic injection
Ignition	electronic
Coolant	liquid
Lubrication	dry sump
Maximum power	485 hp at 8500 rpm
Specific power	127.6 hp/litre

TRANSMISSION
Rear wheel drive

Clutch	dry mono-disc
Gearbox	en bloc with differential, 6 speeds plus reverse

CHASSIS
Unified steel structure

Front suspension	McPherson, lower arms, coil springs, hydraulic shock absorbers, stabiliser bar
Rear suspension	independent, multi-link layout, coil springs, hydraulic shock absorbers, stabiliser bar
Brakes	disc, servo-brake, ABS
Steering	ZF rack
Fuel tank	100 litres
Tyres front/rear	27/65 x 18/31/71 x 18

DIMENSIONS AND WEIGHT
Wheelbase	2350
Track front/rear	1569/1620 mm
Length	4439 mm
Width	1852 mm
Height	1250 mm
Weight	1120 kg

PERFORMANCE
Top speed	-
Power to weight ratio	2.7 kg/hp

911 GT3 RSR and GT3 RSR 4.0   2006

A real racing car developed on the basis of the 911 was introduced in the summer of 2006, after the racing versions of the 997 series GT3 like the GT3 Cup and the Supercup, raced exclusively in mono-marque championships, which were sports preparations in accordance with the regulations of each formula. It was called the GT3 RSR, its body that of the Carrera 4 with widened wheel housings and increased rigidity due to the 10% more welded anti-roll bar cage in relation to its predecessors. The front end was redesigned for aerodynamic reasons, with three large air intakes specifically for the radiators. Wings, boot and engine lids, doors and bumpers were made in composite materials, while the lateral and rear windows were in polycarbonate, all of which meant the car's weight was kept down at 1,120 kg with full tanks, even if the ACO and FIA regulations minimum was 1,225 kg. As the FIA norms permitted cubic capacities of up to 3.8-litres – but with a 30.3 mm aspiration flange - with the cubic capacity at 3795 cc and the power output at 485 hp. The flywheel was lightened and the clutch was a racing multi-disc. But the gearbox was a new conception 6-speed sequential, with components derived from the RS Spyder, even if the donor did make its debut in the 2006 24 Hours of Le Mans with the "old" 'box. Suspension was also revised, the brakes had 380 mm front, 355 mm rear, steel discs with aluminium callipers and the rims were 18 inches in diameter. The 911 GT3 RSR was improved for each season, but the real turnaround happened in 2011 with the debut of the GT3 RSR 4.0, which was derived from the limited series of 600 GT3 RS 4.0 road cars that put out 500 hp at 8250 rpm: cubic capacity was taken to 4-litres to generate 460 hp, limited by aspiration restrictors as imposed by the ACO's LM GTE regulations. Aerodynamics were also completely revised to create more downforce. The openings on the engine cover were replaced by two lateral air intakes similar to those on the Turbo production car.

The 911 Turbo kept the 997's body shell, with its wider wheel housings, extendable rear spoiler, lateral air intakes and front bumper shield, which had three large intakes to cool the radiators and were able to suck in 4,000 litres of air per second. That forced the redesign of the secondary optical groups, with lateral rounded fog lamps.

TECHNICAL SPECIFICATION

ENGINE

Rear, overhanging, longitudinal
6 cylinders horizontally opposed

Bore and stroke	100 x 76.4 mm
Unitary cubic capacity	600 cc
Total cubic capacity	3600 cc
Valve gear	twin overhead camshafts, chain driven
Number of valves	4 per cylinder
Compression ratio	9.0:1
Fuel feed	electronic injection, bi-turbo
Ignition	electronic
Coolant	liquid
Lubrication	dry sump
Maximum power	480 hp at 6000 rpm
Specific power	133.3 hp/litre

TRANSMISSION

4WD

Clutch	dry mono-disc
Gearbox	en bloc with differential, 6 speeds plus reverse

CHASSIS

Unified steel structure

Front suspension	McPherson, lower arms, coil springs, hydraulic shock absorbers, stabiliser bar
Rear suspension	independent, multi-link layout, coil springs, hydraulic shock absorbers, stabiliser bar
Brakes	disc, servo-brake, ABS
Steering	ZF rack, servo-assisted
Fuel tank	64 litres
Tyres front/rear	235/35 x 19/305/30 x 19

DIMENSIONS AND WEIGHT

Wheelbase	2360 mm
Track front/rear	1490/1558 mm
Length	4450 mm
Width	1852 mm
Height	1300 mm
Weight	1585 kg

PERFORMANCE

Top speed	310 kph
Power to weight ratio	3.3 kg/hp

911 Turbo (997)   2006

The new 911 Turbo was unveiled at the 2006 Geneva Motor Show, based as it was on the 997 series. Externally, it had three large front air intakes, bi-xenon headlights, LED direction indicators, bigger and two-part intakes, a larger extendable rear spoiler than in the past and new, forged, 19-inch light alloy rims, into which tyre pressure sensors had been incorporated. The body was further lightened using new doors in vacuum melted light alloy, that weighed only 10.3 kg each – obviously without locks, glass and other elements – each of which was 7.2 kg lighter than those in steel. The 3.6-litre engine had a revised VarioCam Plus system, now with a rotating phase shifter with a 30° excursion and new turbochargers with geometrically variable turbines developed with Borg Warner that reduced turbo lag to a minimum to obtain a more homogeneous and powerful engine torque: 620 Nm in a range of revs from 2100 to 4000 rpm. Using the overboost facility, which was available with the Sport Chrono package, pressure could be increased by 0.2 bar for a maximum of 10", taking torque to a maximum of 680 Nm. In spite of the unchanged cubic capacity, power output increased by 60 hp compared to the "old" Turbo for a total of 480 hp, which could take the car to a 310 kph top speed and a 0-100 kph time of 3.7 seconds. Both a 6-speed manual gearbox and a 5-speed Tiptronic S were available with a lockable phase convertor to achieve even better acceleration times. But 4WD meant the viscose coupling was out and an electronically controlled multiple disc clutch was in, and that better managed the torque. The PASM suspension was standard, but brakes with PCCB discs were optional. The following year, out came the 911 Turbo Cabriolet, the development of which helped retain excellent torsional rigidity to weigh just 70 kg more; the car's Cx was 0.31.

Because key competitors like Mercedes-Benz and BMW were launching ever more powerful SUVs, Porsche decided to re-establish its performance supremacy in the sector with the Cayenne Turbo S that produced a massive 521 hp. The chassis and body were adapted, but the company didn't say no to reduced gear ratios or the pneumatic suspension system.

TECHNICAL SPECIFICATION

ENGINE
Front, longitudinal, V8

Bore and stroke	93 x 83 mm
Unitary cubic capacity	563.8 cc
Total cubic capacity	4511 cc
Valve gear	twin overhead camshafts, chain driven
Number of valves	4 per cylinder
Compression ratio	9.5:1
Fuel feed	electronic injection, bi-turbo
Ignition	electronic
Coolant	liquid
Lubrication	dry sump
Maximum power	521 hp
Specific power	115.7 hp/litre

TRANSMISSION
4WD

Clutch	-
Gearbox	en bloc with engine, 6 speed and reverse automatic

CHASSIS
Unified steel structure

Front suspension	quadrilaterals, air springs, electronically controlled shock absorbers, stabiliser bar
Rear suspension	multi-link layout, air springs, electronically controlled shock absorbers, stabiliser bar
Brakes	disc, servo-brake, ABS
Steering	ZF rack, servo-assisted
Fuel tank	100 litres
Tyres front/rear	275/40 x 20

DIMENSIONS AND WEIGHT
Wheelbase	2855 mm
Track front/rear	1647/1662 mm
Length	4786 mm
Width	1928 mm
Height	1699 mm
Weight	2355 kg

PERFORMANCE
Top speed	275 kph
Power to weight ratio	4.5 kg/hp

Cayenne Turbo S   2006

When it was introduced in 2006 – a year before the model's restyling – the Cayenne Turbo S was the most powerful Porsche that ever went into production with the exception of the Carrera GT, which was on its way out of production at the time. The 4.5-litre's 521 hp V8 engine was enough to even outclass all the 911s. Main modifications to the power unit concerned turbocharger pressure, which was raised 4.3 psi, and the adoption of two bigger intercoolers in aluminium. Normally, the Porsche Traction Management system sent 62% of torque to the rear axle, improving the driving sensation, but in this case it could be distributed in an optimal way on both axles. The pneumatic suspension and the PASM for the electronic control of the shock absorbers were adapted to the new higher performance, the set-up became more rigid due to the enormous 275/40 wheels and 20-inch rims. The tyres were especially designed for the Cayenne Turbo S and its top speed of over 270 kph and were certified for up to 300 kph. There was also more power for the brakes. But apart from top speed and a 0-100 kph dash in 4.9 seconds, performance was higher than that of the normal Turbo, especially in the upper regions. Set-up also gave a lateral acceleration of 0.86g, which was considerable if one considered the vehicle mass and its height from the ground: even the most critical of people appreciated the Cayenne's driveability, emphasising how the driving imposition was similar to that of a grand tourer although it was penalised by a high centre of gravity even though design had resulted in a body shell in high resistance steel. Regardless, Porsche decided not to give up the off-road prerogative of the Cayenne, which once again had low range gears: even if not at the level of the Jeep and Range Rover, the Turbo S was one of the best off-road SUVs. In addition, from 2004 it became available with an optional "Advanced Off-road Technology Package".

After the great success of the first series, a slightly restyled Cayenne was presented in 2007 for the 2008 model year: the 2007 model year was ignored to sell the remaining 2006 cars. The sheet steel was more or less identical, but there were new graphics for the optical groups and the bumpers giving the vehicle a more aggressive and attractive look. There were many new developments, especially from the mechanical point of view.

TECHNICAL SPECIFICATION

ENGINE
Front, longitudinal, V8

Bore and stroke	96 x 83 mm
Unitary cubic capacity	600.2 cc
Total cubic capacity	4806 cc
Valve gear	twin overhead camshafts, chain driven
Number of valves	4 per cylinder
Compression ratio	12.5:1
Fuel feed	direct injection
Ignition	electronic
Coolant	liquid
Lubrication	dry sump
Maximum power	385 hp at 6200 rpm
Specific power	80.2 hp/litre

TRANSMISSION
4WD

Clutch	dry mono-disc
Gearbox	en bloc with engine, 6 speeds plus reverse

CHASSIS
Unified steel structure

Front suspension	quadrilaterals, air springs, electronically controlled shock absorbers, stabiliser bar
Rear suspension	multi-link layout, air springs, electronically controlled shock absorbers, stabiliser bar
Brakes	disc, servo-brake, ABS
Steering	ZF rack, servo-assistance
Fuel tank	100 litres
Tyres front/rear	255/55 x 18

DIMENSIONS AND WEIGHT

Wheelbase	2855 mm
Rack front/rear	1647/1662 mm
Length	4798 mm
Width	1928 mm
Height	1699
Weight	2225 kg

PERFORMANCE

Top speed	252 kph
Power to weight ratio	5.7 kg/hp

Cayenne (MY 2008) 2007

The second generation of the Cayenne according to Porsche was launched in 2007. Externally, the plastic components were updated and the optical groups – LED at the rear – leaving more or less intact the expensive sheet metal panels. Yet as a result of work carried out on the underbody, rear spoiler and bumpers, the Cx dropped from 0.39 to an excellent 0.35, with obvious performance and fuel consumption benefits. The whole engine range was updated with direct petrol injection and, at the same time, the cylinders were increased in size on all versions: the "old" 3.2 V6 was replaced by a similar 3.6-litre unit – still of Volkswagen derivation – that put out 290 hp. The V8's bore was also increased to 96 mm, while the stroke stayed at 83 mm, and the cubic capacity moved on to 3.8-litres due to an increased compression ratio of 12.5:1 that led to 385 hp at 6200 rpm. With the same cubic capacity, the power output of the Cayenne Turbo also went up to 500 hp. Later, a Turbo S that generated 550 hp and had PCCB carbon-ceramic brakes would also go on offer. With the second generation, the suspension and electronic aspects were improved: the Porsche Dynamic Chassis Control made its first appearance and was a system that controlled the body shell's movement (pitch and roll) and gave an optimum behaviour in all driving conditions, independently making the suspension more rigid. A Sport button that was standard on the whole range optimised every configuration in relation to a sportier and more incisive driving style. The GTS version of the Cayenne was unveiled at the 2007 Frankfurt Motor Show, which was mid-way between the S and the Turbo, but with sportier connotations. The power output of the normally aspirated V8 increased by 20 hp more than the S to 405 hp, while the set-up became sportier, being lowered 24 mm. On top of that, the PASM system was combined with the first time by normal steel springs. The light alloy rims were 20 inches in diameter and the body had a distinctive sporting character.

The photograph shows the Boxster RS 60 Spyder with its silver body, windscreen edges in black and red optical groups that recalled the 1960 open top racing car. The illustration shows the Porsche Boxster Design Edition 2, which was especially well finished, an element drawn from the Sport Design line, inspired by the modern, styles aspects of Porsche Design.

TECHNICAL SPECIFICATION

ENGINE
Central, longitudinal
6 cylinders horizontally opposed

Bore and stroke	96 x 78 mm
Unitary cubic capacity	564.5 cc
Total cubic capacity	3387 cc
Valve gear	twin overhead camshafts, chain driven
Number of valves	4 per cylinder
Compression ratio	11.1:1
Fuel feed	Bosch electronic injection
Ignition	electronic
Coolant	liquid
Lubrication	dry sump
Maximum power	303 hp at 6250 rpm
Specific power	89.6 hp/litre

TRANSMISSION
Rear wheel drive

Clutch	dry mono-disc
Gearbox	en bloc with differential, 6 speeds plus reverse

CHASSIS
Unified steel structure

Front suspension	McPherson, lower arms, coil springs, hydraulic shock absorbers, stabiliser bar
Rear suspension	McPherson, lower arms, coil springs, hydraulic shock absorbers, stabiliser bar
Brakes	disc, servo-brake, ABS
Steering	ZF rack, servo-assisted
Fuel tank	64 litres
Tyres front/rear	-

DIMENSIONS AND WEIGHT

Wheelbase	2415 mm
Track front/rear	-
Length	4329 mm
Width	1801 mm
Height	1292 mm
Weight	1355 kg

PERFORMANCE

Top speed	274 kph
Power to weight ratio	4.4 kg/hp

Boxster RS 60 Spyder and Porsche Design Edition 2

2007

The new special version of the Boxster, the RS 60 Spyder, made its first public appearance at the 2007 Bologna Motor Show, all set to go on sale in March 2008. The new model's inspiration was a great racing car of the past, the 718 RS 60 Spyder that won the 1960 12 Hours of Sebring – among others – driven by Hans Herrmann and Olivier Gendebien. And to commemorate that auspicious year, a total of 1,960 units of the Boxster Special were built. Obviously, the colour of the body had to be GT silver, while the rear optical groups were completely red. The windscreen edging was all in black and the 19-inch rims were Sport Design. The front end had a bigger spoiler, as were all the lower parts of the body. The interior was Cartier all-leather with steering wheel, door, tunnel and gear lever details picked out in aluminium. The dashboard and sills had the model's celebrative shield set into them. Mechanically, the starting point was the Boxster S but, due to a new exhaust system, the power output of the 3.4-litre engine went from 295 to 303 hp, all handled by a chassis that was now equipped with the Porsche Active Suspension Management. After having quickly sold all the cars, the Boxster S Porsche Design Edition 2 came out in October 2008 together with the Cayman S Sport. The second Boxster came in Carrara white with three silver stripes along the sides and doors, accentuating the car's speed vocation. The 19-inch star-design aluminium rims were of the Sport Design line, the lateral air intakes were white, as was the internal central console and frames of the three main instruments. And a new accessory was the men's wristwatch "Edition 2 Chronograph" with a white face that was part of the Dashboard Collection. Just 500 of the Boxster Design Edition 2s were produced.

If the 911 GT2 with its 530 hp and rear wheel drive was extreme, Porsche amazed everyone in 2010 with the GT2 RS, the lighter body of which was in composite materials, which were left bare and unpainted, and its power output of 620 hp. The record it set at the Nürburgring left nobody in doubt regarding its level of perfection the 911 had reached. In Europe, the car's price was € 199,500 euros.

TECHNICAL SPECIFICATION

ENGINE
Rear, overhanging, longitudinal
6 cylinders horizontally opposed

Bore and stroke	100 x 76.4 mm
Unitary cubic capacity	600 cc
Total cubic capacity	3600 cc
Valve gear	twin overhead camshafts, chain driven
Number of valves	4 per cylinder
Compression ratio	9.0:1
Fuel feed	electronic injection, bi-turbo
Ignition	electronic
Coolant	liquid
Lubrication	dry sump
Maximum power	530 hp at 6500 rpm
Specific power	147.2 hp/litre

TRANSMISSION
Rear wheel drive

Clutch	dry mono-disc
Gearbox	en bloc with differential, 6 speeds plus reverse

CHASSIS
Unified steel structure

Front suspension	McPherson, lower arms, coil springs, hydraulic shock absorbers, stabiliser bar
Rear suspension	independent, multi-link layout, coil springs, hydraulic shock absorbers, stabiliser bar
Brakes	disc, servo-brake, ABS
Steering	ZF rack, servo-assisted
Fuel tank	89 litres
Tyres front/rear	235/35 x 19/325/30 x 19

DIMENSIONS AND WEIGHT

Wheelbase	2360 mm
Track front/rear	1515/1550 mm
Length	4469 mm
Width	1852 mm
Height	1285 mm
Weight	1440 kg
Performance	
Top speed	329 kph
Power to weight ratio	2.7 kg/hp

911 GT2 and GT2 RS   2007

The 911 GT2 was introduced at the 2007 Frankfurt Motor Show and arrived at the concessionaires in November: it was an extreme version of the 911 Turbo and with its 530 hp it became the fastest 911 ever to go on sale, although it had a fuel consumption of 12.5 litres per 100 kilometres. The heart of the GT2 was its 6-cylinder 3.6-litre engine with two bigger turbochargers able to increase boost pressure, with the flow optimised by a new expansion intake manifold and turn out 50 hp more than the 480 hp of the "normal "Turbo. The exhaust was redesigned with silencers and terminals in titanium. One new aspect was rear wheel drive exclusively via a manual 6-speed gearbox. The car's weight was reduced in that way and with a lightening of the body to just 1,440 kg. Power to weight ratio of 2.72 kg per hp meant a 0-100 kph acceleration time of 3.7 seconds and a top speed of 329 kph. Braking was by the PCCB system, with its carbon-ceramic discs, all of which was standard. A further evolution of the car called the 911 GT2 RS made its appearance in 2010 and was a 500 car limited series. Power output went up to 620 hp and its weight went down to an all-time low of 1,370 kg to produce 2.21 kg per hp due to massive use of composite materials, especially the CFRP or carbon fibre reinforced plastic for the body and a bigger, new rear spoiler. Top speed went up by just 1 kph, but the 0-100 time dropped to 3.5 seconds 0-200 kph to 9.8 and 0-300 kph to 29.8. Testimony to Porsche's chassis research with the suspension perfected and more powerful brakes as it was to the GT2 RS's aerodynamics. A great deal of effort was put into creating the right downforce, a major contributor top speed even if it was only an increase of 1 kph over the GT2. An RS also put in a time of 7 minutes 18 seconds on the Nordschleif of the Nürburgring. On top of that, average homologated fuel consumption was only 11.9 litres per 100 km.

Compared to the previous series, the photograph shows only a few changes in body details were made, among them to the front end and the light alloy rims. But the illustration shows the Cayman R, with its undoubtedly sporty set-up, as is emphasised by its large decals low down on the doors. The interior was simplified with elimination of all that was unnecessary, which lightened the car by 55 kg.

TECHNICAL SPECIFICATION

ENGINE

Central, longitudinal
6 cylinders horizontally opposed

Bore and stroke	97 x 77.5 mm
Unitary cubic capacity	572.6 cc
Total cubic capacity	3436 cc
Valve gear	twin overhead camshafts, chain driven
Number of valves	4 per cylinder
Compression ratio	12.5:1
Fuel feed	Bosch electronic injection
Ignition	electronic
Coolant	liquid
Lubrication	dry sump
Maximum power	330 hp at 7400 rpm
Specific power	95.3 hp/litre

TRANSMISSION

Rear wheel drive

Clutch	dry mono-disc
Gearbox	en bloc with differential, 6 speeds plus reverse

CHASSIS

Unified steel structure

Front suspension	McPherson, lower arms, coil springs, hydraulic shock absorbers, stabiliser bar
Rear suspension	McPherson, lower arms, coil springs, hydraulic shock absorbers, stabiliser bar
Brakes	disc, servo-brake, ABS
Steering	servo-assisted rack
Fuel tank	54 litres
Tyres front/rear	235/35 x 19/265/35 x 19

DIMENSIONS AND WEIGHT

Wheelbase	2415 mm
Track front/rear	1490/1530 mm
Length	4347 mm
Width	1801 mm
Height	1286 mm
Weight	1295 kg

PERFORMANCE

Top speed	282 kph
Power to weight ratio	3,9 kg7hp

Cayman (MY 2008) and Cayman R 2008

The second generation of the Cayman was presented on 21 February 2008, before which it had been subjected to a slight body and interior facelift. At the same time, the base model's was taken to 2.9 litres to put out 265 hp, but due to direct fuel injection, the Cayman S's output had gone up by 20 hp for a total of 320. To emphasise the sporting vocation of both models, the engines had 10 hp more than the Boxster, which cost a little less, despite its greater constructional complexity of the retractable hood. Both cars were available with a PDK dual clutch gearbox with rocker arms on the steering wheel with the much liked paddle as optional, while the self-locking differential was optional. A third version that was a much sportier affair called the Cayman R appeared in 2010. The new model was drastically simplified and that reduced its weight by 55 kg. The casualties included the radio, air conditioning, the glass holder and even the door handles were replaced by cords as per racing cars, while the seats were shell-shaped and he fuel tank's capacity was reduced to 54 litres. Power output went up by 10 hp to 330 hp and the set-up was 20mm lower and modified to produce decidedly sportier handling. The light alloy rims were 19-inch and had their own distinctive design, as was the original body shape and range of colours. A special series came out in 2011, in line with the 911 and Boxster S ranges, called the Black Edition, with its body, interior and details all in black, with the 330 hp Cayman R engine and the especially complete finish. The contract with Valmet Automotive in Uusikaupunki, Finland, came to an end in 2012, so the cars' assembly switched to Karmann of Osnabrück, the property of VW-Audi group.

Specifically prepared for racing, in 2007 26 Cayenne S Transsyberias were assembled and kitted out for extreme use on its namesake's rally, as shown in the illustration. With their mechanics optimised for off-road work and a powerful appearance, in 2009 a road-going version went on sale called the Cayenne S Transsyberia to commemorate the company's victories in racing and offer a special and exclusive vehicle as in the picture.

TECHNICAL SPECIFICATION

TECHNICAL SPEICATION
Front, longitudinal, V8

Bore and stroke	96 x 83 mm
Unitary cubic capacity	600.7 cc
Total cubic capacity	4806 cc
Valve gear	twin overhead camshafts
Number of valves	4 per cylinder
Compression ratio	12.5:1
Fuel feed	DFI direct injection
Ignition	electronic
Coolant	liquid
Lubrication	dry sump
Maximum power	385 hp at 6200 rpm
Specific power	80.1 hp/litre

TRANSMISSION
4WD

Clutch	-
Gearbox	en bloc with engine, automatic, 6 speeds plus reverse and adapter

CHASSIS
Unified steel structure

Front suspension	quadrilaterals, air springs, electronically controlled shock absorbers, stabiliser bar
Rear suspension	multi-link layout, air springs, electronically controlled shock absorbers, stabiliser bar
Brakes	disc and servo-brake, ABS
Steering	servo-assisted rack
Fuel tank	100 litres
Tyres front/rear	255/55 x 18/255/55 x 18

DIMENSIONS AND WEIGHT

Wheelbase	2855 mm
Track front/rear	1681/1696 mm
Length	4798 mm
Width	1928 mm
Height	1748 mm
Weight	-

PERFORMANCE

Top speed	190 kph (tyre limit)
Power to weight ratio	-

Cayenne S Transsyberia   2008

The Transsyberia Rally was a punishing, 7,200 kilometre marathon that started in Moscow and finished at the Mongolian capital of Ulan Bator; it put the crews and vehicles to a severe test as they were called to take on extreme terrain and weather. As early as 2006 two Porsches were prepared by a private team and one of them achieved a brilliant win in the event. The following year, the company decided to compete itself, offering drivers a small production run of 26 vehicles especially equipped for the marathon – and they were called the Cayenne Transsyberia. The base was the normal Cayenne S with the same 385 hp power output as the production cars, but a set-up that privileged engine torque able to reduce fuel consumption by 15%. That was a fundamental result for an event of this kind; the power unit was adapted to 91 octane fuel for the same reason, given the difficulty of finding quality petrol along the route. The transmission was given self-locking differentials, a shorter ratio gearbox for a top speed of 190 kph and specific calibration. The suspension was made more rigid, reinforced and the vehicle had a wider track, with specific rims. The whole body shell was lightened and given a roll bar cage, underbody protection and additional headlights. Porsche had taken the first three places in the 2008 rally and in 2008 an incredible first six places. That's why a special version of the victorious long distance rally vehicle was unleashed onto the market called the Cayenne S Transsyberia in 2009. It was aesthetically very similar to the winning rally car, with powerful lights on the roof and lettering along its sides, which were on request but free, colours with contrasting rims, a spoiler, underbody protection, a bigger fuel tank and a purpose designed interior. The mechanical starting point was the Cayenne GTS with its 4.8-litre V8 engine that put out 405 hp; gear ratios were shortened by 15% to improve acceleration meaning a 0-100 kph squirt in 6.1 seconds, while the chassis was improved with Porsche's Off-road Technology Package.

The illustration is of the Team Brumos Riley-Porsche Mk XX that won the 2009 24 Hours of Daytona, while the photograph is of a sister car prepared by the team itself, that won the following year's Daytona, this time run by the Action Express Racing Team. Despite wins in the most important race, the championships went to the Mk XX powered by Pontiac in 2009 and BMW in 2010.

TECHNICAL SPECIFICATION

ENGINE
Central, longitudinal
90° V8

Bore and stroke	100 x 76.4 mm
Unitary cubic capacity	420.8 cc
Total cubic capacity	3397 cc
Valve gear	twin overhead camshafts, chain driven
Number of valves	4 per cylinder
Compression ratio	-
Fuel feed	electronic injection
Ignition	electronic
Coolant	liquid
Lubrication	dry sump
Maximum power	503 hp at 10,300 rpm
Specific power	148 hp/litre

TRANSMISSION
Rear wheel drive

Clutch	dry mono-disc
Gearbox	en bloc with differential, 6 speeds plus reverse

CHASSIS
Carbon fibre monocoque

Front suspension	double wishbones, torsion bars, gas shock absorbers, stabiliser bars
Rear suspension	double wishbones, torsion bars, gas shock absorbers, stabiliser bar
Brakes	carbon-ceramic discs
Steering	servo-assisted rack
Fuel tank	89 litres
Tyres front/rear	29/65 x 18/31/71 x 18

DIMENSIONS AND WEIGHT
Wheelbase	-
Track front/rear	-
Length	4650 mm
Width	2000 mm
Height	1068 mm
Weight	775 kg

PERFORMANCE
Top speed	329 kph
Power to weight ratio	0.65 kg/hp

Riley-Porsche Mk XX   2008

Alongside the works team's successes and those of privateers, a major chapter has been written in Porsche's motor sport history by cars that were just powered by the company. The best known examples are those of Formula 1 with McLaren and in Formula Indy with March. But there are a good few cases in sports car racing, like that of the Riley-Porsche Mk XX, which won the 24 Hours of Daytona in 2008 and 2009. Riley was established from the ashes of Riley&Scott, which was later bought by Reynard in 1990, but failed in 2000. In 2003, the Grand American Road Racing Association changed the regulations of the Rolex Sports Car Series, abolishing the ultra-fast and expensive open top racers of the period and replacing them with Daytona Prototypes, with closed bodies, chassis in aluminium – no carbon fibre for the monocoque but ok for the body – and engines strictly derived from production cars. The Riley Mk XI powered by Pontiac and Lexus V8 units, first appeared in 2004 and became the absolute dominator of the series with four consecutive Daytona victories. In 2008, GARRA permitted new cars to enter, as for the five previous years' chassis had been frozen. So Riley came up with a perfected Mk XX. As well as the usual Pontiac and Lexus engines, Ford and Porsche units joined the fray – Porsche's the Cayenne V8. And two major names in American motor sport closely associated with Zuffenhausen competed with the Riley-Porsche – Penske and Brumos. A Brumos snapped up pole position with the wafer-thin margin of just one thousandth of a second ahead of its sister car fielded by Roger Penske in the 2009 24 Hours of Daytona and then went on to win the race. And in 2010, the American 24 Hours was dominated by a Riley-Porsche of the Action Express Racing Team, with a specially prepared Cayenne engine.

The second generation 997 made its debut in 2008: few modifications had been made to the exterior, but some aspects of the interior were revised. From the mechanical point of view, the great innovation were engines with direct fuel injection, which greatly improved performance – as well as reducing fuel consumption. Homologation testing confirmed the cars used a record low level of 15 km/litre.

TECHNICAL SPECIFICATION

ENGINE
Rear, overhanging, longitudinal
6 cylinders horizontally opposed

Bore and stroke	97 x 81.5 mm
Unitary cubic capacity	602 cc
Total cubic capacity	3614 cc
Valve gear	twin overhead camshafts, chain driven
Number of valves	4 per cylinder
Compression ratio	12.5:1
Fuel feed	electronic injection
Ignition	electronic
Coolant	liquid
Lubrication	dry sump
Maximum power	340 hp at 6500 rpm
Specific power	94.3 hp/litre

TRANSMISSION
Rear wheel drive

Clutch	dry mono-disc
Gearbox	en bloc with differential, 6 speeds plus reverse

CHASSIS
Unified steel structure

Front suspension	McPherson, lower arms, coil springs, hydraulic shock absorbers, stabiliser bar
Rear suspension	independent, multi-link layout, coil springs, hydraulic shock absorbers, stabiliser bar
Brakes	disc, servo-brake, ABS
Steering	ZF rack
Fuel tank	64 litres
Tyres front/rear	235/40 x 18/265/40 x 18

DIMENSIONS AND WEIGHT

Wheelbase	2350 mm
Track front/rear	1486/1530 mm
Length	4435 mm
Width	1808 mm
Height	1310 mm
Weight	1415 kg

PERFORMANCE

Top speed	289 kph
Power to weight ratio	4.7 kg/hp

911 (MY 2009) 2008

After the great success of the 911's 997 series, a second generation of the car made its first appearance at the 2008 Paris Motor Show as a model for 2009, after the new arrival had been spoken of in advance on the company's website the previous June. The front end was modified with a new-design bumper, which had bigger air inlets and differentiated exhaust terminal, depending on the version. But it was under the skin that the new 911 had been substantially updated, with engines that now had direct fuel injection lowering fuel consumption and reducing emissions. In spite of the 6-cylinder boxers still being defined a 3.6-litre for the Carrera and 3.8 for the Carrera S, their cubic capacities only varied slightly: 3614 cc and 3800 cc against 3596 and 3824. With a marked reduction in fuel consumption, power output still increased to 345 and 385 hp with an increase of 20 and 30 hp respectively compared with the previous generation. The Tiptronic automatic gearbox was replaced by the new PDK dual clutch with seven ratios, which meant it could change gear without interrupting the traction using automatically or manually with the controls on the steering wheel. For the latter, a system of rocker arms was initially considered, but the criticism of a number of clients pointed to the system being little intuitive and that pushed Porsche into offering a normal paddle on the steering wheel. The suspension was also perfected. The new 911 Turbo was unveiled at the 2009 Frankfurt Motor Show: a new 6-cylinder, 3.8-litre power unit with two variable-geometry turbochargers took power output to a maximum of 500 hp, a top speed of 312 kph and a 0-100 kph acceleration in 3.4 seconds, even if some motoring journalists obtained times of under three seconds. Minor aesthetic modifications were carried out on the optical groups. And the GT3, which was also presented at the 2009 Geneva Motor Show had moved on, with its power output now 435 hp for the basic version and 450 hp for the RS.

To launch the Cayenne Diesel, which was sure to infringe a taboo or two, Porsche chose ex-world rally champion and test driver Walter Röhrl, photographed together with one of the SUVs and an old Porsche diesel tractor. The 2010 version in the illustration was a diesel – now legitimised – and with the new 2011 generation was available in two versions, followed by the S that was launched in 2012.

TECHNICAL SPECIFICATION

ENGINE
Front, longitudinal, V6

Bore and stroke	83 x 91.4 mm
Unitary cubic capacity	494.5 cc
Total cubic capacity	2967 cc
Valve gear	twin overhead camshafts
Number of valves	4 per cylinder
Compression ratio	16.8:1
Fuel feed	common rail turbo
Ignition	by compression
Coolant	liquid
Lubrication	dry sump
Maximum power	240 hp at 4400 rpm
Specific power	80 hp/litre

TRANSMISSION
4WD

Clutch	-
Gearbox	en bloc with engine, automatic, 8 speeds plus reverse

CHASSIS
Unified steel structure

Front suspension	quadrilaterals, air springs, electronically controlled shock absorbers, stabiliser bar
Rear suspension	multi-link layout, air springs, electronically controlled shock absorbers, stabiliser bar
Brakes	disc and servo-brake
Steering	rack
Fuel tank	100 litres
Tyres front/rear	255/55 x 18

DIMENSIONS AND WEIGHT

Wheelbase	2895 mm
Track front/rear	-
Length	4846 mm
Width	1939 mm
Height	1705 mm
Weight	2100 kg

PERFORMANCE

Top speed	220 kph
Power to weight ratio	8.7 kg/hp

Cayenne Diesel   2009

After the introduction of the Cayenne, the Porsche "purists" considered it close to blasphemous when the diesel version made its debut at the 2009 Geneva Motor Show; the ultimate taboo had bitten the dust. The company had solid strategic and commercial reasons for making such a decision, but the risk of compromising its integrity was high. Here's what the press kit, given to journalists, had to say on launch day: "The decision was taken following regulation changes, especially in European markets, and concerning the consequent fiscal benefits for vehicles with diesel engines. In addition, Porsche's shareholding in the Volkswagen Group, the biggest manufacturer of new generation diesel engines for cars in the world, has opened up new opportunities for the use of this technology. Porsche will equip the Cayenne with a 3-litre, V6, 240 hp diesel engine supplied by Audi AG, a subsidiary of VW. The average fuel consumption of the Cayenne Diesel is 9.3 litres per 100 km, with 244 grams of carbon dioxide emission per kilometre. The immediate response of the accelerator and substantial engine torque ensures the level of performance expected of a sporty SUV like the Cayenne. A massive engine torque of 550 Nm completes the dynamic characteristics of the chassis, offering high levels of control and driving pleasure typical of Porsche".

In 2010, a new generation of the Cayenne Diesel was launched for the 2011 model year: the engine was the same, but a new chassis further improved performance and fuel consumption. In the summer of 2012, out came the Cayenne S Diesel powered by a 4-2-litre, bi-turbo V8 unit originated by Audi, which generated 382 hp and 850 Nm of torque to take it from 0-100 kph in 5.7 seconds and a top speed of 252 kph.

The Panamera's design was unmistakable and recalled the 911. Four doors and of extremely impressive dimensions make it a real top of the range car, with its luxurious interior and first class equipment. It was available in various versions, with both rear wheel and 4-Wheel drive. And its performance was excellent, in part due to its low 0.29 Cx. The car was a sales success from the start, especially in the USA which was its principle market.

TECHNICAL SPECIFICATION

ENGINE
Front, longitudinal, V6

Bore and stroke	96 x 83 mm
Unitary cubic capacity	600.7 cc
Total cubic capacity	3605 cc
Valve gear	twin overhead camshafts
Number of valves	4 per cylinder
Compression ratio	12.5:1
Fuel feed	direct injection
Ignition	electronic
Coolant	liquid
Lubrication	dry sump
Maximum power	300 hp at 6200 rpm
Specific power	83.2 hp/litre

TRANSMISSION
Rear wheel drive

Clutch	dry mono-disc
Gearbox	en bloc with engine, 6 speeds plus reverse

CHASSIS
Unified steel structure

Front suspension	quadrilaterals, air springs, electronically controlled shock absorbers, stabiliser bar
Rear suspension	multi-link layout, air springs, electronically controlled shock absorbers, stabiliser bar
Brakes	disc and servo-brake, ABS
Steering	servo-assisted rack
Fuel tank	80 litres
Tyres front/rear	245/50 x 18/275/45 x 18

DIMENSIONS AND WEIGHT

Wheelbase	2920 mm
Track front/rear	1658/1662 mm
Length	4970 mm
Width	1931 mm
Height	1418 mm
Weight	1730 kg

PERFORMANCE

Top speed	261 kph
Power to weight ratio	5.7 kg/hp

Panamera S, 4 and 4S   2009

The idea of a real four-seater Porsche, perhaps with four doors, had come to grief a number of times in the company's history, but with the 989 prototype of the late '80s and early '90s it came close to going into production. But to actually see this strange automobile – detested by the purists perhaps even more than the Cayenne SUV – unveiled the world would have to wait until the 2009 Singapore Motor Show, where the Panamera was unveiled. The body had somewhat more than a 911 'family feeling', yet it was almost five metres long. The imposing body and the luxury of the interior created the clear impression of a completely new car at Porsche and to the motoring world in general. The architecture of the liquid-cooled front engine had much in common with the Cayenne SUV, and at the time of the Panamera's presentation the versions available were the rear wheel drive S powered by a 400 hp 4806 cc V8 and the 4S with permanent 4WD, while the Turbo was handled separately. The optimum PDK dual clutch 7-speed gearbox was standard on the 4WD and optional on the other models. From February 2010 two additional versions became available at the bottom of the range, powered by a 3605 cc V6 that put out 300 hp. They were the rear wheel drive Panamera and the Panamera 4 with traction through all four wheels. Despite the car's 1,820 kg kerb weight, its performance was highly respectable, with a top speed of 257 kph and a 0-100 kph dash in 6.1 seconds. The Panamera, which was 90 kg lighter and had a 6-speed manual 'box, still covered the 100 metres in 6.8 seconds. Handling was sporty and precise, sufficient to hide car's real capability from the driver. The Panamera's active suspension and the Porsche Stability Management electronic systems ensured the car would deliver its maximum performance in complete safety without sacrificing the comfort of the four people on board. Boot capacity was substantial at 430 litres and could be accessed via the boot lid, and that went up to 1,300 litres by lowering the backs of the rear seats.

For top of the range performance and equipment there was the Panamera Turbo, which was joined in 2011 by the sporty 550 hp Turbo S. To get the maximum out of the car, there was the Sport Chrono package, which produced specific suspension, engine and transmission settings. And there was also the Sport Plus mode that varied the absorption of the exhaust system that produced a more aggressive sound.

TECHNICAL SPECIFICATION

ENGINE
Front, longitudinal, V8

Bore and stroke	96 x 83 mm
Unitary cubic capacity	600.7 cc
Total cubic capacity	4806 cc
Valve gear	twin overhead camshafts
Number of valves	4 per cylinder
Compression ratio	10.5.1
Fuel feed	electronic injection, turbo
Ignition	electronic
Coolant	liquid
Lubrication	dry sump
Maximum power	550 hp at 6000 rpm
Specific power	114.4 hp/litre

TRANSMISSION
Rear wheel drive

Clutch	dry mono-disc
Gearbox	en bloc with engine, 7 speeds plus reverse

CHASSIS
Unified steel body

Front suspension	quadrilaterals, air springs, electronically controlled shock absorbers, stabiliser bar
Rear suspension	multi-link layout, air springs, electronically controlled shock absorbers, stabiliser bar
Brakes	disc, servo-brake, ABS
Steering	servo-assisted rack
Fuel tank	100 litres
Tyres front/rear	255/40 x 20/295/35 x 20

DIMENSIONS AND WEIGHT

Wheelbase	2920 mm
Track front/rear	1646/1642 mm
Length	4970 mm
Width	1931 mm
Height	1418 mm
Weight	1995 kg

PERFORMANCE

Top speed	306 kph
Power to weight ratio	3.6 kg/hp

Panamera Turbo and Turbo S   2009

The 500 hp Panamera Turbo was launched at the same time as the normally aspirated versions. The engines were the same as the Cayenne, at 4.8-litres with two turbochargers that had an integrated wastegate and intercoolers, one per cylinder bank. Torque was 700 Nm between 2550 and 4500 rpm and that could be increased to 770 Nm by pressing the Sport Plus button that brought in the overboost. The vehicle was revised to lower the centre of gravity, turbos were now arranged in parallel and was equipped with a new ultra-light steel exhaust manifold. The transmission included the modern PDK 7-speed gearbox with dual clutch, while the 4WD was managed by the Porsche Traction Management. The Panamera Turbo had a top speed of 303 kph and did 0-100 kph in 4.2 seconds and four seconds precisely with the Sport Chrono and Launch Control packages with the same fuel consumption of just over 12 litres to the 100 km due to direct fuel injection and VarioCam Plus. The Turbo also had adaptive suspension with air springs and the PASM system. In March 2011 the Panamera Turbo S was introduced, its 4.8-litre V8 with a maximum power output of 550 hp and 750 Nm torque, which became 800 Nm with the Sport Chrono package as part of the Sport Plus, all due to new, part titanium turbochargers that reduced inertia. Top speed went up to 306 kph and the 0-100 kph down to 3.8 seconds. Porsche Dynamic Chassis Control was also standard and managed the suspension as was Porsche Torque Vectoring Plus to better exploit engine torque, distributing it precisely to the rear wheels. Externally, the Turbo S stood out for its 20-inch rims, mini-skirts and active rear spoiler in the same colour as the car. Like the Turbo, the Cx of the S went up to 0.30, providing better downforce.

The Boxster Spyder's interior, as shown in the illustration with its emergency hood in position, whereas the photograph indicates its body clamps, was smartly finished with the central tunnel and dashboard in the body's colour; the exterior – with contrasting Porsche lettering in the lower part of the doors – was available in seven different colours: creamy white, black, red, metallic basalt black, metallic water blue and silver.

TECHNICAL SPECIFICATION

ENGINE
Central, longitudinal
6 cylinders horizontally opposed

Bore and stroke	97 x 77.5 mm
Unitary cubic capacity	572.6 cc
Total cubic capacity	3436 cc
Valve gear	twin overhead camshafts, chain driven
Number of valves	4 per cylinder
Compression ratio	12.5:1
Fuel feed	electronic injection
Ignition	electronic
Coolant	liquid
Lubrication	dry sump
Maximum power	316 hp at 7200 rpm
Specific power	92.9 hp/litre

TRANSMISSION
Rear wheel drive

Clutch	dry mono-disc
Gearbox	en bloc with differential, 6 speeds plus reverse

CHASSIS
Unified steel structure

Front suspension	McPherson, lower arms, coil springs, hydraulic shock absorbers, stabiliser bar
Rear suspension	McPherson, lower arms, coil springs, hydraulic shock absorbers, stabiliser bar
Brakes	disc, servo-brake, ABS
Steering	ZF rack servo-assisted
Fuel tank	54 litres
Tyres front/rear	235/35 x 19/265/35 x 10

DIMENSIONS AND WEIGHT

Wheelbase	2415 mm
Track front/rear	1490/1530 mm
Length	4342 mm
Width	1801 mm
Height	1290 mm
Weight	1350 kg

PERFORMANCE

Top speed	267 kph
Power to weight ratio	4.9 kg/hp

Boxster Spyder 2009

A special version of the Boxster S was unveiled at the 2009 Los Angeles Motor Show, which had sportier lines because it had no electric hood. In spite of its "extreme" characteristics, it would remain in the price list until 2012 as a variant model rather than a limited production series and went on sale in the spring of the following year. The mechanical starting point was the second generation Boxster S and its 6-cylinder, 3.4-litre engine that put out 320 hp. The transmission was a 6-speed manual with a PDK dual clutch available on request. Curiously, the automatic version had a slightly worse Cx of 0.31 instead of 0.30.the door opening lever that was slightly worse at 0.31 against 0.30. The differential was self-locking, the set-up stiffened and 20 mm lower and the exhaust sporty. Top speed was 267 kph and the 0-100 kph dash took 5.1 seconds, which dropped to 4.8 seconds when the Launch Control was inserted. It should be noted that the top speed was limited to 200 kph when the light black hood was up, which was made in two pieces and considered simply an emergency item. Those results, which were a record for the Boxster range, were achieved with a substantial lightening of the body shell and body itself: the elimination of the electric hood saved 21 kg and another 15 kg came from the aluminium doors, of which the bonnet and engine cover were made for all the Boxster models. Another 12 kg improvement came from the lightened 19-inch rims and bucket seats; the 12 kg air conditioning system went, as did the 3 kg audio set-up, the door opening lever – replaced by simple straps - the glass holder and the instrument cluster cover. In total, the Boxster Spyder was 80 kg lighter, sufficient to make it the lightest Porsche in the range. Two faired humps were installed behind the headrests that gave the sides a typical appearance; other modifications were made to the air intakes, now covered by a black grill.

The duck tail spoiler, Fuchs rims, more powerful engine, aluminium doors and a perfected set-up: the 911 Sport Classic just had to be aimed at a passionate public. It was introduced at the 2009 Frankfurt Motor Show three years after the first project and was assembled and super-equipped in a limited series of 250.

TECHNICAL SPECIFICATION

ENGINE
Rear, overhanging, longitudinal
6 cylinders horizontally opposed

Bore and stroke	102 x 77.5 mm
Unitary cubic capacity	633.3 cc
Total cubic capacity	3800 cc
Valve gear	twin overhead camshafts, chain driven
Number of valves	4 per cylinder
Compression ratio	12.5:1
Fuel feed	electronic injection
Ignition	electronic
Coolant	liquid
Lubrication	dry sump
Maximum power	300 hp at 7300 rpm
Specific power	78.9 hp/litre

TRANSMISSION
Rear wheel drive

Clutch	dry mono-disc
Gearbox	en bloc with differential, 6 speeds plus reverse

CHASSIS
Unified steel structure

Front suspension	McPherson, lower arms, coil springs, hydraulic shock absorbers, stabiliser bar
Rear suspension	independent, multi-link layout, coil springs, hydraulic shock absorbers, stabiliser bar
Brakes	disc, servo-brake, ABS
Steering	ZF rack
Fuel tank	64 litres
Tyres front/rear	235/35 x 19/305/30 x 19

DIMENSIONS AND WEIGHT
Wheelbase	2350 mm
Track front/rear	1492/1550 mm
Length	4440 mm
Width	1852 mm
Height	1290 mm
Weight	1425 kg

PERFORMANCE
Top speed	302 kph
Power to weight ratio	4.7 kg/hp

911 Sport Classic   2009

It was a limited series of just 250 cars aimed at the great Porsche enthusiasts linked to the company's traditions and took three years to develop. With that, the 911 Sport Classic was presented at the 2009 Frankfurt Motor Show. The body harked back to a number of characteristics details of cars of the past, especially the duck tail spoiler on the engine cover like that of the legendary 1973 911 Carrera RS 2.7, which eventually became a Porsche symbol after initially causing controversy. Another blast from the past were the 19-inch light alloy rims (with super-low 305/30 ZR 19 tyres at the rear, the widest of the entire Porsche range) with their centres finished in shiny black and the wheels in aluminium that brought back memories of the iconic Fuchs rims of the past. The optical groups were also of special design with their black frames and background; at the front there was an aerodynamic profile in the low area. But the most obvious aesthetic aspect was the roof group, which was tapered in the centre with two "bumps" at the sides, recalling the shape of the Carrera GT as well as a number of '50s racing cars. Inside, the seats were in a Nature Espresso colour and all was particularly well finished, while the small plaque with the number of one out of 250 was fixed near to the glovebox. Mechanically, special attention had been paid to the car's handling: the set-up was lowered by 20 mm, the rear track widened by 44 mm, the brakes had carbon-ceramic discs, there was the PASM system and the Sport Chrono Plus package. The engine's power went out through a 6-speed manual gearbox and was revised to be increased by 23 hp, which took it to 408 hp with tuned injection, a new inlet manifold, with finned resonance apparatus and a special exhaust. And that lot took the 911 Sport Classic to a top speed of 302 kph and a 0-100 kph sprint of 4.7 seconds.

A cut-away of the Cayenne S Hybrid shows the disposition of the mechanical components and the power electronics (the motor was 47 hp) and the battery pack under the boot. Due to the hybrid technology, the vehicle's performance was comparable to that of the Cayenne S and its 4.8-litre V8, but there was a drastic reduction in fuel consumption and emissions.

TECHNICAL SPECIFICATION

ENGINE

Front, longitudinal, V6 electric engine

47 hp at 1150 rpm

Bore and stroke	84.5 x 89 mm
Unitary cubic capacity	600
Total cubic capacity	2995 cc
Valve gear	twin overhead camshafts
Number of valves	4 per cylinder
Compression ratio	10.5:1
Fuel feed	direct injection
Ignition	electronic
Coolant	liquid
Lubrication	dry sump
Maximum power	333 hp at 5500-6500 rpm
Specific power	11.3 hp/litre

TRANSMISSION

4WD

Clutch	-
Gearbox	en bloc with engine, automatic, 8 speeds plus reverse

CHASSIS

Unified steel structure

Front suspension	quadrilaterals, air springs, electronically controlled shock absorbers, stabiliser bar
Rear suspension	multi-link layout, air springs, electronically controlled shock absorbers, stabiliser bar
Brakes	disc, servo-brake, ABS
Steering	servo-assisted rack
Fuel tank	85 litres
Tyres front/rear	255/55 x 18/255/55 x 18

DIMENSIONS AND WEIGHT

Wheelbase	2895 mm
Track front/rear	1655/1669
Length	4846 mm
Width	1939 mm
Height	1705 mm
Weight	2240 kg

PERFORMANCE

Top speed	245 kph
Power to weight ratio	6.7 kg/hp

Cayenne S Hybrid   2010

Porsche's first step towards hybrid technology was at the 2005 Frankfurt Motor Show, when the company announced it would introduce a Cayenne S Hybrid before 2010. A working prototype was presented as early as two years later. But the whole thing was delayed until the unveiling of the new generation Cayenne at the 2010 show at Geneva. The Cayenne S Hybrid, which could only be told from the other models by the external lettering, was powered by a 47 hp electric engine flanked by a petrol thermal unit, a new 3-litre V6 turbo of 333 hp with maximum torque at low revs, through a clutch controlled by a hybrid manager, the control management system. Total power output was 380 hp and maximum torque 580 Nm at only 1000 rpm. As a result of the clutch that separated the two power units, it was possible to use just one of the systems or both at the same time: when particular speed was unwanted, the Cayenne Hybrid could continue for a couple of kilometres on its electric engine alone at a maximum of 60 kph, fed by an NiMh 288-volt battery pack, which took the place of the spare wheel. As soon as the accelerator was pressed down, the petrol unit started instantly, which surged ahead helped by the electric motor. The "soar" function was available at high speed: when power was not required, the thermal motor switches off, leaving the car "free" until the accelerator is depressed again. The various phases come in fast and were imperceptible to the driver, partly due to the optimised and soundproofed engine. With this system, fuel consumption was far less than that of the Cayenne S, which was of similar performance, with a declared 8.2 litres to the 100 km. Handling was exceptionally good, partially because of the boost from the electric unit under acceleration to give a 0-100 kph time of 6.5 seconds and a top speed of 242 kph, while the battery pack of around 200 kg only made its weight felt when driving on the limit.

The design of the 918 Spyder also emphasises the car's sportiness as well as the
innovative technology under the skin. Then
there is the strong Porsche identity, emphasising the many references to the traditions
and styling trends typical of the marque.
With analogue instruments next to "touch"
surfaces, the interior also monitors and
commands at the steering wheel, uniting
tradition and innovation.

TECHNICAL SPECIFICATION

ENGINE
Central, longitudinal
V8 and electric motor front/back 80/90 kw

Bore and stroke	-
Unitary cubic capacity	-
Total cubic capacity	3400 cc
Valve gear	twin overhead camshafts
Number of valves	4 per cylinder
Compression ratio	-
Fuel feed	electronic injection
Ignition	electronic
Coolant	liquid
Lubrication	dry sump
Maximum power	500 hp
Specific power	147 hp/litre

TRANSMISSION
4WD hybrid

Clutch	dry mono-disc
Gearbox	en bloc with differential

CHASSIS
CRFP monocoque

Front suspension	double wishbones, electronically controlled shock absorbers
Rear suspension	multi-link layout, electronically controlled shock absorbers
Brakes	carbon-ceramic discs
Steering	servo-assisted rack
Tyres front/rear	-

DIMENSIONS AND WEIGHT

Wheelbase	-
Track front/rear	-
Length	-
Width	-
Height	-
Weight	-

PERFORMANCE

Top speed	325 kph (150 electric)
Power to weight ratio	-

918 Spyder   2010

"The 918 Spyder prototype combined certain aspects, high technology derived from motor racing and electric mobility to offer a fascinating collection of quality: on the one hand, it emitted just 70 grams of CO2 per km with a consumption of 3 litres per 100 kilometres – a stupefying result, even for an ultra-compact city car – and on the other the performance of a super-sport car. Acceleration from 0-100 kph took under 3.2 seconds, top speed was over 320 kph and a lap of the Nürburgring's Nordschleife took less than 7 minutes 30 seconds, faster than, among others, the Carrera GT". This is a summary by Porsche itself in its press kit of 2 March, 2010. The "manifest" of the 918 Spyder, a futuristic concept-laboratory that interprets the company's approach to the supercar with a hybrid plug-in engine. Under the open top's body there is an extremely light monocoque in CFP (a plastic material reinforced by carbon fibre) with elements in aluminium and magnesium able to offer an ultra-high rigidity to guarantee less than 1,490 kg total weight. An exceptional result if one considers the complexity of the drivetrain: the 3.4 V8 engine, derived from that of the RS Spyder, was centrally installed and produced a maximum power output of over 500 hp at 9200 rpm and was coupled with a double clutch gearbox. Two electric motors were installed on both the front and rear axles for an additional total of 218 hp. The lithium ion battery pack, cooled by liquid, was behind the cockpit and was sufficient to a guarantee an electrical autonomy of 25 km. Obviously, the electric and thermal motors could function separately or together to ensure maximum efficiency on the basis of the request and driving style; on the steering wheel there was a selector that produced four different operational logics. Naturally, a system of energy recovery under braking was also to be provided.

The origins of KERS. In extreme synthesis, that is how one could describe the experience of the 911 GT3 R Hybrid, with its classic 6-cylinder boxer engine to which electric motors were added, which permitted the car to recoup kinetic energy developed by the brakes and transform it into power. In the best traditions of the company, the new car showed it was a winner right away.

TECHNICAL SPECIFICATION

ENGINE

Rear, overhanging, longitudinal
6 cylinders horizontally opposed and two 76 kw
electric motors on the front axle

Unitary cubic capacity	666.6 cc
Total cubic capacity	4000 cc
Valve gear	twin overhead camshafts, chain driven
Number of valves	4 per cylinder
Compression ratio	-
Fuel feed	electronic injection
Ignition	electronic
Coolant	liquid
Lubrication	dry sump
Maximum power	465 hp
Specific power /litre	116.25 hp/litre

TRANSMISSION

4WD

Clutch	dry mono-disc
Gearbox	en bloc with differential, 6 speeds plus reverse

CHASSIS

Unified steel structure

Front suspension	McPherson, lower arms, coil springs, hydraulic shock absorbers, stabiliser bar
Rear suspension	independent, multi-link layout, coil springs, hydraulic shock absorbers, stabiliser bar
Brake	disc, servo-brake, ABS
Steering	rack
Fuel tank	-
Tyres front/rear	27/65 x 18/31/71 x 18

DIMENSIONS AND WEIGHT

Wheelbase	2350 mm
Track front7rear	1569/1620
Length	4439 mm
Width	1852 mm
Height	1250
Weight	-

PERFORMANCE

Top speed	-
Power to weight ratio	-

911 GT3 R Hybrid   2010

The 911 GT3 R Hybrid, a racing car of hybrid technology, was unveiled at the 2010 Geneva Motor Show together with the Cayenne S Hybrid and the 918 Spyder. The starting point was the GT3 with its 4-litre 6-cylinder, 465 hp engine. To this were added two 76 kw electric motors fixed to the front axle which, under braking, acted as generators to recover kinetic energy that would otherwise be wasted as heat while braking. To avoid overheating problems o, charge-discharge speed and weight that could negatively affect a conventional battery during a race, they were replaced by a rotating accumulator. A sophisticated flywheel-generator was fitted into the cockpit in place of the passenger seat. Under braking, the energy generated by the two motor-generators put the mass in movement that could rotate up to 40,000 turns per minute. In acceleration, the flywheel became a generator and gives back to the two motors up to 150 kw for 6-8 seconds. That provided a precious extra-boost when overtaking or accelerating. And an intelligent use of the system also had the advantage of reducing fuel consumption and, therefore, the number and length of pit stops. The car introduced at the Geneva show wasn't just a concept car, as the objective was to enter it for the 24 Hours of the Nürburgring as a laboratory car, although the regulations dictated its unusual mechanics had to be severely limited with restrictors and limiters. But from its debut the car's potential was clear, so much so that it set the fastest lap time and easily won the 2011 American Le Mans Series race at Laguna Seca, driven by Romain Dumas and Richard Lietz even though the 911 GT3 Hybrid was not classified, demonstrating its speed and low fuel consumption.

The 911 Turbo S was available as both a Coupe and the Cabriolet, in the photograph, distinguished by its RS Spyder 19-inch rims fixed by a central nut. As well as its performance, the Turbo S also offered a complete range of equipment. The DFI direct fuel injection system enabled the 3.8-litre 6-cylinder boxer engine to achieve excellent fuel consumption and exhaust emission results.

TECHNICAL SPECIFICATION

ENGINE

Rear, overhanging, longitudinal
6 cylinders horizontally opposed

Bore and stroke	102 x 77.5 mm
Unitary cubic capacity	632.5 cc
Total cubic capacity	3800 cc
Valve gear	twin overhead camshafts, chain driven
Number of valves	4 per cylinder
Compression ratio	9.8:1
Fuel feed	direct injection, bi-turbo
Ignition	electronic
Coolant	liquid
Lubrication	dry sump
Maximum power	530 hp at 6250 rpm
Specific power	137.6 hp/litre

TRANSMISSION

4WD

Clutch	-
Gearbox	en bloc with differential, 7 speed automatic with reverse

CHASSIS

Unified steel structure

Front suspension	McPherson, lower arms, coil springs, hydraulic shock absorbers, stabiliser bar
Rear suspension	independent, multi-link layout, coil springs, hydraulic shock absorbers, stabiliser bar
Brakes	disc, servo-brake, ABS
Steering	ZF rack
Fuel tank	67 litres
Tyres front7back	235/35 x 19/305/30 x 19

DIMENSIONS AND WEIGHT

Wheelbase	2350 mm
Track front7rear	1490/1548 mm
Length	4450 mm
Width	1852 mm
Height	1300 mm
Weight	1585 kg

PERFORMANCE

Top speed	315 kph
Power to weight ratio	2.9 kg/hp

911 Turbo S   2010

Excluding the GT2 RS, the top of the 911 range was unveiled at the 2010 Geneva Motor Show and was the new Turbo S in both Coupe and Cabriolet versions. The lead evolution concerned the car's direct injection 6-cylinder engine which, due to different timing and an increase in turbo pressure of 0.2 to 1.02 bar to a total of 1.2 bar, brought 30 hp more horse power for a total of 530 between 6250 and 6750 rpm and 700 Nm of torque at between 2100 and 4250 rpm. And that generated a top speed of 315 kph, from a standing start 0-100 kph time of 3.3 seconds, 0-200 in 10.8. All that with the same fuel consumption as its predecessor of the Turbo – 11.4 litres per 100 km, a record for its category. Both accelerator response- adjusting the turbine geometry and ignition advance – and the sound can vary in line with the selected setting: the Sport Chrono package makes the Sport and Sport Plus buttons available. Transmission is through a brand new Porsche Doppelkupplungsgetriebe seven speed, double clutch gearbox and, therefore, the 4WD run by the Porsche Traction Management system, with Launch Control. The differential is 22% self-locking under traction and 27% in deceleration, but its effect combines with that of the electronic torque allocation system, Porsche Torque Vectoring. The suspension had the PASM shock absorber active control, while the brake discs were of carbon-ceramic material as standard, which was more effective and less subject to wear compared to those in steel and meant a sizeable weight saving against the steel versions and the car was fitted with 19-inch RS Spyder rims with central nut. The 911 Turbo S was packed with top level equipment: adaptable headlights, electric sports seats and a complete entertainment system. The interior was in leather that was available in two combinations – black and cream or black and blue.

The Cayenne unveiled at the 2010 Geneva Motor Show was a completely new vehicle from the mechanical and aesthetic points of view, with the interiors all redesigned taking into account the Panamera's styling trends. Externally, the car appeared much more compact and dynamic from the sloping roof, the more streamlined front end and sinuous rear, with optical groups that extended onto the hatchback.

TECHNICAL SPECIFICATION

ENGINE
Front, longitudinal
90° V8

Bore and stroke	96 x 83 mm
Unitary cubic capacity	600.7 cc
Total cubic capacity	4806 cc
Valve gear	twin overhead camshafts, chain driven
Number of valves	4 per cylinder
Compression ratio	12.5:1
Fuel feed	electronic injection
Ignition	electronic
Coolant	liquid
Lubrication	dry sump
Maximum power	395 hp at 6500 rpm
Specific power	82.2 hp/litre

TRANSMISSION
4WD

Clutch	-
Gearbox	en bloc with engine, automatic, 8 speeds plus reverse

CHASSIS
Unified steel structure

Front suspension	quadrilaterals, air springs, electronically controlled shock absorbers, stabiliser bar
Rear suspension	multi-link layout, air springs, electrically controlled shock absorbers, stabiliser bar
Brakes	disc, servo-assisted, ABS
Steering	ZF rack, servo-assisted
Fuel tank	100 litres
Tyres front/rear	255/55 x 18

DIMENSIONS AND WEIGHT

Wheelbase	2895 mm
Track front/rear	1655/1669 mm
Length	4846 mm
Width	1939 mm
Height	1705 mm
Weight	2065 kg

PERFORMANCE

Top speed	258 kph
Power to weight ratio	5.2 kg/hp

Cayenne (MY 2011) 2010

Eight years after the first Cayenne was unveiled, the new generation was presented on 8 May 2010 for the 2011 model year. Aesthetically, it was completely new in both the interior, where it continued the styling trends of the Panamera, and externally, where the body looked much more agile, reflecting better aerodynamic profiling and, most important of all, a weight reduction of over 250 kg. Part of the weight saving was accounted for by the body shell, where the extensive use of aluminium saved 33 kg despite an increase in external dimensions and the track by 4 cm to the advantage of habitability, which was one of the of the weak points. An even greater advantage was the contribution of a new four wheel drive system based on an electronically-controlled multi-disc clutch for the division of engine torque to the two axles. The Porsche Torque Vectoring Plus was available for the petrol versions, which was able to divide the torque between the two wheels of the rear axle, creating an evolved system of self-locking differential. Those modifications reflected Porsche's response to the "accusations" of over-engineering the first Cayenne in which the little used offroad ability was much developed, excessively increase the car's weight. Pneumatic suspension was only available for the Turbo, while the others had steel units integrated by PASM. On the engine front, along with the Diesel and Hybrid versions - treated separately – at the bottom of the range there was a 6-cylinder 3.6-litre Cayenne with direct injection which increased its power output to 300 hp. And the generation of the 4.8-litre V8 Cayenne S went from 385 to 400 hp, while the performance increased and fuel consumption went down in both cases due to chassis updates and the new 8-speed Tiptronic S automatic gearbox and Start&Stop. The 500 hp of the Cayenne Turbo was unchanged, but in this case, too, fuel consumption was reduced.

With the objective of bridging the gap performance-wise – the existent one between the Carrera 2 and the GT3 - Carrera GTS was introduced at the 2010 Paris Motor Show. The new arrival was of sporty design and was joined by 4WD versions the following year with a Porsche Traction Management integrated system, based on an electronically-controlled multiple disc clutch.

TECHNICAL SPECIFICATION

ENGINE
Rear, overhanging, longitudinal
6 cylinders horizontally opposed

Bore and stroke	102 x 77.5 mm
Unitary cubic capacity	633.3
Total cubic capacity	3800 cc
Valve gear	twin overhead camshafts, chain driven
Number of valves	4 per cylinder
Compression ratio	12.5:1
Fuel feed	electronic injection
Ignition	electronic
Coolant	liquid
Lubrication	dry sump
Maximum power	402 hp at 7300 rpm
Specific power	105.8 hp7litre

TRANSMISSION
Rear wheel drive

Clutch	dry mono-disc
Gearbox	en bloc with differential, 6 speeds plus reverse

CHASSIS
Unified steel structure

Front suspension	McPherson, lower arms, coil springs, hydraulic shock absorbers, stabiliser bar
Rear suspension	independent, multi-link layout, coil springs, hydraulic shock absorbers, stabiliser bar
Brakes	disc, servo-brake, ABS
Steering	ZF rack
Fuel tank	67 litres
Tyres front/7rear	235/35 x 19/305/30 x 19

DIMENSIONS AND WEIGHT

Wheelbase	2350 mm
Track front7rear	1488/1548
Length	4435 mm
Width	1852 mm
Height	1300 mm
Weight	1420 kg

PERFORMANCE

Top speed	306 kph
Power to weight ratio	3.5 kg/hp

911 Carrera GTS and Carrera 4 GTS   2010

In the autumn of 2010, Carrera GTS was added to the 911 range with Coupé and Cabriolet bodies. Despite the fact that the car put its power out through the rear wheels, the newcomer was given the Carrera 4's body shell with 44 mm wider wheel housings to take bigger section tyres in size 305/30ZR19, the widest in the range. Previously, tyres of that width had only been used for the limited production 911 Sport Classic, but on the GTS they were fitted to RS Spyder black-painted rims. Black finish was also used for other elements of the body, including the lower profile of the special Sport Design front spoiler, the lateral mini-skirts and the area between the two exhaust terminals. Black also dominated the interior, including the sports seat alcantara covering as well as the three-spoke steering wheel, the gear lever and hand brake. From the mechanical viewpoint, the chief development was an increase in power output for the 3.8-litre 6-cylinder engine with its direct fuel injection. Due to a special an aspiration manifold resonance with six movable panels controlled by depression – the Carrera's has only one – power output increased by 23 hp to 408 and the maximum torque of 420 Nm so that had not changed, but it was available at 200 revs lower and 320 Nm were on hand at 1500 rpm to provide an immediate and substantial response from accelerator. The transmission was responsible for much of the car's driving pleasure, with its 6-speed manual gearbox or a PDK double clutch associated with manual self-locking differential. The car did the 0-100 kph sprint in 4.2 seconds with the PDK 'box and Sport Plus from the Sport Chrono package, the top speed was 306 kph. With the Porsche Intelligent Performance system, fuel consumption was 10.2 litres per 100 kilometres with the PDK gearbox. In 2011, the rear wheel drive GTS was joined by the Carrera 4 GTS with permanent 4WD. Externally, it stood out for the reflective strip between the rear optical groups.

In the unmistakable profile of the fourth model of the 911 Speedster it was clear to see whether its hood was up or down, even if the former was considered an emergency position, despite the fact that it is no longer drafty as were the earlier models. The body colour was called Pure Blue, with Carrera White as a free of cost alternative.

TECHNICAL SPECIFICATION

ENGINE

Rear, overhanging, longitudinal
6 cylinders horizontally opposed

Bore and stroke	102 x 77.5 mm
Unitary cubic capacity	633.3 cc
Total cubic capacity	3800 cc
Valve gear	twin overhead camshaft chain driven
Number of valves	4 per cylinder
Compression ratio	12.5:1
Fuel feed	electronic injection
Ignition	electronic
Coolant	liquid
Lubrication	dry sump
Maximum power	402 hp at 7300 rpm
Specific power	105.8 hp/litre

TRANSMISSION

Rear wheel drive

Clutch	dry mono-disc
Gearbox	en bloc with differential, 6 speeds plus reverse

CHASSIS

Unified steel structure

Front suspension	McPherson, lower arms, coil springs, hydraulic shock absorbers, stabiliser bar
Rear suspension	independent, multi-link layout, coil springs, hydraulic shock absorbers, stabiliser bar
Brakes	disc, servo-brake, ABS
Steering	ZF rack
Fuel tank	64 litres
Tyres front/rear	235/35 x 19/305/30 x 19

DIMENSIONS AND WEIGHT

Wheelbase	2350 mm
Track front/rear	1492/1550 mm
Length	4400 mm
Width	1852 mm
Height	1284 mm
Weight	1540 kg

PERFORMANCE

Top speed	305 kph
Power to weight ratio	3.8 kg/hp

911 Speedster   2010

The fourth generation of the Speedster came out in 2010 after the progenitor 356 and the two 911 versions of 1988 based on the 3.2-litre Carrera 2 and the 1993 964 series. The new car was created on the base of the 911 Carrera S Cabriolet from the 997 series and presented in October 2010 at the Paris Motor Show. Like the 911 Sport Classic, the Speedster was also the work of Porsche Exclusive, the offshoot that did extreme personalisation of Stuttgart's cars and the preparation of limited production series. And it was to celebrate the 25TH anniversary of Porsche Exclusive in 2011 that 356 examples of the Speedster were to celebrate; to recall the first body of this kind on the basis of the 356. The front and rear bumpers were of a specific design, the car had lateral mini-skirts and the rear wheel housings were widened by 44 mm, as with the Carrera 4. But the true distinctive characteristics of the fourth generation car were the much more inclined windscreen that was lowered 60 mm compared to the Cabriolet, the flatter profile of the manually operated hood and its cover in a plastic material with the two ever-present "humps". Then there were many details painted in black, starting with the front optical group frames and the windscreen's profile. The interior was home to just about all the optionals on the 911 list and the coverings were in a special black leather with numerous details in the body's colour. From the mechanical point of view, the 911 Speedster was powered by the same 3.8-litre 6-cylinder engine as the Carrera GTS with its 408 hp and was linked to the PDK double clutch automatic gearbox. The differential was mechanically self-locking to improve driving pleasure, while the suspension was the electronically controlled PASM and the brakes had carbon-ceramic discs. The car also had an anti-rollover system relative to all the open 911s' extractable roll bars, which was further evolved for the Speedster.

A cut-away of the Panamera Diesel clearly shows the VW-Audi derived 6-cylinder diesel engine, which was perfected by Porsche's technicians. Few details distinguish the vehicle from the petrol versions, but among the most evident is the lettering that also appears on the doors . The car had special low resistance tyres as optional and could cover over 1,200 kilometres with one tank of fuel.

TECHNICAL SPECIFICATION

ENGINE
Front, longitudinal, V6

Bore and stroke	83 x 91.4 mm
Unitary cubic capacity	600 cc
Total cubic capacity	2967 cc
Valve gear	twin over head camshafts
Number of valves	4 per cylinder
Compression ratio	16.8:1
Fuel feed	common rail, turbo
Ignition	-
Coolant	liquid
Lubrication	dry sump
Maximum power	250 hp at 3800-4400 rpm
Specific power	84.3 hp/litre

TRANSMISSION
Rear wheel drive

Clutch	-
Gearbox	en bloc with engine, 8-speed automatic plus reverse

CHASSIS
Unified steel structure

Front suspension	quadrilaterals, air springs, electronically controlled shock absorbers, stabiliser bar
Rear suspension	multi-link layout, air springs, electronically controlled shock absorbers, stabiliser bar
Brakes	disc and servo-brake, ABS
Steering	rack, servo-assisted
Fuel tank	80 litres
Tyres front/rear	245/50 x 18/275/45 x 18

DIMENSIONS AND WEIGHT

Wheelbase	2920 mm
Track front/rear	1658/1662 mm
Length	4970 mm
Width	1931 mm
Height	1418 mm
Weight	1880 kg

PERFORMANCE

Top speed	242 kph
Power to weight ratio	7.5 kg/hp

Panamera Diesel 2011

After the Cayenne Diesel had legitimised such fuel for the cars from Zuffenhausen, it seemed normal that a Panamera powered by the same fuel should join the Porsche list, as it did in May 2011 with a similar engine to its "high wheel" big sister. At the time, with the crisis in full swing and a taxation that tended to give advantage to reasonably powerful cars in some markets, the newcomer was well on the way to success from the start. Compared to the Cayenne, the Panamera's 3-litre V6 turbo-diesel engine with its crankcase in cast iron, head in light alloy and four valves per cylinder, the engine was given more power so that it put out 250 hp between 3800-4400 rpm, with 550 Nm torque between 1750 and 2750. Such results were achieved due to direct injection common rail with pressure varying between 200 and 2000 bar with electric injectors, electronically controlled variable geometry turbochargers, intercooler and an optimised design of the drive shaft. Performance was excellent, the car sprinting from 0-100 kph in 6.8 seconds and a top speed of 242 kph. The generous engine torque available right from low revs also enabled brilliant handling, helped along by an 8-speed Tiptronic S automatic gearbox with torque converter made by Aisin, which transmitted power to the rear wheels only. So it was no surprise that, according to the NEDC homologation cycles, fuel consumption was 6.3 litres per 100 km with low resistance tyres and 6.5 with standards; and carbon dioxide emissions were 167 and 172 grams per km respectively. So autonomy was 1,200 km with a full 80-litre tank of diesel. Start&Stop and an anti-particulate filter were standard. Suspension, assisted by Porsche Stability Management, were standard with steel springs and optional with the pneumatic version.

Externally, it was only the lettering Hybrid the distinguished, more modern and ecological Panamera from the rest of the range. The new aspects were under the skin, where the same drivetrain was installed with the engine that had already made its debut on the Cayenne S Hybrid and ensured lively performance with contained fuel consumption. Announced in 2008, the car eventually appeared in February 2011.

TECHNICAL SPECIFICATION

ENGINE

Front, longitudinal,
V6 and electric motor 47 hp at 1150 rpm

Bore and stroke	84.5 x 89 mm
Unitary cubic capacity	500 cc
Total cubic capacity	2995
Valve gear	twin overhead camshafts
Number of valves	4 per cylinder
Compression ratio	10.5:1
Fuel feed	direct injection
Ignition	electronic
Coolant	liquid
Lubrication	dry sump
Maximum power	333 hp at 5500-6500 rpm
Specific power	111.3 hp/litre

TRANSMISSION

Rear wheel drive

Clutch	dry mono-disc
Gearbox	en bloc with engine, Tiptronic, 8 speeds plus reverse

CHASSIS

Unified steel structure

Front suspension	quadrilaterals, air springs, electronically controlled shock absorbers, stabiliser bar
Rear suspension	multi-link layout, air springs, electronically controlled shock absorbers, stabiliser bar
Brakes	disc and servo-brake, ABS
Steering	servo-assisted rack
Fuel tank	100 litres
Tyres front/rear	245/50 x 18/275/45 x 18

DIMENSIONS AND WEIGHT

Wheelbase	2920 mm
Track front/rear	1658/1662 mm
Length	4970 mm
Width	1931 mm
Height	1418 mm
Weight	1980 kg

PERFORMANCE

Top speed	270 kph
Power to weight ratio	5.9 kg/hp

Panamera S Hybrid   2011

The S Hybrid version of the Panamera was introduced in 2011 and adopted the same mechanical layout as the Cayenne S Hybrid, in which a 47 hp electric motor worked with a petrol thermal unit, a new 3-litre V6 originated by Audi charged with a 333 hp volumetric compressor with torque at low revs through a clutch controlled by the Hybrid Manager, the system's control unit. So total power output was 380 hp and maximum torque peaked at 580 Nm at just 1000 rpm. Drive was from the rear and the transmission used the 8-speed automatic Tiptronic S gearbox. Due to the clutch that separated the two power units, it was possible to use just one of the two systems, or both of them together. When a particular push was not needed and in residential areas, the Panamera Hybrid could carry on for a couple of kilometres with the electric motor alone at up to 75 kph by pressing the E-power button, prolonging electrical drive as much as possible by adapting performance. As soon as the accelerator was depressed the petrol engine immediately came into play, helped by the electric motor and a system called E-boost. At speeds of up to 165 kph, the "soaring" system was ready to work, but when more was not needed at a constant speed, the thermal engine switched off, leaving the car free without engine brake until acceleration is needed again. The various stages were extremely rapid and imperceptible to the driver with a top speed of 270 kph and the 0-100 kph dash in six seconds, while containing fuel consumption at seven litres per 100 kilometres, 6.8 with special low resistance tyres. Performance sufficient to win the 2011 Intercity Rally Michelin Bibendum Challenge, a competition based on sustainable mobility. The preparation of the car both at aesthetic and mechanical levels was the same as the Panamera S.

The Panamera GTS was destined for the sportier customer that could easily be seen from the outside, starting with the body's rich red colour. The optical groups were the Turbo's dual xenon and LED but with black internal strips, while the 19-inch rims were also Turbo derived. The front bumpers were Sport Design, while the lower part of the car was in matt black.

TECHNICAL SPECIFICATION

ENGINE
Front, longitudinal, V8

Bore and stroke	96 X 83 mm
Unitary cubic capacity	600.7 cc
Total cubic capacity	4806 cc
Valve gear	twin overhead camshafts
Number of valves	4 per cylinder
Compression ratio	12.5:1
Fuel feed	direct injection
Ignition	electronic
Coolant	liquid
Lubrication	dry sump
Maximum power	430 hp at 6700 rpm
Specific power	89.5 hp/litre

TRANSMISSION
Rear wheel drive

Clutch	double
Gearbox	en bloc with engine, 7 speeds plus reverse

CHASSIS
Unified steel structure

Front suspension	quadrilaterals, air springs, electronically controlled shock absorbers, stabiliser bar
Rear suspension	multi-link layout, air springs, electronically controlled shock absorbers, stabiliser bar
Brakes	disc, servo-brake, ABS
Steering	rack, servo-assisted
Fuel tank	100 litres
Tyres front/rear	255/45 x 19/285/40 x 19

DIMENSIONS AND WEIGHT
Wheelbase	2920 mm
Track front/rear	1656/1656 mm
Length	4970 mm
Width	1931 mm
Height	1408 mm
Weight	1920 kg

PERFORMANCE
Top speed	288 kph
Power to weight ratio	4.4 kg/hp

Panamera GTS

2011

The Panamera GTS (Grand Sport Tourer) was aimed at clients who like taking to the track or who wanted a sporty car, but which was perfectly suitable for every-day use. The starting point was the Panamera 4S, but the power output of the 4.8-litre V8 was taken to 430 hp at 6700 rpm, with maximum revs increased by 400 and the car's torque to 520 Nm because the aspiration camshaft had been modified with a greater rise and aspiration improved with a supplementary air filters with openable flaps to achieve a dynamic overfeed. The PDK dual clutch gearbox, which was optimised with the Sport Chrono package able to interrupt fuel feed to the cylinders to speed up a change, transmitted torque to the PTM 4-wheel drive. And the exhaust's sound was improved and had matt black terminals. The brakes, with their callipers painted red, and the 19-inch rims also came from the Turbo S, as did the retractable rear spoiler, which opened at 90 kph and could also extend laterally to improve downforce. Acceleration from 0-100 kph took 4.5 seconds and top speed was 288 kph, all with a declared fuel consumption of 10.9 litres per 100 kilometres and 10.7 litres with low rolling resistance tyres. Set-up was 10 mm lower and the suspension had air springs managed by the PASM system, with its ground height, rigidity and shock absorber function that could be automatically adapted to the driving style of the person at the wheel. Externally, the Panamera GTS distinguished itself with special front bumpers with their lower area matt black and plus numerous body details in shiny black, including the lateral air vents, the rear diffusers, window frames, the Turbo's optical groups with black background. The interior was in leather with alcantara inserts and GTS logos on the seats.

The 991 series of the 911 line looked much more streamlined than previous generations, but its style was still unmistakable. Part of the design was a new exhaust system. It was lighter, had a sound symposer that could select the most attractive exhaust note and transmit it to the cab via a plastic tube that came from the parcel shelf.

TECHNICAL SPECIFICATION

ENGINE

Rear, overhanging, longitudinal,
6 cylinders horizontally opposed

Bore and stroke	97 x 77.5 mm
Unitary cubic capacity	572.6 cc
Total cubic capacity	3436 cc
Valve gear	twin overhead camshaft, chain driven
Number of valves	4 per cylinder
Compression ratio	12.5:1
Fuel feed	electronic injection
Ignition	electronic
Coolant	liquid
Lubrication	dry sump
Maximum power	350 hp at 7400 rpm
Specific power	101.9 hp/litre

TRANSMISSION

Rear wheel drive

Clutch	dry mono-disc
Gearbox	en bloc with differential, 7 speeds plus reverse

CHASSIS

Unified steel structure

Front suspension	McPherson, lower arms, coil springs, hydraulic shock absorbers, stabiliser bar
Rear suspension	independent, multi-link layout, coil springs, hydraulic shock absorbers, stabiliser bar
Brakes	disc, servo-brake, ABS
Steering	ZF rack, servo-assisted
Fuel tank	68 litres
Tyres front/rear	235/40 x 19, 285/35 x 19

DIMENSIONS AND WEIGHT

Wheelbase	2450 mm
Track front7rear	1532/1518 mm
Length	4491 mm
Width	1808 mm
Height	1303 mm
Weight	1380 kg

PERFORMANCE

Top speed	289 kph
Power to weight ratio	3.9 kg/hp

911 Carrera and Carrera S (991)   2011

By early 2011, the 997 series of the 911 was a mature car that was fast and a success, offered with four different bodies and no fewer than 23 alternative versions, but a new generation of symbolic cars from Porsche was in the air. It was the 991 series, which was unveiled at the year's Frankfurt Motor Show. The body shell was completely redesigned, with substantial use of light alloy and high resistance steel, which increased torsional rigidity and contribute to reducing the car's weight by no less than 45 kg compared to the previous generation. A major new aspect was the lengthening of the wheelbase by a significant 10 cm and that gave the car a much slenderer line due to the reduced bumps, but handling was also much improved given that, because of the new compact gearbox, the rear axle had moved a considerable 8 cm closer to the engine. A second unconventional choice was the decision to widen the front track by 6 cm. The Carrera's engine was a new 6-cylinder, 3.4-litre boxer that put out 350 hp, was able to carry the 1,400 kg car from 0-100 kph in 4.6 seconds with its PDK gearbox (4.4 seconds with the Sport Plus function of the Sport Chrono package) with a fuel consumption of 8.2 litres per 100 km. But the Carrera S was powered by a 3.8-litre flat six that put out 400 hp at 7400 rpm and 440 Nm at 5600 rpm and that was able to speed to 302 kph and 0.100 kph in 4.3 seconds (4.1 sec in the Sport Plus mode); in this case, too fuel consumption was reduced at 8.7-litres for the 100 km. There were two different gearboxes available: the dual clutch, 7-speed PDK and a new 7-speed manual with three shafts derived from the PDK. The car had 20-inch diameter rims and the suspension the Porsche Dynamic Chassis Control, which was able to manage roll and optimise road holding. The interiors were also new and were similar to those of the Panamera – but without imposing on the 911's identity: the five-instrument dashboard was "saved" (even if one was a multi-function monitor) as was the ignition key on the right.

The sporty and aggressive appearance of the Cayenne GTS was emphasised by its large bi-plane rear spoiler, the wider wheel housings, 20-inch rims, mini-skirts and aerodynamic devices, as well as its matt black exhaust terminals. The interior was also specific to the model, with sports seats and finish in alcantara. The metallic deep yellowish green peridot was one of the two special colours of the Cayenne GTS.

TECHNICAL SPECIFICATION

ENGINE
Front, longitudinal, V8

Bore and stroke	93 x 83 mm
Unitary cubic capacity	563.8 cc
Total cubic capacity	4511 cc
Valve gear	twin overhead camshafts, chain driven
Number of valves	4 per cylinder
Compression ratio	12.5:1
Fuel feed	electronic injection
Ignition	electronic
Coolant	liquid
Lubrication	dry sump
Maximum power	420 hp
Specific power	93.3 hp/litre

TRANSMISSION
4WD

Clutch	-
Gearbox	en bloc with engine, Tiptronic S 8 speed plus reverse

CHASSIS
Unified steel structure

Front suspension	quadrilaterals, air springs, electronically controlled shock absorbers, stabiliser bar
Rear suspension	multi-link layout, air springs, electronically controlled shock absorbers, stabiliser bar
Brakes	disc, servo-brake, ABS
Steering	ZF rack, servo-assisted
Fuel tank	100 litres
Tyres front/rear	275/45 x 20

DIMENSIONS AND WEIGHT

Wheelbase	2855 mm
Track front/rear	1647/1662 mm
Length	4786 mm
Width	1928 mm
Height	1699 mm
Weight	2355 kg

PERFORMANCE

Top speed	261 kph
Power to weight ratio	5.2 kg/hp

Cayenne GTS   2012

A GTS version of the Cayenne had already become available in 2007, but with the new generation in 2010 a range variant was introduced, not only to closed the gap between the 400 hp Cayenne S and the 500 hp of the Turbo, but also to be able to offer a more dynamic and sporty version that delivered plenty of driving pleasure, especially on the road. The GTS was unveiled at the 2012 Auto China, the Peking motor show. So the set-up was more than rigid, always with the PASM and PTV Plus systems for suspension and traction control, and was lowered by 24 mm compared to the S. In addition, the rims were 20-inch diameter with a special style – RS Spyder Design. The brake callipers had been painted red. The mechanics were those of the S, except for the engine tuning which had direct injection, Start&Stop and Variocam Plus, like its smaller sister, with the engine taken to 420 hp. The maximum torque of 515 Nm also contributed to improving performance, so that top speed went up to 261 kph with a Cx of 0.37, while acceleration from 0-100 kph took 5.7 seconds, 13.3 seconds to 0-160 kph; all this while fuel consumption fell to a declared average of 10.7 litres per 100 kilometres. This level of performance was favoured by a particular set-up of the 8-speed Tiptronic S transmission. The appearance of the GTS had punch both inside and out; the cab had sporty seats in dial-colour leather and had eight adjustment points, finish was in alcantara and details in the body's colour: the front end came from the Turbo but with a bigger air intake, wider wheel housings, mini-skirts, lower aerodynamic profiles and a bi-plane rear spoiler. The wider wheel housings exhaust system had four matt black terminals and a specific sound. Two extra-series colour were on offer for the GTS: there was metallised yellowish green peridot and metallised dark red carminio.

The lines of the new Boxster were much more muscular and dynamic against those of the previous generation and the interiors were of new design, much influenced by those of the Carrera GT and the latest 911s. But the aesthetics were just a mirror of a lightened body shell that was completely new and of perfected mechanics to obtain better performance and efficiency, all to the advantage of performance, fuel consumption and emissions.

TECHNICAL SPECIFICATION

ENGINE
Central, longitudinal
6 cylinders horizontally opposed

Bore and stroke	97 x 77.5 mm
Unitary cubic capacity	572.6 cc
Total cubic capacity	3436 cc
Valve gear	twin overhead camshaft, chain driven
Number of valves	4 per cylinder
Compression ratio	12.5:1
Fuel feed	electronic injection
Ignition	electronic
Coolant	liquid
Lubrication	dry sump
Maximum power	315 hp at 6700 rpm
Specific power	92.9 hp/litre

TRANSMISSION
Rear wheel drive

Clutch	dry mono-disc
Gearbox	en bloc with differential, 6 speeds plus reverse

CHASSIS
Unified steel structure

Front suspension	McPherson, Lower arms, coil springs, hydraulic shock absorbers, stabiliser bar
Rear suspension	McPherson, lower arms, coil springs, hydraulic shock absorbers, stabiliser bar
Brakes	disc, servo-brake, ABS
Steering	rack, servo-assisted
Fuel tank	64 litres
Tyres front/rear	235/40 x 19/265/40 x 19

DIMENSIONS AND WEIGHT
Wheelbase	2475 mm
Track front/rear	1526/1540 mm
Length	4374 mm
Width	1801 mm
Height	1281 mm
Weight	1320 kg

PERFORMANCE
Top speed	279 kph
Power to weight ratio	4.9 kg/hp

Boxster (MY 2012) 2012

The third generation of the Boxster – the first harked back to 1996 – was launched in early 2012 at the Geneva Motor Show. If the second generation could be considered an evolution of the first, the third was a completely new model, in which distinctive Boxster elements could be recognised, including the body shell, which had been completely redesigned. Track and wheelbase had grown, all to the benefit of performance and habitability, but the car's weight had fallen to 1,310 kg as the chassis made considerable use of aluminium, of which the doors, part of the roll bar, engine cover and boot lid were also made. From the design point of view, sides with fewer humps, advanced windscreen and "muscular" shoulders had two large air intakes, the inset of which began just past the front wheel arches. The rear spoiler was still retractable, while the new electric hood opened completely automatically in nine seconds up to 50 kph. As before, there were two versions, the Boxster and the Boxster S, the former with a new 2.7-litre engine derived from the 3.4 of the S that put out 265 hp, 10 hp more than the "old" 2.9-litre. The 3.4-litre unit of the Boxster S had an additional 5 hp in relation to its predecessor for a 315 hp output. Both the engines had direct injection, VarioCam Plus, Start&Stop, an evolved thermal management system and electric utilities, which contributed to a 15% fuel consumption reduction. This with PDK, which also improved performance with a declared 7.7 litres per 100 km for the Boxster and 8 litres for the S. The gearboxes were production 6-speed manuals with the dual clutch PDK optional, as were the Sport Chrono package, Porsche Torque Vectoring and the Porsche Active Suspension Management. The cars' 0-100 acceleration times were 5.7 seconds and 5 seconds respectively. The PCCB braking system with carbon-ceramic discs was optional.

The Martini Racing liveried 918 Spider, which made its debut in July 2012 and it announced the arrival of the definitive car – the one in the picture is a concept car with a number of provisional details. The car's development was already well advanced in both the project and practical areas. Various prototypes were tested at the Nürburgring and the high speed Nardò ring in Italy, which had recently been acquired by the VW-Audi group.

TECHNICAL SPECIFICATION

ENGINE
Central, longitudinal, V8
with electric motors front and rear 80/90 kw

Bore and stroke	-
Unitary cubic capacity	-
Total cubic capacity	4600 cc
Valve gear	twin overhead camshafts
Number of valves	4 per cylinder
Compression ratio	-
Fuel feed	electronic injection
Ignition	electronic
Coolant	liquid
Lubrication	dry sump
Maximum power	570 hp
Specific power	123.9 hp/litre

TRANSMISSION
4WD hybrid

Clutch	dry mono-disc
Gearbox	en bloc with differential, 7 speeds plus reverse

CHASSIS
Monocoque in CRFP

Front suspension	double wishbones, electronically controlled shock absorbers
Rear suspension	multi-link layout, electronically controlled hydraulic shock absorbers
Brakes	carbon-ceramic discs
Steering	rack, servo-assisted
Fuel tank	-
Tyres front/rear	-

DIMENSIONS AND WEIGHT

Wheelbase	2730 mm
Track front/rear	1664/1612 mm
Length	4645 mm
Width	1940 mm
Height	1667 mm
Weight	1750 kg

PERFORMANCE

Top speed	325 kph (150 electric)

918 Spyder

2012

After the 2010 success of the 918 Spyder concept car, it was the turn of the 918 RSR, a racing interpretation of the car, to make its debut first at the Detroit Motor Show and then at Geneva. The newcomer embodied many new styling trends of the definitive model, with its mechanics derived from those of the 911 GT3 Hybrid, with a kinetic accumulator on the 3.4-litre V8 engine that put out 563 hp at 10,300 rpm, and two electric motors each of 102 hp. The completed 918 Spyder first appeared in 2012 with ambitions that went beyond those declared two years earlier: it shot from 0-100 kph in under three seconds and lapped the Nordschleife in less than 7 minutes 22 seconds and on 19 September 2012 it set a lap time of 7 minutes 14 seconds: fuel consumption was 3 litres per 100 km and the car had a 25 km autonomy in electric mode. The 4.6-litre ultra-light V8 thermal engine generated 570 hp at over 9000 rpm, the exhausts of which were inclined upwards for best cooling of the engine bay, in which there were also the lithium ion batteries with their 312 cells liquid cooled. The 120 hp electric motor was on the rear axle, while the second 110 hp unit ensured front traction. The gearbox, an especially refined was a 7-speed PDK, and the system for recovering energy during braking (it had to ensure it did so from a deceleration of 0.5g before the carbon-ceramic discs cut in, but also with that right driving feel. As a result of the modern CFRP monocoque the car's total weight was under 1,700 kg and its top speed was more than 325 kph. The plug-in hybrid drivetrain had five positions: E-power, which was completely electric; Hybrid, electric and thermal for maximum efficiency; Sport Hybrid for sporty driving, with the electrical units helping the thermal; Race Hybrid for maximum performance (the batteries were only recharged when maximum power output was not requested; Hot Lap, which exploited all the available energy until the charge had been used up, to optimise performance for a reduced period of time.

Just a few details distinguished the Carrera 4 and 4S from the rear wheel drive cars. The most evident was the wider rear wheel housings, which had to make room for bigger dimension back tyres. The cars' lines looked slender and slick because the car was lower, had shortened overhangs and the attentive aerodynamic profiling that resulted in an excellent Cx 0.29.

TECHNICAL SPECIFICATION

ENGINE

Rear, overhanging, longitudinal
6 cylinders horizontally opposed

Bore and stroke	97 x 77.5 mm
Unitary cubic capacity	572.6 cc
Total cubic capacity	3436 cc
Valve gear	twin overhead camshaft, chain driven
Number of valves	4 per cylinder
Compression ratio	12.5:1
Fuel feed	electronic injection
Ignition	electronic
Coolant	liquid
Lubrication	dry sump
Maximum power	350 hp at 7400 rpm
Specific power	101.9 hp/litre

TRANSMISSION

4WD

Clutch	dual
Gearbox	en block with differential, 7 speeds plus reverse

CHASSIS

Unified steel structure

Front suspension	McPherson, lower arms, coil springs, hydraulic shock absorbers, stabiliser bar
Rear suspension	independent, multi-link layout, coil springs, hydraulic shock absorbers, stabiliser bar
Brakes	disc, servo-brake, ABS
Steering	rack, servo-assisted
Fuel tank	68 litres
Tyres front/rear	-

DIMENSIONS AND WEIGHT

Wheelbase	2450 mm
Track front/rear	1532 / 1522 mm
Length	4491 mm
Width	1852 mm
Height	1304 mm
Wight	1450 kg

PERFORMANCE

Top speed	285 kph
Power to weight ratio	4.14 kg/hp

911 Carrera 4 and 4S (991)   2012

The rear wheel drive Carrera and Carrera S versions of the new 911 991 series were launched in the autumn of 2011, and in less than a year along came the 4WD Carrera 4 and Carrera 4S, at a time when the rest of the range was still based on the 997 series. The differences between the 4WD cars were minimal: the rear track was widened by 22 mm and the chassis was sorted, taking account of the Porsche Traction Management transmission. Even the red reflective strip between the two rear optical groups were of new design. Compared to the previous generation, performance was improved and fuel consumption had dropped by 16%, contributed to in part by a total lightening of 65 kg. Most of the weight saving came from the new, longer wheelbase body shell, but also the new engines and an exhaust system that saved 2.5 kg alone. The 6-cylinder 3.4 and 3.8 boxer engines with direct fuel injection were also optimised with a cooling system shared with the transmission: on the one hand, it provided more effective management and on the other it permitted all the drivetrain to reach an operating temperature very quickly, reducing fuel consumption and improving yield. Start&Stop and the energy recovery system were standard. The 3.4-litre engine, with DFI direct fuel injection and VarioCam Plus developed 350 hp at 7400 rpm, with a maximum torque of 390 Nm at 5600 rpm. With the Porsche 7-speed dual clutch PDK system the Carrera 4 accelerated from 0-100 kph in 4.9 seconds and to a top speed of 285 kph. The 3.8-litre Carrera 4S put out 400 hp at 7400 rpm and a maximum torque of 440 Nm at 5600 rpm. That was enough for a 0-100 kph dash in 4.3 seconds and a max speed of 297 kph. The suspension and the two gearboxes (manual or PDK, both with three shafts and seven speeds) were common to all rear wheel drive versions.

Two years after the initial news and the first official illustration of February 2012, Porsche finally began to deliver the long awaited new Macan SUV in the spring of 2014. It became available from the time of its launch with three different engine types that had a stunning amount of power ranging from the 250 hp and the 400 hp, the latter from a 3.6-litre V6 turbo.

TECHNICAL SPECIFICATION

ENGINE
Front, longitudinal
6 cylinders

Bore and stroke	83 x 96 mm
Unitary cubic capacity	600.66 cc
Total cubic capacity	3604 cc
Valve gear	4 camshafts
Number of valves	4 per cylinder
Compression ratio	10.5:1
Fuel feed	petrol
Ignition	electronic
Coolant	liquid
Lubrication	dry sump
Maximum power	400 hp at 6000 rpm
Specific power	110 hp

TRANSMISSION
Active 4WD

Clutch	double
Gearbox	PDK, 7 speed plus reverse

CHASSIS
Light monocoque

Front suspension	axis with five aluminium control arms, cylindrical coil springs, gas hydraulic double tube shock absorbers inside
Rear suspension	axis with trapezoidal arms, cylindrical coil springs, gas hydraulic double tube shock absorbers inside
Brakes	disc, with twin circuit braking system and division on the two axles
Steering	servo-assisted
Fuel tank	75 litres
Tyres front/rear	8J x 19 with 235/55ZR19 101Y 9J x 19 with 255/50ZR19 103 Y

DIMENSIONS AND WEIGHT

Wheelbase	2807 mm
Track front/rear	1655/1651 mm
Length	4699 mm
Width	1923 mm
Height	1624 mm
Weight	1925 kg

PERFORMANCE

Top speed	266 kph
Power to weight ratio	147.14 kW

Macan   2013

The name Macan comes from the Indonesian tiger and the new SUV brought honour to that denomination: potent and always ready to surge ahead, it was also agile and tenacious on offroad tracts. The last evolution of four-wheel drive, the Porsche Traction Management (PTM) is one of the most effective systems of its kind in the world. The Macan was unveiled at the Los Angeles Motor Show in November 2013, with sales beginning in April 2014.

The Macan was the first Porsche to enter the compact SUV market, establishing new standards in dynamics and driving pleasure both on and off road, but it still also conserved the Porsches' classical driving characteristics: maximum values in acceleration and braking, power, extreme agility and steering precision. Qualities that combine with a high degree of comfort, also in daily use. Like all other Porsches, the sports DNA of the Macan were immediately recognised from its design. The bonnet was wrap-around and the roof line accentuated the general effect of sporting elegance and potent dynamism. Many of the design elements of the other sporty Porsches were improved and incorporated into the Macan, which was a German SUV produced in the company's Leipzig factory. Porsche had invested 500 million euros in the plant to establish an entire production line and was built to be able to construct around 50,000 vehicles a year. There were three models at the time of the launch, all with 4WD: they were the Macan S with a twin turbo V6 3-litre engine that put out 340 hp (250kW); the Macan S Diesel with a 3-litre V6 turbo diesel power unit of 250 hp (185 kW); and the top of the range Macan Turbo – see the previous page's technical specification – which was the most powerful vehicle in the compact SUV segment. The 3.6-litre twin turbo V6 generated 400 hp (294 kW) and shot from 0-100 kph in 4.8 seconds and to a top speed of 266 kph.

In a panorama of cars and general transport which was increasingly moving towards the hybrid, Porsche could not ignore the process and decided to launch its challenge as part of its premium range. It did so with the Panamera and became the first of the constructors to do so. The performance produced by the company's first attempt was more than satisfactory, with the driver being able to make even long journeys in a completely electric mode.

TECHNICAL SPECIFICATION

ENGINE
Front, longitudinal, V6, electric motor
95 hp at 2200-2600 rpm

Bore and stroke	84.5 x 89 mm
Unitary cubic capacity	499.1 cc
Maximum cubic capacity	2995 cc
Valve gear	4 camshafts
Number of valves	4 per cylinder
Compression ratio	10.5:1
Fuel feed	direct injection
Ignition	electronic
Coolant	liquid
Maximum power	416 hp at 5500 rpm
(thermal and electric)	
Maximum torque	590 Nm at 1250 rpm

TRANSMISSION
Rear wheel drive

Gearbox	Tiptronic S, automatic, 8 speeds plus reverse

CHASSIS
Self-supporting in light alloy of an aluminium, steel and magnesium mixture

Front suspension	axis double wishbones in aluminium, air springs, hydraulic twin tube gas shock absorbers inside
Rear suspension	multisnodo aluminium axis with auxiliary chassis, air springs with insertable additional volume, hydraulic twin tube gas shock absorbers
Brakes	disc, with dual circuit braking system and distribution on the two axles
Steering	servo-assisted
Fuel tank	80 litres
Tyres front/rear	8J x 18 with 245/50ZR18 9J x 18 with 275/45ZR18

DIMENSIONS AND WEIGHT

Wheelbase	2920 mm
Track front/rear	1568/1662 mm
Length	5015 mm
Width	1931 mm
Height	1418 mm
Weight	2095 kg

PERFORMANCE

Top speed	270 kph
Power to weight ratio	141.01 kw

Panamera S E-hybrid   2013

Porsche celebrated the debut of its second generation Panamera at the 2013 Shanghai Motor Show. In the centre of their stand was the Panamera S E-hybrid, the first premium segment car in the world with plug-in hybrid traction. Next to the new model, which combined efficiency with sportiness and comfort, were two prestigious Executive versions with lengthened wheelbase and 3-litre V6 engines, developed with twin turbochargers for the Panamera S and 4S. The S E-hybrid was the coherent development of the parallel Full-Hybrid system, which the company was the first to launch in 2010, when it introduced vehicles with that kind of engine: the Cayenne S-Hybrid and Panamera S-Hybrid. That generation had already become popular throughout the world, becoming a paragon of efficiency and synonymous with driving performance. An example is that the number of Cayenne S Hybrids sold had already more than doubled just a year after its introduction in 2011 compared to the oppositions' cars. The technical specification of the new model lists a power output of 416 hp (306 kw), with a 0-100 km dash in 5.5 seconds and a top speed of 270 kph.

The car's fascination comes from its extraordinary efficiency and its ability to travel a long distance with all-electric power. In the NEDC, the new European driving cycle, the Panamera S E-hybrid consumed 3.1 litres to the 100 kilometres with a CO_2 emission of 71 g/km. The electric autonomy was calculated as 36 km in the NEDC and its top speed in electric mode at 135 kph. A lithium-ion battery with a 9.4 kWh, acted as an accumulator of energy. Based on the electrical contact available, it could be recharged in just a few hours using an electric plug or while travelling due to energy recovery.

The new Porsche 911 GT3, the sportiest in the long tradition of 911s, made its world debut at the 2013 Geneva Motor Show. It was the jewel in Porsche's crown and had truly exceptional performance, with a 315 kph top speed, but startling truth was the time it set on the big ring of the Nürburgring of 7 minutes and 30 seconds.

TECHNICAL SPECIFICATION

ENGINE
Rear, overhanging, longitudinal
6 cylinders

Bore and stroke	102.0 x 77.5 mm
Unitary cubic capacity	633.3 cc
Total cubic capacity	3799 cc
Valve gear	4 camshafts
Number of valves	4 per cylinder
Compression ratio	12.9:1
Fuel	petrol
Ignition	electronic
Coolant	liquid
Lubrication	dry sump
Maximum power	475 hp at 9000 rpm
Specific power	125 hp

TRANSMISSION
Rear wheel drive

Clutch	double
Gearbox	PDK
	7 speeds plus reverse

CHASSIS
Light monocoque

Front suspension	McPherson-type, longitudinal arms and shock absorbers, coil springs with interior shock absorbers, six piston mono-block brake calipers, perforated brake discs and with internal ventilation of a diameter of 380 mm and a thickness of 34 mm
Rear suspension	multi-link axis with wheels inserted singularly in five oscillating arms, cylindrical coil springs with interior coaxial shock absorbers, active steering rear axle
Brakes	perforated discs with internal ventilation
Steering	servo-assisted
Fuel tank	64 litres (90 litres optional)
Tyres front/rear	9J x 20 with 245/35ZR20 12J x 20 with 305/30ZR20

DIMENSIONS AND WEIGHT

Wheelbase	2457 mm
Track front/rear	1551/1555 mm
Length	4545 mm
Width	1851 mm
Height	1269 mm
Weight	1430 kg

PERFORMANCE

Top speed	315 kph
Power to weight ratio	241 kW

911 GT3 2013

This is the fifth generation of the 911, the development of which involved all the main sectors, including the engine, gearbox, chassis and body. The new car is in pole position among the Porsche sports cars with normally aspirated engines due to a technical specification which, among other things, puts out a maximum of 475 hp and accelerates from 0-100 kph in 3.5 seconds, its top speed 315 kph in 7ᵀᴴ gear. On the technical front, the main new development is the active steering rear axle, which has been added to a production Porsche for the first time.

The principal mechanics of the GT3 include effective rear traction, a 3.8-litre boxer power unit, and the Porsche Doppelkupplung (PDK) double clutch gearbox. The 6-cylinder is based on that of the 911 Carrera S, although the two only have a few elements in common because all the gears, valve controls, titanium piston rods and the forged pistons have been either adapted or developed specifically for the GT3. All modifications that led to a fairly high 9000 rpm. The gearbox also marks an important development with characteristics that refer straight to that manual-sequential 'box, as used in motor racing, with additional advantages in terms of performance and driver dynamics.

Absolutely new is the active steering rear axle, which improves precision and transverse dynamics. Based on the car's speed, the system sends the rear wheels in a direction contrary to or the same as the fronts, improving agility and directional stability. The self-locking rear differential is electronically adjusted, but the active engine support system also contributes to improving handling.

The large fixed rear wing is, once again, the distinctive element and produces exceptional aerodynamics, with low resistance values and a high degree of downforce. From a standing start, the GT3 makes 100 kph in 3.5 seconds and 200 kph in under 12 seconds.

Porsche brought out this celebrative version of the 911 at the Frankfurt Motor Show (IAA). Once again, this anniversary 911 is a coupé with the classic overhanging 6-cylinder engine and rear wheel drive. Another significant factor is the number of anniversary cars produced – 1963, representing the year in which this evergreen model first appeared and one that has been such a Porsche symbol.

TECHNICAL SPECIFICATION

ENGINE

Rear, overhanging, longitudinal
6 cylinders horizontally opposed

Bore and stroke	97 x 77.5 mm
Unitary cubic capacity	572.6 cc
Total cubic capacity	3436 cc
Valve gear	twin overhead camshafts, chain driven
Number of valves	4 per cylinder
Compression ratio	12.5.1
Fuel feed	electronic injection
Ignition	electronic
Coolant	liquid
Lubrication	dry sump
Maximum power	350 hp at 7400 rpm
Specific power	101.9 hp/litre

TRANSMISSION

Rear wheel drive

Clutch	dry mono-disc
Gearbox	en bloc with differential, 7 speed plus reverse

CHASSIS

Unified steel structure

Front suspension	McPherson, lower arms, coil springs, hydraulic shock absorbers, stabiliser bar
Rear suspension	independent, multi-link layout, coil springs, hydraulic shock absorbers, stabiliser bar
Brakes	disc, servo-brake, ABS
Steering	ZF rack, servo-assisted
Fuel tank	68 litres
Tyres	235/40 x 19 - 285/35 x 19

DIMENSIONS AND WEIGHT

Wheelbase	2450 mm
Track front/rear	1532/1518 mm
Length	4491 mm
Width	1808 mm
Height	1303 mm
Weight	1380 kg

PERFORMANCE

Top speed	289 kph
Power to weight ratio	3.9 kg/hp

911 50ᵀᴴ   2013

Fifty years of the Porsche legend, from 1963 – 2013. To celebrate this significant anniversary, Stuttgart built a limited number of 1,963 cars – representing the year the 911 first appeared. The 911 50ᵀᴴ anniversary car retraces the technical aspects of the Carrera S of two years earlier.

The equipment of this limited edition included the Porsche Active Suspension Management system (PASM) sports chassis with a wider track and exceptional transverse dynamics. The special 20-inch rims in matt black with shiny spokes were a tribute to the legendary Fuchs wheels. Chrome trim on the front air intakes, the engine cover grill's fins and between the rear optical groups emphasised the elegance of this model, which was available in graphite grey and metallic dark grey, as well as the production black. The dual tone lettering 911 50ᵀᴴ with a 3D effect on the engine cover is also in three colours on the headrests and is the model's logo on both the rev counter, on both the strips underpinned in alluminium; the logo also appears on the cup holder lid, together with limited edition series numbers. The shiny mouldings around the glass and the external SportDesign rear vision mirrors on the door panels are further distinctive elements of the special 50ᵀᴴ anniversary edition. There are also numerous references to the first 911 inside the car: the instrumentation numbers area in green with white needles and relative supports in silver, the central strips of the leather or material seats, are in a typical chequered weft of the '60s., the so-called Pepita fabric for example. The performance of the 911 50ᵀᴴ coincides with that of the 911 S – 0-100 kph acceleration in 4.5 seconds and a top speed of 300 kph. Fuel consumption in the combined NEDC cycle is the same, at 9.5 litres per 100 km (8.7 PDK), the CO_2 emission 224 g/km (205 with PDK).

The 911 GT3 had already broken the 7 minutes 30 seconds barrier on the fearsome "long" section of the Nürburgring. The barrier was broken a second time a few months later by the 911 Turbo, which was also tested on the historic track which, for some, is synonymous with Porsche as it is considered one of the most severe natural "test benches" for ultra-high performance cars.

TECHNICAL SPECIFICATION

ENGINE

Rear, overhanging, longitudinal
6 cylinders

Bore and stroke	102 x 77.5 mm
Unitary cubic capacity	633.3 cc
Maximum cubic capacity	3800 cc
Valve gear	4 camshafts
Number of valves	4 per cylinder
Compression ratio	9.8:1
Fuel feed	direct injection
Ignition	electronic
Coolant	liquid
Lubrication	integrated dry sump
Maximum power	520 hp at 6000-6500 rpm
Specific power	136.8 hp/litre

TRANSMISSION

Active 4WD

Clutch	220/163.5 mm
Gearbox	PDK, 7 speeds plus reverse

CHASSIS

Self-supporting with light body

Front suspension	McPherson, longitudinal arms and shock absorbers, cylindrical coil springs with internal shock absorbers
Rear suspension	multisnodo axis with five oscillating arms, cylindrical coil springs with coaxial gas hydraulic shock absorbers with two tubes
Brakes	disc
Steering	servo, electromechanical
Fuel tank	68 litres
Tyres front/rear	8.5J x 20 with 245/35ZR20 11J x 20 with 305/30ZR20

DIMENSIONS AND WEIGHT

Wheelbase	2450 mm
Track front/rear	1538/1552 mm
Length	4506 mm
Width	1880 mm
Height	1296 mm
Weight	1595

PERFORMANCE

Top speed	315 kph
Power to weight ratio	229.3 kw

911 Turbo

2013

Forty years after the very first, it was once again at the Frankfurt Motor Show that the new 911 Turbo and Turbo S made their debut in 2013, which Porsche considered the pinnacle of technology and driving dynamics of the long 911 series. New four wheel drive, active steering rear axle, adaptive aerodynamics, xenon headlights and a powerful 6-cylinder boxer engine that put out 560 hp with its twin turbos consecrated the 911 Turbo as a car of high technological content, both for the track or daily use on public roads. There were many new aspects, like the renewed, light structure chassis, a wheelbase lengthened by 100 mm and 20-inch diameter rims, the PDCC active roll compensation system, the latter on the 911 Turbo for the first time and standard on the Turbo S. When the cars were launched, it was confirmed that the new 911 Turbo S had lapped the Nürburgring's Nordschleife in just under 7.5 minutes.

The cars' engines had been further developed and the new PTM was determinate in increasing performance. The 3.8-litre 6-ylinder with DFI direct fuel injection turned out 520 hp (383 Kw) and the S 560 hp (412 Kw). Porsche was also the only car manufacturer to use two turbochargers with VTG variable geometry turbines with a petrol engine. Transmission of all that power was by a 7-speed double clutch Porsche Doppelkupplung or PDK gearbox which, in the top models of the 991 range, activated the Start&Stop function, switching off the power unit under deceleration and in the active coasting mode. Another new development for the new 911 was the introduction of active aerodynamics. This was a robust, three position front spoiler, which could be extracted by a pneumatic method. And a rear spoiler could also be extracted to provide a three-position adjustable wing profile. To all of this was added rear wheel steering, which increased handling qualities on the track as well as daily use.

Think of the name Targa together with that of Porsche and you immediately imagine you are driving a car with the hood down and wind in your hair. But what makes the difference with this latest, fascinating version of the evergreen 911 is the speed with which the hood opens and closes – in 19 seconds!

TECHNICAL SPECIFICATION

ENGINE

Rear, overhanging, longitudinal
6 cylinders

Bore and stroke	102 x 77.5 mm
Unitary cubic capacity	633.3 cc
Maximum cubic capacity	3800 cc
Valve gear	4 camshafts
Number of valves	4 per cylinder
Compression ratio	12.5.1
Fuel feed	direct injection
Ignition	electronic
Coolant	liquid
Lubrication	integrated dry sump
Maximum power	400 hp at 7400 rpm
Specific power	105.3 hp/litre

TRANSMISSION

Active 4WD

Clutch	240 mm, 292/153 with PDK
Gearbox	manual, PDK optional, 7 speeds plus reverse

CHASSIS

Self-supporting with light body

Front suspension	McPherson, transverse arms, cylindrical coil springs with internal shock absorbers
Rear suspension	multisnodo axis with five oscillating arms, cylindrical coil springs with coaxial shock absorbers inside
Brakes	disc
Steering	servo steering, electro-mechanical
Fuel tank	68 litres
Tyres front/rear	8.5J x 20 with 345/35ZR20 11J x 20 with 305/30ZR20

DIMENSIONS AND WEIGHT

Wheelbase	2450 mm
Track front/rear	1538/1552 mm
Length	4491 mm
Width	1852 mm
Height	1291 mm
Weight	1550 kg

PERFORMANCE

Top speed	296 kph
Power to weight ratio	180.9 kw

911 Targa   2014

From the moment the 911 Targa was introduced in 1965, it occupied an important place in this model's family, accounting for about 13 per cent of all 911 sales up to now. This latest generation first appeared at the 2014 Detroit Motor Show in January, together with an original Targa look for the first time with an excellent latest generation roof group. The new model was given a characteristic roll bar in place of the central pillars of a part of the openable roof above the front seats, and a wraparound rear window without pillars but, unlike the Targa of time gone by, it had an opening and closing system while the car was standing still that took just 19 seconds by using the buttons in the central console.

The system comprised two mobile elements, a small fabric hood and a glass rear window. With pressure on a certain button, the window, together with the convertible top compartment, was opened and moved back. At the same time, two small wings opened out on the roll bar, which activated kinematics of the fabric hood. That way, the element of the convertible top was unblocked and Z-folded and hidden behind the rear seats. A small transverse grill located behind the seats completed the operation.

Lastly, the roll bar's winglets closed and, lastly, the rear window was folded away. A deflector frame integrated with the windscreen could be raised manually when the roof was open to reduce air flow into the cab.

Two variants of the new generation Targa were sold with 4WD alone with Euro 6 motorisation. The 911 Targa 4 had a 3.4-litre boxer that put out 350 hp (257 Kw). With a Porsche Doppelkupplung PDK double clutch gearbox and the Sport Chrono package that made sure it did 0-100 in 4.8 seconds. With a manual 'box it had a top speed of 282 kph. The top of the range was the 911 Targa 4S with a 3.8-litre 400 hp power unit with a 296 kph top speed.

With the return in grand style of the World Endurance Championship, Porsche decided to compete in the series against its Japanese rivals Toyota and Nissan, and especially its "cousin" Audi, the dominators of the previous 10 years. The results were seen in 2015, when Porsche won the constructors' championship and the 24 Hours of Le Mans, achieving those objectives on its second attempt.

TECHNICAL SPECIFICATION

ENGINE

Central, longitudinal
4 cylinders

Bore and stroke	-
Unitary cubic capacity	500 cc
Total cubic capacity	2000 cc
Valve gear	4 camshafts
Number of valves	4 per cylinder
Compression ratio	-
Fuel feed	Bosch MS5.6 direct injection
Ignition	electronic
Coolant	liquid
Maximum power	500 hp at 9000 rpm. On the rear axle/MGU Hybrid 400 hp on the front axle
Maximum torque	-

TRANSMISSION

Rear wheel drive and 4WD through KERS on the front wheels

Clutch	-
Gearbox	hydraulic sequential, 7 speeds

CHASSIS

Monocoque in carbon fibre

Front suspension	independent on multilink, pushrod system with adjustable shock absorbers
Rear suspension	independent on multilink, pushrod system with adjustable shock absorbers
Brakes	disc
Steering	hydraulic rack
Fuel tank	68.5 litres
Tyres front/rear	310/710 x 18

DIMENSIONS AND WEIGHT

Wheelbase	2475 mm
Track front/rear	1526/1540 mm
Length	4650 mm
Width	1900 mm
Height	1050 mm
Weight	870 kg

PERFORMANCE

Top speed	-
Power to weight ratio	-

919 Hybrid   2014

The 919 Hybrid made its first appearance at the 2014 Geneva Motor Show, a car to compete in the top LMP1 class and one which returned Porsche to being a top contender in the 24 Hours of Le Mans. With the *leitmotiv* Intelligent Performance, a group of engineers started from zero and developed a racing car powered by a hybrid engine, a 2-litre thermal motor and a turbocharger.

In conceiving this revolutionary car, the Stuttgart technicians had to take into consider the parameters imposed by LMP1 regulations: the Hybrid cubic capacity, typology of the engine – whether diesel or petrol – were at the discretion of the team. The limiting factor was the type of energy available, in both terms of the quantity of fuel and the electric power recoverable from the accumulation systems each lap. The 919 Hybrid uses lithium ion batteries, cooled by water and fed by two systems – under braking, the kinetic energy is converted at the front axle into electricity, while at the rear the exhaust energy generates that electricity.

The recovery of thermo-dynamic exhaust energy was unique among the cars that competed the World Championship for Makes. In this a supplementary turbine generator replaced the wastegate valve.

A whole lot of technology that bore fruit in 2015, when the 919 was the star of the World Endurance Championship. Its victories at the Nürburgring, Austin, Japan, Shanghai and Bahrain and the team's great success in the 24 Hours of Le Mans – 17 years after Porsche's last win in the French marathon – driven by Hulkenberg-Bamber-Tandy, followed by Bernhard-Webber-Hartley in second driving a sister car, brought Stuttgart both the constructors' and drivers' world titles.

The GTS name, which stands for Gran Turismo Sport used for the 904 Carrera of the mid-60s, finally reappeared on another of Stuttgart's great classics, the two-seater Boxster. A sports car in name and fact, the car was powered by a 4-litre 6-cylinder engine that produced 330 hp for a top speed of around 280 kph.

TECHNICAL SPECIFICATION

ENGINE
Central, longitudinal
6 cylinders

Bore and stroke	97 x 77.5 mm
Unitary cubic capacity	572.6 cc
Total cubic capacity	3436 cc
Valve gear	4 camshafts
Number of valves	4 per cylinder
Compression ratio	12.5:1
Fuel feed	direct injection
Ignition	electronic
Coolant	liquid
Maximum power	330 hp at 6700 rpm
Maximum torque	370 Nm at 4500-4800 rpm

TRANSMISSION
Rear wheel drive

Clutch	240 mm, 202/153 mm with PDK
Gearbox	manual, PDK optional, 6 speeds plus reverse

CHASSIS
Self-supporting with light body, mixture of steel and aluminium

Front suspension	McPherson, transverse and longitudinal arms, twin tube gas shock absorbers
Rear suspension	McPherson, transverse and longitudinal arms cylindrical coil springs with internal coaxial shock absorbers, stabiliser
Brakes	disc
Steering	servo, electromechanical
Fuel tank	64 litres
Tyres front/rear	8J x 20 with 235/35ZR20 9.5J x 20 with 265/35ZR 20

DIMENSIONS AND WEIGHT

Wheelbase	2475 mm
Track front/rear	1526/1540 mm
Length	4404 mm
Width	1801 mm
Height	1273 mm
Weight	1345 kg

PERFORMANCE

Top speed	281 kph
Power to weight ratio	171.1 kg

Boxster GTS   2014

The Boxster GTS had a higher powered engine and a PASM chassis, calibrated ad hoc. It was a characteristic design both at the front and rear, headlights were bi-xenon as standard with the Porsche Dynamic Light System (PDLS) and the logos in shiny black, which helped to unmistakably characterise this absolutely top performance version. The logo is just a kind of calling card: at Porsche, GTS stands for Gran Turismo Sport and, since the legendary 1963 904 Carrera GTS, is synonymous with extraordinary performance. The GTS's 6-cylinder boxer engine was based on the 3.4-litre units of the Boxster S Euro 6 and with the optimisation of the settings, developed 15 hp (11 kW) more, taking the new GTS to an output of 330 hp (243 kW). The new version also had the Sport Chrono as standard, with a double clutch gear-box or Porsche Doppelkupplung (PDK) as optional and an active Sport Plus button, which enabled the GTS to accelerate from 0-100 kph in 4.7 seconds. This roadster was the first Boxster to break the 280 kph barrier.

The GTS combined optimum driving dynamics typical of Porsche with maximum comfort and exclusive equipment. The standard PASM enabled the driver to move from an aggressive driving style to handling also suited to long journeys. The front 235/35 and rear 265/35 tyres on 20-inch Carrera rims were totally suited to the car's characteristics. The seats helped emphasise the sporting pedigree of this model, as did the leather interior, highlighted by Alcantara inserts. A further component standard on the GTS was the sports exhaust system: the driver could activate it by pressing the Sport Plus button on the central consol. On the basis of a specific driving situation, the control motor then operates the insertion valve. Externally, the sporty exhaust system could be recognised by its double black chromed terminals.

With the Cayenne that appeared at the start of the 2000s, Porsche moved to the head of the SUV segment which, considering its successful sales figures, produced such good results that other prestigious marques like Maserati had to dip their collective toe in the SUV market. No fewer than five versions of this new Cayenne went on sale: the S, Turbo, Diesel, S Diesel and the S-E-Hybrid.

TECHNICAL SPECIFICATION

ENGINE
Front, longitudinal
V6

Bore and stroke	96 x 83 mm
Unitary cubic capacity	600.6 cc
Total cubic capacity	3604 cc
Valve gear	4 overhead camshafts
Number of valves	4 per cylinder
Compression ratio	10.5:1
Fuel feed	direct injection
Ignition	electronic
Coolant	liquid
Maximum power	420 hp at 6000 rpm
Specific power	116.6 hp/litre

TRANSMISSION
4WD

Torque converter diameter	272 mm
Gearbox	Tiptronic S, automatic, 8 speeds plus reverse

CHASSIS
Unified steel structure

Front suspension	double wishbone arm in aluminium, steel springs and hydraulic twin-tube gas shock absorbers
Rear suspension	multilink axis with transverse lower arm, two single arms in the upper part, steel springs and dual tube hydraulic gas shock absorbers
Brakes	disc
Steering	servo-assisted
Fuel tank	85 litres
Tyres front/rear	8J x 18 with 255/55 R 18

DIMENSIONS AND WEIGHT

Wheelbase	2895 mm
Track front/rear	1655/1669 mm
Length	4855 mm
Width	1939 mm
Height	1705 mm
Weight	2085 kg

PERFORMANCE

Top speed	259 kph
Power to weight ratio	143 kw

Cayenne S   2014

A refined design and ample standard equipment are the main characteristics of the Porsche Cayenne restyling, press tested for the first time in Spain in September 2014. The new generation of the Cayenne made its market debut in no fewer than five different versions, the S, Turbo, Diesel, D Diesel and S E-Hybrid.

The Cayenne has been a unique success for Porsche from the time the first generation was introduced in 2002, transforming the idea of a sporting SUV into reality and setting new standards of reference. By 2010, over 276,000 first generation Cayennes had been produced. The second generation of the Porsche SUV did even better still with more than 300,000 of them being built and sold up to 2015. The Cayenne not only turned out to be important for Porsche's growth, it has guaranteed and continues to guarantee an economic base for investments from which future cars will be produced. The Cayenne S's new 3.6-litre twin-turbo V6 engine was entirely developed by Porsche: its NEDC consumption was between 9.5 and 9.8 litres over 100 kilometres (223-229 g/km CO_2) developing a maximum power output of 420 hp (309 kW) at 6000 rpm. The 550 Nm torque came up at between 1350 and 4500 rpm. The power/litre ratio was increased by 40% compared to the Cayenne, passing from 83 hp (61 kW) per litre to 117 hp (86 kW). The Cayenne S, which has an 8-speed Tiptronic S as standard, accelerated from 0-100 kph in just 5.5 seconds, but with the Sport Chrono package that improves by a tenth. The main design differences are at the front, with completely new front wheel housings and bonnet, as were the fins of the lateral air intakes which, positioned on both the right and left, direct air to the intercooler, also becoming an attractive design detail. The bi-xenon headlights, which are standard on the base model and the S and were of the typical technique of four "hovering" LEDs, characterise the Cayenne at first glance.

Wheel housings widened for the rear axle is one of the distinctive characteristics of the new 911 Carrera series. Of course, there was also an increase in power output to 430 hp and performance leading to a 306 kph top speed. The model was on offer with the classic rear wheel drive or 4WD.

TECHNICAL SPECIFICATION

ENGINE

Rear, overhanging, longitudinal
6 cylinders

Bore and stroke	102 x 77.5 mm
Unitary cubic capacity	633.3 cc
Total cubic capacity	3800 cc
Valve gear	4 camshafts
Number of valves	4 per cylinder
Compression ratio	12.5:1
Fuel feed	direct injection
Ignition	electronic
Coolant	liquid
Lubrication	dry sump integrated
Maximum power	430 hp at 6000-6500 rpm
Specific power	113.2 hp/litre

TRANSMISSION

Clutch	240 or 202/153 mm
Gearbox	manual, PDK optional, 7 speeds plus reverse

CHASSIS

Self-supporting with light body

Front suspension	McPherson, wishbones, cylindrical coil springs with internal shock absorbers
Rear suspension	multisnodo axis with 5 oscillating arms, cylindrical coil springs with inside coaxial shock absorbers
Brakes	disc
Steering	servo-assisted electromechanical
Fuel tank	64 litres
Tyres front/rear	9J x 20 with 245/35ZR20 11.5J x 20 with 305/30ZR20

DIMENSIONS AND WEIGHT

Wheelbase	2450 mm
Track front/rear	1538/1560 mm
Length	4509 mm
Width	1852 mm
Height	1295 mm
Weight	1425 kg

PERFORMANCE

Top speed	306 kph
Power to weight ratio	210.6 kw

911 Carrera GTS   2014

In 2014, Porsche launched the second generation of the 911 Carrera GTS and it did so with four models: the Coupé, and Cabriolet with rear wheel drive and 4WD respectively, which bridged the gap between the 911 Carrera S and the GT3. Power output was 430 hp (316 kW); the Sport Chrono and PASM and the active shock absorber adjustment system with a 10 mm lower set-up were some of the technical characteristics of these new models. Quicker acceleration and higher speed are additional effects of the greater efficiency, accompanied by unchanged overall fuel consumption values, similar to those of the already positive S models. Together with the double clutch gearbox, the Porsche Doppelkupplung (PDK), the 911 Carrera GTS shot from 0-100 kph in precisely four seconds, while the Cabriolet took two tenths longer. Top speed of each GTS model exceeded 300 kph; the Coupé with its manual gearbox and rear wheel drive reached 306 kph.

Another characteristic of the 911 GTS was its wealth of equipment as standard, like bi-xenon headlights, included in the Porsche Dynamic Light System (PDLS) and the sports exhaust system as well as the exclusive interiors in Alcantara. Outside, the 911 GTS distinguished itself from that of the other Carrera models by its widened wheel housings at the rear and a wider track. Rims were 20-inch diameter with central nuts and their standard finish was in the exclusive matt black. The front had a special finish and the dark bi-xenon headlights, while the black slats on the air intake grill and the black chromed exhaust terminals defined the rear.

The 911 GTS soon became widely popular to the point that, from the time of its introduction in 2010, a quarter of 911 Carrera Cabriolet purchasers chose the GTS model, while 23% of the Carrera Coupés on the roads have the GTS lettering on their tail.

A short while after the introduction of the new Cayenne series, out came the GTS, which was positioned between the S and the Turbo. The difference was in a cubic capacity reduction to 3.6-litres and with six cylinders instead of eight. But that didn't bring with it a drop in performance. In terms in horse power, output was increased to 440 hp.

TECHNICAL SPECIFICATION

ENGINE
Front, longitudinal
V6 twin turbo

Bore and stroke	97 x 83 mm
Unitary cubic capacity	600.6 cc
Total cubic capacity	3604 cc
Valve gear	4 camshafts
Number of valves	4 per cylinder
Compression ratio	10.5:1
Fuel feed	direct injection
Ignition	electronic
Coolant	liquid
Maximum power	440 hp at 6000 rpm
Unitary power	122.2 hp/litre

TRANSMISSION
4WD

Torque converter diam.	272 mm
Gearbox	Tiptronic S, automatic, 6 speeds plus reverse

CHASSIS
Unified steel structure

Front suspension	double wishbone in aluminium, steel springs and twin-tube gas shock absorbers
Rear suspension	multilink axis with lower control arm, two single arms in the upper area, steel springs and twin-tube gas shock absorbers
Brakes	disc
Steering	servo-assisted
Fuel tank	85 litres
Tyres front/rear	9.5J x 20 with 275/45 R 20

DIMENSIONS AND WEIGHT

Wheelbase	2895 mm
Track front/rear	1660/1678 mm
Length	4855 mm
Width	1954 mm
Height	1688
Weight	2110 kg

PERFORMANCE

Top speed	262 kph
Power to weight	154,02 kw

Cayenne GTS   2014

The Cayenne GTS, which was unveiled at the 2014 Los Angeles Motor Show, bridged the gap between the S and the Turbo. The 3.6-litre V6 twin-turbo put out 440 hp (324 kW) and 600 Nm and was an evolution of the new power plant of the Cayenne S, a clear example of downsizing. It had a lower cubic capacity and number of cylinders compared to the V8, but with 20 hp and 85 Nm more. That contributed to a fuel consumption reduction, which dropped by about 0.9 of a litre per 100 kilometres.in respect of the base model. And its sound was impressive with the adoption of the sporty Sound Symposer exhaust. So the GTS was the "emotional" variant that was most effective of the Cayenne series. Its chassis, which was expensive and complex, ensured excellent transverse dynamics and as a result of the interaction between the traction of 440 hp (324 Kw) AND 600 Nm of traction, it was an agile and sporty SUV. All that doesn't just come from the traction, but also from the standard active shock absorber system, the Porsche Active Suspension Management system (PASM) and a 24 mm increase in stroke with steel suspension as standard or of 20 mm with the optional pneumatic version. The Cayenne GTS could zip from 0-100 kph in 5.2 seconds, a tenth of a second faster with the Sport Chrono package for an increase of 0.5 and 0.6 seconds against the previous model. Like all Porsche sports cars, the Cayenne GTS had to pass a tough baptism at the Nürburgring, where it stopped the clock at 8 minutes 13 seconds

The GTS also had a strong personality with its 20-inch rims of RS Spyder design as well as the front end, which boasted large air intakes and specific LED headlights and fog lamps. Also note the vehicle's lateral mini-skirts of sharper profiles and the bigger wheel housings as well as the use of black for the specific connotation for the lettering, wheels, exhaust terminals, internal masking of the bi-xenon optical groups and blackened LED rear lights.

A lap of the Nürburgring's Nordschleife, a no excuses testbed, proved the quality of this version of the Cayenne. In fact, the potent twin-turbo 8-cylinder engine made it possible for the car to break the eight-minute barrier, an unthinkable time just a few decades ago when Porsche competed in Formula 1.

TECHNICAL SPECIFICATION

ENGINE

Front, longitudinal
twin-turbo V8

Bore and stroke	96 x 83 mm
Unitary cubic capacity	600.75 cc
Total cubic capacity	4806 cc
Valve gear	4 camshafts
Number of valves	4 per cylinder
Compression ratio	10.5:1
Fuel feed	direct injection
Ignition	electronic
Coolant	liquid
Lubrication	-
Maximum power	570 hp at 6000 rpm
Specific power	118.6 hp/litre

TRANSMISSION

4WD

Torque converter	272 mm diameter
Gearbox	Tiptronic S, automatic, 8 speeds plus reverse

CHASSIS

Unified steel structure

Front suspension	double wishbones in aluminium wishbones, steel springs and hydraulic gas twin-tube shock absorbers
Rear suspension	multi-link axis with lower control arm, two individual arms in the upper area, steel springs and hydraulic gas twin tube shock absorbers
Brakes	disc
Steering	servo-assisted
Fuel tank	100 litres
Tyres front/rear	10J x 21 with 295/35ZR21

DIMENSIONS AND WEIGHT

Wheelbase	2895 mm
Track front/rear	1661/1675 mm
Length	4855 mm
Width	1954 mm
Height	1702 mm
Weight	2123 kg

PERFORMANCE

Top speed	284 kph
Power to weight ratio	196.2 kw

Cayenne Turbo S 2015

Launched in January 2015, the Cayenne Turbo S is the top version of this model range, bringing together high performance and driving versatility in a single vehicle, even in every day traffic.

Among the car's strongpoints are a twin-turbo V8 4.8-litre engine that drums up 570 hp, as well as a latest generation chassis with Porsche Traction Management or active 4WD, with the rear wheel drive sharing a variable force with the front axle – the active Porsche Dynamic Chassis Control – active roll stabiliser that reduces lateral sway and the Porsche Torque Vectoring Plus system, which ensures better driving dynamics with intervention aimed at the brakes and self-locking differential with electronic adjustment.

And the braking system is well up to date, with 10-piston callipers on the front axle and 420 mm discs, while the rear had another four pistons with 370 mm discs. The integral turbochargers were located right in the exhaust manifolds for the shortest reaction time, better combustion that translates into maximum return from fuel: those are the key elements of the Turbo S.

Other standard equipment includes the Sport Chrono package with an analogue stopwatch and Sport Plus button, 21-inch diameter tyres like the 911 Turbo, with shiny black rims.

On the styling front, the model stands out for its large frontal air intake, new conception LED optical group and fog lights. The air intakes are painted shiny black, as are the lower parts of the vehicle plus the external mirrors' base, while the roof spoiler and wheel arches are in the same colour as the body.

Certainly not the ideal car in which to go shopping, but people who see it in the store's car park, imagining it with race numbers and sponsors logos on the body, would have no problem transferring the GT3 RS to its natural environment – the pit lane, with an army of mechanics intent on sorting the vehicle, ready for a new test session or stint in an actual race.

TECHNICAL SPECIFICATION

ENGINE
Rear, overhanging, longitudinal
6 cylinders

Bore and stroke	102 x 81.5 mm
Unitary cubic capacity	666 cc
Total cubic capacity	3996 cc
Valve gear	4 camshafts
Number of valves	4 per cylinder
Compression ratio	12.9.1
Fuel feed	direct injection
Ignition	electronic
Coolant	liquid
Lubrication	integrated dry sump
Maximum power	500 hp at 8250 rpm
Specific power	125 hp/litre

TRANSMISSION
Active 4WD

Clutch	202/153 mm
Gearbox	PDK, 7 speeds plus reverse

CHASSIS
Self-supporting with light body

Front suspension	McPherson, wishbones, cylindrical coil springs with internal shock absorbers
Rear suspension	multisnodo axis with five oscillating arms, cylindrical coil springs with internal coaxial shock absorbers
Brakes	disc
Steering	electro-mechanical servo, active on the rear axle
Fuel tank	64 litres (90 litres optional)
Tyres front/rear	9.5J x 20 with 265/35ZR20 12.5J x 21 with 325/30ZR21

DIMENSIONS AND WEIGHT

Wheelbase	2457 mm
Tack front/rear	1538/1557 mm
Length	4545 mm
Width	1880 mm
Height	1291 mm
Weight	1420 kg

PERFORMANCE

Top speed	310 kph
Power to weight ratio	246.9 kw

911 GT3 RS   2015

The Porsche 911 GT3 RS bowed in at the 2015 Geneva Motor Show and it is a car with which Porsche has once again crossed the divide between sports cars and racers. The GT3 RS has the most sophisticated motor sport technology available in a 911, developed for daily use and homologated for use on public roads.

The new RS is powered by a 4-litre 6-cylinder 500 hp (368 kW) engine capable of 480 Nm of torque, paired with a Porsche Doppelkupplung (PDK) double clutch especially developed for this model. The potent aspirated engine with more cubic capacity than any other in the entire 911family, takes this supercar from 0-100 kph in 3.3 seconds and 200 kph in 10.9. Functions like the Paddle-Neutral clutch disengage and a speed limiter that can be operated by a Pit-Speed button, were specifically conceived for use in racing. Those short cuts offer the greater driver freedom of management providing much more support on the track.

The GT3 RS's body is unique. The roof has been made in magnesium for the first time, the engine cover and boot lid are in carbon fibre, while other components are of alternative materials. That's why the RS weighs about 10 kilos less than the 911 GT3. The body shape is of the 911 Turbo, as the specific aerodynamic components of the RS defined the status of a racing car, to which the small front spoiler also contributes as well as the ample rear wing.Some of the distinctive aspects of the GT3 RS include a depression that crosses the engine cover and the roof, and the sporty ventilation grill of the front wheel arches.The GT3 RS's chassis has been conceived to obtain the maximum precision and the best handling. In that sense, there are a number of other aspects to point out, like rear wheel steering, Porsche Torque Vectoring Plus with the rear differential variably controlled and the wider track for both the front and rear axles.

The picture shows the key new technical and aesthetic developments made by Porsche to the Cayman. The front end has three air vents for cooling and a substantial fixed wing in this case, and is just distinguishable from the rear, which is wider than that of the previous model.

TECHNICAL SPECIFICATION

ENGINE
Central, longitudinal
V, Euro 6

Bore and stroke	102 x 77,5 mm
Unitary cubic capacity	633,3 cc
Total cubic capacity	3800 cc
Valve gear	4 camshafts
Number of valves	4 per cylinder
Compression ratio	12.5:1
Fuel feed	direct injection
Ignition	electronic
Coolant	liquid
Maximum power	385 hp at 7400 rpm
Unitary power	101,3 hp/litre

TRANSMISSION
Rear wheel drive

Clutch	dry mono-disc
Gearbox	manual, 6 speeds plus reverse

CHASSIS
Unified steel structure

Front suspension	McPherson, transverse and longitudinal arms, cylindrical coil springs, with internal shock absorbers
Rear suspension	McPherson, transverse and longitudinal arms, cylindrical coil springs, with coaxial internal shock absorbers
Brakes	disc
Steering	electromechanical, servo
Fuel tank	54 litres
Tyres front/rear	8.5J x 20 with 245/35ZR20 11J x 20 with 295/30ZR20

DIMENSIONS AND WEIGHT

Wheelbase	2484 mm
Track front/rear	1539/1533 mm
Length	4438 mm
Width	1817 mm
Height	1266 mm
Weight	1340 kg

PERFORMANCE

Top speed	295 kph
Power to weight ratio	172.3 kw

911 Cayman GT4   2015

The Cayman GT4 is a member of the Porsche GT family based on the Cayman, but with components derived from the 911 GT3, and has confirmed itself at the top of its market segment by lapping the Nürburgring in 7 minutes 40 seconds. The car's engine, chassis, brakes and aerodynamics have been conceived to ensure maximum driving dynamics, but at the same time the top of the range model maintains such a versatility that it is ideal for daily use. The GT4 has a 3.8-litre 6-cylinder boxer power unit that puts out 385 hp (283 kW) and is derived from that of the 911 Carrera S. Transmission is a 6-speed manual gearbox with active engine support system. The Cayman GT4's performance is absolutely top for the segment, with a 0-100 kph time of 4.4 seconds and a maximum speed of 295 kph (with NEDC consumption of 10.3 litres per 100 kilometres. The chassis with the body lowered 30 mm and the more powerful braking system mainly use components from the 911 GT3.

The GT4 has three front openings and a bigger fixed rear wing. Additional equipment is optional, and includes for an even sportier drive a braking system in carbon ceramic PCCB, bucket seats in synthetic reinforced material with carbon fibre (CfK), a specific Sport Chrono package with the extraordinary Track Precision App or preparation called Clubsport. The interior of the Cayman GT4 has been conceived to guarantee pure driving pleasure and extremely high standards of comfort for the passenger. The seats are leather and Alcantara covered and ensure optimum lateral containment. As well as the umbilical cord that links it to the 911 GT3, as a sports car with a mid-engine, the GT4 conceptually continues the tradition of cars like the 904 GTS, 911 GT1, Carrera GT and the 918 Spyder.

With the new version of the Spyder, Porsche decisively took in hand the now celebrated Boxster model, and also revised its aesthetics. It has the performance of an ultra-sports car, especially for one without a roof group. Other details have been added, like the three vent front end, which recalls the one that has just appeared on the new Cayman series.

TECHNICAL SPECIFICATION

ENGINE
Central, longitudinal, V6

Bore and stroke	102 x 77,5 mm
Unitary cubic capacity	633,3 cc
Total cubic capacity	3800 cc
Valve gear	4 camshafts
Number of valves	4 per cylinder
Compression ratio	12.5:1
Fuel feed	direct injection
Ignition	electronic
Coolant	liquid
Maximum power	375 hp at 6700 rpm
Unitary power	98,7 hp/litre

TRANSMISSION
Rear wheel drive

Clutch	dry mono-disc
Gearbox	manual, 6 speeds plus reverse

CHASSIS
Self-supporting with light aluminium-steel body

Front suspension	McPherson, wishbones, cylindrical coil springs with internal shock absorbers
Rear suspension	multisnodo axle with five oscillating arms, cylindrical coil springs with coaxial internal shock absorbers
Brakes	disc
Steering	servo, electro-mechanical
Fuel tank	54 litres
Tyres front/rear	8.5J x 20 with 235/35ZR20 10.5J with 265/35ZR20

DIMENSIONS AND WEIGHT

Wheelbase	2475 mm
Track front/rear	1538/1552 mm
Length	4414 mm
Width	1801 mm
Height	1262 mm
Weight	1315 kg

PERFORMANCE

Top speed	290 kph
Power to weight ratio	198,5 kw

Boxster Spyder   2015

This "pure" version of the roadster made its debut at the New York Motor Show and is the top of the range Boxster - the fastest and most potent produced by the company today. It conserves the personality of the Spyder that preceded it, in the meantime having become a cult car and a collectable. And it offers, once more, the classic canvas hood put up or down by hand; the gearbox is also manual.

As is fitting for an open car in the most classic of definitions, the Boxster Spyder enables the driver to enjoy a sporting performance at high level due to its rigid chassis with suspension lowered 20 mm, 911 Carrera brakes, its more direct steering and, naturally, the potent 3.8-litre 6-cylinder engine that develops 375 hp (276 kW). Performance is stunning for a car without a roof, with an acceleration from 0-100 kph in just 4.5 seconds and a top speed of 290 kph.

The original design of the car embodies styling elements of the legendary sporting Porsches and racers of the past. This repertoire includes two large items of fairing that join into two headrests with the bot lid, having a clear aerodynamic function, but which also constitutes a reference to the 718 Spyder barchetta of the '60s. And the hood partially operated manually bring back memories of a roadster of times gone by. In the front and rear views of the car there is an evident association with the Cayman GT4. The interior of this new top of the ranger is conceived to give the driver the maximum pleasure and to be able to drive in complete relaxation. Driver and passenger are accommodated in sports bucket seats with plenty of support from the sides, and the sporty steering wheel is new. The "purist" interpretation of this model and the consequent necessity to reduce weight to the minimum meant there had to be no radio or air conditioning, but they are available as options.

A year after the launch of the 911 Carrara GT3's four versions, Porsche came up with the 991/II for its clientele. Two new 3-litre twin turbo engines have different levels of performance, with about 50 hp less for the base model of 370 hp, and 420 hp for the S.

TECHNICAL SPECIFICATION

ENGINE

Rear, overhanging, longitudinal
6 cylinders

Bore and stroke	91 x 76,4 mm
Unitary cubic capacity	496,8 cc
Total cubic capacity	2981 cc
Valve gear	4 camshafts
Number of valves	4 per cylinder
Compression ratio	10:1
Fuel feed	direct injection
Ignition	electronic
Coolant	liquid
Lubrication	integrated dry sump
Maximum power	370 hp at 6500 rpm
Unitary power	124,1 hp/litre

TRANSMISSION

Rear wheel drive

Clutch	28 mm, 202/153 mm with PDK
Gearbox	manual, PDK optional, 7 speeds plus reverse

CHASSIS

Self-supporting with light aluminium-steel body

Front suspension	McPherson, wishbones, cylindrical coil springs with interior shock absorbers
Rear suspension	multi-link axis with five oscillating arms, cylindrical coil springs with coaxial shock absorbers inside
Brakes	disc
Steering	servo, electro-mechanical
Fuel tank	64 litres
Tyres front/rear	8.5J x 19 with 235/40ZR19 11-5J x 19 with 295/35ZR19

DIMENSIONS AND WEIGHT

Wheelbase	2450 mm
Track front/rear	1541/1518 mm
Length	4499 mm
Width	1808 mm
Height	1303 mm
Weight	1430 kg

PERFORMANCE

Top speed	295 kph
Power to weight ratio	181,3 kw

911 Carrera

2015

The 911 Carrera 991/II is a milestone in the history of Porsche, with the adoption of the new 3-litre twin turbo engines: 370 hp (272 kW) for the basic version and 420 hp (309 kW) for the S, with 60 Nm more torque. At the same time, the car's 7500 rpm exceed the conventional number of revolutions of a turbo power unit while benefitting fuel consumption at 12% lower.In performance terms, the 911 Carrera with its double clutch gearbox Porsche Doppelkupplung (PDK) and the optional Sport Chrono package goes from 0-100 kph in 4.2 seconds, while Carrera S with PDK and the Sport Chrono package enables the driver to do it in 3.9 seconds. In terms of top speed, the 911 races up to 295 kph, the Carrera S 308 kph. With the optional Sports Pack, the 911 Carrera has for the first time the Mode switch on the steering wheel, which gives a choice of driving programmes, Normal, Sport, Sport Plus and Individual. With the PDK gearbox, the Mode switch there is a supplementary control, the so-called Sport Response Button which, once it has been activated, controls the transmission chain for 20 seconds in relation to maximum acceleration, for example to help overtake. At the same time, the optimum gear is inserted automatically and in that fraction of time that engine management is calibrated to have an even more punctual response. On the aesthetics front, the 911 Carrera has a number of retouches, like four-point daytime headlights, door handles flush with the body, a newly configured rear engine cover with the traditional slatted air intake, while the sharp rear optical groups of great elegance. Once the driver is aboard, the new development he will immediately notice is the standard Porsche Communications Management, with its multi-touch screen, which offers a whole range of significantly increased functions and much simpler controls.

Almost two years after it went on sale, Porsche once again raised the level of their new Macan by adding the GTS to the range. Changes had been made to both the chassis and the vehicle's absolute performance. The braking system was improved and a slight increase in horse power combined with a lower set-up which, together with a new interior, made the car that much more appetising, so it sold well from the start.

TECHNICAL SPECIFICATION

ENGINE
Front, longitudinal,
6 cylinders

Bore and stroke	83 x 96 mm
Unitary cubic capacity	600,66 cc
Total cubic capacity	3604 cc
Valve gear	4 camshafts
Number of valves	4 per cylinder
Compression ratio	10,5:1
Fuel feed	petrol
Ignition	electronic
Coolant	liquid
Lubrication	dry sump
Maximum power	400 hp at 6000 rpm
Unitary power	110 hp/litre

TRANSMISSION
Active 4WD

Clutch	double
Gearbox	PDk, 7 speeds plus reverse

CHASSIS
Light monocoque

Front suspension	axis with five aluminium control arms, cylindrical coil springs, gas hydraulic shock absorbers with internal double tube
Rear suspension,	axis with trapezoidal arms, cylindrical coil springs, hydraulic gas shock absorbers with internal double tube
Brakes	disc, with a dual circuit braking system and distribution to the axles
Steering	servo-assisted
Fuel tank	75 litres
Tyres front/rear	8J x 19 with 235/55ZR19 101Y 9J x 19 with 255/50ZR19 103 Y

DIMENSIONS AND WEIGHT

Wheelbase	2807 mm
Track front/rear	1655/1651 mm
Length	4699 mm
Width	1923 mm
Height	1624 mm
Weight	1925 kg

PERFORMANCE

Top speed	266 kph
Power to weight ratio	147.14 kw

Macan GTS   2015

The new GTS version of the Macan is inspired by motor sport like all Porsche cars which, by tradition, carry this logo. A power output increased by 20 hp in respect of the S, a revised upwards chassis and a more potent braking system, which are some aspects of this new model, which was launched at the 2015 Tokyo Motor Show.

The car's technical specification shows its maximum power output at 360 hp and 500 Nm of torque, all of which comes from a 3-litre twin turbo V6 engine, which had already been installed in the Macan S, linked to double clutch Doppelkupplung (PDK) as well as the Porsche Traction Management (PTM) with variable distribution of the driving force between the front and rear axles. That's why the Macan GTS accelerates from 0-100 kph in 5.2 seconds, but with the optional Sport Chrono package it knocks two tenths of a second off that, with a top speed of 256 kph.

Extremely high performance that the GTS combines with great drivability and versatility typical of a vehicle for everyday use. Its equipment also includes the PASM chassis with its set-up lowered by 15 mm, 20-inch rims identical to those of the RS Spyder, painted in matt black with different sized tyres of 235/55ZR19 front and 255/50ZR19 rear.

Aesthetically, the Macan GTS has shiny black elements above the belt line and matt satin in the lower parts of the body. Like a special version of the SportDesign package, which is standard and presents the vehicle in a specific colour. LED headlights are available for the first time as an optional, including the Porsche Dynamic Light System Plus, which guarantees optimum illumination in all conditions.

The GTS has special seats as standard, with a central strip in Alcantara, which is also used for many interior details. The vehicle also gave the new Porsche Communictions Management (PCM) its debut, available for the first time on a SUV.

The Cayman GT4 Club Sport's world unveiling took place at the Los Angeles Motor Show in November 2015, but the vehicle did not begin to challenge the opposition's products on the tracks of the world until the following spring, starting in Italy where Porsche intended to organise the Cayman GT4 Trophy.

TECHNICAL SPECIFICATION

ENGINE
Central, longitudinal, V6

Bore and stroke	76.4 x 102.7 mm
Unitary cubic capacity	633.3 cc
Total cubic capacity	3800 cc
Valve gear	4 camshafts
Number of valves	4 per cylinder
Compression ratio	12.5:1
Fuel feed	direct injection
Ignition	electronic
Coolant	liquid
Lubrication	integrated dry sump
Maximum power	385 hp at 7400 rpm
Specific power	101.3 hp/litre

TRANSMISSION
Rear wheel drive

Clutch	dry mono-disc
Gearbox	manual, 6 speeds plus reverse

CHASSIS
Unified steel structure

Front suspension	McPherson, transverse and longitudinal arms, cylindrical coil springs with internal shock absorbers
Rear suspension	McPherson, transverse and longitudinal arms, cylindrical coil springs with internal coaxial shock absorbers
Brakes	disc
Steering	electro-mechanical servo-steering
Fuel tank	90 litres (90/100 litres optional)
Tyres front/rear	9J x 18 with 25/64 x 18 10.5J x 18 with 27/68 x 18

DIMENSIONS AND WEIGHT

Wheelbase	2484 mm
Track front/rear	1539/1533 mm
Length	4438 mm
Width	1817 mm
Height	1266 mm
Weight	1300 kg

PERFORMANCE

Top speed	-
Power to weight ratio	172.3 kw

Cayman GT4 Club Sport   2015

The Cayman GT4 broadened the Porsche GT family, which was meant for road use but it was also destined for racing. The Club Sport has a purely sporting vocation and it was conceived to take part in the 2016 Italian Grand Touring Championship and the National GT4 Trophy, within which Porsche Italy has established the Italian Cayman GT4 Trophy with the trophies going to the three top scoring drivers or teams, who will receive a special award, free entries for the Italian Carrera Cup of the following season.

The Cayman GT4 Club Sport has widened the Porsche racing car offer and is conceived specifically for beginners and not so experienced in motor sport and is not homologated for road use. The Club Sport is powered by a 3,8-litre 6-cylinder boxer engine of 385 hp, installed directly behind the driver and is combined with Porsche Doppelkupplung double clutch 6-speed gearbox plus a rear mechanical self-locking differential for racing. The light-structured spring-shock absorber group of the front axle comes from its 911 GT3 Cup big sister, while the rear axle has a light, reinforced spring-shock absorber group with wishbones that also come from the 911 GT3Cup. The braking system has 380 mm large dimension discs and fixed mono-block callipers in aluminium, the fronts with six pistons, the rears with four. The wheels' anti-blocking system can be adjusted in 12 levels, the electronic stability programme has been extended by the use of slick tyres, while the servo steering works electro-mechanically.

In the technical specification of this thoroughbred racer its weight is listed as just 1,300 kilos, it has a standard 90-litre fuel tank – the 70 litre and FT3 safety tank of 100 litres are optional. And the Club Sport has 18-inch five hole forged rims with Michelin tyres in sizes 25/64 x 18 front and 2768 x 18 rear.

Like the Sport Club, the new 911 GR3 R has been conceived as a racer to compete in the superior GT3 class. Introduced in mid-2015, the car was delivered to the various teams for the 2016 season, when Porsche intended to win national titles, aiming at leadership among the GTs, a role that is almost its right, also because the World Endurance Championship was won by the RSR.

TECHNICAL SPECIFICATION

ENGINE
Central, longitudinal, V6

Bore and stroke	102 x 81,5 mm
Unitary cubic capacity	666 cc
Total cubic capacity	3996 cc
Valve gear	4 camshafts
Number of valves	4 per cylinder
Fuel feed	direct injection
Ignition	electronic
Coolant	liquid
Lubrication	integrated dry sump
Maximum power	500 hp at 8250 rpm
Specific power	125 hp/litre

TRANSMISSION
Rear wheel drive

Clutch	dry mono-disc
Gearbox	sequential, 6 speeds plus reverse

CHASSIS
Self-supporting in aluminium-steel

Front suspension	McPherson, optimised by Porsche, height adjustable, toe-in and camber, adjustable anti-roll bar
Rear suspension	multi-link, adjustable in height, toe-in and camber, adjustable anti-roll bar Brakes disc
Steering	two braking circuits subdivided by front and rear axle
Fuel tank	64 litres (90 optional)
Tyres front/rear	8.5J x 20 with 245/35ZR20 11J x 20 with 295/30ZR20

DIMENSIONS AND WEIGHT

Wheelbase	2463 mm
Track front/rear	1538/1557 mm
Length	4604 mm
Width	2002 mm
Height	-
Weight	1220 kg

PERFORMANCE

Top speed	-
Power to weight ratio	246,9 kw

911 GT3 R

2015

This model is based on the 911 GT3 RS and has been developed for clients compete in the GT3 series. In developing the already potent 500 hp 911, the Stuttgart technicians lightened the chassis and body, improved aerodynamics and reduced fuel consumption, keeping service and replacement component parts cost reduction in mind.

The 911 GT3 R has taken from the production model the typical aerodynamic profile of the roof and wheelbase was lengthened by 8.3 cm. That's how the technicians ensured a more equilibrated weight distribution and stable handling compared to the GT3 R.

The hybrid structure of the aluminium and steel body of the RS was an excellent base for a racing car. Roof, engine cover and part of the front end, wheel arches, doors, sides, the rear area and boot lid are all made in composite synthetic material with carbon fibre (CFK). For the first time, the windscreen and windows are in polycarbonate.

The new 911 GT3 R is powered by a 4-litre 6-cylinder boxer engine, much of it identical to that of the 911 GT3 RS, which is homologated for normal road use.

The 911 GT3 R's aerodynamics also come from the road car. The marked cooling vents in the front wheel arches increase the downforce of the front axle. The rear spoiler, which is two metres wide and 40 cm deep, ensures aerodynamic equilibrium. The GT3 R also adopted the central radiator of the 911 RSR, improving its centre of gravity and the flow of exhaust gas towards the vents on the bonnet. The new car's braking system has also been optimised for endurance racing.

The 911 Turbo made its debut in Detroit in January 2016 at the North American International Auto Show. A few weeks later, it was test driven by the press in South Africa where the company and its guests used the renewed Kyalami circuit.

TECHNICAL SPECIFICATION

ENGINE
Rear, overhanging, longitudinal
6 cylinder

Bore and stroke	102 x 77 mm
Unitary cubic capacity	633.3 cc
Total cubic capacity	3800 cc
Valve gear	4 camshafts
Number of valves	4 per cylinder
Compression ratio	9.8,1
Fuel feed	direct injection
Ignition	electronic
Coolant	liquid
Lubrication	integrated dry sump
Maximum power	540 hp at 6400 rpm
Specific power	142.1 hp/litre

TRANSMISSION
Active 4WD

Clutch	220/163.5 mm
Gearbox	7-speed PDK plus reverse

CHASSIS
Self-supporting with light aluminium and steel body

Front suspension	McPherson, wishbones, cylindrical coil springs with internal shock absorbers
Rear suspension	multi-link axis with five oscillating arms, cylindrical coil springs with internal coaxial shock absorbers
Brakes	disc
Steering	electro-mechanical servo-steering
Fuel tank	68 litres
Tyres front/rear	9J x 20 with 245/35ZR20 11.5J with 305/30ZR20

DIMENSIONS AND WEIGHT
Wheelbase	2450 mm
Track front/rear	1541/1590 mm
Length	4507 mm
Width	1880 mm
Height	1297 mm
Weight	1595 kg

PERFORMANCE
Top speed	320 kph
Power to weight ratio	248.9 kw

911 Turbo 2016

The Turbo version of the 911 (with a capital T) was a new design that was immediately launched in Coupé, Cabriolet and S versions, the latter the top of the range. The twin-turbo 3.8-litre 6-cylinder engine puts out 540 hp at 6400 rpm, a power increase made possible with the use of modified intake ducts, a new injector and higher fuel pressure. As a result of using new turbos of greater pressure – Porsche was the only constructor to use turbo chargers with a variable turbine geometry together with petrol engines – the 911 Turbo S puts out a substantial 580 hp. The engine has the Dynamic Boost function to further improve response. Fuel feed pressure remains constant during the load variations, so every time the driver even slightly lifts his foot from the accelerator, the only interruption is fuel injection but leaving the throttle open, so that the power unit responds almost immediately with a new acceleration impulse. To that extent, the 911 Turbo S accelerates from 0-100 kph in 2.9 seconds and charges up to a top speed of 330 kph, 10 km more than the base model.

Fuel consumption is 9.1 litres per 100 kilometres for the Coupé and 9.3 litre/km for the Cabriolet, with a reduction of 0.6 litres for every 100 kilometres throughout the range.

The Porsche Stability Management (PSM) of the Turbo now has a new operating method called the PSM Sport: with slight pressure on the PSM button on the central tunnel, the system moves to a highly sporty mode, independent of the driving programme selected. PSM Sport, which can be activated separately, has a function that enables the driver to use the PSM more effectively, permitting the car to reach even more extreme levels of sporty driving, especially on the track. Even so, the new 911 Turbo with PASM as standard always keeps its eye on the relationship between performance and comfort. As far as the Turbo S is concerned, that car has the PDCC roll stabilisation system and a PCCB ceramic braking system as standard.

Almost 20 years have gone by since the introduction of the first Boxster. At the 2016 Geneva Motor Show, Porsche presented a new generation of this historical model, the 718 and the 718 S, inspired by the 718 that takes enthusiasts back to the company's origins in the second half of the 1950s.

TECHNICAL SPECIFICATION

ENGINE
Central, 4-cyinder boxer

Bore and stroke	91 x 76.4 mm
Unitary cubic capacity	497 cc
Total cubic capacity	1988 cc
Valve gear	Variocam Plus system
Number of valves	4 per cylinder
Compression ratio	9.5:1
Fuel feed	direct injection
Ignition	electronic
Coolant	liquid
Lubrication	?
Maximum power	300 hp at 6500 rpm
Specific power	151 hp/litre

TRANSMISSION
Rear wheel drive

Clutch	240 mm
Gearbox	manual, 6 speeds plus reverse, PDK optional

CHASSIS
Self-supporting, with light aluminium-steel body

Front suspension	McPherson, light structure shock absorbers
Rear suspension	light structure shock absorbers
Brakes	disc
Steering	electro-mechanical servo-steering
Fuel tank	64 litres
Tyres front/rear	8J x 18 ET 57 with 235 35ZR18 – 9.5J x 18 ET with 265/45ZR18

DIMENSIONS AND WEIGHT

Wheelbase	2457 mm
Track front/rear	1515/1532 mm
Length	4379 mm
Width	1801 mm
Height	1281 mm
Weight	1335 kg

PERFORMANCE

Top speed	275 kph
Power to weight ratio	164.7 kw

Boxster 718 2016

Under the new Boxster's engine cover, beats a new conception 4-cylinder boxer engine with turbo: the 718 puts out 300 hp with a 2-litre cubic capacity, while the 718 S generates 350 hp with its turbocharged 2.5-litre unit that has a variable turbine geometry (VTG). Both of them have a 6-speed manual gearbox as standard and PDK as an option. Due to the turbocharger, the cars have a significant torque increase to 380 Nm, which is available between the 1950 and 4,500 rpm on the base model and 420 Nm between 1900 and 4500 rpm with the 2.5-litre power unit. Performance? Simple: the 718 with a double clutch gearbox or Porsche Doppelkupplung (PDK) and the Sport Chrono package does 0-100 kph in 4.7 seconds, the 718 Boxster S with the same equipment in 4.2 secs. Top speed? Base model 275 kph and the S 285 kph. First class performance, but with a fuel consumption reduction, the 4-cylinder 718 taking 6.9 litres per100 km in NEDC and the 2.5-litre 7.3 litres by the S. The new 718 is recognisable at first glance by its front end with a much more marked profile that increases its presence and personality; there are the same air intakes but much bigger and expresses its power and aggressiveness. The main Bi-Xenon headlights are of new configuration, with LED day lights - optional4 LED day lights – complete the front of the 718.

The lateral view shows the new roadster with its redesigned wheel housings and mini-skirts; the bigger vent-type two-bladed air intakes are also new, as are the door handles. The 718 Boxster S has 19-inch rims as standard with 20-inch as optional. The rear end was wider, especially because of the connecting strip with the Porsche name located between the optical groups, which are recognisable by their characteristic three dimensional LED lights and 4-point stop lights.

The 911 R developed by Porsche's motor sport department was unveiled at the 2016 Geneva Motor Show. As result of a weight of just 1370 kg, it is the lightest of the 911s. To make the car even more exclusive, Porsche has decided to limit its production to 991 of them, another highly significant number in the history of the- Stuttgart company and in that of the 911 in particular.

TECHNICAL SPECIFICATION

ENGINE

Rear, overhanging, longitudinal
6 cylinders

Bore and stroke	102 x 81.5 mm
Unitary cubic capacity	666 cc
Total cubic capacity	3996 cc
Valve gear	4 camshafts
Number of valves	4 per cylinder
Fuel feed	direct injection
Ignition	electronic
Coolant	liquid
Lubrication	-
Maximum power	500 hp at 8250 rpm
Specific power	125 hp/litre

TRANSMISSION

Rear wheel drive

Clutch	228 mm
Gearbox	manual, 6 speeds plus reverse

CHASSIS

Coupé with light aluminium-steel body

Front suspension	McPherson with light structure shock absorbers
Rear suspension	light structure multi-link
Brakes	disc, carbo-ceramic
Steering	variable electro-mechanical power steering, rear wheel steering
Fuel tank	64 litres
Tyres front/rear	9J x 20 ET 55 with 245/35ZR20 12J x 20 ET 47 with 305/30ZR20

DIMENSIONS AND WEIGHT

Wheelbase	2463 mm
Track front/rear	1551/1555 mm
Length	4532 mm
Width	1852 mm
Height	1267 mm
Weight	1370 kg

PERFORMANCE

Top speed	323 kph
Power to weight ratio	268.6 kw

911 R   2016

With a normally aspirated 4-litre boxer engine that puts out 500 hp through a manual 6-speed gearbox, the 911 R is steeped in the original model's tradition that first appeared in 1967: a sporty car homologated for road use. The 911 R of times gone by (when the R stood for Racing) was used in rallying as well as endurance racing, the Targa Florio at the top of the list. The new 911R is like a chip off the old block, a top car in terms of both lightness and performance. It is powered by the now noted 6-cylinder 3996 cc boxer of the 911 GT3 RS, which generates 500 hp at 6250 rpm. From a standing start, the R hits 100 kph in just 3.8 seconds and has a spine-tingling top speed of 323 kph! In line with the minimalist traditions of a sportier 911, Porsche's newcomer is only available with a 6-speed manual gearbox with a reduced excursion. Mixed routes are certainly those that makes the qualities of the new R stand out, because of the standard steering rear axle designed specifically for this car, that guarantees precision of manoeuvre combined with a high degree of driving stability, and the mechanical self-locking rear differential that provides maximum traction in all conditions. The job of the Porsche Ceramic Composite Brake (PCCB) with 410 mm diameter front discs and 390 mm rear – is to stop the beast. Contact with the asphalt is ensured by ultra-high performance tyres on 20-inch forged light alloy rims with the central torque in opaque aluminium. The double de-clutching function activated by a specific button for perfect changes to a lower gear and the single mass flywheel option return to the 911 R repertoire. The front boot lid and wheel arches in carbon fibre, roof in magnesium, rear window and the back laterals in synthetic material and an interior of reduced insulation, with no rear seats, air conditioning (optional) or radio are other characteristics of this car born to race. Clear references to Porsche's glorious past include the company's name along the sides of the R, strips of red or green and bucket seats with a central area in two colour check Pepita. An aluminium plaque on the passenger side indicates the number of this limited edition 911.

Porsche's motor racing victories

Porsche is certainly one of the car manufacturers most closely associated with the world of motor racing, having made its debut in 1951, although some of the company's cars had been entered in races in previous years. There followed decades of commitment to all levels of the sport and in all categories, an undertaking that still hasn't diminished; on the contrary, Porsche is still heavily committed in pursuing in new seasons, new stimuli and new victories.

In reproducing Porsche's results list it is once more necessary to select. Next to the official victories and those in the most important events in the world – among them the Mille Miglia, the 24 Hours of Le Mans, Formula 1, world championship rallies, the Targa Florio and Can-Am (a full list would be even longer that that) – there is an imprecise number of triumphs achieved by private teams and drivers. Sometimes modified by Stuttgart, others prepared personally: and yet others built from scratch with Porsche engines.

So the pages that follow list the company's most important successes scored in the great international competitions, a testament to a role in motor racing that certainly goes way beyond a simple list of names and numbers. It is one that is made of technology, commitment, tenacity, cars and men. One of great victories and bitter defeats, always benefiting from the glow of pride and passion.

THE GREAT ENDURANCE RACES

24 HOURS OF LE MANS

Year	Drivers	Car
1970	Richard Attwood (GBR) / Hans Herrmann (GER)	917K
1971	Gijs van Lennep (HOL) / Helmut Marko (AUT)	917K
1976	Jacky Ickx (BEL) / Gijs van Lennep (HOL)	936
1977	Jürgen Barth (GER) / Hurley Haywood (USA) / Jacky Ickx (BEL)	936/77
1979	Klaus Ludwig (GER) / Bill Whittington (USA) / Don Whittington (USA)	935-K3
1981	Derek Bell (GBR) / Jacky Ickx (BEL)	936/81
1982	Derek Bell (GBR) / Jacky Ickx (BEL)	956
1983	Hurley Haywood (USA) / Al Holbert (USA) / Vern Schuppan (AUS)	956
1984	Klaus Ludwig (GER) / Henri Pescarolo (FRA)	956B
1985	Paolo Barilla (ITA) / Klaus Ludwig (GER) / John "Winter" (GER)	956B
1986	Derek Bell (GBR) / Al Holbert (USA) / Hans-Joachim Stuck (GER)	962C
1987	Derek Bell (GBR) / Al Holbert (USA) / Hans-Joachim Stuck (GER)	962C
1994	Mauro Baldi (ITA) / Yannick Dalmas (FRA) / Hurley Haywood (USA)	Dauer Porsche 962LM
1996	Davy Jones (USA) / Manuel Reuter (GER) / Alex Wurz (AUT)	TWR Porsche WSC95
1997	Michele Alboreto (ITA) / Stefan Johansson (SWE) / Tom Kristensen (DEN)	TWR Porsche WSC95
1998	Laurent Aiello (FRA) / Allan McNish (GBR) / Stephane Ortelli (FRA)	911 GT1-98
2015	Nico Hülkenberg (GER) / Earl Bamber (NZL) / Nick Tandy (GBR)	919 Hybrid

TARGA FLORIO

Year	Drivers	Car
1956	Umberto Maglioli (ITA)	550A RS 1500 Spyder
1959	Edgar Barth (GER) / Wolfgang Seidel (GER)	718 RSK 1500 Spyder
1960	Joakim Bonnier (SVE) / Hans Herrmann (GER)	718 RS60 1700 Spyder
1963	Joakim Bonnier (SVE) / Carlo Mario Abate (ITA)	718 GTR 2000 Coupé
1964	Colin Davis (GBR) / Antonio Pucci (ITA)	904 GTS
1966	Willy Mairesse (BEL) / Herbert Müller (CH)	906 Carrera 6
1967	Paul Hawkins (AUS) / Rolf Stommelen (GER)	910/8

1968	Umberto Maglioli (ITA) / Vic Elford (GBR)	907/8
1969	Gerhard Mitter (GER) / Udo Schutz (GER)	908/2
1970	Joseph Siffert (CH) / Brian Redman (GBR)	908/3
1973	Herbert Müller (CH) / Gijs van Lennep (HOL)	911 Carrera RSR 3000

12 Hours of Sebring

1968	Hans Herrmann (GER) / Jo Siffert (CH)	907
1971	Vic Elford (GBR) / Gerard Larrousse (FRA)	917K
1973	Peter Gregg (USA) / Hurley Haywood (USA) / Dave Helmick (USA)	911 Carrera RSR
1976	Al Holbert (USA) / Mike Keyser (USA)	911 Carrera RSR
1977	George Dyer (USA) / Brad Frisselle (USA)	911 Carrera RSR
1978	Bob Garretson (USA) / Charles Mendez (USA) / Brian Redman (GBR)	935
1979	Bob Akin (USA) / Rob McFarlin (USA) / Roy Woods (USA)	935
1980	Dick Barbour (USA) / John Fitzpatrik (GBR)	935-K3
1981	Hurley Haywood (USA) / Al Holbert (USA) / Bruce Leven (USA)	935
1982	John Paul Jr. (USA) / John Paul Sr. (USA)	935
1983	Wayne Baker (USA) / Jim Mullen (USA) / Kees Nierop (CAN)	934
1984	Hans Heyer (GER) / Stefan Johansson (SWE) / Mauricio De Narvaez (COL)	935
1985	A.J. Foyt Jr. (USA) / Bob Wollek (FRA)	962
1986	Bob Akin (USA) / Jo Gartner (AUT) / Hans-Joachim Stuck (GER)	962
1987	Jochen Mass (GER) / Bobby Rahal (USA)	962
1988	Klaus Ludwig (GER) / Hans-Joachim Stuck (GER)	962
2008	Timo Bernhard (GER) / Emmanuel Collard (FRA) / Romain Dumas (FRA)	RS Spyder

24 Hours of Daytona

1968	Vic Elford (GBR) / Hans Herrmann (GER)	
	Jochen Neerpasch (GER) / Rolf Stommelen (GER)	907
1970	Leo Kinnunen (FIN) / Brian Redman (GBR) / Pedro Rodriguez (MEX)	917K
1971	Jackie Oliver (GBR) / Pedro Rodriguez (MEX)	917K
1973	Peter Gregg (USA) / Hurley Haywood (USA)	911 Carrera RSR
1975	Peter Gregg (USA) / Hurley Haywood (USA)	911 Carrera RSR
1977	John Graves (USA) / Hurley Haywood (USA) / Dave Helmik (USA)	911 Carrera RSR
1978	Peter Gregg (USA) / Toine Hezemans (HOL) / Rolf Stommelen (GER)	935/77
1979	Ted Field (USA) / Hurley Haywood (USA) / Danny Ongais (USA)	935/78
1980	Reinhold Joest (GER) / Volkert Merl (GER) / Rolf Stommelen (GER)	935
1981	Bob Garretson (USA) / Bobby Rahal (USA) / Brian Redman (GBR)	935-K3
1982	John Paul Jr. (USA) / John Paul Sr. (USA) / Rolf Stommelen (GER)	935
1983	Claude Ballot-Lena (FRA) / A.J. Foyt (USA) / Preston Henn (USA) / Bob Wollek (FRA)	935
1985	Thierry Boutsen (BEL) / A.J. Foyt (USA) / Al Unser Jr. (USA) / Bob Wollek (FRA)	962
1986	Derek Bell (GBR) / Al Holbert (USA) / Al Unser Jr. (USA)	962
1987	Derek Bell (GBR) / Al Holbert (USA) / Chip Robinson (USA) / Al Unser Jr. (USA)	962
1989	John Andretti (USA) / Derek Bell (GBR) / Bob Wollek (FRA)	962
1991	Hurley Haywood (USA) / Frank Jelinski (GER)	
	Henri Pescarolo (FRA) / John "Winter" (GER)/ Bob Wollek (FRA)	962C
1995	Christophe Bouchut (FRA) / Jurgen Lassig (GER)	
	Giovanni Lavaggi (ITA) / Marco Werner (GER)	Kremer K8 Spyder
2003	Jorg Bergmeister (GER) / Timo Bernhard (GER)	

	Kevin Buckler (USA) / Michael Schrom (USA)	996 GT3 RS
2009	David Donohue (USA) / Antonio Garcia (SPA)	
	Darren Law (USA) / Buddy Rice (USA)	Riley MK XI Porsche
2010	Joao Barbosa (POR) / Terry Borcheller (USA)	
	Ryan Dalziel (SCO) / Mike Rockenfeller (GER)	Riley MK XI Porsche

1,000 KILOMETRES OF MONZA

1969	Jo Siffert (CH) / Brian Redman (GBR)	908LH
1970	Pedro Rodríguez (MEX) / Leo Kinnunen (FIN)	917K
1971	Pedro Rodríguez (MEX) / Jackie Oliver (GBR)	917K
1976	Jochen Mass (GER) / Jacky Ickx (BEL)	936
1978	Reinhold Joest (GER)	908/3
1981	Edgar Dören (GER) / Jürgen Lässig (GER) / Gerhard Holup (GER)	935 K3
1983	Bob Wollek (FRA) / Thierry Boutsen (BEL)	956
1984	Stefan Bellof (GER) / Derek Bell (GBR)	956
1985	Manfred Winkelhock (GER) / Marc Surer (CH)	962C
1986	Hans-Joachim Stuck (GER) / Derek Bell (GBR)	962C
1997	Thomas Bscher (GER) / John Nielsen (DEN)	Kremer K8 Spyder

1,000 KILOMETRES OF THE NÜRBURGRING

1967	Joe Buzzetta (USA) / Udo Schütz (GER)	910
1968	Vic Elford (GBR) / Jo Siffert (CH)	908
1969	Jo Siffert (CH) / Brian Redman (GBR)	908/02
1970	Vic Elford (GBR) / Kurt Ahrens Jr. (GER)	908/03
1971	Vic Elford (GBR) / Gérard Larrousse (FRA)	908/03
1977	Rolf Stommelen (GER) / Tim Schenken (AUS) / Toine Hezemans (HOL)	935
1978	Klaus Ludwig (GER) / Hans Heyer (GER) / Toine Hezemans (HOL)	935/77
1979	Manfred Schurti (FL) / Bob Wollek (FRA) / John Fitzpatrick (GBR)	935/77
1980	Rolf Stommelen (GER) / Jürgen Barth (GER)	908/3 Turbo
1983	Jochen Mass (GER) / Jacky Ickx (BEL)	956
1984	Stefan Bellof (GER) / Derek Bell (GBR)	956

1,000 KILOMETRES OF SPA-FRANCORCHAMPS

1969	Brian Redman (GBR) / Jo Siffert (CH)	908
1970	Brian Redman (GBR) / Jo Siffert (CH)	917K
1971	Jackie Oliver (GBR) / Pedro Rodríguez (MEX)	917K
1982	Jacky Ickx (BEL) / Jochen Mass (GER)	956
1983	Jacky Ickx (BEL) / Jochen Mass (GER)	956
1984	Stefan Bellof (BEL) / Derek Bell (GBR)	956
1986	Thierry Boutsen (BEL) / Frank Jelinski (GER)	962C

200 MILES OF THE NORISRING

1970	Jürgen Neuhaus (GER)	917K
1972	Leo Kinnunen (FIN)	917/10 TC
1973	Leo Kinnunen (FIN)	917/10 TC
1975	John Fitzpatrick (GBR)	911 Carrera RSR
1976	Toine Hezemans (HOL)	934

1977	Rolf Stommelen (GER)	935
1978	Bob Wollek (FRA)	935/77A
1979	Rolf Stommelen (GER)	935J
1980	John Fitzpatrick (GBR)	935 K3/80
1981	Bob Wollek (FRA)	935 K4
1982	Jochen Mass (GER)	956
1983	Stefan Bellof (GER)	956
1984	Manfred Winkelhock (GER)	956B
1985	Klaus Ludwig (GER)	956
1986	Klaus Ludwig (GER)	956B
1987	Jonathan Palmer (GBR) / Mauro Baldi (ITA)	962C GTi
2008	Jörg Bergmeister (GER) / Marc Basseng (GER)	997 GT3

1,000 KILOMETRES OF ZELTWEG

1966	Gerhard Mitter (GER) / Hans Herrmann (GER)	906
1968	Jo Siffert (CH)	908
1969	Jo Siffert (CH) / Kurt Ahrens Jr. (GER)	917
1970	Jo Siffert (CH) / Brian Redman (GBR)	917K
1971	Pedro Rodríguez (MEX) / Richard Attwood (GBR)	917K

FIA WORLD CHAMPIONSHIP

1962	International Grand Touring Manufactures, Division II
1963	International Grand Touring Manufactures, Division II
1964	International Grand Touring Manufactures, Division II
1965	International Grand Touring Manufactures, Division II
1966	International Manufactures, Prototypes 2000
1966	International Sport Car, Division II
1967	International Manufactures, Prototypes 2000
1967	International Sport Car, Division II
1968	International Championship for Makes
1968	International Grand Touring Trophy
1969	International Championship for Makes
1969	International Grand Touring Trophy
1970	International Championship for Makes
1970	International Grand Touring Trophy
1971	International Championship for Makes
1971	International Grand Touring Trophy
1972	International Grand Touring Trophy
1973	International Grand Touring Trophy
1974	FIA Cup for Grand Touring Cars
1975	International Grand Touring Trophy
1976	World Championship for Makes
1976	World Sport Car Championship, Group S
1977	World Championship for Makes
1978	World Championship for Makes
1978	FIA Grand Touring Cup
1979	World Championship for Makes
1980	World Championship for Makes
1981	World Championship for Makes
1982	World Endurance Championship
1983	World Endurance Championship
1983	FIA Grand Touring Cup
1984	World Endurance Championship
1985	World Endurance Championship (Team)
1986	World Endurance Championship (Team)
2015	World Endurance Championship, LMP
2015	World Endurance Championship, GTE

PORSCHE IN FORMULA 1

First...

1962	GP France	804	Dan Gurney

...later

1984	GP Brazil	McLaren MP4/2 TAG Porsche P01	Alain Prost
	GP South Africa	McLaren MP4/2 TAG Porsche P01	Niki Lauda
	GP San Marino	McLaren MP4/2 TAG Porsche P01	Alain Prost
	GP France	McLaren MP4/2 TAG Porsche P01	Niki Lauda
	GP Monaco	McLaren MP4/2 TAG Porsche P01	Alain Prost
	GP Britain	McLaren MP4/2 TAG Porsche P01	Niki Lauda
	GP Germany	McLaren MP4/2 TAG Porsche P01	Alain Prost
	GP Austria	McLaren MP4/2 TAG Porsche P01	Niki Lauda
	GP Holland	McLaren MP4/2 TAG Porsche P01	Alain Prost
	GP Italy	McLaren MP4/2 TAG Porsche P01	Niki Lauda
	GP Europe	McLaren MP4/2 TAG Porsche P01	Alain Prost
	GP Portugal	McLaren MP4/2 TAG Porsche P01	Alain Prost
1985	GP Brazil	McLaren MP4/2B TAG Porsche P01	Alain Prost
	GP Monaco	McLaren MP4/2B TAG Porsche P01	Alain Prost
	GP Britain	McLaren MP4/2B TAG Porsche P01	Alain Prost
	GP Austria	McLaren MP4/2B TAG Porsche P01	Alain Prost
	GP Holland	McLaren MP4/2B TAG Porsche P01	Niki Lauda
	GP Italy	McLaren MP4/2B TAG Porsche P01	Alain Prost
1986	GP San Marino	McLaren MP4/2C TAG Porsche P01	Alain Prost
	GP Monaco	McLaren MP4/2C TAG Porsche P01	Alain Prost
	GP Austria	McLaren MP4/2C TAG Porsche P01	Alain Prost
	GP Australia	McLaren MP4/2C TAG Porsche P01	Alain Prost

THE GREAT MARATHONS

Parigi-Dakar

1984	Renè Metge (FRA) / Dominique Lemoyne (FRA)	911 4x4
1986	Renè Metge (FRA) / Dominique Lemoyne (FRA)	959

PORSCHE AMONG THE MONSTERS

La CAN-AM

1972	George Follmer (USA)	917/10
1973	Mark Donohue (USA)	917/30KL

PORSCHE IN THE PRINCIPALITY OF MONACO

Monte Carlo Rally

1968	Vic Elford (GBR) / David Stone (GBR)	911T
1969	Björn Waldegård (SWE) / Lars Helmer (SWE)	911S
1970	Björn Waldegård (SWE) / Lars Helmer (SWE)	911S
1978	Jean-Pierre Nicolas (FRA) / Vincent Lavergne (FRA)	911 Carrera

PORSCHE IN THE MOUNTAINS

European Mountain Championship

1958	Sport: Wolfgang Von Trips (GER)	RSK
1959	Sport: Edgard Barth (GER)	RSK
1960	GT: Huschke von Hanstein (GER)	Carrera
1960	Sport: Heini Walter (CH)	RSK
1961	GT: Heinz Schiller (CH)	Carrera
1961	Sport: Heini Walter (CH)	FS
1962	GT: Hans Kuhnis (CH)	Carrera
1963	GT: Herbert Muller (CH)	Abarth
1963	Sport: Edgar Barth (GER)	Spyder 718 W-RS
1964	GT: Heini Walter (CH)	904 GTS
1964	Sport: Edgar Barth (GER)	904
1965	GT: Herbert Muller (CH)	Abarth
1966	GT: Ebergard Mahle (GER)	911
1966	Sport: Gerhard Mitter (GER)	904
1967	GT: Anton Fischhaber (GER)	911S
1967	Sport: Gerhard Mitter (GER)	910
1968	GT: Holger Zarges (GER)	911T
1968	Sport: Gerhard Mitter (GER)	910
1969	GT: Seep Greger (GER)	911T
1970	Cat. A: Claude Haldi (GER)	911
1971	Cat. A: Wilhelm Bartles (GER)	911S
1972	Cat. A: Anton Fischhaber (GER)	911S
1973	Cat. A: Seep Greger (GER)	Carrera
1974	Cat. A: Anton Fischhaber (GER)	Carrera
1975	Cat. A: Jean Claude Bering (CH)	911
1976	Cat. A: Jean Claude Bering (CH)	911
1978	Cat. I-II: Jeacques Almeras (FRA)	934 Turbo
1978	Cat. III: Jean Marie Almeras (FRA)	935
1979	Cat. I-II: Jeacques Almeras (FRA)	934 Turbo
1979	Cat. III: Jean Marie Almeras (FRA)	935
1980	Cat. I-II: Jeacques Almeras (FRA)	934 Turbo
1980	Cat. III: Jean Marie Almeras (FRA)	935
1982	Cat. I-II: Jeacques Guillot (FRA)	930 Turbo

Printed by D'Auria Printing - Ascoli Piceno (AP)

april 2016